DATE DUE

NOV 16 1984		
MAR 18 1985		
SEP 2 1986		
MAY 2 9 1991		
FEB 08 1996		
NOV 01 2012		

DEMCO NO. 38-298

JAN 21 1982

THOMAS ALVA EDISON

THOMAS ALVA EDISON

Wyn Wachhorst   An American Myth

The MIT Press
Cambridge, Massachusetts, and
London, England

This book was set in Fototronic
Baskerville by The Colonial
Cooperative Press Inc. and printed
and bound in the United States of
America.

**Library of Congress Cataloging in
Publication Data**

Wachhorst, Wyn.
  Thomas Alva Edison, an American
myth.

  Bibliography: p.
  Includes index.
  1. Edison, Thomas A. (Thomas
Alva), 1847–1931. 2. Inventors—
United States—Biography. I. Title.
TK140.E3W3   621.3′092′4 [B]   81-751
ISBN 0-262-23108-5   AACR2

For Rita,

who is also a bringer of light.

CONTENTS

1

INTRODUCTION

"Master Mind of the Machine Age,"
by Rafael Valdivia, 1926. Edison National Historic Site.

A story has come down concerning one of the famous camping trips which Edison took with Henry Ford, Harvey Firestone, and the naturalist, John Burroughs, in the hills of West Virginia shortly after the First World War. A village mechanic was inspecting the motor of their ailing car when a tall man climbed out of the driver's seat and said, "I am Henry Ford and I say the motor itself is in perfect order." The rustic then suggested that it might be the electrical system. "I am Thomas A. Edison," spoke up the stout man in the front seat, "and I say the wiring is all right." Whereupon the village mechanic, squinting into the back seat at John Burroughs and his long, white beard, remarked, "An' I s'pose that must be Santa Claus." [1] Although the anecdote is apocryphal, it is a fact, which this study seeks to explain, that Edison came to rank with Santa Claus as a major folk hero.

This book is not a biography. It chronicles the stages in the evolution of a culture hero, analyzing the factors in Edison's life and character which transformed man into myth; but its final concern is with the myth rather than the man, the image rather than the reality. Cultural images, such as the *Mayflower,* the log cabin, the cowboy, or the Statue of Liberty, are symbols by which members of a society may communicate a common identity and purpose. At the simplest level, the culture hero is such an image: Lincoln splitting logs, Washington on the Delaware, or a young and curious Ben Franklin munching his roll as he wanders up Market Street in the early morning of America. Yet the psychocultural meaning of these images derives in each case from a larger mythology.

The Edison symbol has been a vehicle for every major American cultural theme: the gospel of technological progress, the rural Protestant virtues (hard work, initiative, perseverance, prudence, honesty, frugality, etc.), the success mythology of the self-made man, individualism, optimism, practicality, anti-intellectualism, the American Adam and the New World Eden (America as a new beginning for mankind), the sense of world mission, democracy, egalitarianism, the idealization of youth, and others. Analysis of the symbol reveals not only interrelationships of these themes within American mythology but also suggests some larger insights into the psychodynamics of the American value structure itself.

As a form of myth, the culture hero functions to resolve mechanically contradictory cultural values into a single paradoxical reality. Charles

Lindbergh, for example, incarnated the conflicting American ideals of nostalgic, agrarian individualism and the promise of a technological society.[2] Neither a separation nor a synthesis of the two poles is necessary; rather, the paradox itself provides a schematic diagram of a reality directly perceived only in symbol and myth. Thus for each of the overt themes in the Edison symbol there has been a covert antithesis. The myth of reentering Paradise with the machine, for example, is subtly joined with the pastoral myth of Paradise lost, and advocates of the success mythology take great pains to show that the individualism of the "self-made man" has deep communal roots—that his power is the flowering of innocence.*

The complexity of the Edison image, in fact, leaves almost no facet of the American mythology untouched. There is Edison the Wizard, "the alchemist alone in his tower at midnight conjuring mysterious forces of Nature while the world sleeps." On the surface, this is a Merlin-like figure; in a larger sense it resembles Ethan Brand or Captain Ahab, with boundless Faustian drive and unfathomable intellect. In contrast, there is the Tom Sawyer image (as a boy he is always "Tom Edison"): the rural, Midwestern, prankish, Eternal American Boy, stringing up his homemade telegraph line, interested in everything but school, setting fire to his father's barn "just to see what it would do," or talking another boy into swallowing Seidlitz powder on the hypothesis that it would make him lighter than air. Young Edison adrift on the train, where he sold papers and conducted chemical experiments in the baggage car, and his confident schemes to outwit the cruel world bear a strong resemblance to Huck Finn and his river journey. By far the most important aspect of the Edison boyhood image, however, is the Horatio Alger figure: the enterprising newsboy who rose with pluck and luck to fame and fortune. The early part of Benjamin Franklin's classic *Autobiography* also figures strongly in the image of Edison's youth. Like Ben, arriving in Philadelphia by ship from Boston, destined for success,

* It has been suggested by such theorists as Jung, Levi-Strauss, and their disciples that the central purpose of all myth is the resolution of overt-covert, paradoxical polar tensions and that all such polarities ultimately reflect some universal psychic dichotomy such as individualization versus communion, conscious versus unconscious, autocentric versus allocentric (David Gutmann), or even the left and right hemispheres of the brain.

Edison's turning point was his arrival in New York by the same route, where he too wandered the streets with his dollar. The democratic, equalitarian, Lincolnesque Edison appears often, as does the optimistic prophet of progress and apologist for the special destiny of America—of which he himself is viewed as living proof. Still another Edison is the earthy Yankee with a frontier spirit, the tinkerer with know-how, horse sense, and a disdain for intellectuals. One also finds Edison as the "Rotarian," the apotheosis of all good business values. Often he is a modern Prometheus, stealing fire (light) from the Gods (Nature) and giving it to humanity; sometimes he is God himself. Whatever the image, it is almost always presented as the perfection of the typical American.

THE SIXTH GREATEST AMERICAN?

In his eighty-four years (1847–1931) Thomas Alva Edison took out 1,093 patents, the most ever granted to any one person. In addition to the light bulb and phonograph, these included fundamental contributions to the telegraph, telephone, typewriter, microphone, motion picture camera and film, storage battery, and electric railway. The awesome variety of his other accomplishments ranged from synthetic chemicals and rubber, mining machinery, waxed paper, Portland cement, and the mimeograph to the dynamo and the whole basis for the modern system of power distribution (including sockets, switches, fuses, fixtures, meters, etc.). The world responded to these gifts with countless banquets, prizes, celebrations, expositions, titles, tributes, medals, monuments, and memorials.

In spite of all the acclaim awarded Edison during his lifetime (he once commented that he could count his medals by the quart), the attention naturally declined sharply after his death. Thus some quantitative estimate of the actual magnitude and endurance of the Edison image in the twentieth century would be of interest.

Returning to "Middletown" for their follow-up study in 1935, sociologists Robert and Helen Lynd found that many linked Edison with Washington and Lincoln as the third greatest American. Earlier, the readers of *Independent* magazine had voted Edison "the most useful American" (1913), and a *New York Times* poll had named him the greatest living American (1922). In 1945 the National Opinion Research

Center asked a nationwide cross section to name the greatest men who ever lived in this country; Edison placed fourth after Franklin Roosevelt, Lincoln, and Washington. Later in the same year a Gallup poll asked: "Who is the greatest person, living or dead, in world history?" Edison was outranked only by Jesus, FDR, Lincoln, Washington, and General MacArthur—all of whom were believed to have saved mankind, or at least the entire nation, from total destruction. These and many more opinion samples indicate that the Edison image shifted from "great specialist" to "great man" during the second decade of this century; that Edison had a healthy hold on third place in the American pantheon of the 1920s; and that he fell to sharing fourth or fifth place with a number of others by the late 1940s. Although there have been no authoritative polls relating to the question for more than a third of a century, Edison did rank third in 1971 when *Nation's Business* asked its readers to name the ten greatest men in American business history.[3]

My own speculation, based on opinion polls and bibliographic samples from the past half-century, is that Edison has dropped from an indisputable third in the 1920s to sharing sixth place with two or three others in the 1970s. He has definitely been outranked by Lincoln, FDR, Washington, and Franklin. The popularity of Jefferson, and recently Truman, has been rising, while that of charismatic and topical figures from the fifties and sixties continues to decline. Among the top ten only Lincoln, Washington, Franklin, and Jefferson have stood the test of time, although by that criterion Edison would rank at least fifth. During the 1970s the frequency of press items on Edison has risen again to approximately that of the 1940s. Although the phonograph and light centennials have contributed to this increase, factors more fundamental than these appear to be at work. The concluding chapter, which reevaluates the Edison legacy in the perspective of contemporary society, suggests a number of reasons why the enlargement of the Edison symbol may continue for some time to come.

The sheer bulk of printed material on Edison over the past century leaves little doubt about his general popularity. For this study, 62 books, 21 pamphlets, 326 more chapters and excerpts, 936 periodical articles, 3,218 newspaper items, 148 book reviews, four plays, five films, and four television documentaries were examined. A representative distribution of this material over time is indicated by the graph, which converts radical

annual fluctuations into an annual average for each decade.[4] The descending slope of this graph after the 1920s closely approximates the
fate of all traditional heroes in a modern, fragmented, demythologized
culture. Within the late nineteenth and early twentieth centuries, a
phase of American history which could symbolically be called the Age
of Edison, is a watershed dividing rural, small-town America, with its
relatively strong value consensus, from urban, industrial America and a
collapse of consensus which is still under way. It is a common observation that one shift during this period was from "idols of production"
(statesmen, industrial leaders, scientists) to "idols of consumption" (mass
media celebrities), from the moral to the amoral, the active to the passive, from the culture hero, the symbol of shared values, to the celebrity,
known only for his "well knownness." [5] Edison lived to see this transition affect his own image. His life and career, in fact, paralleled almost
to the year the rise and decline of the broad cultural phenomena—both
the reality and mythos—which he came to symbolize.

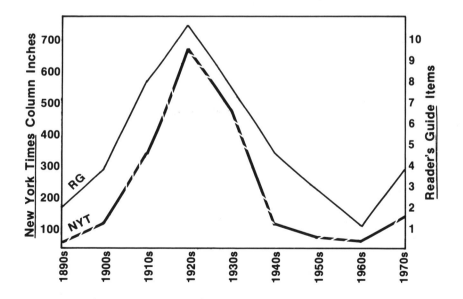

AN AMERICAN EPIC

Born in the 1840s during what has been called the "take-off period" in
our economic history, Edison grew along with the West, the cities, the
railroads, and the productive power of America. Inventors were prerequisite to industrialization and were in turn spawned by the process. In
1847, the year of Edison's birth, the United States Patent Office issued
a total of 576 patents. In 1869, when Edison received his first patent,
13,813 others were granted (by comparison, 81,274 were issued in 1974).
Edison's industriousness reached its peak in the early 1880s, when non-
agricultural workers were beginning to outnumber those in agricultural
pursuits and the output of manufactured goods was overtaking that of
farm products in dollar value. It is interesting that Edison's inventive
activity moves generally parallel to national patent totals (which have a
chicken-and-egg relationship to the general state of the economy), rising
sharply in the 1870s and again in the early 1890s, then falling off suddenly to recover at the turn of the century. But by the 1920s, when the
urban population officially exceeded the rural and consumption was a
greater goal than production, Edison himself had become primarily an
item to be consumed by readers of the popular press, radio listeners, and
visitors at public events. He died in 1931, on the eve of the worst period
in the depression and in the twilight of the four-hundred-year boom in
Western civilization. In 1933, when Edison was posthumously granted
his last patent, the annual total issued in the United States began a long
downswing, not to reach the former high until the 1960s.*

There is little coincidence, of course, in the fact that America, its railroads, and its greatest inventor grew up together. In 1847 a new spurt of
growth put railroad mileage permanently ahead of canals; in that same
year, Edison was born in the booming canal town of Milan, Ohio. He
was six years old when the railroad began to shape the course of his life.
Rejected by the wary town fathers, the Lake Shore Railroad bypassed
Milan in 1853, diverting commercial traffic and draining eighty percent
of the population from the town. In 1854 Sam Edison left the ruins of
his lumber business and took his family across Lake Erie to Port Huron,
Michigan, but the Edisons never regained their former prosperity.

* U.S. patent totals fell from 53,458 in 1932 to 20,139 in 1947, rose to 81,274 in
1974, and then declined steadily to 69,781 in 1977; the decline continues.

Building northward from Detroit, the Grand Trunk Railroad reached Port Huron in 1859. Edison, now twelve years old, supplemented the family income by selling newspapers and candy aboard the train. He soon began spending his spare hours in a section of the smoker car (the baggage car, according to legend) experimenting with some chemicals brought from his cellar laboratory at home. After giving part of his earnings to his parents, he would spend the rest on books and chemicals. Later he brought an old press aboard and began printing the *Weekly Herald,* a small sheet containing primarily railroad news and advertisements, but often accompanied by a joke or epigram and occasionally news of the Civil War acquired from railway telegraphers.

The Grand Trunk Railroad was a part of the Michigan Central system, which had been the first to install a telegraph line along its routes in order to prevent collisions—the early railroads having built only single tracks, with side tracks for passing. At every station, therefore, was a telegraph, which fascinated boys in the mid-nineteenth century just as planes, radios, and rockets have in the twentieth. At fifteen, Edison learned telegraphy from a stationmaster whose small son he had earlier plucked from the path of a rolling boxcar. In the Horatio Alger tradition, this incident is usually cited as the piece of pluck and luck which set Edison on the road to success—and the road was again the railroad.

At first he worked nights in railway stations as a telegraph operator and continued to experiment with electrical gadgets and various modifications of the telegraph itself. So that he might sleep part of the night, he devised a clockwork mechanism which automatically sent the required periodic signal showing that he was on the job. To practice receiving messages more rapidly he took the strips of paper on which dots and dashes were imprinted by the old Morse embossers and created a "repeater" which converted these strips back into electrical signals at any speed desired. Then he developed a telegraphic printer which translated signals into roman characters—all the while experimenting incessantly with the idea of duplex telegraphy (sending two messages simultaneously over one wire). As a result of his tricks, experimental mishaps, and personality clashes, he was frequently fired. Adolescent America incarnate, Edison drifted about the country in the 1860s, riding or walking the rails, working in telegraph offices. At one desperate point he actually joined a railroad gang laying track across a river in Arkansas.

Original tin foil phonograph. Edison
National Historic Site.

Replica of Edison's first successful incandescent lamp. Edison National
Historic Site.

Edison in Washington, D.C., with the
phonograph he demonstrated to President Hayes, 1878. Edison National
Historic Site.

Eventually he wandered to Boston, which was then the center of American scientific and electrical research. His work on the telegraph printer led to his involvement with the stock ticker (a specialized printer), first in Boston and then in New York, where he developed an improved ticker of his own. With the money and backing received from his stock ticker patents he was able to set up his first "invention factory" at Newark, New Jersey, later moved to Menlo Park.

The succession of Edison's inventions followed as naturally as the events in his life. He continued his work on the telegraph, eventually developing the quadruplex system. His interest in automatic telegraphy (eliminating the hand-powered telegraph key with faster encoding and decoding devices) led to an intensified study of chemistry and chemically treated paper and hence to the mimeograph. His crucial improvements on Bell's telephone (which was called a "speaking telegraph transmitter," and which in effect substituted sound vibrations on a diaphragm for a hand-powered key) involved refinements in the quality of voice reproduction. The final product, the carbon-button telephone transmitter, was derived from his discovery, during automatic telegraph experiments, that the conductivity of carbon varied according to the pressure it was under.

Also during his experiments with automatic telegraphy, which involved a stylus (contact point) and chemically treated paper, Edison discovered that if he wrapped the paper around a cylinder and connected both the stylus and the rotating cylinder to a battery, the friction of the stylus against the paper increased or decreased according to the strength of the current. He called this apparatus an "electromotograph" and attempted to find uses for its principle in a number of areas in which he had been working simultaneously: the mimeograph, autographic telegraphy (transmitting handwriting or drawings), a telephone speaker, and a means of somehow electrically encoding voice messages from the telephone onto paper so that Western Union might convert to it without prohibitive longhand transcription. Edison had been at Menlo Park little more than a year when these lines of experimentation converged in an aura of serendipity. Although his electromotographic telephone speaker failed to transmit his shouts when tested, the slight impressions they had made on the paraffined paper vibrated the diaphragm as he continued to turn the cylinder. The musical hum haunted him for days.

What would happen if he simply ran a strip of paraffined paper under the stylus? He tried it, shouting "Halloo!" into the diaphragm, and then ran the strip back through. There was a distinct sound, Edison later related, "which strong imagination might have translated into the original Halloo!" It was at that instant, on a hot July afternoon in 1877, that both the phonograph and the Wizard of Menlo Park were conceived.

In the following year Edison applied the principle of the carbon-button telephone to a heat-sensing device (tasimeter); this led him to the idea that a heat sensor might solve the main problem then confronting experimenters in incandescent lighting: an overheating filament. Although his eventual solution was different, this idea set him to work on the light bulb. With the exception of his contributions to the motion picture camera and projector, which resulted from his attempts to synchronize the phonograph with an existing zootropic device (pictures on a rapidly rotating wheel reflected in a mirror), all of his other major inventions were outgrowths of his work on the light bulb. His initial search for platinum as a filament substance led to his development of magnetic ore-separating machinery, later applied to iron mining. His plans for the installation of lighting systems demanded that he create a greatly improved generator along with all the aspects of the distribution system. The generator was converted into an electric motor to drive machinery, leading him to designs for electric locomotives and cars, and to his final major invention (1909), a storage battery to power them.

It has been noted that the scope of Edison's achievements rests largely on the fact that he invented the profession of inventing. Ironically, while much of the Edison symbol derives from the image of a lone individual succeeding through extraordinary physical, mental, and spiritual powers, Edison actually initiated the kind of team research, involving machinists, technical men, and trained scientists, that served as a pilot model for the huge industrial research laboratories such as those later organized by General Electric or Bell Telephone. Others have observed that an inventor of the Edison type is not a wizard but a patient plodder, trying all possible combinations and permutations, aiming for that logical but infinitesimal step which follows from the fund of previous knowledge. This process, primarily the search for materials and the struggle for practicability, is what Edison had in mind when he said that "genius is one percent inspiration and ninety-nine percent perspiration." Such a view is supported by the fact that the same innovation is often introduced almost simultaneously by separate individuals. The derivation of calculus, the discovery of the planet Neptune, the introduction of the decimal point, and the Darwin and Wallace theories of natural selection are among many examples. Bell's application for a patent on the telephone was given precedence over that of Elisha Gray because it was submitted a few hours earlier. Yet the hero remains mythopoeic; for if he is not outside of history, he *is* history. The argument from cultural determinism misses the point. The inexorable logic of Edison and America maturing together is the very genesis of symbol and myth.

A child of the steam age and chief engineer of the electrical age, Edison was a living illustration of how developments in transportation fathered those in communications. He and his dynamo stand as transitional symbols between the brute snort of the locomotive and the soft dissonance of the computer.

THE MAKING OF A WIZARD

Shaped by a transitional time, the Edison image bridged a number of cultural transformations. Chapter 2 touches on the shift from steam to electricity as part of that broader technological ascent, which Lewis Mumford has termed a shift from "paleotechnic" to "neotechnic." Later chapters relate the Edison image to the displacement of idols of production by idols of consumption and to the value shift from form to function, static to dynamic, and fixed to relative. More important, the most fundamental transition during the last one hundred years of American history has been a paradoxical one: Both America and Americans have experienced a vast increase in power and leverage over the environment while the world itself has appeared to close in from all sides. The encounter with limits that has increasingly characterized the twentieth century has cast doubt upon the organizing myth of the American world view: a New World Garden in which the American Adam is ordained to a millennial mission. Our faith in this destiny has rested primarily on a belief in the unique gift of Yankee technological know-how. It is for this reason that the Edison myth, perhaps better than that of any other American culture hero, has illustrated some of the psychocultural dynamics of the "Great American Watershed," centering in the years 1890 to 1920 (the very years in which the Edison image crystallized), but continuing into our own time.

I have noted that it is the function of the culture hero to resolve rationally contradictory cultural values into a single paradoxical reality—to mediate polar tensions. As emphases change within the Edison image, we can discover inversions of emphasis within some fundamental polarities in the American experience: the technological versus the pastoral ideal (the machine in the garden, or Paradise to be regained versus Paradise lost), individualization or isolation versus communion, power versus innocence, allocentrism versus autocentrism, and others, all of which seem to manifest some single root paradox structuring the human condition.

Bringing all of these and other general observations together, the concluding section suggests that the legacy of Edison for the late twentieth century has shifted from the myth to the man himself. The larger perspective of the book, after the degree of legend-debunking inevitable in any analytical study of heroism, is that the man who remains is finally greater than the myth.

The body of the study, however, is concerned primarily with the evolution of the myth. It attempts to determine what cultural themes have been associated with the image; which themes have been stressed most heavily; how these emphases have shifted over time; and, to some degree, what subcultures have been responsible for particular emphases at different times. The final picture, of course, is a product not just of collective psychology but of its interaction with the personality traits of the real Edison and the particular events of his real life.

The first and most obvious question, therefore, is concerned with the genesis of the myth itself. At what point in Edison's life did "the Wizard" emerge in the public mind? A schoolboy who knew only one fact about Edison would most likely cite the invention of the light bulb. It is upon this event, of course, that the greatest formal emphasis has come to rest. After ransacking the New Jersey countryside for pieces of the original lumber, Henry Ford reconstructed the Menlo Park laboratory, along with other Edisonia, at Greenfield, Michigan. Here, in 1929, on the fiftieth anniversary of the invention of the incandescent lamp, Edison reenacted his success over national radio. As he turned up the replica of the old carbon-filament lamp, with President Hoover looking on, special lamps in cities throughout the country suddenly blazed up, while Graham McNamee, the well-known radio voice of the day, proclaimed: "And Edison said: '*Let there be light!*' " Two years later, on the night of Edison's funeral, Hoover suggested that the lights throughout the nation be dimmed for a few moments. But the real tribute to the inventor lay in the fact that the idea of a complete blackout—of halting even for a moment the vast network of power which had spread over the nation from the seed planted at Menlo Park—was abandoned for fear of incalculable disaster.

The idea of the light bulb, however, was not original with Edison, and his trial-and-error discovery of the long-sought filament that made it practicable was not the event which initially set him apart from other inventors in the public mind. Nor was his system of power distribution, a far more imaginative creation, widely acclaimed. The filament, of course, which may have been his most practical single discovery, greatly reinforced the image of Edison as the American Prometheus, but under the particular circumstances it probably could not have given birth to such an image. The public mind does not dwell in the world of matter-of-fact; it lives in the realm of myth.

If one were to seek out the primordial moment when "the Wizard" materialized, it would not be the night in 1879 when the carbon lamp gave off its soft, red glow, but almost two years before, when Edison arrived out of the blue at the offices of the *Scientific American* and pushed a quaint-looking contrivance across the editor's desk.

"Here you are," Edison said. Spying a crank, the editor instinctively turned it.

"Good morning!" said the machine. "What do you think of the phonograph?" [6]

In those same West Virginia hills where Edison camped with Ford and "Santa Claus," inhabitants of sleepy hamlets believed that his name was "Mr. Phonograph." And as late as the 1920s the Lynds found that the citizens of "Middletown" thought the phonograph the "most wonderful invention of the age." In spite of the Edison tower, illuminating the modern New Jersey sky with its thirteen-foot, 5,200-watt bulb, it was the phonograph that caught the fancy of America.

2

THE WIZARD OF MENLO PARK

Edison in a Napoleonic pose after a
60-hour struggle with the "perfected"
phonograph in 1888. Edison National
Historic Site.

A reporter from the New York *Daily Graphic* visited Edison one spring afternoon in 1878 shortly after the appearance of the phonograph. "Aren't you a good deal of a *wizard*, Mr. Edison?" he asked. "Oh no!" Edison laughed, "I don't believe much in that sort of thing." But the public had made its choice. The conversation was printed; and Al Edison, the tinkering telegrapher, would live and die "the Wizard of Menlo Park."

It is not that Edison was unknown before 1878. His reputation was national—even international—for a half-decade prior to the phonograph. His duplex and quadruplex telegraphs (1873, 1874), electric pen (1874), and mimeograph (1875) were well publicized. In 1874 a "telegraphic war" was in progress between Western Union and the Automatic Telegraph Company, owned by Jay Gould. One of the skirmishes, reported in the national papers, involved a race between Gould's company, using Edison's printing telegraph, and Western Union, using manual operators. Edison's device won by a hair: With two senders and thirteen receivers it conveyed an 11,130-word message of President Grant from Washington to New York in sixty-nine minutes; Western Union's eight senders, eight wires, and eight receivers required seventy. In the same year a Western Union suit for patent infringement threatened Gould's telegraphic empire with extinction. Gould called in Edison, who saved the company by substituting an entirely new device—the electromotograph—for the Page relay system.* Edison had become a scientific soldier of fortune who could be called upon in an emergency to improvise any device needed to evade the restrictions imposed by some existing patent.

In 1874, however, Edison's international reputation was confined almost entirely to the telegraphic community. Newspapers and technical journals reported his activities to a limited, scientific public. Nor was he considered above ridicule. In 1875, while involved in telegraphic experiments, Edison noticed some strange sparks which he attributed to a new force. This "etheric force," as he called it—actually electromagnetic waves—later formed the basis of radio communication. Although he did

* Edison reversed the story for his authorized biographers, Dyer and Martin, claiming to have saved Western Union from the unscrupulous Gould (*Edison: His Life and Inventions,* vol. I, pp. 157–167). The error was repeated in most of the subsequent biographies.

not pursue it, he did announce that he had discovered a "new force." The resulting ridicule by university professors contributed to his long-lasting prejudice against all theoretical scientists. This experience, along with the attacks of academic skeptics during his work on the electric light and his boyhood inability to comprehend Newton's mathematics, helps to account for his subsequent anti-intellectualism.

In 1877 Edison replaced the crude mechanical diaphragm in Bell's telephone with what was essentially a microphone. This improvement added volume, clarity, and distance to what had previously been no more than a fascinating toy. He also invented a better receiver than Bell's. Yet even these crucial steps in the communications revolution were apparently insufficient to set Edison apart from the common inventor. At one point, he attached his receiver to an old-style dulcimer, which functioned as a speaker, and sent popular songs over a telephone wire into the Newark Opera House, where the singing and music could be heard clearly throughout the large hall. When a business associate was franchised to promote the musical telephone at various East Coast resorts, as many as 8,000 people gathered for the concerts. Although the musical telephone far surpassed Bell's crude instrument in the public mind, its impact was nothing like that of the phonograph. The telephone, which was initially called the "speaking telegraph," was apparently viewed simply as an extension of the telegraph; its working was perhaps envisioned by the lay public as somehow similar to the familiar act of speaking through a tube. But the phonograph—a machine that spoke by itself—was inexplicable.

The first reaction was often one of skepticism. Prominent scientists ridiculed Edison's announcement of the invention. At demonstrations he was even accused of ventriloquism, and a Methodist bishop came to Menlo Park to test the machine by uttering a long string of abstruse biblical names which he alone had mastered.

In each case, of course, skepticism gave way to amazement. When Edison placed his first model of the phonograph on the desk of the editor of *Scientific American,* word went through the building until people had packed themselves so tightly into the office that the editor feared the floor would collapse. Edison was invited to demonstrate the invention at the National Academy of Sciences in Washington, D.C., where the doors had to be taken off their hinges to accommodate the crush of the curious. Congressmen assembled in the Capitol to hear the talking machine; and President Hayes detained Edison at the White House until 3:30 A.M.

As the crude, tin-foil phonographs were exhibited and demonstrated all over the country, public interest assumed the proportions of a national fad. Widespread speculation on the future uses of the invention included the suggestion that a phonograph be placed in the forthcoming Statue of Liberty so that she might give "salutes to the world." The phonograph craze was boosted by the popular press, which depicted typical American families gathered about the machine in their overstuffed parlors. Reporters, discovering that Edison had patented 158 other inventions and that his models filled an entire case at the patent office, hailed him as the nation's greatest inventor. Journalists became regular visitors at Menlo Park, where Edison and his interviewers seemed to encourage one another in their mutual love of the sensational. On April 1, 1878, the New York *Daily Graphic* went so far as to print an April Fool's bannerline: "Edison Invents a Machine that will Feed the Human Race—manufacturing Biscuits, Meat, Vegetables and Wine out of Air, Water, and Common Earth." Other papers around the country picked up the story and ran it straight; no feat seemed beyond the power of a wizard who could make a machine that talked.

THE NEOTECHNIC REVOLUTION

To understand this quantum leap in Edison's reputation it is necessary to appreciate the larger impact of the phonograph on the public mind. If someone today were to announce the invention of a machine that could record the precise details of a man's thoughts, we would probably be less astounded than those who jammed into entertainment halls to hear Edison's crude, tin-foil talking machine. For the phonograph appeared on the eve of two great transformations in the history of technology: the shift from steam to electric power and the convergence of technology and science, particularly chemistry and physics. Both shifts correspond to the distinction made by Lewis Mumford between the "paleotechnic" and "neotechnic" phases of technology. The former, associated with coal and iron, was based primarily on the steam engine. The latter, associated with such things as alloys, synthetics, elasticity, electronics, and automation, was born with the dynamo.[1] In the steam age, the machine was a super-beast of burden requiring the physical degradation of men for its operation; the tasks accomplished were primarily those that could have been achieved by a sufficient quantity of manpower; most machines were but an extension of man's larger muscles. Early in the electrical age, on the other hand, the view of the machine as a benevolent superhuman which increased leisure and physical comfort became more compelling and more explicit. Machines began to do things that no quantity of men could do, becoming not only extensions of the finer muscles but of the eye, ear, and even the brain itself. The goal of Faustian man seemed within reach; and few were ready to equate the machine with Mephistopheles.

With much justice, Edison came to be viewed as the father of the new electrical age. Not only was his phonograph the precursor of all modern forms of mechanical memory and his light bulb and "Edison effect" the forerunners of the vacuum tube (the seed of electronics), but his system of power distribution took the machine from the exclusive hands of the producer and put it in the home of the everyday consumer. The machines with which Edison usually worked were not mammoth mechanical brutes like the locomotive, the essence of which did not extend much beyond the valves, pistons, tubing, and vapors visible to the eye. Rather, his reputation rested on small and delicate contrivances with obscure "magical" powers, such as the ability to duplicate a human voice, capture living motion on a two-dimensional surface, or dispel darkness at a finger's touch. A content analysis of the Edison material for adjectives used to describe his inventions reveals that, for the period 1870–1914, "simple" was the most common, followed by "beautiful," "delicate," "sensitive," "curious," and "fragile." Adjectives denoting smallness outnumber those describing bigness in the period 1870–1889 by a ratio of 10 to 1. (The obviousness here is not what it may seem. Although Edison did invent small things, the adjectives disproportionately emphasize such words as "tiny" and "minute"; more important, much of the stress is on delicate parts—especially the lamp filament—rather than whole devices.)[2]

In other words, instead of the traditional image of crude power achieved through complicated snarls of tubing, valves, and cogwheels,

Edison, to a greater degree than any man before him, suggested to Americans of the 1870s and 1880s a new concept of the machine: the achievement of spectacular ends through inconspicuous means. It was the first glimmering of the fantastic button-pushing leverage that was to characterize the electric age. Some insight into the nature of the changes implied might be gained by contrasting the ages of steam and electronics: heat, sweat, and grime give way to the glistening, flawless, indestructible, mathematically perfect shapes of mass-produced alloys and synthetics, the cool glitter of a metropolis at night, the inscrutable song of the computer, the ballet of the astronaut on the surface of the moon. It is the image of physical power under the absolute control of intellect.*

The phonograph seems to have been the first machine to awaken the mass mind to the potential of the neotechnic revolution. It is not surprising, then, that with its invention the "Wizard of Menlo Park" emerged suddenly as a national hero. Nor was the idea of wizardry misplaced. For if wizards have any universal trait it is the absence of muscle power; the wizard traditionally uses his fingers, tongue, or eyes, and his devices are the simplest: a wand or staff. He is an intellectual figure, the cerebral control of nature being the goal common to both magic and science.

WHILE THE WORLD SLEPT

During 1878 and 1879, when the phonograph and incandescent lamp appeared, the use of supernatural imagery in popular descriptions of Edison was in fact far out of proportion to all subsequent years. One of the more responsible writers of the time suggested that the journalists, running short of material, had been forced to draw upon their imaginations and create "a scientific hermit, shut up in a cavern in a small New Jersey village, holding little or no intercourse with the outside world, working like an alchemist of old in the dead of night, with musty books and curious chemicals, and having for his immediate companions per-

* When the Associated Gas and Electric System bought space in many papers during the fiftieth anniversary of the light, their tribute consisted of a large bust of Edison flanked by two drawings depicting, respectively, 1879 and 1929, the latter being represented not by the locomotive but by an electric crane effortlessly lifting it.

sons as weird and mysterious as himself." Eight days after releasing its
scoop announcing the successful test of Edison's light, the *New York
Herald* printed a piece suggesting that one's mental image of Edison
resembled that of "the Merlins" and "the Fausts":

Invisible agencies are at his beck and call. He dwells in a cave, and
around it are skulls and skeletons, and strange phials filled with mystic
fluids whereof he gives the inquirer to drink. He has a furnace and a
caldron and above him as he sits swings a quaint old silver lamp that
lights up the long white hair and beard, the deep lined inscrutable face
of the wizard, but shines strongest on the pages of a huge volume written in cabalistic characters. . . . The furnace glows and small eerie
spirits dance among the flames.

Such images of the old wizard, the article explained, were to Edison "as
the shadow is to the substance."

A passage from *Harper's Weekly* in the summer of 1879 contains most
of the imagery found elsewhere:

It is utter, black midnight, and the stillness and awe of that lonely hour
have settled upon the pleasant hills and pretty homes of the remote
New Jersey village. Only one or two windows gleam faintly, as though
through dusty panes, and the traveller directing his stumbling steps by
their light, enters a door, passes to a stairway guarded by the shadows of
strange objects, and gropes his way upward.
    A single flaring gas flame flickers at one end of a long room, disclos-
ing an infinite number of bottles of various sizes, carved and turned
pieces of wood, curious shapes of brass, and a wilderness of wires, some
straight, others coiled and spiral and kinked, the ends pinched under
thumbscrews, or hidden in dirty jars, or hanging free from invisible
supports—an indiscriminate, shadowy, uncanny foreground. Picking his
way circumspectly around a bluish, half-translucent bulwark of jars
filled with azure liquid, and chained together by wires, a new picture
meets his bewildered eyes. At an open red brick chimney, fitfully outlined from the darkness by the light of fiercely smoking lamps, stands a
roughly clothed gray-haired man, his tall form stooping under the
wooden hood which seems to confine noxious gases and compel them to
the flue. He is intent upon a complex arrangement of brass and iron
and copper wire, assisted by magnets and vitriol jars, vials labelled in
chemical formulae, and retorts in which to form new liquid combinations. His eager countenance is lighted up by the yellow glare of the unsteady lamps, as he glances into a heavy old book lying there, while his
broad shoulders keep out the gloom that lurks in all the corners and

hides among the masses of machinery. He is a fit occupant for this weird scene; a midnight workman with supernal forces whose mysterious phenomena have taught men their largest idea of elemental power; a modern alchemist, who finds the philosopher's stone to be made of carbon, and with his magnetic wand changes everyday knowledge into the pure gold of new applications and original uses. He is THOMAS A. EDISON, at work in his laboratory, deep in his conjuring of Nature while the world sleeps.

Another observer reported that the "simple inhabitants" of Menlo Park, glimpsing brilliant flashes of light from the laboratory and seeing midnight figures gliding about the fields with lanterns and equipment, "were minded of the doings of the powers of darkness." Alchemy, wonder, magic, mystical, mysterious, miracle, supernatural power, and the search for the Philosopher's Stone are commonly-found terms and phrases. The frequent use of "weird," "ghostly," and "spooky" characterizes another group of images which includes the "big iron gate," "vast gloomy corridors," "creaking stairs," and "tall, gloomy buildings, whose ghostly lights glowed in the mist." The subject of witchcraft provides numerous associations and calls forth such words as "necromancy," "conjurer," and "caldron." Referring to the thousands of different materials that Edison had collected during his search for a filament substance, one journalist suggested that if, two centuries ago, "the good people of Salem had taken an awed peep at the uncanny materials in his stock room," Edison would not have escaped the stake. "In these multitudinous drawers and shelves," he added, "lurk unearthly relics of birds, beasts, plants, and crawling things."

When Edison was not credited with a "mysterious power over nature," he was often accused of refabricating its laws. His notebooks were collectively referred to as the "Edisonian book of Genesis"; and according to *Scribner's Monthly*, one western journal represented him as

predicting a complete overthrow of nearly all the established laws of nature; water was no longer to seek its level; the earth was speedily to assume new and startling functions in the universe; everything that had been learned concerning the character of the atmosphere was based on error; the sun itself was to be drawn upon in ways that are dark, and to be made subsidiary to innumerable tricks that are vain;—in short, all nature was to be upset.

During those first years of the phonograph and the light, said a later
co-worker, "no feat would have been considered too great for his occult
attainments. Had the skies overspreading Menlo Park been suddenly
darkened by a flotilla of airships from the planet Mars" bringing a dep-
utation of Martian scientists, "the phenomenon would have been accepted as a proper concession to the scientist's genius." Fantastic rumors
arose; many believed, for example, that the evening star was a light
bulb suspended by Edison from a balloon.* The blacks in Florida,
where Edison later had a summer home and laboratory, had heard
many stories of Edison's "mysterious and wonderful power with machinery" and had come to look upon him as "something supernatural."
"They were inclined," as one reporter described it, "to give his house
and machinery a wide berth. It was difficult to get hands to take his apparatus from the boats. They won't touch any of it, for fear, as they say,
'some ob dem infernal machines gwine to bust.' " Even the native
whites, he added, looked upon Edison as an "all-powerful magician."
Inevitably, in 1890 the *Catholic World* actually went so far as to offer as a
scholarly article a "mathematical" analysis of Edison's name (the occult
figures are spread over six pages) in an attempt to demonstrate that the
Wizard was Satan himself. "There!" the author concludes, the "results
as given in this essay would all appear as plain as day."

Comparisons of Edison standing "before a white hot retort, with the
oven door open, cooking something in a small crucible" to "an alchemist at work with his big apron," along with the imagery of flickering
flames and shadows, open chimneys, fiercely smoking and glaring lamps,
and glowing furnaces, all bring to mind the kind of archetypal scene described by Hawthorne in "Ethan Brand," a classic variant of the Faust
legend (p. 27). Brand was a lime-kiln tender who went in search of the
Unpardonable Sin, only to find it within his own breast in the form of the
desire for knowledge as an end in itself. Like Edison, Ethan Brand worked
at night. The tale, which begins at sundown and ends at dawn, centers
around the kiln, or "furnace," which stood on a mountainside. Serving
as a motif throughout the story is the opening and closing of a massive

---

* The rumor seems to have originated in the fact that Edison's experiments in
1885 with etheric force (the basis of radio) involved an attempt to transmit an
electric charge from one hot-air balloon to another. Because transmission was
better at night, the balloons required lights to mark their location.

FRANK LESLIE'S ILLUSTRATED NEWSPAPER

Entered according to the Act of Congress, in the year 1879, by FRANK LESLIE, in the Office of the Librarian of Congress at Washington.

No. 1,267—VOL. XLIX.]   NEW YORK, JANUARY 10, 1880.   [PRICE, WITH SUPPLEMENT, 10 CENTS. $4.00 YEARLY. $2 WEEKLY $1.00.

Drawing of Edison before a lighted oven, carbonizing a paper lamp filament. From *Frank Leslie's Illustrated Newspaper,* 1880. Edison National Historic Site.

The Menlo Park laboratory in the
winter of 1880–1881. The main laboratory is in the center of the yard. Edison National Historic Site.

Second floor of the Menlo Park laboratory in 1880. Left to right: Ludwig K. Boehm, Charles L. Clarke, Charles Batchelor, William Carman, Samuel D. Mott, George Dean, Thomas Edison (wearing a cap), Charles T. Hughes, George Hill, George E. Carman, Francis Jehl, John W. Lawson, Charles Flammer, Charles P. Mott, and J. U. Mackenzie (who taught Edison telegraphy). Note the incandescent lamps in the old gas fixtures and the organ in the background. Edison National Historic Site.

iron door, periodically exposing the dark forest to the intense heat and "insufferable glare" of the "curling and riotous flames." With the smoke and jets of flame issuing from the chinks and crevices of this door, "it resembled nothing so much as the private entrance to the infernal regions." It was said that Ethan Brand "had conversed with Satan himself in the lurid blaze of this very kiln," and that in the course of his "vast intellectual development" he had become "a cold observer, looking on mankind as the subject of his experiment." [3]

The significance of all this imagery in the Edison literature is that it indicates a popular ambivalence toward the advance of technology. There is a dark side to the scientific-industrial revolution which has always been associated with age-old archetypes of evil—with images carried over from primitive magic and medieval alchemy. As Malinowski, Frazer, and others have observed, magic is akin to science in that it is governed by a system of internally consistent principles which dictate the means to effective action. Both magic and science seek a predictability in the material world based on an assumption of order and uniformity in nature. The logical end of both is nothing short of man's domination of the universe.

Thus, the underside of science and technology bears the same burden of evil as the myth of Original Sin or the legend of Faust; that is, the perception that the drive to knowledge and power—collectively, science and technology—involves a progressive loss of communion with anything larger than the conscious self. Good has been universally equated with the serving of some such transcendent reality, be it group, community, institution, nation, Nature, or God. Evil, on the other hand, has been defined by the world's religions as overindividualization or the drive toward the self-sufficient mastery of experience—ultimately, the dream of omniscience and omnipotence, of becoming God.

Paradoxically, there is the need, on one hand, to achieve self-definition through conflict—to establish the boundaries of the self through confrontation with external reality; on the other hand, there is also a need to find some meaning for this limited self within the context of the transcendent whole—through harmonious relationships with family, community, Nature, God, or ultimately, perhaps, our species imperatives (Jung's "archetypes of the collective unconscious"). The greater the definition of the self through knowledge and power, the greater one's isolation from the transcendent sources of meaning. Conversely, the less distinct one's individuality, the greater one's identification, or communion, with the transcendent whole (the infant's inability, for example, to distinguish itself from the mother). At the extremes of these two tendencies—toward power on one hand and innocence on the other— man becomes God; in either case he becomes, in the absence of limits, simultaneously zero and infinity. The ultimate imperative, therefore, is toward an equilibrium between these two heuristic poles of the human condition. Mythically, they represent Paradise lost and Paradise to be regained—the myth of the Garden and the myth of the Machine. The mediation of this polar tension is the function not only of the Edison image but of all modern culture heroes.[4]

At the level of cultural values, then, the myth of the Machine represents the aggressive, individualizing side of this paradox, the side which seeks to delimit a unique self through conflict. Modern Western attitudes toward material progress and individual agency have reflected an overt affirmation and a covert denial of this pole of the paradox in the form of a tension between the Promethean and the Satanic. In Greek mythology, Prometheus had not only taught man the useful arts and crafts but had stolen fire from the gods and had given it to man as a source of light, heat, and power. Fire became the symbol of technology; but in the Christian context it also came to represent the Satanic lust for self-glorification.

As the practical-minded giver of light, Edison became the American Prometheus, the prophet of technological progress. But at the same time, the sinister, occult flavor of some of the early accounts of Edison reflected popular misgivings about the myth of the Machine. Indirectly, some of these misgivings may have been related to the fact that industrial technology in the 1870s and 1880s was still in its man-consuming, steam-powered phase and, as such, was compromising the image of America as the new Eden. In this period, when the physical abuses of labor still exceeded the psychological and production took precedence over consumption, the machine had yet to produce the standard of living that would later make all misgivings sound academic.

The supernatural aura surrounding Edison was far more the product of neotechnics than of paleotechnics. The Promethean-Satanic tension was present in the initial mystery surrounding the phonograph, the light, and electricity itself to an exponentially greater degree than in the older technology, which simply exchanged brute mechanical strength for physical oppression and aesthetic blight. It was the dynamo, not the locomotive, that Henry Adams juxtaposed to the Virgin in contrasting the organizing symbols of modern and medieval history.* Most important, as I noted, the aura of neotechnics suggested new dimensions of intellect, and it is intellectual power, not brawn, that has always been at the center of both the Promethean and the Satanic visions of control over nature.

At the simplest level, of course, the public's projection of an intellectual wizard was an untutored response to new unknowns. Perhaps electricity would cure all of man's ailments as the lightning bolts on the labels of "electric" remedies proclaimed.** Perhaps man would walk on the moon as Jules Verne predicted. Or perhaps he would become a sorcerer's apprentice in a Kafkaesque society where means had become ends in themselves.

THE PROFESSOR

The misgivings, however, remained covert in the Edison literature, as they did in American writing in general. Overtly, the new extensions of intellect were hailed as harbingers of the millennium. (Table 4 in the appendix indicates the dominance of intellectual traits in the public

* A note to the structuralist: If the parallel reference to different polarities (Machine-Garden, Promethean-Satanic, dynamo-Virgin) is confusing, it should be kept in mind that any polarity is actually a quaternal matrix, since each pole has its own unique positive and negative expression. The basic duality for our purpose is the Machine versus the Garden, described as symbolizing the basic paradox of the psyche: self-definition (agency, power, means) versus self-transcendence (communion, meaning, ends). The Promethean-Satanic tension represents positive and negative expressions of the self-definition pole. The self-transcendence pole, often associated with the archetypal feminine, or Great Mother of classic mythology, has frequently found its positive and negative symbolism in an all-nurturing Good Mother and a castrating, devouring Terrible Mother.

** Edison himself was not above peddling such nostrums in the 1870s. His "Inductorum," a Ruhmkorff induction coil, was guaranteed to cure rheumatism, gout, sciatica, and nervous diseases. For neuralgia he concocted "Polyform," a mixture of morphine, chloroform, ether, chloral hydrate, alcohol, and spices.

conception of Edison's character, an emphasis also found in the boy-hood image, as shown in table 3.) An early description of the first lighting system, installed by Edison in the town of Menlo Park, explained that

all this light is generated at one point—Edison's laboratory on the plateau. From that one point he can control it all. A touch of his hand—it vanishes, and all is dark. Another touch—and all is light again. He seems to have one of the great forces completely in his control; and when he stands in his laboratory and illuminates the surrounding country, as far as his system extends, by a simple gesture, the light appears to us for a moment as the iridescence of his bright intellect.

It was, in fact, the comparable but more worldly idea of "Genius" which quickly replaced the idea of "Wizard" in the Edison symbol. Although he retained the pet names "Wizard" and "magician," by the 1890s elaborations on the terms remained only in children's books or historical references to his earlier image.

The image of Edison as a profoundly intellectual theoretical scientist, like its occult counterpart, the Wizard, dates from the invention of the phonograph. It is interesting to note the synonyms used by writers in place of Edison's name before and after the appearance of the phonograph. Prior to the event we find, in addition to "the inventor," such phrases as "the discoverer" (1875), "the first inventor of the inductive balance" (1876), and "the renowned electrician of New Jersey" (1877). Immediately after the invention of the phonograph, however, Edison became not only "the Wizard of Menlo Park" but "the Napoleon of Science," "America's great inventor," "the Professor," "Doctor," and even "philosopher." One of the reasons for such titles was that the subjects with which he worked were still matters of academic speculation; it was he himself who brought them into the practical realm of technology. Edison's critics—those who were informed about such matters as electricity—were all professors, so people naturally granted the same status to Edison. The frequent use of "Professor" during 1878 and 1879 * also illustrates the fact that the public had not as yet conceived of the

* References to Edison as "Professor" occur only during those two years. If we include uses of "Doctor," the "academic" Edison accounts for 30 percent of all synonyms used in place of, or titles used in conjunction with, Edison's name during 1878–1879.

professional commercial inventor, which is understandable when one realizes that Edison was the first to become such in the modern sense.

It seems also to have been a popular assumption that the inventor of revolutionary devices discovers the underlying theoretical principles as well. Thus Edison is repeatedly credited with having "reached out into the universe to grasp the unknown forces and capture, break and harness them to service in our daily life." One recent historian of science and technology argues that this conception of the technologist is not entirely inaccurate. The commonly accepted model of the relationship between science and technology holds that science creates new knowledge that technologists then apply. This model, asserts Edwin Layton, "is not so much false as misleading. It assumes that science and technology represent different functions performed by the same community. But a fundamental fact is that they constitute different communities, each with its own goals and systems of values." Science begets science and technology leads to further technology. This situation, which developed during the nineteenth century, had reached a point by 1900 where "the American technological community was well on the way to becoming a mirror-image twin of the scientific community." The rise of the engineering sciences enabled technology to develop its own methods, formulas, and bodies of knowledge, which were the "equivalents to the theoretical and experimental departments of physical science." Layton illustrates the difference between the two with an historical example of a physicist and an engineer who separately made essentially the same discovery. Each interpreted the event in his own conceptual vocabulary; thus, the engineer had no idea that he had uncovered a new principle, and the physicist was completely unaware that he had solved a basic problem in electrical engineering. "For information to pass from one community to the other," says Layton, "often involves extensive reformulation and an act of creative insight." [5]

Layton's model helps to explain the American paradox of apparent scientific excellence and the overwhelming antitheoretical emphasis on applied technology. To the extent that we have required pure scientists, we have more often than not imported them. It also helps account for how a man like Edison could become a scientist in the public view; for not only was the American concept of science realistically technological, but, as Layton observes, "prestige and power in engineering went to the 'doers,' not the 'theorists.' " "While Huxley, Tyndall, Spencer, and other theorists talk and speculate," said the *Scientific American* in 1878, Edison "produces accomplished facts, and with his marvelous inventions is pushing the whole world ahead in its march to the highest civilization." Edison himself epitomized the practical outlook. Referring to an assistant at Menlo Park, he complained:

He knows a lot but he doesn't stick to the job. I set him at work developing details of a plan. But when he happens to note some phenomenon new to him, though easily seen to be of no importance in this apparatus, he gets side-tracked, follows it up and loses time. *We can't be spending time that way!* We have got to keep working up things of commercial value—that is what this laboratory is for. We can't be like the old German professor who as long as he can get his black bread and beer is content to spend his whole life studying the fuzz on a bee!

If Americans have always shared some of Edison's disdain for the "old German professor," the disdain has been mutual. Britisher Harold Laski, for example, satirically commented in 1948 that the American "recognizes the great scientist in Thomas Edison." But even Laski may not have been aware of the extent to which he was correct. He might have italicized "the" had he read the 1929 newspaper comment that "no one disputes Thomas A. Edison's right to the title 'King of Science' " or heard the 1940 speech in the House of Representatives in which Edison was referred to as "our country's greatest contribution to the world list of scientific men."

Yet, in the end, science was one of the factors that was most damaging to Edison's image. This was true in two respects: First, Edison was not even a technological scientist in Layton's sense, for this involved much abstraction—including mathematics—and required increasingly greater academic training and specialization. With his practical, empirical, cut-and-try methodology, his ignorance of mathematics, and his utilitarian contempt for "*the*-o-retical science," he became more and more an outsider in the twentieth century. His image, of course, was insulated not only by his past achievements and by the other themes which it represented but also by the fact that he spoke constantly as though he were intimately acquainted with every aspect of modern science. His use of the word "science" in interviews during his lifetime seems to have increased in rough proportion to the decrease in his current knowledge of the subject. In addition, the utopian nature of his pronouncements probably encouraged public credulity. "Science will give us anything," was a typical statement. Eventually, when scientific sophistication reached the point where even college undergraduates who met him became disillusioned, this failing began to affect the image.

The fact that Edison was seen in 1879 as equal or superior to any scientist in history owed much to the novel aura of neotechnics. The fading image of Edison as scientist was probably related less to the increasing obsolescence of his knowledge and more to the fact that his inventions became household items. Furthermore, although the academic titles soon disappeared, the image of intellectuality persisted for decades, partly because it was perpetuated by reporters dressing up mundane interviews and partly because Edison himself deliberately encouraged it.

Science itself was increasingly romanticized in the late nineteenth and early twentieth centuries. Science fiction and the figure of the megalomaniacal mad scientist were born together in Mary Shelly's *Frankenstein* (1818). The stereotype, further developed by Jules Verne, entered serialized and pulp science fiction between the 1890s and 1930s. The mad-scientist stereotype may actually have gained some of its particulars from early popular photographs of Edison in his laboratory. One of the most common of these—showing him in his white smock in a dingy room full of bottles, flasks, funnels, beakers, and tubing, holding up a test tube with an expression of grim intensity—is especially suggestive (p. 87). One particularly curious item appeared in the *New York Times* as late as 1910. There is a photograph of Edison's laboratory similar to the one just mentioned, but without Edison; set part way into the picture is a small circle framing a fiendish sorcerer hovering over a spherical beaker; to the left of the frame the artist drew a bottle of nitric acid, to the right a bottle of glycerine.

By the 1890s, Edison himself had become the hero, in the "mad-scientist" mold, of a number of pulp science-fiction pieces. The terms "Wizard" and "Professor" had simply been precursors of the super-scientist, working for good or evil in the neotechnic age. When a turn-of-the-century biographer wrote that "this man of almost magical powers who worked at all hours of the night in the lonely laboratory, whence the sounds of explosions, and flashes of light more brilliant than sunlight, often issued, began to be regarded almost with a feeling of awe," he was very likely chuckling at the naiveté of wizard-worshipers while simultaneously brandishing the image of super-scientist before his readers.

THE BEST YEARS

The image of Edison as erudite intellectual and Faustian scientist continued to obscure the real man until well into the twentieth century. When the public did become aware of his raw, folksy, Midwestern personality, the myth took a quantum leap from "great inventor" to "great American." The legend began to assume a life of its own over which Edison himself had waning control. After the 1880s, in fact, as he accomplished increasingly less, the legend rose in inverse proportion to the decline in patents (see appendix, graph 1). The achievements that had generated the myth—the improved telephone, the phonograph, the incandescent lamp, and the basic elements for a system of power distribution—were confined to the brief period at Menlo Park from 1876 to 1881. Edison always sought to recreate the patterns of that period, the most productive in his life, and his nostalgic memories of its excitement, frustrations, triumphs, and comradeship intensified as he approached old age.

Most of the stock components of the Edison myth have their origin in the lore of the Menlo Park years, largely the creation of the numerous newspapermen from nearby New York who frequented the laboratory. Always on jovial terms with reporters, the Barnumizing Edison seldom failed to cook up a good story—an exaggerated claim about the imminent success of some project, a sensational prediction, a colorful opinion. From the resulting reports arose Edison's reputation for "ceaseless activity," "indomitable perseverance," "extraordinary propensities for work," and, above all, the sixty-hour sleepless marathons. (Actually, Edison's frequent catnaps on the laboratory floor or workbenches more than made up for the lack of scheduled sleep; he could sleep soundly on anything, anywhere, anytime.)

The same enthusiasm, talent, and expansive geniality that won him favor with reporters also earned Edison the extreme loyalty of the handful of men who worked with him at Menlo Park. He described them as his "friends and co-workers," and they called their thirty-year-old, unkempt, chemical-stained boss "the Old Man." His personal example, along with his self-confidence and rash optimism, kept the men working to capacity in an intense atmosphere of high anticipation. John Ott, one of the old timers, later described the "sacrifices" he had made:

"My children grew up without knowing their father. When I did get home at night, which was seldom, they were in bed."

"Why did you do it?" he was asked.

"Because Edison made your work interesting. He made me feel *I was making something with him.* I wasn't just a workman."

It became a ritual to take a break at midnight for a snack, followed by cigars, jokes, tales, and spontaneous entertainment. Some of the men might do a clog dance; or Boehm, the glass blower, would sing German songs, accompanying himself on the zither. "Another of the boys," one of them later reminisced, "had a voice that sounded like something between the ring of an old tomato can and a pewter jug. He had one song that he would sing while we roared with laughter. He was also great in imitating the tin-foil phonograph." One man would play the organ that stood at the end of the room while another strummed the guitar, and all would join in singing sentimental songs like "Sweet Genevieve," or such wee-hour standards as "Good Night, Ladies" and "We Won't Go Home Until Morning." So inviolable was the ritual of the midnight supper, observes Edison's recent biographer, that "even on the stormiest, wind-swept nights one of the apprentices was sent to the Woodward farm-house, nearly a mile away, to return with hot coffee, pie, and a steaming kettle of food." Occasionally Edison and his band would work on into morning. Reporters who missed the 9:30 train back to New York on such nights would share in the supper and singing and return "bleary-eyed on the morning train" to write of "Edison's Herculean endurance and the lab that never slept."

Menlo Park is variously described as "a quiet spot," "the merest ham-let," and "a little knot of houses near a diminutive railway station. All about it stretched open country." A picture of Edison's laboratory and outbuildings in winter, found in an 1892 biography, resembles one of those quaint, geometric, New England Christmas card scenes. A snow-covered meadow, set against a delicate background of bare trees, con-tains a number of two-story structures, the porches and peaked roofs of which are piled high with snow; sleigh tracks lead out through the gate.

From the side, the long, clapboard laboratory looks more like a barn; from the front, the porch and upper balcony give it the appearance of a farmhouse. The pastoral image is enhanced by a rectangular white picket fence enclosing the whole complex (p. 28). The contrast between the pastoral exterior and the Faustian interior, with its array of dingy jars, metals, batteries, machinery, and cobwebs of wire, is an excellent example of the "Machine in the Garden" symbolism which Leo Marx has associated with nineteenth-century attempts to reconcile pastoralism and technology (again, the polarity of innocence and power, harmony and conflict, Paradise lost and Paradise to be regained, communion and individualization). After the invention of the phonograph, the one-store hamlet of Menlo Park became famous overnight as the "village of science." Over the decades, this kind of contrast became increasingly important to the Edison image.

It was also significant that the laboratory, which was referred to as the "tabernacle," bore a resemblance to a meetinghouse or church; for Edison's move to Menlo Park was essentially a retreat to a monastery where he could devote a cloistered life to what he called "communion" with Nature—the probing of her secrets. Edison and his disciples, who, according to legend, were locked into the laboratory for days at a time pending the completion of a project, were in fact an order of ascetics in the religion of scientific and technological progress. "The truth is," wrote his authorized biographers, "there was very little social life of any kind possible under the strenuous conditions prevailing at the laboratory." Edison himself said he moved to Menlo Park to get away from the "vulgar" curiosity of throngs of visitors to his Newark shop. "When the public tracks me out here," he said, "I shall simply have to take to the woods." But—reminiscent of Emerson's man in the woods with the better mousetrap—the world soon made a beaten path to Menlo Park.

With the appearance of the phonograph in 1877, the village became the mecca rather than a monastery for the faith in technological progress. "A continuous pilgrimage of scientists and curiosity hunters," as Matthew Josephson described them, "came from cities and farms, by carriage or wagon and by train. . . . Foreigners arriving in New York by transatlantic steamer would ask their way to Menlo Park." "Follow the yellow-brick road," they might have been told, had Baum's novel been known.* The Pennsylvania Railroad organized special excursions to the town. Two years later, on New Year's Eve, 1879, extra trains were added for the first public exhibition of the light. Three thousand people poured into the town to see the globes strung between the railway station, the laboratory, and the half-dozen houses in the village. "They might have turned the place into a carnival," notes Robert Conot, "but most had a sense of historic witness. They came in wonder, they walked in awe, they left touched by the magic."

IMAGE TROUBLE

The invention of the incandescent lamp removed Edison's subordination to his financiers, radically reduced anyone's inclination to dispute him, and solidified his image as the world's greatest inventor. So exaggerated was the exaltation, in fact, that it actually worked against his popularity for some years after 1880.

Our contention that the Edison star rose with the phonograph rather than the light bulb (the evening star rumor notwithstanding) is supported by the fact that his popularity declined during the very years in which he produced the bulb and installed the lighting system in New York; it reached its former height only with the introduction of the perfected phonograph in 1888. In the 1870s, after most people had heard the instrument once, the phonograph craze died out. With its crude caricature of the human voice, the phonograph had been introduced prematurely; it remained a mere scientific curiosity for more than a decade. In spite of the temporary resurgence of celebrity after the success of the light, Edison's image continued to fade along with interest in the talking machine. If this seems strange in retrospect, it should be remembered that the light had little practical significance for the nation at large until the dynamo and a system of power distribution put it into use. A writer in 1884 observed that although Edison was very recently regarded as a wonder, a miracle, a prodigy, now he is generally considered a failure. Then the papers were full of his plans and achievements;

* Frank Baum's *The Wizard of Oz*, which did not appear until 1900, may have owed some debt to the Edison image. The self-glorifying and Barnumizing but well-meaning, good-hearted Midwestern Wizard of Oz was at home with electrical tricks, balloons, and audio and visual projection.

now his name is very seldom printed. . . . The failure of the phonograph did much to destroy the popularity of Mr. Edison. So did his subsequent failure to utilize the electric light in private dwellings to take the place of gas. So did his connection with the telephone, the honors of which discovery were carried off by his competitors. The truth is that the public expected too much, and judged the inventor, not by what he had done, but by the miracles which the newspapers had predicted for him. He has gone on inventing; but the public have [sic] ceased to expect from him a daily marvel.

The writer evidently shared the public's misconception of the significance of Edison's Pearl Street power station, inaugurated in 1882 with 85 customers and 400 lamps. But he was correct in noting that Edison's "image trouble," to use the modern PR phrase, was a result of overexpectation on the part of the public.

First of all, the rapid-fire impact of invention—Bell's telephone, for example, appeared only two years before the phonograph—had raised popular expectations to an extremely high level. Second, Edison himself made premature, barkerlike pronouncements in the papers about the success of his light. This occurred partly because of the interest of the *Herald, Sun,* and *Tribune* in Edison as "good copy," but also because Edison's lawyer hoped to draw Wall Street money to the project. Edison trumpeted his first claims to a successful light in the fall of 1878, but he was subsequently forced to abandon platinum as a filament substance and search fervently for a new material. About halfway through the year's delay, in the spring of 1879, negative reactions in the press began to multiply. Some of the criticism emanated from academic circles, but much of it was gas company propaganda. Nor were the skeptics quieted when the *New York Herald* finally announced Edison's first successful test of the incandescent lamp on December 21, 1879. In spite of the Promethean headline, "Giving Light to the World," which appeared the following day, other experimenters with incandescent light, such as Henry Morton and William Sawyer, expressed a profound distrust of Edison, citing his past false alarms. Although it was said that "among the scientific men of Europe, certainly of England, Edison stands very much higher than he does here," the *Boston Daily Advertiser* printed the comments of a French electrician which depicted Edison as a lucky tinkerer. Edison, he said, "trusts to luck." His "methods are purely empirical, and . . . he has no scientific knowledge of the force with which he is experimenting by rule of thumb."

Most of the reporting on the light during the three weeks after the *Herald*'s announcement was highly technical in nature; the few items which did treat Edison the man greatly overdramatized him, again in the context of wizardry. "It seems very probable," said one paper, "that if Edison lives much longer we shall have to destroy our primers of science and take new lessons from him in the philosophy of fact and truth." But as Edison settled into the problem of developing a longer lasting filament and a system of distributing current, the excitement again died.

He therefore dreamed up what was in large part a publicity stunt. Having finally succeeded in his exhaustive trial-and-error search for a filament by carbonizing a strip of bamboo from a fan that was lying around, he would now send explorers around the world in search of the "most perfect" vegetable fiber. This scheme, which repeated Edison's empirical method on a global scale, not only caught the fancy of all popular newspapers but has captured the imaginations of many subsequent biographers. The Dicksons, for example, in 1892, devoted two entire chapters—eight percent of their ponderous volume—to a description of two explorers' trips into the Amazon, southern India, and Ceylon, complete with a score of photographs on native life and customs. (It should be noted that the book was first serialized in *Cassier's Magazine*.) Nearly every biographical sketch explains how Edison "ransacked" or "scoured" the world for the most perfect filament material. The contemporary newspaper accounts, of course, played up the heroism and hardships of "Edison's lieutenants." Explorer McGowan, who did not taste meat for 116 days and did not change his clothes for ninety-eight,

penetrated the wilderness of the Amazon, and for a year defied its fevers, beasts, reptiles, and deadly insects in his quest of a material so precious that jealous Nature has hidden it in her most secret fastnesses.

No hero of mythology or fable ever dared such dragons to rescue some captive goddess as did this dauntless champion of civilization. Theseus, or Siegfried, or any knight of the fairy books might envy the victories of Edison's irresistible lieutenant.

The campaign, which one biographer called "the quest for a scientific Holy Grail," was a literal embodiment of the war of science upon Na-

ture. Readers needed no longer symbolize Nature with flasks and cruci-
bles, for here was a "lieutenant" of Napoleon-Edison "penetrating" the
actual "wilderness" in search of a laboratory material and undergoing
all the hardships of battle contained in Nature's arsenal. It would have
been the night-journey of a flesh-and-blood Prometheus in every minute
detail were it not for one fact: By the time the last knight of civilization
returned in 1889, bearing no better strain of bamboo than that supplied
by a single Japanese plantation owner since 1880 (a few wagonloads
sufficed for millions of lamps), carbonized bamboo itself was being replaced by "squirted" cellulose, a product perfected by chemists like
Joseph Swan, "who had stayed at home and pursued the methods of
theoretical, as well as empirical, science." But while they lasted, the explorations resembled Jules Verne's science-fiction voyages, which the
same readers encountered in the Sunday supplements.

Edison himself enjoyed Jules Verne. Although it is not certain that he
had the author in mind when he instigated the explorations, there is little question that publicity was a principal object. During the height of
Edison's public career one writer argued that his inventions were no
more significant than those of Burbank, yet only Edison's name had become a household word. "Publicity," he declared, has made Edison rich
and "the lack of it has caused Burbank to remain poor." Edison had
what Burbank lacked: a "selling organization." Although the writer
may have overlooked the symbolic differences between the garden and
the machine, he was correct in observing that Edison "became one of
the most persistent of advertisers. His name was upon all his products,
and his products were advertised in almost every conceivable way."
Even those who knew him well admitted that Edison was "a great be-
liever in advertising." One of Edison's most bitter defeats was the decision of General Electric to override his protests and remove his name
from the company title. The *New York Times* once commented that Edison has "a way of making not a few things mean" a "vast amount of
newspaper space" for himself, and that "spiteful rivals whisper that it is
quite the most remarkable of his achievements." Edison's ease with "the
boys" of the press dated from his days as a press telegrapher. He delighted in shocking and provoking statements and was always good
copy. Like his friend Henry Ford, Edison had a capacity to dramatize
his career and to generate myths about himself which gained him a

great deal of free advertising. Yet he seems to have been unaware of his own motives. "I don't propose to be Barnumized," he once protested. It would be difficult to imagine a more Barnum-like figure than the "Edison Darky," a dancing performer wired for light, who appeared at many expositions and fairs in the mid-eighties.

In spite of publicity, however, Edison's notoriety was again on the wane in the early 1880s. In fact, to the degree that overexpectation was the cause, the fading was *because* of publicity. A few days after the announcement of the new light, a New Orleans paper commented that some of the visitors to Menlo Park, "many of whom had come a great distance, seemed grievously disappointed. They evidently expected to see the rays of the sun rivaled, if not excelled." Within a year the *Boston Journal* observed that "Edison has been disciplined by his last three years of experiment, and he is beginning to be rational in estimating his own inventions and cautious in his claims." The other side of the coin was that the public was taking invention—especially Edison's—more and more for granted. When Edison threw the Pearl Street switch, lighting up a small section of New York (not the entire city, including a dazzling Broadway, as in the Hollywood version), the event appeared only on the inner pages of the papers. Yet the same switch had moved the world out of the steam age into the electrical age.

Another reason for Edison's waning notoriety in the early and middle 1880s is that he turned from experimenting and concentrated on perfecting and overseeing his power system in New York; he got himself an office on Fifth Avenue and became a businessman. By 1886 assets of the combined Edison organization approached ten million dollars, big business for those days. In addition, Edison's associates introduced him to a beautiful young socialite, Mina Miller, the daughter of Lewis Miller, a wealthy manufacturer of farm tools and co-founder of the Chautauqua Association, whose career was the subject of one of Samuel Smiles's essay-sermons on self-help. Edison's docile first wife, having led a dull and lonely existence, fattened up on chocolates and finally died of "congestion of the brain" in 1884. The following year Edison met Miss Miller and braved high society just long enough to court her into marriage in 1886. The purchase of a large stately house, called "Glenmont," in West Orange, New Jersey, completed the requirements for the role of "electricity baron." But the American public was not as interested in the business barons as the history books might suggest. Although Edison, who was a baron with an added dimension, was constantly visited by journalists, relatively little was published (see appendix, graph 1). Not only did newspaper and periodical coverage drop significantly during the period, but there were no books and only one biographical book chapter on Edison published during the 1880s, and that one lamented the decline of public interest in Edison. It was not until 1888, when competition forced him to renew his work on the phonograph, that Edison's image resumed its growth.

Alexander Bell and an associate were about to market a slightly improved model of Edison's phonograph which they called the "graphophone." In May 1888, Edison, who had been making his own improvements, locked himself and his associates into the laboratory at West Orange and produced a perfected phonograph after what the more sensational papers called a sleepless, five-day orgy of toil (actually it was only seventy-two hours). The "phonograph vigil" captured the American imagination. A photograph taken at the end of the vigil was reproduced in a Napoleonic oil painting and distributed as an advertising poster by the Edison Phonograph Company (p. 17). Edison's image was boosted not only by the "vigil" but by the fact that the new phonograph was marketable. In England, Edison's notoriety soared with the introduction of the new model and he was probably the best-known American in civilian life. In the 1890s the nickelodeon became an American institution. The Wizard had again stepped before the public eye, but this time to stay.

THE GREENING OF A WIZARD

In the decade between the tin-foil phonograph of 1877 and the perfected model of 1888, while the image of Wizard, Professor-scientist, and erudite intellectual had its ups and downs, another dimension of the legend steadily took shape. On the simplest level, the popular picture of the Wizard was a response not only to the unknowns of neotechnics but to the mystery of the inventor himself. As the Menlo Park interviews increased, however, a plain, rough-hewn, democratic Edison began to emerge. Sightseers wandering through the laboratory found a good-humored, quaint, and unpolished Midwesterner who was always happy to explain his devices. When he demonstrated the phonograph at the National Academy of Sciences in Washington, "the thirty-one-year-old Edison, looking, with his shaggy brown-gray hair standing out at all angles, like a mechanic straight from the workshop, sat shy and withdrawn, a rubber band twisting around his fingers." * In the press, almost from the beginning, nearly every item depicting the Faustian figure of the Wizard went on to qualify it with a description of the "real" Edison—the enterprising trainboy, the solid businessman, and the practical, nonconforming, egalitarian, hard-working Yankee tinkerer.

Between the first book on Edison, by J. B. McClure in 1879, and the authorized *Life and Inventions of Thomas Alva Edison* by co-worker W. K. L. Dickson and his stepsister in 1892, a standardized biographical outline had taken shape. It was a tale of how an honest, optimistic trainboy, without formal schooling, had risen to fame and fortune through perseverance and hard work. Like Franklin in Philadelphia, he had arrived in New York in rags and had conquered the city; defeating the shrewd and the skeptical with candor and talent, and in ascetic and indomitable pursuit of nature's puzzles, he had become the benefactor of mankind.

The Algeresque story of Edison's rise became a classic in the moral education of America's youth, the first juvenile piece appearing in *Stories of Great Inventors* in 1897. Although the main themes centered on the success mythology of the self-made man, along with the motif of the Eternal American Boy, the underlying dynamic was the rooting of the American Prometheus in the New World Garden.

* The parallels to Lindbergh are not surprising. Most of the basic observations which John Ward makes in his article on the aviator would also apply to Edison ("The Meaning of Lindbergh's Flight," *American Quarterly* X (Spring 1958), pp. 3–16).

3

INNOCENCE AND POWER:
THE MYTHOLOGY OF EDISON'S
YOUTH

Edison at age 14. Edison National
Historic Site.

"The happiest time of my life," Edison once said, "was when I was twelve years old. I was just old enough to have a good time in the world, but not old enough to understand any of its troubles." The same might almost be said of American society in the decade of Edison's birth. When Americans become nostalgic about the innocent and irresponsible youth of their country, they seem to favor eras of prosperity and rapid transition such as the turn of the century or the antebellum decades, setting their reveries in Grant Wood's Iowa, Lincoln's Indiana and Illinois, or Tom Sawyer's Missouri. The Midwest has been viewed as America's heartland, where the "Good Old Days" were once real; more exactly, it is the romanticized, Disneylike, Midwestern small town over which Americans become pensive, harboring visions of rambling twilight talk on a porch swing, a Fourth-of-July picnic, or a druggist who knows the family history. The nostalgia is intensified by combining the innocence of rural, small-town America with that of Huck Finn drifting down the Mississippi on his raft, embodying the collective search for identity peculiar to immigrant, mobile, restless America itself. The Eternal American Boy, often flanked by his dog, his taciturn father, and his sympathetic mother, must have flourished luxuriantly, we are sure, somewhere around the 1840s. It was right around the time when Tom Sawyer was whitewashing his fence, in fact, that the mythic Tom Edison was born to just such parents in a small town in the heartland state of Ohio.

There is more to the appeal of all this than nostalgia and simplicity. The pastoral idealization of pre-urban, pre-industrial small-town culture is a collective counterpart to the individual's reflection on his own childhood. The innocence, irresponsibility, and what Jung might call the "archetypal numinosity" of one's youth is equated with an Edenic cultural past, while the stifling complexity of adult responsibility is equated with modern, fragmented, impersonal, demythologized civilization. Just as the collective mourns the loss of an arcadian Golden Age when social conflict was absent and all the world was benevolent, the individual longs to restore his autocentric, narcissistic childhood—a holistic universe where all things had meaning and reality only to the degree that they revolved about his personal well-being. Once the child has undergone the rite of separation from the parents and has developed the power of abstraction (the rational fragmentation of experience), he is less able to escape the "knowledge of evil"—the awareness that conflict with an alien "other" is the final reality. The same contrast between power and innocence operates at the collective level, where a Faustian technological society envisions an idyllic past more in harmony with Nature and the natural, a pastoral "middle way" between the evils of the wilderness on one hand and those of civilization on the other. Leo Marx has called this ideal the myth of the Garden, suggesting that during the nineteenth century it came increasingly into conflict with the myth of the Machine—the idea that if the pristine paradise of the American Adam and his New World Eden had been *lost,* it could nevertheless be *regained* through technology.[1]

During the era of Edison's birth, the intrusion of the Machine into the Garden, like the shriek of the locomotive whistle penetrating Walden, was becoming a common experience. As the dark side of the Machine became ever more evident in the pre-electric phase of industrialization, the prophets of technological progress began to develop a new mythology: The new social order was ultimately benevolent because its *roots* were in the Garden. Descendants of purified Puritans, Jeffersonian farmers, and Jacksonian democrats, our great industrial innovators were born on the soil or in small country towns, and they were nurtured in the Garden without the unnatural advantages of wealth or formal education. In the new success mythology, the individualistic power of the self-made man was rooted deeply in communal innocence.

If the culture hero functions to resolve rationally contradictory cultural values into a single paradoxical reality, the fundamental paradox of the American culture hero has been the belief that only the New World Garden could nurture the growth of a new technological Eden. The men who built the machines and the factories in the midst of the Garden were said to be a very special kind of man: the American Adam, a powerful innocent who thrived only in the equalitarian soil of the New World Garden. Here we find Lincoln's log cabin and Edison's baggage car.

The attempt to resolve this paradox has produced a constellation of themes and images known as "the American myth of success." Though its roots run deep in Western civilization, the success mythology took on its familiar outlines in the late nineteenth century when the need was strong; for men like Rockefeller, Vanderbilt, Carnegie, and Hill were mechanizing the Garden at an exponential rate. The story of Edison's beginnings, along with that of Lincoln's, was one of the prototypal chapters in the American mythology of success.

EVERYTHING COMES TO HIM WHO HUSTLES

The perception that the development of Edison the man so closely paralleled and embodied the evolution of American society itself gave rise to the feeling that the mythology of Edison's roots—his boyhood character and environment—was somehow inseparable from the root meaning of the American epic. Thus the images of Edison's youth emphasize the idea that success is almost automatic if one's roots are in the New World Garden and the resulting American character traits are carefully nurtured.

Most of the accounts of Edison's early life consist of little more than a series of loosely joined anecdotes designed to communicate the image of a precocious, yet typically American boy whose success is foreordained by these few basic traits of character. The boyhood story has become so inseparable from the anecdotes that the sketch offered in the introduction does little more than reflect their frequency.

This study reviewed approximately 350 accounts of Edison's first sixteen years, 1847–1863 (see appendix, table 1, for a breakdown over time.) Forty of the 50 or more anecdotes discovered comprise 1,972 out of approximately 2,100 instances in which an anecdote was offered. The 13 most frequent—accounting for 1,491, or 76 percent, of those 1,972—are as follows: (1) printing the *Weekly Herald*; (2) the train fire resulting from his chemical experimenting and the ejection of both boy and equipment by the conductor; (3) saving the child; (4) the laboratory on the train; (5) the laboratory in the cellar at home and the labeling of all the bottles with the word "POISON" so that no one would disturb them; (6) the teacher calling him "addled" and his removal from school; (7) reading great literature with his mother; (8) reading books indiscriminately "by the foot" in the Detroit Free Library during train stopovers; (9) stringing a telegraph between his house and that of a friend; (10) the ear-boxing by the conductor in response to the fire, and Edison's subsequent deafness;* (11) talking the managing editor of the Detroit *Free Press* into advancing him a thousand copies on credit after learning of the battle at Shiloh from the telegraph, arranging for a telegrapher friend to wire the headline ahead to the train stops, and selling all of his papers to the waiting crowds at increasingly higher prices; (12) sitting on goose eggs at the age of six in an attempt to hatch them; (13) raising fruits and vegetables and selling them (prior to acquiring the job as trainboy). (Of the 1,972 printings of anecdotes in the sample, these 13 account, respectively, for the following percentages: 10, 9, 9, 9, 7, 5, 5, 4, 4, 4, 4, 3, 3.)

The general image conveyed by these events is that of a doer, a practical, worldly boy leading a life of hustle and bustle—the type of person likely to accompany the shriek of the locomotive into Hawthorne's "Sleepy Hollow." The figure is Franklinesque in its youthful enterprise, self-reliance, and buoyant enthusiasm. Much of this is communicated in the only existing photograph of Edison during his newsboy days. It appears again and again in books, periodicals, and newspapers, showing him in cap and scarf with a suggestion of color in his cheeks and an inscrutable expression of mischievous amusement (p. 47). A typical passage demonstrates the degree to which the literature conveys the image of intense activity:

He thought he could get a job as newsboy on that train. And from selling papers and magazines he would go on to peddling candy and fruit to the passengers. He delighted his mother by saying he would spend the mid-day in Detroit, between his goings and comings, at the public library. Yes, he had every hour of the day accounted for. . . .

In addition to his work on the train, he set up two stores in Port Huron, one for periodicals, the other to continue his vegetable marketing. The first closed abruptly when Thomas found his partner holding back part of the daily profits. But the vegetable shop did a thriving business. To supplement the products of his father's gardens, the boy lugged to the shop huge baskets of produce from the Detroit markets along with the butter and eggs he picked up at small country stations.

* Edison's near-deafness has also been attributed to an incident in which he was late for the train and the conductor pulled him aboard by the ears. In truth, his hearing problem, which worsened throughout his life, was either congenital or a result of the scarlatina he had had as a child, although a blow or a yank on the ears might have accelerated the deterioration.

He had two years of such successful selling experience when news of the Civil War began to flash along the wires to Detroit. Immediately, Thomas saw his chance and took it. [The anecdote of the Battle of Shiloh newspaper bonanza follows.]

[Within days of the bonanza he was publishing his own newspaper.] Then he rolled up a list of five hundred regular subscribers who with three hundred chance buyers added $45 a month to his income.

Life was certainly moving fast for Tom, and profitably. But, while giving enough attention to his publishing, his trade in papers and candy, and his vegetable markets to keep them going successfully, his real heart and best thinking were centered in the smoking car laboratory. . . .

Of the thirteen most frequent anecdotes, there are three that at first glance may not seem to be in line with the image of intense, practical activity. The point of the first of these—being pronounced "addled" by the teacher and withdrawing from school—is that formal education in Edison's day was neither practical nor active. (Actually, Edison received considerably more schooling than the three months allowed by the mythology.) The intended irony, often explicitly stated, is that the teacher could not tolerate Edison because he asked too many practical questions, and he was bored by the rote memorization of information which he could not apply to his everyday life. The teacher is not the only skeptic depicted. The townspeople also viewed Edison as "a dunce" and a misfit because of his "foolish questions," the implication being that the adults were embarrassed by their ignorance of the world about them (if they answered "I don't know," Edison asked "Why don't you know?"). Sometimes, however, the reactions were sparked by Edison's attempts to answer his questions for himself; for example, he set fire to his father's barn "to see what it would do" and filled a friend with gas-producing Seidlitz powder to see if he would fly. The critical reader cannot help but suspect that Edison was at least "different" as a child, though the opinion of almost all biographers is clearly that the skeptics were the real "dunces." If nothing else, as some recent writers have suggested, Edison was a hyperactive child. Such instances, however, are presented not only as evidence of intellectual precocity but in a "boys will be boys" tone with the implication that Edison was a boy's boy.

The second anecdote which may seem to conflict with the image of practical, worldly activity is that relating the hours spent in the Detroit

Free Library. "I started," Edison later wrote, "with the first book on the bottom shelf and went through the lot, one by one. I didn't read a few books. I read the library." The consensus of the more realistic accounts seems to be that he read about six feet of books on one shelf before the librarian convinced him that he should use greater discrimination. One writer actually accepted the idea that Edison read the entire library; his point was that Edison could accomplish whatever he set out to *do*. Another author has him reading "a foot a week." Edison's reading, in other words, was quantitative rather than qualitative; success was measured by the energy expended or the sheer bulk of facts acquired.

The third anecdote in question, relating how Edison and his mother read such authors as Gibbon, Hume, Sears, and Shakespeare, is obviously incongruous with the image of the practical doer. The biographers, however, seem to include the anecdote primarily to provide Edison with the same kind of token culture indulged in by late nineteenth-century "doers" who bought massive gilt-framed oils in Europe to hang in their gingerbread mansions. Occasionally one encounters a suggestive comment such as "You will not find one great man in a hundred who has had several years of schooling, who has read the above learned but hard and dry books." One wonders how much the nine-, ten-, and eleven-year-old Edison really absorbed.

The primary image of Edison's early life, then, is that of a busy, energetic, industrious, enterprising, highly motivated and ambitious, self-reliant, and worldly boy. At the center of this picture is a profound concern for two major canons of nineteenth-century success mythology: the Protestant Ethic, that is, the older Puritan virtues relating to diligence and industriousness at one's occupation; and the later emphasis on social mobility through competition in that occupation. The first of these dominated the success literature of the early nineteenth century. Written primarily by Protestant clergymen, these success tracts, self-help handbooks, Christian sentimental novels, and children's books were highly moral in tone, espousing the great Trinity of the Protestant Ethic—Industry, Frugality, and Prudence—while seeking generally to preserve the traditional social hierarchy and the values geared to a static, agrarian society. The success writers idealized the man who knew his Bible from cover to cover, who exhibited the virtues of the Protestant ethic, and who had risen from rural poverty—with the aid of a good

mother—to the mastery of some occupation that offered a sound competence. "Poverty," however, did not mean slum tenancy or migrant farm
labor; it referred rather to the literate, preferably self-educated, middle-
class boy brought up on a farm, or in a small town, where the family
had to struggle to make ends meet. Accumulation was not an end in itself; wealth without labor was ignoble. Writers on success did not simply
give advice on how to get ahead in the world; they presented an entire
world view—a spectrum of merchant-agrarian values that included
piety, devotion to hearth and home, and usefulness to the community.[2]

Although the rural, Protestant mythology was upstaged in the late
nineteenth century by more ruggedly individualistic themes centering
on social mobility, much of the older tradition survived. Most of those
who describe Edison's early life, for example, are captivated by the boy's
capacity for work. "He found his 'fun,' " we are frequently told, "in doing things which most boys would have called work." "Putting aside
sleep, rest, and amusements of the idler sort, for years [the boy] worked
fifteen to twenty hours a day. Any man who sets for himself the ideal of
hard work is certain to go far on the road to success." "The more to do
the more to be done," the fifteen-year-old Edison himself wrote in his
Weekly Herald, noting that two porters never seem to accomplish as
much as one alone. And when he learned that his truck farming had
made $600 he said, "I guess hard work pays." Selling papers on the
streets while waiting for a reply to his application for the job of trainboy, he exemplified one of his favorite proverbs: "Everything comes to
him who hustles while he waits."

For most writers, the very notion of a job, any job, is held in reverence. One overenthusiastic biographer has Edison earning his own living
from the age of eight. Combing all of the boyhood material for nouns or
adjective-noun phrases used in place of Edison's name, almost exactly
one-half of the terms refer to economic occupations such as "newsboy,"
"editor," "merchant," or "proprietor." [3]

It is as a young "businessman" or "capitalist" (the terms are frequent)
that the teenage Edison is most admired. The most menial tasks became
"business" if young Edison was engaged in them, and his "business acumen" is noted repeatedly. He always tried, for example, "to get one person buying at the front end of the car, as he noticed that, if one bought,
others were sure to follow." The Battle of Shiloh newspaper bonanza

anecdote, especially, is used to demonstrate "what kind of a businessman he was." Another less popular anecdote, appearing in about twenty
percent of the books (it was too long for use in most of the briefer
items), involves a haughty Southerner aboard the train who asks for all
of Edison's magazines and flings them out the window, instructing his
slave: "Nicodemus, pay the boy!" After seeing to it that all his other
wares were out the window and paid for, Edison dragged a huge trunk
full of all his unsalable items down the aisle along with his own shoes
and shirt; all were ejected, and a sizable settlement was made with
Nicodemus.

The attitude toward the money made by all this pluck is ambivalent.
It is generally asserted that Edison was not interested in profit for its
own sake but conducted all his enterprises only for the purpose of earning enough money to purchase chemicals and books on practical science.
We are told that he often took the money handed him by his helpers
without counting it. Yet a number of authors are concerned with profit
to the point of offering complicated estimates after each of Edison's ex-
ploits. Sometimes it is suggested that he made more than most men at
the time. Estimates range from five to ten, even to the ridiculous sum
(for the 1860s) of twenty dollars a day.

"It does not matter much what I do," young Edison says, "so long as
the work is honest and brings in the cash!" An anecdote encountered
only seven times (and only once in the youth-oriented literature), however, involves a trick Edison had of scooping into the customer's pocket
only half the amount of peanuts paid for. A variation (counted in the
seven instances) is Edison's later reminiscence that the bottoms in his fig
boxes "were at least an inch thick." To make the case for honesty, however, one juvenile book attempts to update the Parson Weems story of
Washington: "I did it," Tom says after burning down his father's barn.
But it was closer to the Smothers Brothers' version of Weems (Washington's father "looked at him with tears in his eyes—and smashed him
in the mouth") in that Edison was publicly whipped.

Although industriousness is the most prominent, all the traits in the
rural, Protestant tradition are evident in the Edison material (see appendix, table 3). The lesson drawn from Gibbon by Edison's mother is that
"idleness, pride and indulgence bring the downfall of individuals as
surely as they do empires," and, again, that "pride and sloth come be-

fore destruction." Edison, we are told, "never lost sight of the goal of success, never allowed his brain to rust or his splendid energies to be exhausted in excess or dissipation"; he was "willing to work hard, dress poorly, and eat plain food for the sake of his laboratory."

The rural, Protestant success mythology, or self-help literature, as it was called, persisted into the post-Civil War period, where, with the Mugwumps and the Populists, it took a futile stand against the fundamental consequences of industrialization. At the same time, another success tradition arose alongside that of the Protestant clergy. The great increase in success writing after the Civil War was due primarily to this second stream of literature, which stressed competition, enterprise, the power of will, and the pursuit of wealth, and readily accepted a society governed solely by economic and political motives.

OUT OF A BAGGAGE CAR

With the rapid industrialization and large-scale consolidation in late nineteenth-century America, the successful industrialist became the leading oracle of the success mythology. Espousals of what came to be called "rugged individualism" continued to include the Protestant virtues but developed the individualistic implications at the expense of the communal, laying far greater stress on social mobility: ambition, initiative, energy, drive, shrewdness, the will to win, and a religious dedication to material progress.

Of the three major ideals in the mobility theme, two are contained in the statement that Edison "rose from a poor newspaperboy with very little schooling to be one of the greatest inventors the world has ever known." The first ideal is that America is a place of equal opportunity where one can succeed regardless of his origins. This was emphasized during the fiftieth anniversary celebration of the incandescent lamp when President Hoover said on the radio: "Mr. Edison by his own genius and effort rose from modest beginnings to membership among the leaders of men. His life gives renewed confidence that our institutions hold open the door of opportunity to all those who would enter."

There is, however, some confusion about Edison's beginnings. Of those writers who, explicitly or implicitly, make some commitment on the question, 42 percent (57 out of 135) say his family was poor, 37 percent say the Edisons were comfortable, and 21 percent say they were well-to-do. The main source of confusion lies in the decline in family status following their move from Milan to Port Huron. The conflict seems to date from the fact that the first book-length biography (Mc-Clure, 1879), referring to Milan, described the family as well-to-do, while Edison himself, thinking of Port Huron and his later days as a wandering telegrapher, told interviewers that he had been poor. The fact that Edison was not born in poverty has usually found its way from the major biographies into the juvenile literature (where 42 percent say he was comfortable, 28 percent well-to-do), partly because it fits the image of the typical middle-class American boy with whom most of the readers can identify. The journalists, however, aware of the aura surrounding humble beginnings in America, did not question Edison's assertion.

The license encouraged by this confusion has resulted in much romantic exaggeration, especially in the periodicals, where 61 percent of the statements about early status imply that Edison's beginnings were Lincolnesque in their humble simplicity. The fact that many people knew nothing else about his youth except that he "began life as a newsboy" also perpetuated the image. Popular writers were fond of phrases that described Edison as having been "born of a poor family in an obscure Ohio canal village," in a "humble brick cottage," the "modest dimensions and design" of which "serve as a constant reminder that in America a humble beginning is no deterrent to success." "Never has there been an American inventor," declared *Mentor* magazine in 1913, "who has achieved greatness under a heavier handicap of early disadvantages."

The second ideal in the mobility theme, contained in the frequent phrase "very little education," complements the first. One says that you will not be prevented from climbing the ladder by artificial social restraints; the other says that neither do formal institutions *aid* any person or group in the ascent. Behind both ideals, of course, is an equalitarian belief in democracy. "Common men regarded [Edison] as one of themselves," we are told, "because he rose from their social ranks." "Edison stands for opportunity in a democracy," said the *New York Times* on the centenary of his birth. "He came not out of a great university, nor even out of a high school, but out of a baggage car where he had set up a little laboratory, and out of railway telegraph offices, where he conceived his first inventions. In a word, he was the uncommon man who always emerges from the mass of common men and who proves that democracy works not only in politics, but in science and invention." Compared with the success virtues, good genes and formal education are of little importance and may even be a hindrance: "School?" Edison once exclaimed to an assistant, "I've never been to school a day in my life! D'you think I would have amounted to anything if I had gone to school?" Many biographers agree that he was "blest with little formal schooling, which might have ruined him." "Whenever a boy wants to learn," one writer tells his juvenile readers, "he will learn whether he goes to school or not." "Edison was born without riches or extraordinary mental equipment," writes another, "his achievements were accomplished entirely through hard work and perseverance." An article entitled "How They Got Their Education," which appeared during the "normalcy" of 1922, at the height of a controversy over Edison's attack on university education, leaves the impression that no great American in history ever finished grammar school. "Any man with a backbone can educate himself," explained the author.

No one denied that men differed in intellect. The issue was whether those differences, within limits, were important to success in America. More simply stated, the issue was equality of opportunity. The conflict lay between *experience,* or practical, self-educated "know-how," and *intellect,* or an abstract body of knowledge that was not only more accessible to the genetically superior brain but was a sacred lore, ritually passed down by the intellectual oligarchies of formal education. The former was associated with democracy, the latter with theocracy and aristocracy. It was never asserted that Edison's talents had no bearing on his success. But his talents were practical. "In the rush of the metropolis," one writer tells us, "a man finds his true level without delay, especially when his talents are of so practical and brilliant a nature as were this young telegrapher's."

The third component of the mobility myth is the contention that the "school of hard knocks," where the self-made man is self-educated, is a crucible for the virtues of atomistic individualism. Edison got his hard knocks as a newsboy and telegrapher. "In the ups and downs of this rugged calling Edison found his university education," explained one obituary, and it was this "process of relentless self-education which eventually made him the best known and most representative American." The emphasis is on "struggle," "lifting oneself," and "step by step advancement," phrases that abound in the Edison material. Self-reliance is an especially strong trait; the biographers are impressed by "the necessity of [Edison] going out in the world and taking care of himself." The image is supported by the aggressive self-confidence that characterizes his enterprises. As late as 1950, a Pennsylvania Chief Justice proclaimed that Lincoln spent "less than one whole year, and Edison spent less than three months, in a schoolroom. . . . They faced difficult problems, not with wishbones, but with backbones. . . . Lincoln and Edison each paddled his own canoe. . . . Nancy Elliot Edison raised her son to be self-reliant and self-supporting. He was taught to seek his security in what he could acquire by his industry and conserve by his thrift."

The reference to Edison paddling "his own canoe" is suggestive of Turner's thesis that the frontier takes the European "from the railroad car and puts him in the birch canoe." "To the frontier," he said, "the American intellect owes its striking characteristics. That coarseness and strength combined with acuteness and inquisitiveness; that practical, inventive turn of mind, quick to find expedients; that masterful grasp of material things, lacking in the artistic but powerful to effect great ends; that restless, nervous energy; that dominant individualism, working for good and for evil and withal that buoyancy and exuberance which comes with freedom." [4] Turner might just as well have been describing the boyhood image of Edison. The irony, as Edison himself demonstrated, is that these traits are more suited to the railroad car than to the canoe. The machine did not invade the Garden; in America it was born there.

The frontier thesis, written in 1893, three years after the census announced the disappearance of the frontier, stands, like the success mythology itself, at an ideological crossroads. Behind was the image of the wilderness Garden of America with its log cabins and canoes. Ahead lay the image of a mature and powerful nation, regaining Eden through her own indomitable energy. Paradoxically, however, it was believed that such energy belonged only to the American Adam and could only have taken root in the frontier Garden. The parallel between the self-made nation and the self-made man is obvious. America, like its greatest men, had begun in poverty. The theme dominates most of our cultural images, from the ragged men at Valley Forge to the words inscribed on the Statue of Liberty, beckoning the tired, the poor, the "huddled masses" and "wretched refuse" of the world.

TATTERED TOM THE MICHIGAN TRAIN BOY, OR, THE IMPOSSIBLE DREAM

The speaker who praised Edison for paddling his own canoe may not have heard of Turner, but he had most certainly heard of the author of *Strong and Steady, Or, Paddle Your Own Canoe,* a novel written in 1871 by Horatio Alger, Jr. One of the most popular novelists of all time, Alger wrote over one hundred books for boys, the hero of which was usually the ambitious country boy who broke home ties to seek his fortune in the great migration from farm to city during the last half of the nineteenth century.

In the popular mind, the mythical Alger hero is a ragged boy who is plunged into the maelstrom of city life but works conscientiously as a newsboy or bootblack until—through initiative, enterprise, and the Protestant Decalogue—he eventually rises to fame and fortune. On the basis of this unqualified image, a number of concepts have been inaccurately attributed to Alger, confusing his stories with the success apologetics of later industrial capitalists, stressing economic mobility and the accumulation of wealth. He belongs instead with the McGuffey readers in the rural, Protestant, middle-class reform tradition.

First of all, Alger did not glorify the common man; his street waifs are always middle rather than lower class. Second, he did not equate the pursuit of money with the pursuit of happiness. Alger's heroes strive for moderate economic security and middle-class respectability. Even more important than the Protestant virtues are those qualities of character and intellect, such as fidelity, punctuality, and courteous deference, which make the hero a good employee. The third misconception is that the Alger hero was a rugged individual who rose by his own efforts. The Alger plot (which, in spite of inept attempts to camouflage the fact, never varied) always involved a Providential stroke of luck. The struggling hero barely maintains himself on the sale of his papers, finding it impossible to accumulate any savings. Then suddenly he rescues a child.

Edison was once permitted to drive
this locomotive when he was a newsboy on the Grand Trunk Railway.
Edison National Historic Site.

The wealthy father, who just happens to be in the line of business toward which the hero aspires, rewards him with a junior partnership. We are assured, however, that luck never comes to the wicked and that the boy had prepared himself through goodness, industry, and perseverance to seize the opportunity when it arrived (reminiscent of the Calvinist notion of an inscrutable God who saves only, but not all of, the virtuous).

Two incidents in the mythology of Edison's youth have been placed in the Alger tradition. The first, the rescue of the station agent's child, enables him to learn telegraphy and ultimately sets him on the road to New York and electrical invention (although it appears that the stationmaster was a friend of the family prior to the incident and might have been induced to teach him anyway). The second, receiving the $300-a-month job in return for making the simple repair on the stock ticker, alleviates his poverty and provides him with a benefactor who eventually pays him $40,000 for an improved stock ticker; Edison uses this money to establish his shop for manufacturing and invention. (Again the facts are distorted; apparently the $300-a-month job never materialized, so that the repair had little direct bearing on subsequent events.) While these two mythic incidents are correctly placed in the Alger tradition, other aspects of Edison's early image seem to qualify the association..

Even if Edison was not a street urchin living in dire poverty and his aggressive enterprise was more in line with the "rugged individualism" of Rockefeller or Vanderbilt than with Alger's employee-hero, the resemblance of "tattered Tom" to Tom Edison remains striking. Edison, after all, *was* a newsboy, a train boy, and a telegraph boy, and there is continual reference to his having "faced the world hunting for a job." Alger's titles include *The Telegraph Boy* (interestingly, written in 1879 immediately after Edison achieved his first notoriety with the phonograph), *The Train Boy* (1883), *Number 91 or, The Adventures of a New York Telegraph Boy* (1887), *The Erie Train Boy* (1890), *Facing the World* (1893), *Mark Mason's Victory: The Trials and Triumphs of a Telegraph Boy* (1899), and nine others containing the name "Tom," only two of which fall before 1878. The picture of Edison as he "trudged up the middle of the dusty street with a bundle of papers under each arm" is certainly Algeresque, as is the pronouncement that selling papers is "the first avenue for a boy." And if he was not "adrift in the city" as a small boy, he certainly was adrift as a wandering telegrapher. To what degree Edison

provided material for the Alger stories and to what extent Alger provided patterns for the Edison myth may never be known. The fictionalized juvenile literature often bears a strong resemblance to the Alger
style. One passage, accompanied by a picture of young Edison with his
cap in his hand facing a man with a top hat and a walking stick, reads

"Please Sir," he said eagerly . . . "if you need a boy to sell newspapers, I—I'd like the job."
"You sound like a hustler, young fellow!" he exclaimed, "that's the
kind of fellow we need!"

Some of the Edison material also falls into the Alger pattern by virtue
of its concern for employee traits. Edison was "so faithful in his duties as
a newsboy that he had made and saved quite a little sum of money."
Moreover, "people liked his bright face and pleasant manners," and "his
stock was neat and clean"; they "liked to buy things from this friendly
train-boy." One of the anecdotes, another which was too long to be
found anywhere but in books, tells of the night when Edison was paid
fifteen dollars to fetch a ship captain who lived fourteen miles from the
nearest railway station. Terrified of bears, and tripping over stumps in a
heavy rain, Edison forced himself to go on through the black night.
When his companion became weak-kneed, Edison declared, "I promised
to deliver the message," and "young Edison's reputation as a boy who
always carried a 'Message to Garcia' was known throughout the Michigan country." Elbert Hubbard's "A Message to Garcia" was a tract
honoring self-reliant and conscientious perseverance; next to Franklin's
Way to Wealth, it was, according to Richard Huber, "the most effective
and widely distributed tract in the history of success literature." [5] It was
essentially a well-timed defense of the success mythology that shifted
praise from the builders of oligopoly to the men within it who got the
job done.

While Alger's concern with the white-collar worker mirrored a social
transition, his use of luck reflected an ideological shift within the success
mythology. His outlook was expressed by a 1908 reviewer commenting
on Edison's rescue of the station-agent's child: "Fortune is ever on the
alert to serve him who is worthy of her favors." (Although Edison seized
the child with considerable time to spare, 40 percent of the accounts describe close calls to the point of Edison's heel being touched by the

wheel.) A 1929 article entitled "Making Friends With Luck" used the
Nicodemus anecdote to say approximately the same thing; but a new
dimension was added. The author agreed with Alger that "good luck is
a wise chooser of its companions," but it also "prefers to run with the
man who sees his way clearly and is prepared to act quickly when approaching decisive moments. . . . The really lucky man is the one who
knows good fortune when he sees it and then pushes it to the limit." In
1952, a book called *How to Attract Good Luck and Make the Most of It in
Your Daily Life* again distorted the Nicodemus incident to produce the
same moral: "Edison's mind was ready to recognize chance because he
understood his own requirements. When chance offered him an opportunity to fulfill the most urgent of these [the purchase of science books],
he seized it quickly."

If Franklin's *Way To Wealth* and Hubbard's "A Message to Garcia"
were the two most popular tracts in the history of the success mythology, Russell Conwell's *Acres of Diamonds* was probably third. His point
was that poverty is invariably the result of the individual's failure to
recognize the opportunities that lay right under his feet. The emphasis
on opportunity was a part of the Pollyanna-like optimism, the belief in
willpower, mindpower, or "positive thinking" and the evangelistic faith
in the transcendental power of the single individual that began to characterize the success mythology around the turn of the century. Popular
middle-class magazines such as the *Saturday Evening Post* and *Success*
offered dramatic stories of success or failure in parable form or short biographies describing the rise from rags to riches of well-known figures in
business, politics, and the professions. At the same time, the Alger myth
was altered to fit the new ideology: People succeeded because they expected to succeed.

Edison's cheerful acceptance of his deafness gave rise to much comment in the mindpower tradition. People were impressed when he
reflected on the boyhood causes of his affliction and declared, "Spilt
milk doesn't interest me." One author devotes an entire essay to the
point that Edison was superior to the average man in his ability to remain confident while "stricken by handicap." Edison's willpower and
"try, try again" nature were popular knowledge. He "persisted in behav-
ing as if his body were strong enough and tough enough to enable him
to bear any amount of exertion and fatigue, and it ended by becoming

so," said one mindpower advocate. The enterprising experiences of
Edison's youth were the first signs that "older men could be influenced
by his will." In the Dale Carnegie spirit it is observed that three friend-
ships were "landmarks in his progress as a boy": the managing editor
who advanced him the papers with the Shiloh headline, the man who
sold him the press cheaply, and the station agent who taught him
telegraphy.

The self-help, mindpower, positive-thinking success tradition, which is
at least as old as Christian Science and which became one and the same
with the official business creed in the 1920s, has survived to the present
in Norman Vincent Peale, TM, EST, and numerous other fads. Beneath
this tradition lies a view of the universe as ultimately benevolent. The
key disposition is optimism. "The drive for him was interest, 'radiant
interest,' another definition of genius," wrote one of Edison's better biographers. The early period of his life "is a wonderful tribute to the
willingness of people to help," says another. "If a boy is in dead earnest
and can convince others that he is worthwhile, he will find thousands
ready to help him. The half-hearted desire gets nowhere." Optimism,
however, is not confined to the mindpower success mythology; it lies in
the vision of Eden at the center of American culture. The very first
book-length biography of Edison (1879) proclaims that "he was taught
the presence, power and possibilities of human resources, and what he
himself might ultimately accomplish if 'faithful to the end'; that the
world was one great, broad field of activities, and that Nature was
brimmed with law, order, the beautiful and good." This core faith
emerged in the aura surrounding the discovery of the New World, when
the boom in land, bullion, and opportunity gave the individual an unprecedented feeling of existential freedom and self-worth.

Any collective identity is rooted in the experiences which have shaped
it. If there is an American spirit, it has been forged by the immigrant
experience, westward movement, urban migration—quests after the
impossible dream by people willing to undergo radical uprooting and
unknown threats. Certain group traits were prerequisite: hope, the self-
confidence to risk change, optimism about the potential of the future,
and the courage to endure what was necessary to realize it. There had
to be a collective sense that one could break away, that one *could* escape
history. Held short of blind millennial dogma, this basic affirmative

spirit is the lifeblood of any collective. It is this archetypal faith in the future that Edison embodies perhaps better than any other American symbol.

THE ADVENTURES OF TOM EDISON

Nowhere is this Edenic sentiment more visible than in our obsession with beginnings, nascent activity, and the promise of youth in the Garden of America. Although the thirteen most frequent anecdotes in the Edison material were primarily connected with the success mythology, the next eleven were suggestive of the "typical American boy"—that barefoot, adventurous, mischievous, curious, and imaginative sprout who is nevertheless imbued with Yankee ingenuity, canniness, practicality, and horse-sense. Significantly, MGM's *Young Tom Edison,* which grossed over a million dollars at 1940 prices, starred Mickey Rooney, who began his career in the "Our Gang" series and *Boy's Town,* went on to play Huck Finn, and became the number one box office attraction in 1939 and 1940 as Andy Hardy, the typical American Boy.

Beginning with number fourteen, the next eleven most frequent anecdotes in the Edison literature are: (14) the barn-burning incident; (15) a friend swallowing gas-producing Seidlitz powder for Edison, who wanted to see if he would fly (inspired by the sight of the "mad Miller of Milan" disappearing in his balloon); (16) a serious scratching by a cat that Edison was rubbing in an attempt to produce electric power; (17) *Paul Pry,* a gossipy expansion of the *Weekly Herald* that (18) got Edison thrown into the river by an angry subscriber; (19) the six-year-old Edison falling into the Milan canal; (20) making his own telegraph set after the station-master's offer to teach him the trade (an "achievement" which is still in the cub scout handbooks); (21) climbing his father's backyard tower (built simply for the view), where he played Captain Kidd and Robinson Crusoe; (22) pretending to forget to bring his papers home so that his news-conscious father would agree to let him stay up and practice the telegraph by getting the news from a friend over the wire; (23) falling into the grain bin in Milan; and (24) running a locomotive while the engineer slept and blowing soot all over the engine and himself because he failed to stop for water.

There are many other yarns: he is butted by a ram; he cuts off part
of a finger while trying to shorten a skate strap with an axe; he feeds a
choregirl a concoction of worms (trying again for that elusive flight); he
and some others get into a scrape across the border with some Canadian
boys after ridiculing the visiting Prince of Wales; and he often sneaks up
on an army post in the dark, commanding the corporal of the guard to
report, until finally he avoids capture only by hiding in a barrel in his
cellar. All of these "Tom Sawyer" yarns are disproportionately emphasized in the juvenile literature.*

None of these tales receive anywhere near the emphasis of the success
stories (they account for 18 percent of all instances in which an anecdote
is given, as opposed to 76 percent for those associated with the success
mythology). Nevertheless there is a general attempt to exaggerate the
"typical boy" image. One biographer lists most of these anecdotes and
then says that "such things were all in a day's adventures." The movie,
Young Tom Edison, portrays the American Boy far more than it does
Alger's Ragged Dick. It even goes so far as to invent two new anecdotes:
Tom almost burns down the school while experimenting in the cloak
room where he was sent as punishment; later he nearly blows up a train
with a bottle of nitroglycerin. Hollywood also structures the Seidlitz
powder incident in direct parallel to the fence-whitewashing section of
Tom Sawyer, only Tom Edison uses his clever psychology toward the
more exotic end of human flight. Tom's interests were closer to Tom
Swift's than to Tom Sawyer's. (In reality, Young Edison was called
"Al," for Alva.)

The whole attempt to "Tom Sawyerize" Edison probably arose out of

* The anecdotes receiving disproportionate emphasis in the juvenile literature
were, in descending order, numbers 24, 12, 6, the corporal of the guard incident,
3, 15, 19, 5, 8, 4, an unmentioned episode in which a train wreck spills his wares
over the ground and he attempts to eat all the candy to avoid waste, 23, 21, 2,
and the worm concoction. Those receiving disproportionate emphasis in the literature for older youth were, in descending order, the corporal of the guard, the
night message to the ship captain, 22, being butted by the ram, seeing the
"Great Western Panorama" painting (the irony being that it anticipated the
motion picture), failing to report that a playmate had drowned, a visit to the
Page farm, the Prince of Wales incident, the worm concoction, 23, 20, copying
store signs as a small child, running the locomotive, the skate strap, Nicodemus,
9, 11, 12, 19, and 13.

the fear that it would be difficult for young readers to identify with a laboratory recluse. "This lad," declares Mary Nerney,

was no Penrod, smoking hayseed cigarettes and scribbling lurid romances on his stable retreat while the faithful 'Duke' thumped approval with his tail. Dancing school and Sunday school seem to have been as remote from his young life as children's parties. Nor is there any record that he ever blacked his shoes, brushed down his cowlicks, or donned his best suit to call on a girl. There was no Fanchon, no Marjorie Jones to distract him from the lure of experimenting. Nor as adolescence sped toward manhood does he seem to have entertained any of those common questionings of youth about the soul.

"He never had any boyhood," said his father. "His earliest amusements were steam-engines and mechanical forces." This, along with the statement by a few other writers that he was "essentially a dreamer," sounds closer to the truth. Most of the "adventures," if one puts them in perspective for a moment, are duller than those of the great mass of American youth. Even the success aspects are greatly played up. There is a reproduction of Edison's "baggage-car laboratory," with the inventor's seal of approval, created by Ford at the Edison Institute at Dearborn, Michigan. It is an unprepossessing model: a little wooden table and a half dozen bottles. This is not to say that he would be more admirable as Tom Sawyer; it is only to say that the emotional impact of the literature, as is true for any culture hero, is far in excess of the mundane reality. But none need have feared for the image. For, as Dixon Wecter said, "Edison was the American boy's special hero. Every youth with a work-bench in the barn, or an evil-smelling chemical set in the cellar, adored him."

Yet the evil-smelling cellar does not figure prominently in the mythology of Edison's youth. Instead, the aura is closer to the pastoral myth of the Garden—manifest in the Edison literature as the farming frontier, the Midwestern small town or countryside, or simply "the outdoors." The outdoors in general is stressed primarily in the juvenile literature. Here we find descriptions of the changing seasons, the surrounding countryside, and Edison swimming in "the cool waters of the river," digging caves and exploring the banks of the canal, skipping stones over the water, and ice skating on moonlit nights. His mother "let him have plenty of fresh air and sunshine so that he would get stronger." The boy was "a healthy, hearty, rosy-cheeked youngster . . . an out-of-doors boy who played vigorously with other boys," and his was the "strength that came from generations of good living and of hard work in the open air." Two authors even try to attribute his failure in school to the fact that he was "accustomed to outdoor activity" and could not be "shut up in the stuffy schoolroom away from the blue sky." Other writers for juveniles describe such rural, small-town scenes as pig-catching and pie-eating contests and the coming of the circus.

Particularly strong is the image—more often implicit than explicit—of Turner's Jacksonian Middle West. When Edison was born, said the *New York Times,* "Milan, Ohio, was a frontier settlement, a prosperous and growing one. Around it lay the wheat fields of the Middle West. . . . The young Edison drew in with his first breath the Middle West's buoyant spirit, its courage and enterprise." When Edison stepped out of the "stuffy laboratory" onto the train's platform, wrote another pastoral-minded biographer, "he would see farmers, cutting wheat with tired strokes of old-fashioned scythes and flailing out the grain on threshing floors. He waved back at carpenters, sitting on the beams of half-finished houses, before the train carried him on past wood lots where the brush piles looked like Indian tepees." The image of a sunny, pre-industrial prosperity produced by men who were frozen in time somewhere between innocence and power, still in contact with the archetypes, and content in self-sufficient labor, is captured magnificently here.

The special milieu of the American Boy, of course, is the American Family. The family is one's personal Garden, the point of contact between inner and outer reality. The juvenile literature, especially, contains traditional imagery of the American family, such as reading and talking on the front porch or before the fire. In fictionalized material there are many domestic images such as clicking knitting needles and the licking of frosting from utensils. The Milan home is pictured with picket fences, arched elms, red bricks, and "good Ohio clay."

The Garden, as any psychologist knows, is feminine. The central symbol is Mother: Mother Nature, the Earth Mother, and one's own mother in that primordial unconscious time when mother, sustenance, and self were one organism—at first literally, later functionally, and finally symbolically. In the legend of Edison's boyhood it is his mother who symbolizes that autocentric, benevolent universe that is a prerequisite medium for the success mythology. "My mother was the making of me," Edison once told a reporter, "She was so true, so sure of me; and I felt that I had some one to live for, some one I must not disappoint. The memory of her will always be a blessing to me." The image of Nancy Elliot Edison has more than just a name in common with Nancy Hanks Lincoln. Both are depicted as possessing unusual intelligence, deep religious feeling, exemplary character, devotion to home and family, a love of beauty and a strong, self-reliant spirit. Both are said to have been remembered by their famous sons for their sympathy, understanding, moral guidance, and intellectual stimulation.[6] In neither case (though even less seems to be known about Nancy Hanks) are we dealing with an attempt to communicate the image of a real person, but rather the American symbol of "Mother." (Edison's mother, in fact, beat him frequently with a birch switch.)

In our demythologized culture the phrase "as American as apple pie and Mother" is considered humorous but nevertheless accurate. In a 1929 poll, Edison himself placed third behind Lindbergh and "Mother" among living characters most admired. And only in America could the idea of a Mother's Day have originated (Father's Day was thrown in as an afterthought). Permeating the Edison material is the belief that all great Americans have had mothers similar to Edison's. Sketches of the mothers of a long list of famous Americans are grouped, along with Edison's, in a book entitled *Mothers—Makers of Men*.

"Will you quit worrying about better ways to light a house and go get me some stove wood?" asks Edison's mother impatiently. "You're not going to blow up the world this afternoon." The same image of timeless, down-to-earth common sense is imparted by Fay Bainter (a type-cast mother in the 1940s), who played the mother in the film *Young Tom Edison*. The hot-tempered, egocentric, individualized father, whom the mother must placate, regains his faith in the boy only after he does something mechanically progressive. The mother, on the other hand, representing the benevolence of the child's holistic universe, responds to the father's loss of faith with a knowing, "Someday they'll understand him the way we do."

The idea of delicate potential—of embryonic greatness which can so easily be squelched by adults—is communicated strongly by almost

Edison's parents, Nancy Elliot Edison
and Samuel Edison, Jr. Edison National Historic Site.

Edison's birthplace in Milan, Ohio.
Edison National Historic Site.

every aspect of Edison's boyhood story. The literature conveys a feeling for the beauty of a child who is curious and excited about life and whose development must be essentially autonomous and free of corruption from the outside. The ideal symbol for such an environment is again the Garden. Archetypally, the unconscious, out of which ego-consciousness evolves, Nature, out of which civilization evolves, and Mother, out of which human existence evolves, are all equated in one primordial symbol of origin and nurture: the Great Mother. In the American psyche, then, the New World Garden is identical with the Good Mother. And in the same way that aggressive, individualistic, progressive America was nurtured in the Garden, her legendary, driving individuals must derive from good mothers.[7]

The emphasis on individual uniqueness has reflected Americans' romantic attachment to the tale of the ugly duckling: a lonely, castoff hero whose creative achievements are an egoistic triumph over the rejecting group and whose "success" is attained in spite of the social context in which he must ultimately find his identity. Such an overtly abstract, linear, reductionist, individualized outlook must maintain a covert belief in concrete, cyclic, holistic, communal symbols. This resolution of masculine and feminine is achieved through paradoxical images. Growing up with America, Edison became a symbol whose paradox—Paradise lost versus Paradise to be regained—was that of the nation itself.

EDISON'S NIGHT-JOURNEY

In the 1860s, leaving childhood innocence behind, Edison and America set out together on a restless quest for identity. The Civil War and Reconstruction formed an "initiation" period for both the man and the nation. The years from 1863, when Edison became a wandering telegrapher, to 1869, when he set up his factory in Newark, constitute what in mythology would be called his "night-journey" of the soul.

It was once a tradition, carried over from European folkways, for a journeyman in certain trades to kick about for a year or two—his *Wanderjahre*—before settling into his career. Many writers speak of Edison's "wanderyears" as the time between 1864 and 1869, when he drifted from Stratford Junction, Ontario, to Adrian, Michigan, to Fort

Wayne, Indianapolis, Cincinnati, Nashville, Memphis, Louisville, New Orleans, and Boston as a "tramp telegrapher." During the Civil War telegraph operators were a wild, irresponsible, nomadic lot who could nevertheless always find a job, both armies having recruited so many operators from the civilian circuits. The common image of Edison during these years is that of an unkempt, destitute young man, seen as an eccentric hayseed by his fellow operators, who continually loses jobs as a result of inattention to duty. The shirking was due not just to the dullness of the work but primarily to incessant experimenting with chemicals and electrical gadgets. We are assured that Edison's years in the bohemian underworld of drunken companions and bug-ridden boarding houses were in fact a time of dedicated preparation for his work in the world.

After leaving home Edison worked as a telegrapher in ten different cities, his average stay being about six months—actually a considerable period of time for an itinerant telegrapher to remain in one place. Almost half of the references to his job changes, however, use the word "drift" or "wander," the latter accounting for one-third of the total. The word "wander" and the third most frequent choice, "roam," are used in spite of the fact that Edison often moved because he had been fired. These words, along with others such as "adventurer," "nomad," "on the move," "on the road," "roving," "bird of passage," "Bohemian," and "Ishmael," suggest a subtle distinction between "aimlessness"—a word used only once—and a restless spiritual quest.[8]

In the same sense that the boyhood image of Tom Edison, like that of Tom Sawyer and Huck Finn, is a nostalgic embodiment of the innocent Garden of early America, Edison the wandering telegrapher is postbellum, adolescent America incarnate. The transportation and communications revolutions—which Edison, as trainboy and telegrapher, knew intimately—created a national market, forcing small-town America into a kind of social puberty; that is, men lived for a time in a "distended society," attempting to conduct affairs that were ultimately national in scope in the same personal and informal manner in which they had handled local matters. Edison, the typical, restless, mobile, individualized American "wandering" across the heart of the country not only represents his own search for self but parallels the beginnings of a national search for order.

There is a sense in which Edison's trek resembles the heroic pattern of classic mythology: Jason sets sail on the night-sea-journey and returns with the Golden Fleece, or the prophet wanders into the desert and returns with the word of God. The stories, which symbolize both the psychic regeneration of individuals through archetypal dreams and the cycle of spiritual renewal in whole cultures, are structured around the rites of passage: separation, initiation, and return. During his night-journey the hero is torn from his former relationship to the mother or the group, overcomes his ego-personal limitations on a "road of trials," and is finally, in the "meeting with the Goddess," put in touch with transcendent, archetypal sources of meaning—ultimately, one's own unconscious. He then returns to society with the "boon," a gift or sacrifice which ultimately causes the group to move toward a similar transcendence.[9]

In a collective, historical context the same thing occurs when an orthodox mythology loses its numinosity—its living force—and becomes a hollow, brittle shell that must be supported by authoritarian power. The Old Order "goes to seed," spawning mystics and prophets from whose night-journeys are sown new religious consensuses, new organizing myths. Christ and Columbus are the obvious Western examples: Each brought the myth of Paradise to be regained, one spiritual, the other secular. As the prophet of neotechnic progress, Edison is at least a first-order saint within that central myth.

The mythology of Edison's wanderyears, set on the eve of the Great Watershed in American history, conforms to the classic model in many of its details. There are shades of the supernatural origins of mythological heroes in references to the endurance feats of Edison's father, Samuel, "six feet tall and broad of shoulder," who boasted he could outjump any man in the county, and who, when the Canadian revolt failed in 1837, almost literally ran "180 miles to the border, in bitter winter, tramping through wilderness and hostile Indian country." Others add that during his flight Samuel "never slept, and dispensed almost entirely with food and rest," finally crossing the frozen St. Clair River into the United States where "destiny's child" was to be born. The baby, Thomas Alva, we are told, "seldom cried." Edison's grandfather is described as godlike in appearance, "an ancient person a hundred and two years old," sitting with the sunlight on his "crown of white hair." And Edison is linked to the mother of the American pantheon, the Revolution, through great-grandfather Edison, Thomas the first, who helped finance the Continental Army. One author describes him reading the Constitution and then proceeds to quote the document at length.

The initial stage of the mythologic night-journey, which Joseph Campbell designates "the call to adventure," often occurs when "a blunder—apparently the merest chance—reveals an unsuspected world, and the individual is drawn into a relationship with forces that are not rightly understood." The frequent appearance of a "herald" who reveals these forces functions as a sign that "the time for the passing of a threshold is at hand." The chance happening in Edison's case is the rescue of the stationmaster's child; the herald is the grateful father who insists on teaching him telegraphy, thus introducing him to the mysterious forces of electricity which he must master during his journey. Or, again, MacKenzie (the father of the child saved by Edison) could represent the "protective figure," often a man in some humble occupation, who "provides the adventurer with the amulets against the dragon forces he is about to pass." Edison's telegraphic skill not only gains him his food and shelter but also provides the means of buying experimental equipment.

The protective figure of classic mythology is often a little old crone (Jung's Old Wise Man archetype), representing the benign, protecting power of destiny. At one point in his journey Edison, in desperation, agreed to accompany two young Southern telegraph operators into the Brazilian jungle, where many Confederate veterans were moving to new slave plantations. Arriving in New Orleans, however, they found that the steamer had been delayed. At this point a figure appears who is usually referred to as "an old Spaniard." Having long lived in South America, he paints a picture of the Amazon region which is so dismal that Edison, after listening "to the old man's words of wisdom," is persuaded to abandon the whole adventure. His companions, who proceeded on the journey, got only as far as Vera Cruz, where they died during a great plague of yellow fever. The Spaniard's wisdom is sometimes embellished with such admonishments as "the United States is the best country in the world for a man who wants to get somewhere" or "this is the land of opportunity—which can't be equaled anywhere on the face of the earth."

Classic mythology also features a "threshold guardian," an ogre or monster at the gate that leads from the known to the unknown. Working as a telegrapher at Stratford Junction, Ontario, only forty miles from Port Huron, Edison had no intention of setting out on a journey, let alone encountering an ogre. But his habit of catnapping nearly caused the collision of two freight trains, and the railroad's general manager threatened to make an example of him with a prison sentence. The arrival of an important business delegation, momentarily distracting the manager, enabled Edison to slip by the ogre and jump a fast freight for the border, thus beginning his five-year night-journey.*

Another facet of the threshold is the frequent presence of sirens drawing the hero ever further into the dangers of the unknown. One of the first biographical pieces suggests that Edison's trials "seem to have been the result of an uncontrollable impulse. His inventions were calling him with a sort of siren voice. Under the charm he was deaf and semi-callous to everything else." Still another aspect of the passage through the gate, which Campbell calls "the belly of the whale," is the symbol of the unconscious realm itself. The self-annihilation of consciousness is accomplished when the hero is temporarily swallowed by a monster or by some vast, unknown region. In real-life sagas this region may be a desert, a jungle, or the social leviathan itself where the hero is but a drop in the ocean of humanity. Edison the dispensable employee, "moving about over the enormous empty land," fits this image.

It is convenient to the idea of a night-journey—"the darkest period of his history," as one writer phrased it—that Edison always seems to be working the night shift, his purpose being to free his days for experimenting. Although in fact he worked the night shift less and less, the literature sets almost all of his trials and hardships in dimly lit telegraph shacks across the Midwest, and against the black setting of night. During the incident of the near-collision Edison ran toward a lower station

* While the near collision and Edison's escape is brushed over as just another adventure by most American authors—who often seem even adolescently amused—the British authors, less ready to give unqualified praise to rugged individualism, declare him "guilty of a serious breech of duty." A similar contrast applied to his earlier failure to report the drowning of a playmate.

in a forlorn hope of catching the train, but, he later recalled, "the night was dark and I fell into a culvert and was knocked senseless." Another night the sulphuric acid from a carboy, upset while Edison was experimenting, went through the floor and ate up the desk and carpet in the manager's room below; as on other similar occasions, Edison was fired the next morning. One night at 3 A.M., as Edison walked along one of the dark streets of Louisville carrying a package of books, a policeman who took him for a thief opened fire on him; because of his deafness, Edison had not heard the loud warnings.

The main body of the night-journey, the "road of trials," is a series of tests, ordeals, and temporary triumphs that the hero must endure before his rebirth and return to the world with the boon for mankind. In the accounts of these years Edison seems always to be cold, hungry, and ill-clad; one also gets the impression that his entire journey was on foot. Wearing only a linen duster, he once walked 150 miles from Decatur, Alabama, to Nashville, Tennessee, arriving in the midst of a snowstorm. This fact has caused his biographers collectively to set him walking to almost every city in his itinerary, always in the middle of winter and always insufficiently clad. For example, he "finally arrived [in Louisville] worn out and half-famished. To add to his miseries, a blinding snowstorm suddenly whirled up and raged for hours. Wearing his linen duster for an overcoat, Edison breasted the cutting gales." An excerpt from a biography serialized in *Cassier's Magazine* between 1892 and 1894 demonstrates the extreme form in which the story often reached the mass audience. Edison arrived at Nashville

one bleak and cheerless morning, toward the beginning of winter. The church bells were clanging the hour of six, and the great city, with its ice-locked streets, seemed the external projection of the colder hearts within its gates. Nothing more desolate can be conceived than the figure of this slender, eager-eyed lad, stranded on the margin of this desert, faint with hunger and fatigue, paralyzed with cold, and disheartened with injustice and rough usage. . . . Soleless shoes clung fragmentarily to his aching feet, a straw hat covered his head, thin summer underwear mocked the searching blasts, and a miserable linen duster threw its poor protection over the stained and threadbare raiment. That vacuum, which nature so cordially abhors, was visible in his pockets, and a handkerchief, suspended over his shoulders, carried the bulk of his worldly gear. In this humble fashion he presented himself at the telegraph office, where he was distrustfully and superciliously received.

"But," says author, "the indomitable spirit within refused to yield to the forces arrayed against it. . . ." After a very similar passage, another early writer adds: "But, through all these episodes and trials, poverty stricken and beset by failure, his brave young heart buoys him up and beats a march to victory, and, through it all his studying and experimenting and inventing go on." "He preferred to freeze in inadequate clothing rather than not buy chemicals, wire, and batteries to test his scientific ideas," said another; and "while he worked on his telegraph repeater he continued to subsist in a bare room on poorly cooked food." Thus the hero prepared for his return from the wilderness and the bestowal of the boon upon man.

Edison's "rebirth," or return to the world—his arrival in New York at the end of his wanderyears—is a near-exact copy of the landing in Philadelphia of that other Promethean American culture hero, Benjamin Franklin. Both Edison and Franklin arrived by boat from Boston; both left most of their belongings behind; both were poorly dressed, friendless, and "very hungry." While the sum attributed to Edison's pocket varies from zero to forty-two cents in most accounts, actually both he and Franklin possessed a dollar. Most important for American mythology, both men secured work almost immediately.

What makes the arrivals of Franklin in Philadelphia and Edison in New York archetypal American experiences is the aura of expansive optimism combined with the omniscient reader's knowledge of inevitable triumphant success. Both scenes take place in particularly creative and formative periods in American history; the promise of the future for Franklin and Edison, then, is the promise of the future of America. Inherent in these legendary stories is the image of American material progress, unlimited individual opportunity, and existential freedom—the open-ended universe accompanying the four-hundred-year boom in the West.

The awakening from the night-journey and the reentry into the everyday world of men is enhanced by the imagery of dawn and morning as Edison enters the city. "When the night boat from Boston sailed down through the Hell Gate," one writer told his young readers, the sun was rising over the City of New York. This morning in 1869 was the dawning of a new day for Thomas Edison. . . . The morning sunlight glistened on the scene before his eyes like the magical Kingdom of Cathay.

As he stepped down the gangplank, it was like another young Columbus starting out to conquer a new world. Here he was—twenty-two years old—in debt—penniless and without a friend in the great city. . . . Like the first Americans who had thrown overboard the tea in Boston Harbor, he had thrown overboard everything he possessed on earth to make the new venture.

The description of Edison wandering "among the booths, pushcarts, and fish stalls of Washington Market, marveling at the throngs of people shouting their wares" certainly suggests his return to the world. Yet one comes away from all these accounts with a sense that, unlike the classical hero, Edison had never really left the world—that his "night-journey of the soul" was somehow two-dimensional. His "road of trials" did not involve the meditation or the tormented soul-searching of the religious hero. Rather, it seemed more in the spirit of Dos Passos's epitaph:

Edison traveled round the country taking jobs and dropping them and moving on, reading all the books he could lay his hands on, whenever he read about a scientific experiment he tried it out, whenever they left him alone in a telegraph office he'd do tricks with the wires . . . always broke, his clothes stained with chemicals, always trying tricks with the telegraph. . . . he worked all day and all night tinkering with cogwheels and bits of copperwire and chemicals in bottles, whenever he thought of a device he tried it out. He made things work . . . whenever he got a hunch he tried it out.[10]

Almost all of the triumphs of this hero's dark journey involved the clever construction or operation of a mechanical gadget. The anecdotes concerning his wanderyears, in descending order or frequency, were: (1) He invented an automatic vote recorder which was rejected by Congress because of the damage it would do to the filibuster (the story is coupled, more often than not, with Edison's statement that the experience taught him never again to invent anything that was not practical and in commercial demand). (2) He developed the clockwork device which automatically sent the required periodic signal, enabling him to sleep on the job. (3) When Edison arrived at his new job in Boston his hayseed appearance caused his fellow telegraphers to put him on the line with New York's fastest sender; not only did Edison meet the test but he cut in and advised the "speed king" to "change off and send with your other foot." (4) Instead of sleeping, it was said, Edison spent the entire day between work shifts reading Faraday's *Experimental Researches in Electricity,* a book which took an empirical, experimental approach that was wholly free of complicated mathematical formulas. (Faraday, poor and self-educated in his youth, an empirical, practical doer, seems to have been Edison's boyhood idol.) (5) At his Memphis post Edison developed a repeating telegraph which relayed messages on to other cities; when his boss, who had been striving for the same result, discovered his success, Edison was fired. The next ten anecdotes involved (6) the near collision of the two freight trains; (7) his buying books and equipment with his pay; (8) an electric cockroach killer developed at one especially bug-ridden post; (9) the bright idea of sending Morse code messages via locomotive whistle when an ice jam had severed the telegraph cable between Port Huron and Sarnia across the St. Clair River (apocryphal); (10) the invention of an automatic telegraph recorder, enabling him to read the messages at his leisure; (11) the loss of his job after spilling the acid; (12) the costly failure of the demonstration of his first major invention, the duplex telegraph; (13) the walk to Nashville; (14) the attempted South America trip; and (15) an electric "rat paralyzer," also developed at one of his pest-infested posts. Additional stories concerned (16) arriving late and unkempt to give a lecture which turned out unexpectedly to be at a girls' finishing school; (17) being shot at by the policeman; (18) unknowingly doing the night's work during an operator's strike and being promoted as a result; (19) taking messages so fast that he recorded Lincoln's assassination without realizing it; (20) wiring up an electric water dipper as a practical joke on fellow workers; and (21) making nitroglycerin and having to dispose of it with a string through a sewer opening in the street. Of the fifty-four anecdotes counted in connection with Edison's wanderyears, these were the top twenty-one (718 out of 835 or 86 percent of instances in which an anecdote was related).

The most striking feature about this list of episodes is its lack of any meaning beyond showing mere cleverness and common sense practicality. An interpretation of Edison in the light of myth, in fact, suggests

the "trickster" hero more than any other. Hero myths do not always
present the whole cycle from birth to death; there are special forms of
the hero story to reflect each stage in the evolution of the human personality. The "trickster" hero (Bre'r Rabbit or Reynard the Fox) corre-
sponds to the earliest and least developed period of life. Interestingly,
David McClelland found that Hermes, the trickster of the Greek pantheon, is the mythological type which best reflects the "achievement personality." Hermes is a technological innovator who "pursues his career
in a spirit of restless energy in which there is much motion and little
waste of time." Hermes was, in fact, the patron of the *nouveaux riches*
merchant classes in ancient Greece.[11]

More commonly, however, Edison was compared to the greatest trickster of them all, Prometheus. Although the Promethean stature of Edison as the giver of light and electric power was frequently noted, the
parallel goes further. Both heroes also had in common a stunted night-
journey; in neither case was there a "meeting with the Goddess" who
bestows spiritual enlightenment. Rather, in the state of war that exists
between Nature and a technologizing culture, the Goddess will bestow
nothing. She must be tricked; the boon must be stolen from her. Thus
Prometheus darts directly to his goal and returns with fire but without
humbling self-knowledge. For this he is chained to a rock, much as the
technological society has been chained to the rock of what Jaques Ellul
(in *The Technological Society*) called a pervasive, hyperrational "technique."
Likewise, although Edison is depicted traversing the forms of the night-
journey, it strikes us more as the trek of a tin woodsman who never
reaches the Land of Oz. As depicted in the standard accounts, the trials
and triumphs of his wanderyears are either minor or overdramatized,
and the boon is placed within his reach through a sheer stroke of luck.

Edison, the story goes, happened to be studying the mechanism of the
gold indicator at the Central Gold Exchange when it suddenly stopped
functioning. Since this was at a time, shortly before the famous "Black
Friday," when Gould had cornered the market and speculation in gold
was at a fever pitch, the owner of the indicator company lost his head in
the emergency. Edison, who noticed that one of the main contact
springs had slipped out of place, soon repaired the indicator. (One account has him fixing the indicator "instantly," "without even troubling

to take his left hand out of his pocket," while others assert that he appeared on the scene on Black Friday itself and miraculously saved Wall Street.) Explaining that he had been sleeping in the basement of the indicator company while looking for a job, Edison was offered a job supervising the maintenance of the central indicator at a larger salary than he had ever received before. With this income, and in this setting, he was able to develop a stock ticker of his own for which he was paid $40,000. The story that he had expected only two or three thousand has caused this incident to be dramatized in Alger fashion also. With the money received for the ticker he set up his first "invention factory" at Newark, New Jersey. Although the salaried job actually did not materialize and the $40,000 for rights to his stock ticker patents was no surprise to Edison, the inaccuracy of the story is unimportant. We are concerned not with the reality but with the mythology in which the $40,000, Edison's arrival in New York, and the indicator repair, respectively, are the three most frequently recorded anecdotes for the period from 1863 to 1869, accounting for 419 out of 1,282 or one-third of all instances in which any of 34 selected anecdotes are related.

THE POWERFUL INNOCENT

The extreme emphasis is placed on the Alger-like stroke of earned luck has a larger significance. Luck comes only to the deserving. Both the Alger hero and Edison are depicted as pristine innocents fresh from the New World Garden. Edison's innocence is implied, for example, by the story that he did not know how to cash the $40,000 check, that he subsequently decided the whole thing must be a joke, and that he had to be taken back down to the bank by a friend, at which time the teller gave him the whole amount in small bills; Edison then sat up the whole night guarding the money with a shotgun. The frequent use of the term "lad," especially in connection with terms such as "eager-eyed," in spite of the fact that the Edison referred to is often in his early twenties, correlates with some of the drawings in the juvenile literature that depict him as a child of twelve during this period. The image of innocence in a world of power is thus retained. The trickster is a childlike innocent because in his helplessness he must rely on cleverness. The Promethean myth asserts this innocence in technological man, who filched fire from the cookie jar of parental gods. Likewise, the Edison lore proclaims at least the innocence of American technological superiority, at most the immaculate power of Faustian man himself. In the end, the Edison legend takes its place alongside the cowboy and the superhero as part of an American monomyth: that of a powerful innocent who redeems the community at the price of his own isolation.

We shall return to these and related ideas in later sections. At present it must suffice to note that the success mythology was a symptom of America's coming of age. In the nineteenth century most Americans lived in a socially atomized and insulated world. The individual, the family, the farm, the rural small town, the nation itself, had few ties to the outside. The essential condition of the twentieth century has been the growth of interdependence, accompanied by a sense of limits. Transportation and communications revolutions produced a national market, urban organisms, vast bureaucracies, and our irreversible and utter dependence on one another and on technology. As a result, conflict is the condition of life; responsibility—both individual and collective—is inescapable. The Fall has always been a symbol of passage from the insulated innocence of childhood to the responsibilities of power in an organic network of adults. The child may enjoy the luxury of caricaturing good and evil as the rational designs of the virtuous and the villainous, the impotent and the powerful; adults must accept the paradox that evil often emerges from community itself as a set of power relationships among the virtuous.

But one retreats from such realities. Man is finally a social animal who would rather be loved for his innocence than feared for his power. Thus we have the myth that the most powerful among us are dependent on virtue and luck rather than talent and intellect and that success has nothing to do with power or conflict because the New World Garden raises no obstacles—one need only stay awake, persevere, hustle. In America, the Machine, the ultimate symbol of power, was not the product of Faustian intellect but was spawned by the plodding know-how and democratic practicality of rural, Protestant Midwesterners who, as was said of Edison, were "the apotheosis of barnyard tinkering." The success mythology, in short, especially when applied to the father of the electrical age, puts upon the machine the imprimatur of the Garden. Although Edison was "the god of the Machine," as Dixon Wecter has called him, it was not until the mythology of his innocent youth in the Garden of America was well known that he soared to Lincolnesque heights, becoming a symbol of the paradoxical tensions in the national psyche.

4

PROGRESS TOWARD THE
ULTIMATE: EDISON AND THE
AMERICAN MONOMYTH

Edison at work in his West Orange
laboratory in 1890. Edison National
Historic Site.

There are at least three discernible periods in the half-century of Edison's public life. During the first of these, roughly the decade from the invention of the phonograph in 1877 to its perfection in 1888, Edison did his most intensive work and secured his reputation. This included the Menlo Park period, the invention of the incandescent lamp, and the development of the first system of power distribution. The second period, covering approximately the last decade of the nineteenth century and the first decade of the twentieth, was transitional. Growing ever older, less energetic, and more disillusioned, Edison increasingly talked more and invented less. It was during this second period that the image began to take on a life of its own, gradually becoming separate from the man. A standardized biographical outline arose, especially, as we have seen, with reference to his boyhood and youth; anecdotes crystallized and traditions and rituals emerged. By no later than the second decade of the twentieth century, the image, far more than the man, determined what was reported in the press; it even conditioned, to some degree, what Edison himself said and did. During the third period, which took shape in the decade prior to 1914 (the year that Edison's West Orange laboratory burned down) and extended to his death, Edison seemed more willing to rest on his laurels, pretending always to be maintaining the old pace. While this is the chronology of most careers, the uniqueness of Edison's experience is found in the fact that an entire culture shared not only his values but his growing sense of limits and, therefore, supported his personal illusions.

In the second period of Edison's career, three developments proceeded simultaneously. First, Edison personally experienced a decline in energy, enthusiasm, and productivity. Second, his public role as the Promethean prophet of scientific and technological progress grew ever more stereotyped, becoming, in the end, almost a caricature of itself. Finally, the mythology took on a new dimension as Edison moved from "great inventor" to "great American." The erudite wizard gave way to the kindly, venerable, and democratic benefactor of mankind. The anecdotal boyhood, standardized once and for all in William H. Meadowcroft's *The Boy's Life of Edison* (1911), entered American folklore. This humanizing trend in Edison's image continued after his death. The paternalistic, senatorial aura faded, while the grandfatherly eccentricity remained. By the 1930s the tinkering, vernacular, rough-hewn, Midwestern folk figure

was beginning to dominate the image. Thus the polar tension characteristic of all primary culture heroes was evolved not only by rooting the
god of the Machine in the New World Garden but ultimately by allowing him his finite humanity—that rural, practical individualism directed
to communal ends.

This transformation of the image, which began with the standardiza-
tion of the anecdotal boyhood, will be the organizing concern of succeeding chapters. It is first necessary, however, to look at the other two
developments in Edison's second period: the decline of the man himself and the reduction to caricature of the far-seeing and fathomless
intellectual.

SEVERAL THOUSAND THINGS THAT WON'T WORK

The year 1889 marked the pinnacle of Edison's life and career. At West
Orange, New Jersey, where he lived in a fine mansion with his beautiful
new wife, he had just completed construction on the most extensive laboratory in the world. His electrical enterprises had made him an industrial capitalist, with an income surpassed by only a handful of men in
America. The phonograph was perfected, the courts had finally declared
him indisputably the inventor of the incandescent lamp, and his imagination was bursting with plans and projects. When he toured Europe in
the summer of 1889, the most popular exhibit at the great Paris Exposition was the phonograph. The European press treated him as a scientific
prophet. He was received by heads of state; enormous banquets were
held in his honor; titles were bestowed on him; and the French President decorated him with the highest rank in the Legion of Honor. When
Edison and his party entered the presidential box at the Paris Opera,
the orchestra struck up "Hail Columbia!" and the audience gave him a
standing ovation.

In a sense, however, the applause was a curtain call on the best years
of his life. For there were already signs that these now lay behind him.
"In 1879," writes a recent historian of technology, "Edison was a bold
and courageous innovator. In 1889 he was a cautious and conservative
defender of the status quo." Although the observation concerns Edison's
bitter opposition to George Westinghouse's advocacy of alternating cur-

rent, there is a sense in which it was increasingly true of his general outlook. The shift from youthful abandon to middle-aged conservatism is,
of course, nothing unusual; yet the mere notation of this tendency is always inadequate as explanation. Nor does it suffice simply to state that
by 1889 Edison was one of America's ranking industrial barons, thereby
disposing of him unimaginatively by way of a categorical preconception.
The truth is that Edison was no cautious consolidator, as evidenced by
the ore-milling project he took up after 1888. Rather a sequence of personal experiences seems to have nurtured a growing disillusionment.

The sense of reward gained from his early accomplishments was
largely canceled by constant ridicule and belittlement from the very
men who should have appreciated the significance of those achievements
and by the fact that slight alterations or outright patent infringements
seemed so often to quickly supersede his original product. The litiga-
tional bickering and bitter court battles over patent rights seemed un-
ending. Edison's famous quip might well have been revised to read:
"Inventive genius is one percent inspiration and ninety-nine per cent
litigation." Against this background, a series of personal disappointments and setbacks between 1888 and 1914 seemed, along with aging itself, to gradually drain his energy and weaken his will.

A particularly bitter experience occurred in 1888 when he was
swindled out of an astronomical sum of money by the close friend and
associate who had introduced him to his second wife. After this, wrote
Matthew Josephson, "Edison, the once open-hearted country boy, became fairly secretive." A decade of experimenting with an electric railway had also come to naught by the end of the 1880s.

Perhaps the most telling blow was the treatment Edison received from
General Electric, formed from the Edison power industries in 1889 and
merged into a trust under J. P. Morgan in 1892. The company was sold
over Edison's head, the Edison Lamp Works were removed from his
control, and his name was deleted from the company title. But even before he became disassociated, Edison was given bureaucratic treatment
by company managers when he expressed interest in experimenting with
the products. Edison's most profound realization, in fact, was that the
technology of the power industry was falling under the direction of engineers like Steinmetz, who had the formal training of a mathematical

physicist. Trapped in his empirical method and lacking in the power of abstraction, Edison sensed within himself that he could not confidently play the role of a leader in the new ground of electrodynamics. "Something had died in Edison's heart," his secretary Alfred Tate related, "he had a deep-seated, enduring pride in his name. And his name had been violated, torn from the title of the great industry created by his genius through years of intensive planning and unremitting toil."

"Tate," he said, and I never before had heard him speak with such vehemence, "if you want to know anything about electricity go out to the galvanometer room and ask Kennelly [his physicist]. He knows far more about it than I do. In fact, I've come to the conclusion that I never did know anything about it. I'm going to do something now so different and so much bigger than anything I've ever done before people will forget that my name ever was connected with anything electrical."

For the next few years, during the 1890s, Edison severed himself from society and worked furiously in the New Jersey highlands with his steam shovels and gargantuan rock-crushers. It is almost as though, in the iron-mining project, Edison took the "Napoleon of Science" title to heart and deliberately set out on a massive mechanical conquest of Mother Nature herself. In a New Jersey wilderness he literally established what a *McClure's* headline called "mills that grind up mountains." The accompanying article contained some of the better machine versus nature imagery. "The way to the plant," it explained, led

through virgin forests undergrown with rank, dank masses of ferns; upward, always upward, until the 1,200-foot level is reached; and the snorting, puffing little engine darts forward into a nest of tall red buildings from which a dull booming noise sounds forth and a choking white dust blows out. The activity roundabout is of that massive order which reduces one to a condition of awe and helplessness similar to that experienced in an earthquake-ridden country. One feels that the very ground under one's feet may suddenly yawn at the displeasure of the master mind which created the community. On all sides the roar and whistle of machinery, the whir of conveyors, and the choking white dust proclaim this to be some quite extraordinary enterprise. . . . Big wheels revolve in the engine-houses; big dynamos transmit their heavy currents through overhead wires to the various parts of the plant. Little narrow-gauge locomotives puff their way in and out between the buildings; a line of freight cars moves slowly along, with shrieking and whistling wheels and brakes. Far off one can see a great bridge-crane, its top lifted above the tree-line; and presently the cry of a child startles one into a quick view of "Summerville," a hamlet where the miners live.

The stressing of "upward" gives the site (which was called "Edison, New Jersey") an Olympian quality. Here is the American Adam subduing the wilderness, not in the pedestrian manner of a Daniel Boone but as an American Prometheus, god of the Machine. Near the beginning of the article is a photograph of a dense wilderness with the small figure of Edison in the center leaning against a tree. The caption reads: "The wilderness about Edison. Before the timber had been felled, previous to the blasting and steam-shoveling." The author goes on to describe the process by which the mountain was literally being pulverized to dust by the giant machinery and the iron ore was magnetically removed from the dust.

The figure of Edison dwarfed by the wilderness recalls the habit which late nineteenth-century romantic landscape painters had of placing tiny humans in awesome and majestic scenes, depicting the wilderness as the face of God. Just as the miniature figures suggested the American ambivalence toward nature, descriptions of technology often carried a covert fear of the machine. The same sort of ambivalence that Leo Marx found in the rhetoric of praise for the railroads[1] pervades the *McClure's* description of the ore-milling project. "Monster!" cries the author in response to the one-hundred-ton steam shovel:

Its thick neck has all the stockiness of invincibility; and its great square head, with the three steel teeth protruding like the fangs of an under-shot bulldog, give it quite the air of a great animal, even in repose. But it is when it is in action that the personality of the thing becomes apparent. The beams of the derrick slide against one another like the sinewy tendons in the neck of a mastodon, the great head lowers itself for the charge, and the teeth fairly glisten as they attack the hillside. Then when some hidden obstacle is encountered and the way becomes temporarily blocked, the pent-up steam within it breaks forth as from its nostrils, and the great thing trembles all over and shrieks out its rage, the shrill tones only dying down to a satisfied grunt when the obstruction has been conquered.

There is a similar description of the spiked "giant rolls" which broke up the great boulders. They were "monster crushers," "studded with great

Edison as an industrial baron, 1892.
Edison National Historic Site.

Edison seated before his ore-milling
office in Edison, New Jersey, 1895.
Edison National Historic Site.

Edison's second wife, Mina Miller
Edison, circa 1886. Edison National
Historic Site.

Glenmont, the home Edison bought
for his bride on a ridge overlooking
West Orange. Edison National Historic Site.

Edison and wife shortly after their
marriage in 1886. Edison National
Historic Site.

teeth" and "wicked," "relentless fangs, constantly traveling inward and downward," forming "the most awe-compelling abyss in the world," a "bottomless pit." Thus, on the one hand, Edison again becomes the Satanic master—this time of monster-machines; on the other hand, he remains a Promethean protector against the swallowing threat of the wilderness. In the ore-mining setting he took on the added dimension of a technological midwife, drawing from the womb of the earth the very essence of the machine.

The whole idea of applying steam to stone was not in line with the public image of Edison as the neotechnic wizard. From its very beginning in 1892, the whole ore-milling campaign was largely ignored by the press. Seven years and $1,750,000 later the project lay in ruins as a result of the Mesabi range development. The losses represented the money gained from the sale of his electrical enterprises, the stock value of which would then have been about four-and-a-quarter-million dollars. Edison's response, when reminded of this fact, is a favorite of those seeking to demonstrate his indomitable American spirit of optimism: "Well, it's all gone, but we had a hell of a good time spending it!"

No sooner had Edison abandoned his white elephant in the New Jersey highlands than he became embroiled in disputes over his right to claim the invention of the movie camera, developed in the early 1890s. It later came to light, in fact, that the chief credit for the motion picture work did lie with his employee, W. K. L. Dickson. On top of these disappointments, Edison's successful invention of a fluoroscope, shortly after Roentgen discovered X-rays in 1895, was marred by the fatal overexposure of a laboratory assistant.

Although many biographers catalog some of Edison's setbacks as examples of his reputedly unquenchable spirit, none seem to have perceived the profound and increasing disillusionment that character and circumstances so strongly indicate. In a way, Edison epitomized the dilemma as well as the content of the American success mythology. Ironically, the public set up an image which Edison could not help but believe to some degree; as a result, the unreality of the image seems to have involved him in chronic frustration and, as the years wore on, defeat. The saddest examples are his later pronouncements on religion and education, the "brush-off" which the navy gave his actual experimentation during the First World War, and his poignant collapse during the fiftieth anniversary celebration of the invention of the light. But all of these took place in the third period of his career; in the second period Edison was not as yet ready to give himself over entirely to his public image.

Appropriately, Edison turned his attention in the first year of the twentieth century to the advent of the automobile. He was convinced that the future of the automobile lay in stored electricity rather than internal combustion. Thus he set out on his last great "campaign": the invention of a storage battery which would actually power the car (rather than simply ignite a gasoline engine as do present-day car batteries). It was a sad campaign, lasting through ten laborious years. In spite of considerable demand, Edison conscientiously retrieved his battery from the market to make lengthy improvements only to encounter, at the end, Ford's Model N, the precursor of the Model T. With the electric car obsolete, the battery was limited to uses which, although valuable, were extremely narrow by comparison.

Far more poignant, however, was the self-emulating spirit in which Edison conducted the campaign. Back in the Menlo Park days, when he was searching for the proper filament substance, he had claimed to possess "a steadfast faith in the fullness of Nature, a profound conviction that, if a new substance were demanded for the carrying out of some beneficial project, that substance need only be sought for. . . ." Years later he made the widely publicized statement that he did not "think Nature would be so unkind as to withhold the secret of a *good* storage battery if a real earnest hunt for it is made." As with the incandescent lamp, he began a publicity campaign way ahead of the fact. Back in Menlo Park he had said that he had "constructed three thousand different theories in connection with the electric light . . . yet in only two cases did my experiments prove the truth of my theory." Edison probably conducted over *fifty* thousand experiments on the battery; when a friend came to offer his condolences on the lack of results Edison replied: "Why, man, I have gotten a lot of results! I know several thousand things that won't work." To a degree we all pattern our efforts on the warm memories of past successes which have become archetypal for us. In the battery campaign we see only the first glimmering of a process that in later years would become blatantly transparent: Edison's attempt to relive his youthful years of intense achievement at Menlo Park.

As Matthew Josephson perceived, the ten-year search for a good storage battery was "a prevailingly somber period." In 1900 Edison was fifty-three years old; in 1910 he was sixty-three and his hair had turned white. An operation for mastoiditis in 1905 had almost completely removed what little hearing he had had.* In 1907, not only did Ford's Model N cut the heart out of Edison's battery campaign but the nationwide depression hit even the phonograph industry. Part of the problem was that Edison had clung to the cylinder too long; Emil Berliner's disk record was gaining in popularity. Significantly, it was in 1907 that Edison announced his "retirement." By this he meant that he was turning from commercial invention to "pure science" (again, the attempt to regain the image of the 1870s). In practice, it turned out to mean only that he devoted less time to the same activities. He suffered another disappointment the following year when it became obvious that his "poured cement house" (a low-cost dwelling made entirely from prefabricated molds) would fail to win acceptance. That same year his treasurer shot himself and Edison underwent a second critical operation on his ear. Throughout the decade his relationship with his first-born, Thomas A. Edison, Jr., was estranged. Edison, Jr., became involved in marital scandal and business fraud to the extent that in 1904, when he was associated with a patent medicine carrying the Edison name, his father, partly for his own legal protection, stated publicly that his son had "never shown any ability as an inventor or electrical expert" and was "incapable of making any invention or discovery of merit." And finally, in 1910, came the death of the closest friend and co-worker that Edison had ever had. Charles Batchelor had joined him in Newark, five years before the move to Menlo Park. Like Edison, he was a creature of the night, and together, writes Robert Conot, "they had struggled side by side with the same problems, they had experienced the failures and shared the successes; theirs was an intimacy that required no expression. With Batchelor's death, part of Edison's own life died."

* Edison's health problems seem also to date from his "peak" years in the late 1880s. After months of recovery from near-fatal pneumonia in 1887, he was operated on for abscesses below his ear. During the following two years he experienced breakdowns from overwork.

Most symbolic, however, was the disaster of 1914. That year, historically favored as the eve of the twentieth century in America, was also
the evening of Edison's career. Just as returning American soldiers would
have found both a personal and a cultural meaning in Thomas Wolfe's
title, *You Can't Go Home Again,* so Edison himself, whose career so closely
paralleled the American epic, crossed a symbolic threshold when his
West Orange laboratory burned to the ground shortly before Christmas
1914. Henceforth—and especially during the war itself—he was to be not
so much an American inventor as an American symbol.

Although the transition may not have been complete until the 1920s,
we find—as Henry May found in the case of "the end of American
innocence"—a prelude in the prewar period. Wading through the Edison
material in the popular press, one can sense the points of shift: 1905,
1908, 1911, and 1914. Table 2 in the appendix, which provides a rough
analysis of newspaper subject matter, reflects these shifts. Progressively,
Edison talks more and does less; increasingly, the image becomes standardized, with archetypes lying almost entirely in the Menlo Park years.
Occasional attempts to rechristen him the "Wizard of West Orange,"
despite improved alliteration, were totally ignored. He would always be
the Wizard of Menlo Park.

DISINTEGRATORS AND DOOMSDAY MACHINES

During all of these personal setbacks in the second period of Edison's career, his image had enlarged to the degree that it became independent
of the man. To Al Edison, America's "Thomas A. Edison" must have
seemed increasingly remote, yet ever more confining.

One of the more sensational signs that Edison's image was getting
away from him was a serialized adventure in the *New York Evening Journal* depicting "Edison's Conquest of Mars." Appearing in 1898 immediately after the publication of H. G. Wells's *War of the Worlds,* the serial's
theme was the "second invasion." The hero, Edison, invents a "disinte-
grator" that is capable of reducing to atoms any substance at which it is
aimed, and the world sings his (and America's) praises: " 'Let them
come,' was the almost joyous cry. 'We shall be ready for them now. The
Americans have solved the problem. Edison has placed the means of victory within our power.' "

The popularity of science fiction was growing rapidly in the late nineteenth century. The modern themes began with Jules Verne's accounts of voyages to the moon, the center of the earth, the bottom of the sea, and around the world. Published in the early seventies at almost the same moment when Edison began his career, *Twenty Thousand Leagues Under the Sea* and *Around the World in Eighty Days* each reached the million mark in American sales. In 1889, sixteen years after the publication of Phileas Fogg's eighty-day journey around the world, the *New York World* suddenly decided to send its star girl-reporter, Nelly Bly, on a trip to beat Phileas's record; she returned in seventy-three days amid a blaze of fireworks and glory. One must conclude that the stunt was suggested by the "world-ransackers" whom Edison had sent in search of the ideal filament substance, the last of whom had returned that same year surrounded by similar publicity. Edison himself not only read Jules Verne but agreed to collaborate with a popular journalist in the writing of their own science-fiction novel. He made some notes on projected gadgets of the 1940s but abandoned the idea when he took up ore-milling. Always straightforward and practical, he planned to title the novel "Progress." But Edison did not need to write fiction; the public fantasized his everyday activities. Wild, uninformed speculation as to the possible uses of his fluoroscope, for example, were rampant in the late nineties.

Edison as the military savior of the nation and world in the serialized Martian invasion was prototypical of a theme which clung to the Edison image from the Venezuelan crisis in 1895, when America became concerned about her military prowess, until after the First World War. The only weapon which Edison actually invented prior to 1916 (and even then his work was solely with submarine *defense*) was a torpedo for which W. Scott Sims shared credit. It was to be controlled from shipboard by long electrical cables, but its lack of speed rendered it useless. Nevertheless, this invention, along with interviews during the late nineties in which Edison pulled many ideas for defense off the top of his head, was responsible for a degree of smug confidence at home and panicky rumors abroad. Edison was reprimanded in the British papers for the misuse of his powers. In 1892 it was rumored in France that Edison was building an "infernal machine" for the German Emperor "that would destroy the largest cities from a distance of thirty miles and which would annihilate a whole army corps." A derivation of this rumor, perhaps, was the portrayal in a Parisian paper in the late nineties of Edison's "doomsday machine." The skit describes an assistant bursting into Edison's laboratory shrieking that war has been declared. Edison calmly inquires where the enemy is embarking.

"At Liverpool."

"At Liverpool—yes. Now, my friend, would you please join the ends of those two wires hanging there against the wall? . . ."

He then curtly informs the wild-eyed assistant that "there is no British army." As an afterthought, he destroys all England with "button No. 4."

As one might expect, Edison was considered a primary national asset during the First World War. The fact that his antisubmarine efforts came to naught had no effect on the adoration exuded by the public. Although he was appointed head of the Naval Consulting Board primarily as a symbolic figurehead, rumors soon spread that he was conducting "mysterious experiments" and "working literally night and day for the government." In Washington, he was given Admiral Dewey's old office, which had been vacant since Dewey occupied it. "When I went to Mr. Edison to ask him to accept the Chairmanship," said Secretary of the Navy Daniels, "I told him that I did not ask him for myself, that I did not even ask him for the navy, but that I asked him for the whole United States." The Menlo Park legend persisted in such headlines as "Inventor has worked 18 hours a day ever since break with Germany." "For months," it was reported, Edison had "scarcely left his laboratory and his home," and it was suggested that he had "invented an epoch-making device for use against the submarine." After his appointment to the Naval Board a photograph appeared in the *Times* in which Edison stood with his head literally in the clouds, which were sketched in; from behind his head and the clouds, the sun was breaking magnificently. Few could miss the message that Edison was the hope of the nation. Those who did were sure to encounter it spelled out somewhere: "Thomas A. Edison is one of this country's greatest assets in the fight for civilization." The image of Edison as national savior had penetrated the public mind so thoroughly that it appeared matter-of-factly in a Mutt and Jeff comic strip in 1918. There were also overtones of a real-life version of "Edison's Conquest of Mars," or the "doomsday machine." A few years after the war, journalists observed retrospectively that "credulous persons" had expected Edison to devise a "marvelous electric machine to annihilate at one stroke the armies of our enemies" or one which would "extract the venom from German natures and bottle it to be used in shells against them."

The truth, however, as Rear Admiral Grant declared in 1920, was that Edison had "little to do" with the perfection of submarine detecting devices or, for that matter, any other defense developments. Edison himself later complained that he had offered the navy forty-five inventions but that every one of them had been rejected. The navy, he said, was a "closed corporation" which seemed "to resent ideas for the betterment of the navy." But all this had little effect on the public faith. As late as 1922 Americans still read that "the one intellect in the world which might conceivably be able to abolish war from the earth is that of Edison."

Edison's role as a science-fiction–like hero illustrates how, as the prophet of progress, he was gradually reduced to caricature. It was as though this dimension merely supplied a stereotyped framework around which the broader American symbol was to be built. For the emphasis within the image, initially on the erudite wizard and Promethean harbinger of the technological millennium, shifted, during the second period in his career, to the practical democrat, self-made individualist, and kindly benefactor. The construction of the human Edison, as noted in the boyhood discussion, was an attempt to balance power with innocence, a need which grew along with the dark realization that the natural tendency in a technological society is for means to become ends in themselves.

There is a sense, however, in which the caricaturing of Edison as the god of the Machine was itself an attempt to resolve the power-innocence paradox. This becomes especially evident when the writings take on metaphysical overtones, as with discussions of science in the abstract or depictions of Edison as the science-fiction hero. The psychocultural significance of this aspect of the image is best understood as an expression of what has been called the "American monomyth," a structural pattern that has permeated our popular culture. The following section attempts to clarify this contention.

". . . JUST ABOUT THE PERFECT GUY, DISREGARDING SEX FOR A SECOND"

Historically, Americans have tended to deny the reality and necessity of limits, a trait which has led to an apocalyptic view of conflict and a refusal to acknowledge its natural role in human experience. (To a degree, the South has been the exception.) Such an outlook involves a rejection of one's interconnectedness with the world and others; it is an attempt to preserve the boundless potential of childhood, to avoid becoming the finite being whose delineation would enable one to interact meaningfully with the social organism. This "eternal child" syndrome may occur because one refuses to accept the limits which accompany mutual responsibilities; or it may persist, as in the case of American innocence, simply because a peculiar set of circumstances has made such interdependence less vital.

For at least four interrelated reasons, America has been exempt, until very recently, from the kind of interdependence which has characterized most of human history. First, seemingly infinite resources have enhanced autonomy at every political and environmental level. Second, prior to the transportation and communications revolutions, the nation's continental isolation was paralleled by the rural insulation of the individual. Third, the uprootedness of a nation of immigrants, the restless geographic and social mobility even of those born here, and the lack of institutions rooted in tradition have exaggerated the general fragmenting forces of modern history, producing a pluralistic and abstract society where each individual atom must find its own self-contained meaning. Finally, all of these factors coincided with the historical moment of technological "take-off," providing, in the short run, even greater independence from one another and from nature.

The belief in boundless potential, however, also derives from the larger context of Western history, in which America was simply the leading edge. The per capita increase in land and bullion after the discovery of the New World not only launched a four-hundred-year boom but also expanded human opportunity to such a degree that men of imagination could not help but experience a new awareness of man's ability to control his own destiny. The New World, in fact, became the magic kingdom in a large literature of utopias. One historian has argued impressively that the idea of "Paradise to be regained" is the organizing image of modern history.[2] Certainly the spirit of the Enlightenment, with its faith in the rational perfectibility of man and his environment, was largely a product of this expansion, as was the accompanying scientific revolution. It is no accident, then, that America, which epitomized the new conditions, was settled by millennial sects and shaped by Enlightenment principles. The absence of limits—Freedom—became the core of the American faith, from the rejection of colonial, church, and governmental authority to the success mythology, "manifest destiny," and unlimited economic growth.

Near the end of the nineteenth century, however, Americans began to sense not only a shrinking globe and a fading frontier but, with the coming of the railroads and the resulting national markets and bureaucracies, a loss of local autonomy and small-town informality. The reactions resembled those of any adolescent encountering the finite world of communal responsibility; for the revolt was more fantasized than real (Populists and Progressives notwithstanding). As the natural response to feelings of impotence, fantasy allows the destruction of one's barriers by omnipotent surrogates such as the cowboy, the sports star, or the superhero. Thus the limitless horizons of childhood are preserved by annihilating anything that threatens to bind one to finite mortality. For if confrontations with limits are unnatural to the human condition, they can occur only if one is the object of some evil intent.

It was exactly this sort of fantasy that increased radically in America around the turn of the century. An "American monomyth" emerged which has since pervaded most of the basic genres of our popular culture. Although the myth has found its ideal expression in science fiction, it was prototyped in the classic western:* An innocent and helpless Edenic community, threatened by villains who come from *outside* the town, is saved by a hero who embodies the American paradox. While he possesses power similar but superior to that of the villains, he also shares the Puritan innocence of the New World community. Does he ever

* Both the science-fiction and western genres emerged in the late-nineteenth century. It is no accident that both were inherited in the mid-twentieth century, in the form of samurai and monster movies, by Japan, a culture uprooted far more thoroughly and rapidly than our own.

drink, smoke, swear, gamble, or kiss dirty women? Is he nice to his horse? Does he ever draw first? Faster, but not first. Does he ever ask for thanks? He is, as a childhood companion of mine once commented, "just about the perfect guy, disregarding sex for a second." The paradox of the powerful innocent can be resolved only in myth: he lives in ascetic isolation, never functioning in everyday society (those hours, days, or months which pass between fade-outs and fade-ins); he has no identity, comes out of nowhere, and disappears into the sunset. (Who *was* that masked man, anyway?)

It was not until the first severe encounter with limits, in the depression of the 1930s, that the monomyth came into its own. Western heroes proliferated; lone private eyes materialized; the comic-book superheroes were conceived; Disney launched his special version of the Edenic myth; and the popularization of the science-fiction hero, who saves not the town but the universe, began in earnest.* In all of these fantasies, a selfless redeemer possessing some form of superior power emerges to rescue an innocent, Edenic community from an alien threat. The real world of limits, conflict, and communal interdependence is thus eluded, while the hero has it both ways. He becomes omnipotent, defeats the projection of his own omnipotence, and achieves a form of communion, the entire community being utterly dependent upon him.[3]

My contention is that Edison was as much a part of this monomyth as Buffalo Bill, Babe Ruth, the Lone Ranger, Superman, or Captain Kirk. For as late nineteenth-century Americans began to encounter limits they looked more and more to technology for salvation. If the area of free land was disappearing and if imperialistic adventures were disappointing, technology would become the new frontier. If one's per-

---

* The classic science-fiction film plot involves a megalomaniacal scientist who seeks the power of God at the expense of innocent humanity; the world is saved by the Good Scientist hero who, if his instrumental powers are not quite a match for the villainous scientist, gains the day because his heart is pure—his intuitive *human* dimension finally confounds mere mechanical rationality. Among the better examples are many of the *Star Trek* episodes. This twist reflects the paradox that one's own drive to omnipotence is projected upon those who seek to limit it and is defeated in that form by an ascetic, disciplined self. The psyche, in other words, is not really so simple. Its very essence is paradox: While seeking to become God, it also perceives that dependence is necessary to its survival—ultimately, that the life of the ego requires its death.

sonal universe was radically diminished by the move to the city, technology would more than compensate with an exponential increase in one's impersonal power. Chronicling the growing tendency to equate progress with the machine in the nineteenth century, Leo Marx observes that "the awe and reverence once reserved for the Deity" was redirected "toward technology, or, rather, the technological conquest of matter." The machine "captured the public imagination," and popular discussions of technological progress assumed that inventors were "uncovering the ultimate structural principles of the universe." [4] Invention became to America what painting had been to Italy, or sculpture to Greece, and inventors were the romanticized heroes of the age.

The technological version of the monomythic hero, epitomized by Edison, served as a cultural image for what one biographer called "the redemption of this earth through the use of machinery." At all levels, American innocence would be preserved. As a science-fiction hero per se, Edison is depicted with a repertoire of gadgets that saves the nation in international and interplanetary war. As the American Prometheus, he dispels distance, bestows power, and extends the area of freedom. But above all, as the twentieth century moved into its second decade, Edison became the unparalleled, Pollyanna-like spokesman for the open-ended future. "Everything, anything, is possible," he proclaimed in a *New York Times* headline; the article went on to describe him jumping out of his chair and stretching "his arms wide apart in sheer distraction of the scientific possibilities of the future." "He will not believe," another interviewer reported, "that any problem will arise of which solution is essential to human advance which will not find its solver." "In our art," said Edison, " 'impossible' is an impossible word." A number of interviews written up between 1909 and 1911 by the socialist Allan Benson had, as one might expect, a strong millennial flavor. They all centered on Edison's belief that science and technology—especially automation—would increasingly expand leisure, material comfort, and happiness. "Talk about coming to the limits of knowledge!" Edison exclaimed. "Why, we are scarcely on the threshold; we have just begun to suspect a few things, that's all!"

The leverage to move all limits lay in machines. One of the most common types of observation about Edison's laboratory was that "some of the machines were powerful enough to crush bars of steel and others delicate enough to polish the eyes of needles." The implication is that the machines "seem almost like sentient beings themselves, as they perform their allotted tasks . . . for these iron and brass levers and cogwheels seem capable of doing all that man can do, and more." "Man has found his muscles short," wrote Allan Benson, "and has lengthened them with machinery." In so doing, he "has transformed the world."

But when Edison called machines the "hope of humanity" he did not limit their effects to automation and man's physical emancipation. "If we continue to increase machine production and the number of machines engaged in it," he said, "the next generation will be far beyond where we are now in its intelligence." Nor do we have "to bother about eventual overproduction and stagnation and all that, for enough additional intelligence will by then have been created to solve the problems which the new conditions create." "We are just emerging from the chimpanzee state mentally," he said on another occasion. An official historian of the New York Edison Company, writing in 1913, referred to Edison's first lighting system as "another step in man's toilsome climb up from primeval darkness—the darkness of ignorance as well as of night." *

America's machine-worship and aesthetic feeling for the functional becomes overt in references to Edison's laboratory as the "Temple of Invention" or the "Vatican of Science." Writers refer to the "cathedral-like airiness" of "noble machine shop No. 2," to the "shapes of beauty and utility" within, and to the "cyclopean activity" of "miles of machines whose roar is that of the sea." If Edison was the pope of this secular faith and his laboratory its Vatican, the light bulb was its symbol. Just as Prometheus' fire kept away the beasts or the good Christian's cross frightened off the emissaries of Satan, so Faustian man burned the

* The image of Edison as the seeker of knowledge for its own sake would contradict his earlier disdain for "the old German professor" who spent "his whole life studying the fuzz on a bee" were it not for Edison's own insistence, especially after he reached sixty, that it was "all science, pure science, no commercialism with me henceforth." He had "had enough of business," he said in 1907. "I am not bothering my head as to whether it produces money or not, so long as it adds to the sum total of human knowledge." That he nevertheless retained until death his bias against what he called "*the*-o-retical" science shows, if nothing else, that Emerson's warning about a "foolish consistency" was not lost on him.

electric light before the black infinity of inscrutable Nature. Resembling a great votive candle, the Edison Tower, at the site of the old Menlo Park laboratory, supports a blazing thirteen-foot, 5,200-watt bulb. And in cartoon symbolism, the light bulb still represents the ingenious idea.

The associations of Edison with science fiction are particularly significant in that the genre has provided the classic parables for the faith in man's infinite potential for knowledge and power. In their concern for *absolute* control, *utter* reality, and *final* solutions, the better science-fiction plots usually involve a breakthrough to some new plane of existence. The implication is that quantitative change (technological progress) will ultimately provide the leverage for qualitative change (the discovery of ultimate meaning). In effect, the modern individual's impotence before the vast indifference of his social and natural milieu is alleviated by the faith that the hero will find the Great Mother or that by brandishing gadgets he will become God.

This obsession reflects the fact that the motion of modern history has been toward an ever greater isolation of the individual from all transcendent contexts of meaning. Until very recently in man's evolution, self-definition was most commonly achieved through an *identification* with something larger than the self—a sense of functioning in harmony with the tribe, community, church, or some other collective. As the commercial, industrial, and urban revolutions have progressively fragmented cultural institutions and consensuses, creating abstract and impersonal societies, the means of self-definition has increasingly become *individualization*—the realization of one's limits through reality testing or confrontation with the alien "other." [5] When this condition of acquiring identity through conflict is combined with a denial of limits, the result is a search for the ultimate confrontation—the final and absolute victory that will define one as omnipotent. This leads to the paradoxical assumption that the key to self-definition lies tangibly "out there" rather than "in here"—that The Answer will suddenly appear one day under the electron microscope or on one of NASA's viewing screens.*

* Rush Welter's distinction between the European idea of progress as "moral and upward" (inner limits) and the peculiarly American idea of "material and forward" progress (outer limits) fits America's historical role at the leading edge of individualization.[6]

An unintentional travesty of this quest appeared in 1913 when one biographer envisioned it as a kind of classical night-journey animated by Disney: "Of all mortals," he wrote, Edison alone

had crept quietly out of the City of the Living, on his long, lonesome journey passed [sic] all earthly borderlands, till he penetrated the uncharted land wherein elemental forces are set in motion; and robing himself in his cloak of invisibility, like the genii in the fairy tale, had managed to pass the guards at the outer walls and had slipped into the mysterious Castle of Inspiration, where he sees the giants at work over their brew-pots . . . with their lightnings and their thunders, and their oxygen, and their carbon, and their star-dust. . . .

Looking on for a stolen hour, while the celestial guards sleep, this earth-mortal sees and wonders, and charges his mortal mind with some fragments of the why and how and the wherefore of things, as they fall out in the Universe. . . .

Similarly, in 1878, after the invention of the phonograph, Edison was referred to as "the first mortal who has removed the veil of Isis from one of the innermost shrines of Nature's temple."

More aggressively, the heroes who extended man's boundaries "out there" were those who, like Edison, could "get into Nature's intrenchments and make her give up." Edison's inventions, it was predicted in 1879, were victories "which will be far more renowned than the triumphs of Caesar or of Bonaparte." "The real war," it was said in 1914, was "for progress and welfare." Edison was "at the front"; his laboratory was "the world's military headquarters" where he "pressed Nature's obstinate resistance from stronghold to stronghold, and finally to unconditional surrender. Compared with the campaign he had waged, those of Caesar and Frederick seemed the idle, tiring play of boys. Beside his victories, those of Hannibal and Napoleon seemed insignificant." A woman who claimed to have discovered an analytical method of putting the signatures of great men to music gave the following examples: over the musical notation for Woodrow Wilson was the instruction "With deep feeling"; over Theodore Roosevelt, "With great energy"; over Caruso, "dramatically"; but over Edison: "March time." Edison himself spoke of his experimental projects as "campaigns," and a wide variety of phrases occur asserting Edison's power to "subdue Nature." One reads of "conquering," "mastering," "controlling," "subjection," "conquest,"

"Herculean" tasks, and "wresting from Nature inch by inch the domains she would have kept hidden." Edison, "pitted against the forces of nature," "reaches far out into the regions of the unknown, and brings back captive the requisites for his inventions."

Thus Edison, as the monomythic hero, defeats the attempts of Nature, as villain, to impose limits on man. A selfless ascetic, never misusing his power, working alone in his laboratory at night while the innocent world sleeps, Edison leads the hero's life of sacrificial isolation. The team may have infinite potential, but only with Edison on the field calling signals is it assured of victory. His reputation for personally overcoming such human limitations as the need of sleep or unproductive diversion enhanced the heroic symbol. His kinship with the cowboy, the superspy, and the science-fiction hero is reinforced by the fact that their power also rests finally on a masterful use of technology. Edison, however, defeats even the ultimate limits of time and death. For the phonograph and motion picture preserve the present moment for the future and provide immortality for the past, while light, representing life, displaces darkness, the symbol of death in the life-cycle of night and day.

In comparing the night-journey of Edison's youth to that of classical mythology, we found that Edison's odyssey fell short of the ancient monomyth, where the rites of passage—initiation, separation, and return—represented a process of maturation, involving the acceptance of a limiting communal reality greater than the ego-self. The American monomythic hero seeks exactly the opposite end: a trickster-like defeat of all that threatens to impose limits on his boundless potential. If the mythology of Edison's boyhood sought to root power in innocence, the Promethean image reflected the complementary faith that innocence could be regained through power.

As American values in the twentieth century became increasingly polarized between those who accepted and those who rejected limits, Edison tended to remain the special hero of the latter. Ideally, of course, one seeks to balance these two poles of the human condition. In the concluding chapter we shall discuss the fact that the Edison image has recently moved in this direction. At the beginning of the century, however, the Promethean Edison, like the pulp heroes and the rhetoric of their admirers, became ever more caricatured and stereotyped.

RICE, RICE, RICE, RICE FOREVER

The caricaturing was accelerated between 1909 and 1914 when Edison began to offer his opinion on a great many subjects which were far removed from his field of competence. Above all, of course, he was the front-page prophet of technological progress. One writer's remark that Edison "puts the impress of progress on whatever he touches" actually applied most accurately to his impact on the media, where he spoke more or less *ex cathedra* on anything relating to the future.

One of his favorite topics was efficiency. The measure of a man's intelligence, or of a people's stage in evolution, was their ability to emulate the machine. A second measure appeared to be the degree to which they valued change for its own sake, pursuing means as ends in themselves. When Edison returned from a trip abroad in 1911, he praised Germany for throwing off the domination of tradition, especially of the church; he was impressed by the newness, constant change, and high level of activity in that country. "The fringe of Berlin is always wet with paint," he said, "and what is the fringe today is belted with another layer of buildings tomorrow." In France, on the other hand, "people are living in houses that were built two hundred years ago"; they are "obsolete." "The truth is," he sadly confided, "the French are not a 'machinery people.'" In Edison's mind the French were grouped with the Chinese; and "rice-eating nations never progress. They never think or act anything but rice, rice, rice, rice forever." While abroad he measured the efficiency of various peoples "by noting the difference in time required by people of different countries to get off the road after he blew his automobile horn." "I never tried the automobile experiment upon Americans," he said. "I don't need to. They are the quickest people in the world to think, and therefore the best workmen. A Chinaman can tend two looms at once, a German five, and an American seven." "This is the machine age," Edison reminded readers, describing his plan for an "automatic, clerkless shop"; "in an automatic shop," he said, "there will be no wasting of time in talk." "Wherever man's power or horsepower can be eliminated," he added, "speed, accuracy, and economy are the result. . . . Eventually nearly everything in this world will be got down to a mechanical basis."

If the unconditional worship of progress were to be described in a word, it would probably be "hyperrationalism." The backwardness of other peoples was attributed to their irrationality. "All real progress made on this earth," explains one biographer, "must be forced on the rabble by the lashings of whippers-in, who point out the true path over Mountains of Superstition," and Edison was "one of the great whippers-in of latter-day slaves to superstition." The same author imagines Edison—whose inventions were "victories of pure reason"—on trial in Salem for witchcraft. At the stake, Edison engages in a tirade against "old, worn-out gods by the hundreds" which would perish as men "advanced in the light of reason." Another writer blamed the irrationality of "traditionalism" and "institutionalism" for the lack of interest which caused "Tony" to run away from school. Edison would remedy this by throwing out "every last schoolbook" and "teaching entirely with motion pictures."

Most irrational of all were music and poetry. Edison felt that music should be put on a "scientific" basis. "I am going to do for music exactly what I did for electricity when I invented machines to measure it," he announced. Nor was he deterred by the fact that he had never studied music, could not sing a note, played no instrument but the phonograph, and listened to the latter, because of his deafness, largely by biting the wood with his teeth. His favorite piece was "The Little Gray Home in the West." He turned away many of the twentieth-century greats from his recording studio, including Rachmaninoff, whose audition he interrupted with "Who told you you're a piano player? You're a pounder—that's what you are, a pounder!" Asked to comment on Carnegie's list of "twenty-one world-movers," Edison replied that he would bar poets and most writers, since they were not world-movers. (Had he been a contemporary, Archimedes—who said "give me a long enough lever, with the moon as fulcrum, and I'll move the earth"—would surely have been Edison's write-in choice for president.)

To move the world, then, man must emulate the mechanical. The ultimate compliment, in fact, is to liken him to the machine. "This brain of ours is a queer and wonderful machine," Edison once said, "machinery pure and simple." "Food," he told another interviewer, "should be to the body only what coal is to the boiler of a steam engine." "We are nothing but machinery, meat machinery." Fittingly, Edison himself was sometimes compared to a machine. The first announcement of Edison's light in 1879 advised the reader: "Remember, then, that before Edison you are in the presence of the greatest machine of the present generation, his brain the motor. It is the modern fancy that the faces of the old gods were expressionless of emotion, because they were indifferent to pain or pleasure, simply looking straight on in the plane of their power. Edison's face, like theirs, is expressionless." Another author was impressed with Edison's "ability to carry in his mind all the minutiae of numerous and diverse problems simultaneously, and to do an immense amount of intellectual labor and mechanical manipulation without breaking down. He does everything with the least amount of friction . . . and his mind moves with the celerity and certainty of an electric current in the opening and closing of a circuit." But the ultimate caricature was still to come—a painting, done for the dust jacket of George Bryan's *Edison: The Man and His Work* (1926), showing Edison's profile composed entirely of mechanical and electrical parts (p. 1).

Edison's tendency to see the present as the beginning of the future rather than as the end of the past and his inclination toward change for its own sake further illustrate the fact that the religion of progress stops at no such practical objective as human comfort. Rather, as Lewis Mumford observes, there is a constant resynthesis—steam for horsepower, rayon for silk, plastic for wood, and so on.[7] Although greater convenience is provided for greater numbers, population control would often serve as well. Few critics blame the machine; they only note, with Jaques Ellul, that "the technological society" tends to take on a life of its own when technology reaches a point where it is almost entirely consumed in solving the problems technology creates; most advocate only intelligent planning and control to prevent losses from exceeding gains. At the dawn of the twentieth century, however, Edison spoke for the average middle-class American when he said that many views concerning current events were 'inconsequential because the things they deal with are going to get nowhere into the future. . . . [T]he folks that hold many of them are too absorbed in what's right around them. They don't project themselves far enough into the future. . . ." The ambiguity of ends in this future orientation, which characterized Enlightenment liberalism and thus the American experience as well, is highlighted in a conversation which occurred at the end of one of Edison's interviews:

"Why, it is all a phase of human progress toward the—" The great inventor paused.

"The what?"

"The ultimate, if there is any ultimate. All things progress or retrograde. Humanity progresses."

The belief that change is good in itself facilitates the flight from limits. For a static condition is one of fixed and finite relationships, the ultimate manifestation of which is death. The paradox, however, is that innocence—the absence of limits—is actually an existing state of perfection to which change can only be a threat. Change, and the power prerequisite to it, are thus viewed as simultaneously good and evil by those seeking escape from limits. Covert misgivings about technological progress did not fade along with early occult allusions to Edison as Wizard but persisted in many guises, as evidenced in descriptions of the ore-mining project or in recurrent rumors of Edison's doomsday machine.

The same sort of ambivalence is evident in Sarah Bernhardt's account of her visit to Edison's laboratory in West Orange in 1908. One is reminded of biblical allusions to the strait and narrow path from which a slip of the foot sends the sinner plunging into Hell. The actress followed Edison "up staircases as narrow and steep as ladders, crossing bridges suspended in the air above veritable furnaces." As they "leaned over a slightly unsteady bridge, above the terrible abyss in which immense wheels, encased in wide thongs, were turning, tacking about, and rumbling, he gave various orders in a clear voice and light then burst forth on all sides, sometimes in sputtering, greenish jets, sometimes in quick flashes or in serpentine trails like streams of fire." Amid "the deafening sound of the machinery" and "the dazzling rapidity of the changes of light" (now the image is closer to that of the battlefield) Edison reminded her of Napoleon—another archetypal blend of the good redeemer and the evil megalomaniac.

A similarly qualified reverence was directed toward the "heart" of Edison's machine shop—a great wheel which turned all the belts to drive the other machines. One writer visiting the shop could not help but "admire the powerful giant with his tireless arms turning forever, like Ixion, the huge wheel which represents the motive power of all those whirring machines in the great throbbing building." Like Prometheus, Ixion had been punished by Zeus for reaching beyond his limits; he was bound to an eternally revolving wheel in Tartarus, a region even below Hades. Whether suggesting an endless cycle of technology solving technology's problems or a perpetual, alienated search for identity, the image seems to represent more than an author's stuffy attempt to display a classical education.

Another form of reservation about the machine and progress appeared in Edison's own imagination in the late 1880s. His secretary, A. O. Tate, was riding with him in an open carriage "behind a handsome team of horses with his coachman Thomas on the box":

Edison, pointing to a valley we were skirting through which a stream wandered, said:
"Tate! see that valley?"
"Yes," I replied, "it's a beautiful valley."
"Well," he responded, "I'm going to make it more beautiful. I'm going to dot it with factories!"

The image invoked by Edison reminds us of George Inness's painting, *The Lackawanna Valley* (1855), which attempts to reconcile the machine and the garden, and exemplifies, as Leo Marx observes, the nostalgic, "ambivalent, look-both-ways kind of native progressivism" that a number of historians have analyzed.[8] "Dot" is the key word in Edison's comment, for it suggests that the pastoral landscape would still dominate the scene.

TECHNOLOGY AND THE NATIONAL COVENANT

Such attempts to place the machine within a pastoral setting represented a transitional stage in the American Edenic myth. The idea of America as a new beginning for mankind and the American as the new Adam rested on a belief in the redeeming powers of nature. "Nature" meant a pastoral "middle way" between the threat of the wilderness and the decadence of Old World civilization; it was the idealized way of the Puritans, Jefferson's yeomen farmers, and Jackson's and Turner's frontier democrats. In the late nineteenth and early twentieth centuries, however, with the disappearance of the frontier and the *fait accompli* of urbanization and industrialization, the man in the street began to see technology itself as the redeeming force that would preserve the national covenant—the agreement with God and nature that America would be delivered from the vicissitudes of history as long as her society was kept pure and simple. Technology, then, would be the new frontier. The complexity of a technological society, however, exceeded even that of the corrupt and decadent Old World. A covenant with the machine, in other words, seemed to violate all former contracts. Two alternative views suggested themselves: Either nature became the enemy—the physical, social, and psychic wilderness that threatened to place limits on man's knowledge and power—in which case he would crash through the barriers astride the machine, or else the machine was the violator of everything sacred, a dissenting view which became almost a cult of the wilderness in the Progressive era, expressions of which ranged from the intensity of the conservation movement, to the novels of Jack London, to the founding of the Boy Scouts of America in 1910.

The ideal, of course, was the resolution of the positive and negative, or overt and covert, sides of both nature and the machine by viewing the New World Garden as the source of technological superiority. As technology became ever more pervasive, Edison, as its symbol, was increasingly associated with the redeeming qualities of nature and frontier democracy.

Thus, as the American Adam, Edison was identified with both nature and technology as the two sources of American exceptionalism. In the Promethean caricature that has been discussed, the identification with technology of course prevailed. It remains only to look at this caricature in connection with the notion of American superiority itself; for not only would technology eliminate the barriers to an equal distribution of wealth and make possible a society in which equal education, equal standards of living, and equal happiness would prevail but this was seen as having been the special *destiny* of America from the beginning. Technology, like nature before it, would free each individual, and, collectively, America would escape history. The irony of the fact that mass uniformity seems to increase in proportion to the decrease in communal limits on individual freedom (*E Pluribus* Uniformity), though recognized as early as 1835 by Tocqueville, was not a significant concern at the turn of the century. In seeking to regain Paradise by the very means responsible for its presumed loss, the American seemed to believe, like his prototype, Columbus, that he could reach the East by sailing west.[9]

Steaming westward in October, 1911, after his second look at the Old World, Edison "felt like kissing Miss Liberty" as he entered New York Harbor. Headlines proclaimed: "We Are Still Ahead, Says Mr. Edison." Asked if he saw anything "better than what we have here in America," he answered, "No, I did not, and what I saw convinced me that America is still the greatest of them all." "I found no people so intelligent, so honest, so companionable as our own," he added. But heading his list of European comparisons, of course, was America's greater efficiency and technological superiority. The articles about his visit made an attempt to camouflage national egotism with such titles as "Where Europe Can Give America Valuable Points," "Edison Says Germany Excels Us," and "Lessons We Can Learn From Other Countries, Especially Germany." It turned out, however, that the French excelled us in "cooking," and German chemical industries had slipped ahead of us; the bulk of the text explained that we were superior in most of the remaining areas, especially automatic machinery, and large illustrations showed the European use of women as "beasts of burden."

The idea that America's strength has derived from a proximity to nature emerges in Edison's criticism of the hunting methods of the Kaiser, who "uses a cannon and a thousand men to drive the game in front of him as he shoots. That's not hunting to my mind. I like old Buffalo Jones' way better." And he "would rather live in a corrupt American city where there is a lot of hesitation about legislation, than in one of your orderly German cities." By "order," he of course meant bureaucratic rigidity rather than mechanical efficiency. But no one pressed him on these distinctions because all shared his Machine-in-the-Garden vision of America.

The reserve exercised in depicting Edison as a symbol of American superiority was comparable to Uncle Sam's taste in clothes. Uncle Sam, in fact, often appeared in Edison cartoons. In one, for example, he holds up a portrait of Edison before a little animated globe which is jumping for joy; the caption reads: "One of America's Greatest Gifts to Human Progress." In the same vein, a play written for school children to perform includes a scene in which a "great scientist of Italy" and another from France have come to Edison after his invention of the bulb:

"Then you will help, Signor," asks the Italian, "you will give Europe the electric light?"

"Yes," answers Edison, "certainly."

"Europe will rejoice, Monsieur Edison," says the French scientist, "you are a true benefactor of mankind."

"I told you, Chief, the world would be coming to you to give them the electric light," exclaims a lab assistant in the tradition of the better mousetrap.

"If one were to ask what person best symbolized the industrial regeneration for which we, as a nation, stand," said one typical American writer in 1902, "it would be marvelously easy to answer, Thomas Alva Edison. The precocious self-reliance and the restless energy of the New World; its brilliant defiance of traditions; the immediate adaptation of means to ends; and, above all, the distinctive inventive faculty, have reached in him their apogee." (It would be difficult to find a more succinct list of traits related to self-definition through conflict.) "He is not in the least European," the school children of 1915 were told. "He is just good, plain, solid American. . . . Just exactly the same things that have brought the United States to the top among the nations of the world have made Edison what he is today." Edison's career "would be impossible in any other country but America," said former Postmaster General James Farley in 1953. "A celebration of his genius amounts, indeed, to a celebration of the genius of our nation," added the president of NBC in 1962. "For Edison is uniquely of our America and of our· times. He was an individualist through and through, ceaselessly breaking new ground, a pioneer pushing dauntlessly across new frontiers, exploring unknown continents of matter and energy." He was, in short, a pioneer from a day when the technological frontier was as wide open as the land had been for Daniel Boone.

To the degree that Americans have achieved a group identity, it has rested largely on their technological superiority. The type of American exceptionalism that appears most frequently in the Edison image, as one would expect, is that which glories in "American inventive genius," of which Edison is naturally seen as the "incarnation." The literature is saturated with such phrases as "we are the most ingenious people in the world," and "America is the chosen home of invention." Almost always, inventiveness is treated as prerequisite to any accredited civilization. "The United States," one journalist told American youth, "quickly adopt the newest things under the sun, thus helping to make true the poetic prophecy, 'Westward the course of empire takes its way.' " "The day of ignorance and poverty is passing," said Edison, "the newspapers and American inventions are doing it." Some of the loudest boasting, of course, was done in wartime. Under the 1916 headline, "36 Reasons Why We Are Proud," was a "list of epic-making inventions by the people of the United States." If one "compares the dull intelligence, the empty lives of the human beings whom he finds in China with the alert mentalities and the full lives which characterize men and women in America," said Edison in 1915, "he will see at once how much machines are capable of accomplishing for the development of man." In the same year, an historian of the telephone, noting that there were fewer phones in Asia than in Philadelphia, asked: "Does this not establish a new gauge of civilization?" And the comment in 1953, at the height of the Cold War, that the record of inventions compiled by Edison "must be one to make the genius-hungry Russians fret with envy" showed that the attitude was unchanged. But one feels that Edison himself had the last word: "The English are not an inventive people; they don't eat enough pie."

American superiority was not attributed entirely to geography and institutions. "It is no chance system," wrote one biographer,

that makes Mexico, with its mineral wealth, poor, and New England, with its granite and ice, rich; that bids the elements in one country become subservient to the wants of man, and in another to sport idly and run to waste; it is thought that makes the difference. Ideas do not stir the Hindu and Mexicans as they do the American. Here they beget enterprise and invincible courage that defy difficulties and surmount obstacles. They assure victory.

"Since 'men do not gather grapes from thorns or figs from thistles,' " said another as late as 1950, "we know that there was back of Washington and Lincoln and Edison superior racial stock." Just as the Puritans had suspected, then, Americans were God's chosen people.

Two extremes have alternated within the idea of America's millennial role. The first is isolationist withdrawal into a private Eden; the second is the messianic attempt to make over the world in its own Edenic image. Prior to each of the great wars the former sentiment prevailed; but, once accepted, the battle was equated with Armageddon.[10] In the years surrounding the First World War, Edison played a significant part in both of these phases. On the eve of the war, when the supply of carbolic acid from abroad was cut off, Edison converted in record time to the manufacturing of his own supply. This chemical declaration of independence was hailed as an expression of "the splendid spirit of '76." "Going into war is the very last thing we should think of at present," he said in 1915, "the United States is the only bright spot on the earth's surface today, and we should keep it bright." When the country became militarily involved, however, Edison supported the Wilsonian crusade, insisting that the nation "must make good its pledge to the world." "This nation," he declared, "has agreed to save democracy from despotism, and at no matter what cost it must carry out its contract." Although the results of his work with the navy during the war were less practicable than symbolic, the resurgent rumors of his doomsday machine revealed the Jehovian image that Americans held of the nation and its monomythic hero.

AN EDISONIAN BULL

Although the Promethean face of the Edison image, with its expansive aura of Faustian intellect and fathomless vision—what we might conceive as a kind of *Reader's Digest* Dr. Frankenstein—was a household icon well before the 1890s, an event occurred in 1910 which, more than any other, drove the cosmic-sage caricature deep into the collective psyche. This was the famous interview on the immortality of the soul.

After the death of William James in 1910, the newspapers were full of comment on the alleged reappearance of his soul on earth. In response, journalist Edward Marshall "turned to Edison," explaining that the public was "puzzled" and that the existence of the soul had "lately become largely a scientific question"; and "no one," he added, "has studied the minutiae of science with greater care than Edison." After "searching the inner structure of all things for the fundamental," Edison told him that "he had come to the conclusion that there is no 'supernatural,'" and "that all there is, that all there has been, all there ever will be, can or will, soon or late, be explained along material lines." There was no soul, no immortality, no "merciful and loving Creator." The supreme power was Nature, and "Nature is not merciful and loving, but wholly merciless, indifferent." The bannerline on the front page of the

Times magazine section read: "No Immortality of the Soul Says Thomas A. Edison." "In Fact," the headline went on, "He Doesn't Believe There Is a Soul—Human Being Only an Aggregate of Cells and the Brain Only a Wonderful Machine, Says Wizard of Electricity." Beneath the bannerline is a large drawing of Edison posed philosophically in an academic-looking chair with his index finger against his temple. In the course of the interview, Edison suggested to Marshall that he read a book on the brain by Dr. W. H. Thomson. The following Sunday, in the same magazine section of the *Times,* Thomson came at Edison with the declaration that "people who do not believe in immortality are abnormal, if not pathological." "As a historical fact," he added, "disbelief in the unseen world does not prevail among nations until they begin to rot." This time the pondering figure in the academic chair was Thomson. Below this illustration was a group of reader responses to the Marshall interview, most of which concluded that belief in immortality was indispensable to the human spirit and Edison was out of his field.

A noted Baptist preacher offered the same opinion the following Sunday when his Fifth Avenue church overflowed with people who had come to hear his answer to Edison. Within a month the Edison interview had been reprinted in half a dozen languages, attacked in pamphlets, and commented on so extensively in the press that Marshall himself declared the reading of the clippings "a task impossible." In the *Columbian Magazine* for January 1911, Marshall published another interview defending Edison. He reminded his readers that "to be the greatest of inventors means to be among the greatest thinkers" and asserted Edison's belief in a "Supreme Intelligence" (though not a personal god) and his commitment to the Golden Rule. The same affirmations had appeared in the papers a month earlier.

Yet in the course of the interviews Edison had asserted that "the brain is a piece of meat-mechanism" and the men in the pulpits should "stop declaring the unprovable, and give their time to what is really Truth." "Proof, proof! That is what I always have been after," he said. "Mercy? Kindness? Love? I don't see 'em. Nature is what we know. We do not know the gods of the religions. And nature is not kind, or merciful, or loving."

Most of the protests that appeared after the Edison interview came from Catholics, Baptists, and denominations that leaned heavily toward

Calvinism. Cardinal Gibbons himself replied to Edison, asserting that the inventor had "maimed his mind as Darwin did" by specializing too completely. In the fashion of one enamored with authority, he asked what "school" the inventor represented other than his own uneducated intuition, unintentionally answering his own question by calling Edison "a scientist who proclaims dogmas to the public." An entire issue of *Columbian Magazine* (published by the Catholic Knights of Columbus) was devoted to replies to Edison.

The outcry of the stricter orthodoxies was misleading, given that the stridency of minorities tends to increase in inverse proportion to its numbers. The percentage of persons who congratulated Edison for his "courageous stand" was significant when one allows that the compulsion was less. My contention is that the broader implications of Edison's pronouncements on religion actually reflected the prevailing American mood.

While it is true that moral absolutism was still intact, Protestant theology was not, and Edison's statements were metaphysical rather than moral. Even then he denied only immortality, not God. True, he rejected a personal God, but Americans have never been too concerned with what kind of God one believes in as long as it resembles something to which the term can be applied. More than this, Edison not only failed to lose face with many Americans but it is likely that he actually *grew* in stature as a result of the interview.

"By every test but that of influence the church had never been stronger than it was at the opening of the twentieth century," writes Henry Steele Commager. "Everyone was a Christian, and almost everyone joined some church, though few for reasons that would have earned them admission to Jonathan Edwards' Northampton congregation. . . . Never before had the church been materially more powerful or spiritually less effective." "Victims of their own success," added Winthrop Hudson, the churches "lost their sense of a distinct and specific vocation in society and devoted their energies to social activities, humanitarian enterprises, and the building of costly edifices." This theological barrenness was the natural outcome of a revivalism that had stressed the emotional regeneration of the individual (who was assumed to be inherently good) at the expense of emphasis on doctrine. Into the theological vacuum flowed the prevailing standards of the marketplace. Closely identified with the success mythology, the "New Theology," as preached by men like Beecher, Brooks, and Conwell, was basically the identification of Christian virtue with the socioeconomic rationales of late nineteenth-century, middle-class America.[11]

Intellectually, the most important factor weakening the traditional theology was the theory of evolution, to which there were two basic responses: fundamentalism and modernism. Modernism, which dominated urban middle-class religious thought, combined the New Theology's optimistic view of man and his destiny with an acceptance of scientific truth; both fit the secular idea of progress. To the modernist, the spiritual realm was moral rather than magical. The chief aim of modernism was "to rise above all theologies, creeds and cults to a universal faith grounded in universal evolution." Where the Bible clashed with scientific conclusions, the former was interpreted loosely; the six days of creation were simply very long days. In effect, the leading ministers preached that whatever was responsible for the existing culture was good. Just as Henry Ward Beecher had seen laissez-faire as a sacred pillar in the prevailing order, so a man like Lyman Abbott saw that the hallowed idea of progress depended more on science than the Bible. "I believe," he said, "that the great laws of life which natural science has elucidated from a study of natural phenomena are analogous to, if not identical with, the laws of the spiritual life, and that the latter are to be interpreted by the former." [12]

It would have been difficult to distinguish Edison's pronouncements from those of a modernist preacher of the time, especially those statements reflecting his faith in the future—as opposed to the past—as the source of knowledge, his affirmation of the efficacy of science as the means to absolute truth, and his belief that the function of the church is moral and that theology is but a ruse obstructing man's evolution. "I am an optimist by nature, and believe that good prevails," he said, "but I have never had time to bother my mind about creeds, dogmas and the like." "Religious faiths and creeds have greatly hampered our development. . . . Moral teaching is the thing we need most in this world, and [the] scientific search for rock-bottom truth, instead of wasting . . . time expounding theories of theology which are not in the first place firmly based. . . ." The churches should "learn to take this rational view of things" and "become true schools of ethics and stop teaching fables . . . which keep them from the proper emphasis on that one great Truth, the Golden Rule." If religious leaders "would turn all that ability to teaching this one thing—the fact that honesty is best, that selfishness and lies of any sort must surely fail to produce happiness—they would accomplish actual things."

It is true that Edison rejected three fundamental tenets of Christianity: the divinity of Christ, a personal God, and immortality. His insistence that Christ was "the greatest moral teacher of them all" was certain to mitigate much of the concern over his alleged metaphysical error, especially in the eyes of morally-oriented, this-world modernists and Social Gospelers, who were undoubtedly all the more impressed by the democratic, humanitarian image that pervaded Edison's activities. The saving fact with regard to the second tenet was his avowal of faith in a "Supreme Intelligence," the existence of which he later stated he could demonstrate in his own laboratory.

Earlier, however, in an interview published in *Harper's* in 1890, Edison was asked: "Do you believe, then, in an intelligent Creator, a personal God?" And Edison had answered: "Certainly. The existence of such a God can, to my mind, almost be proved from chemistry." The article then concluded:

Surely it is a circumstance calculated to excite reflection, and to cause a good deal of satisfaction, that this keen and penetrating mind, so vigorously representing the practical side of American intelligence—the mind . . . of a brilliant and prolific inventor who has spent his life in dealing with the material part of the world—should so confidently arrive at belief in God through a study of those media that often obscure the perception of spiritual things.

Five years later, when again asked if he believed in a "personal God," Edison replied: "Most assuredly I do. Nature and science both affirm His existence, and where the layman believes the man of science knows." "A refreshing statement this," concluded the author, "in an age of doubt and unbelief, to come from the great Democrat of Science." It is possible that Edison, like Mark Twain, altered his beliefs with age and disillusionment; it is also possible that the writers misunderstood his deism. It is far more likely, however, that in this area—as in all others, from inventiveness and practicality to optimism and the belief in progress—Edison was no more than a sharply focused reflection of his time.

Edison's denial of the third tenet, immortality, requires two qualifications. First, Edison in effect reversed his position on immortality in the 1920s. But more important, the respectability of "freethinking" as a philosophical position reflected the optimistic excitement accompanying rapid change; as always, material expansion devalued the inner mode of reality. Edison's interment of the soul along with gaslight and zootropes signified to prosperous Americans in 1910 that they had indeed gained the world.

Edison's "papal bull" on the place of religion in technological society has been discussed in some detail not only because biographers have neglected to put it in its cultural context but also because it emerged at a critical point in the development of the Edison image. Edison was slowing down. He had announced his "retirement" in 1907, and his work on the storage battery, his last great "campaign," terminated in 1910. In "retirement" Edison could be severed in the public mind from immediate technological concerns and set in perspective as the Grand Old Man of Science and Invention. It seems that at this critical point in the crystallization of an image, as it breaks its last major ties with the living man, the quick finishing touches assume great importance. It would have been far more difficult, in other words, for Edison to add a new dimension to his image in 1920 than it was in 1910. It is for this reason that the Marshall interview of 1910 seems to have done more than startle a few complacent pew owners. The paradox of Edison's religious pronouncements was that they denoted radical individualism while safely connoting the mainstream of American values. The result was that any previous restrictions were removed from Edison's license to serve as national sage.

The religious controversy enlarged the image of the "remote, heavy-faced scientist"—the Edison so often described as a brilliant and imaginative genius with awesome powers of concentration and an insatiable thirst for knowledge. This is the Edison who said (after hitting a batter with his ceremonial pitch) that he "was always too busy a boy to play baseball" and who impressed one reporter with his "substance and repose and granitelike immobility, like an heroic statue." "The average man," said one journalist, "pictures Thomas Alva Edison, his scientific brow 'sicklied o'er with the pale cast of thought,' his head sunk in the hollow of his hand, pondering unutterable things in the depths of some picturesque chair, his eye fixed upon remote horizons of the intellect inaccessible to ordinary flesh and blood." (This description, written in 1922, sounds suspiciously like the sketch of Edison in the academic chair in Marshall's religious interview.) The descriptions given by reporters did frequently resemble this image:

He smiled softly, as though the query seemed childish to the verge of absurdity. His facial expression indicated that he had not only looked ahead that far, but beyond, and far beyond. Shadows of prophecy were in the far-away gaze, as though he were mentally following a road which extended world beyond world.

But as a former employee suggested, Edison often assumed this pose intentionally:

While the reporter was being ushered in, the Old Man disguised himself to resemble the heroic image of 'The Great Inventor, Thomas A. Edison' graven in the imagination of those who have no imagination. Suddenly gone were his natural boyishness of manner, his happy hooliganism. His features froze into immobility, he became statuesque in the armchair, and his unblinking eyes assumed a faraway look like a circus lion thinking of the Nubian desert. He did not stir until the reporter tiptoed right up to him, then he slowly turned his head, as if reluctant to lose the vision of the Nubian desert.

The interview on the soul expanded this image during the very years when the Promethean caricature was approaching its zenith. The religious issue arose again in the twenties; but by then a fundamental shift had occurred within the Edison symbol.

5

LOOKING BACKWARD: FROM
GREAT INVENTOR TO GREAT
AMERICAN

Portrait of Edison painted by Ellis M.
Sylvette, 1926. Edison National Historic Site.

During the quarter-century in which Edison suffered a series of personal disappointments, roughly 1890 to 1915, he had become reified to a degree that the myth might easily have jettisoned the mortal man. The press began to seek him out less as the genesis of the symbol than as its pedestrian housing. On one hand, the Paradise-to-be-regained aspect of his image—the front-page prophet of progress—became ever more conventionalized, culminating in the comic-book vision of Germany crying "aagh!" in the clutches of his doomsday machine. On the other hand, the Paradise-lost aspect—the rooting of technology in the New World Garden of innocence—was picking up momentum. By 1920, when disillusioned America itself had turned toward normalcy and nostalgia, Edison as the practical, democratic individualist had begun to overshadow the Promethean wizard. Yet, as always, both sides of the symbol were indispensable; for the twenties, more radically than any decade before, became polarized between past and future, farm and city, innocence and power. The paradox was blatant in all the heroes of the period, from Harding and Coolidge to Ford and Lindbergh.

A partial explanation for Edison's shift from "great inventor" to "great American" after the turn of the century probably lies in the growth of the electrical industry. One of the reasons that Edison's reputation in the 1870s and 1880s was based mainly on the phonograph rather than the electric light was that the former depended on a hand crank rather than a vast system of power distribution. As electrification became more pervasive, so did the Edison image. The decade from 1904 to 1914 as a transitional period for the image may be understood in this context. Although the greatest *acceleration* in the production of electric power took place in the 1890s, it was roughly during the second and third decades of the twentieth century that the mass of urban Americans came to experience electricity in the home.* At the same time,

* The annual residential consumption of electric power in kilowatt-hours per household unit of population was probably about 13.5 in 1902 (an extrapolation); it was 43 in 1912, 74 in 1917, 130 in 1920, 367 in 1930, 685 in 1940, 1,658 in 1950, 3,718 in 1960, and 7,205 in 1970. Although the increase between the early 1880s and 1902 was probably around 1300%, falling to 320% between 1902 and 1912, and 302% from 1912 to 1920, the actual number of consumers of electricity rose at a geometric rate, expanding very little in the 1890s when compared, for example, to the 1920s.

exhibitions and advertising increasingly publicized the miracles of electricity. Although the Chicago World's Fair in 1893 was not designed as an electrical exhibition, it turned out to be such; it was the first international exposition in which separate buildings housed electrical exhibits, and along with the electrical fountain, admired by millions of visitors, they became the chief attractions.[1] But while the spread of electric power enhanced Edison as the god of the machine, it was the growth of the technological society itself which brought a longing for the garden and suggested the need for a "human" Edison. The gradual increase in covert themes of innocence within the Edison symbol during the last two decades of his life is the organizing concern of this chapter.

THE MENTOR OF CIVILIZATION

In 1904 an exposition was held in St. Louis to celebrate the centennial of the Louisiana Purchase. Since it was also the twenty-fifth anniversary of the invention of the incandescent lamp, the Association of Edison Illuminating Companies (organized in 1885 as a means of maintaining good business relations among local power companies using Edison equipment) brought together for the fair an extensive collection of "Edisonia," illustrating the early stages of the Edison electric lighting system. Edison had become an historical figure: the Founding Father of the Electrical Age.

A few weeks before the opening of the Exposition, and also in honor of the twenty-fifth year of the incandescent lamp, the American Institute of Electrical Engineers paid homage to Edison with a huge banquet at the Waldorf-Astoria on his fifty-seventh birthday. The tables were placed together to form a giant "E," at the head of which sat Edison

in front of a grand display of flags, lighted by a brilliant pyramid of fifty-seven electric bulbs. Above his head was a little painting of his birthplace at Milan, Ohio. . . . Miniature models of his various inventions, made of sugar, stood here and there about the table; the menus were elaborate works of art, stamped with a bronzed bust of the inventor and bearing his autograph; while the ices were frozen in the shape of dainty electric bulbs and borne in models of motors, dynamos, switchboards, phonographs, and what not. . . . Thousands of electric bulbs strung along the galleries, and festooned about the walls lent a wondrous brilliance to the scene.

It was at this banquet that the first Edison Medal was awarded to a promising young engineer. "There should be encouragement in the founding of this medal tonight for every struggling, ambitious youth in America," began the toastmaster's speech. The liturgy which followed lacked only altar-bells and incense:

Let our sons recall and applaud the cheery little newsboy at Detroit; the half-shod, half-frozen operator seeking bravely a job along the icy pikes of the Central States; the embryonic inventor in New York grub-staked by a famous Wall Street man for his first stock-ticker; . . . the genius, our comrade, who took this little crystal bulb in his Promethean hand, and with it helped to give the world a glorious new light. . . .

The most important aspect of this birthday celebration, however, was the large number of articles and interviews which appeared in the New York papers. From that day on, the Edison birthday interview became an annual event, growing eventually into an American ritual in which the same themes were reiterated with almost identical words each February 11.

The major theme of the birthday interviews was work, especially the idea that Edison did not consider his birthday an excuse to stop work even for a moment. Typical birthday headlines over the years were: "Edison's Birthday Just a Work Day. No Time Even to Go Home"; "Wife Will Make Him Quit Work Long Enough to Dine with Friends"; "Celebrates by Beginning the Day at Five, after Four Hours Sleep"; "Family Decoys Inventor from Laboratory for a Birthday Dinner"; "Thomas Edison, 73, Will Work All Day"; "Still a Two-Shift Man"; and "Edison, at 80, Finds Work a Pleasure." "Why should idleness, a release from work, a desertion from usefulness be the goal of the civilized and, presumably rational, responsible human being," scolded one writer after praising Edison's hard labor on his sixty-ninth birthday. One of the standard questions in the ritual was "When do you plan to retire?" to which Edison would reply liturgically, "The day before the funeral." One of his favorite observations was that he was really one-hundred-and-some-odd years old because he had slept so much less than the average man.

The work theme had been romanticized from the beginning: Laying power lines in the streets of New York, Edison "went down on his hands and knees in her [America's] very dirt to give her the use of Electric light and power." He is "one of the very few ditch diggers," said another writer, "who can express poetry in terms of toil." A drawing of Edison with gnarled, toil-worn hands appeared in Ripley's "Believe It Or Not" with the caption, "Edison has been granted more than 1000 patents." And the obituaries explained that his emphasis on work was "a mark of his Americanism."

"Most of those who come in looking for work want to know how much we pay and how long we work," Edison once explained. "Well, we don't pay anything and we work all the time." The press loved to play up this sacrificial aspect of the work theme. A number of articles in 1913 and 1914 told of him working in spite of bad health and against the advice of family and physicians. He had little interest in profit, it was noted; yet in 1911 he was taking "his first vacation in twenty years." In 1915, after an incident in which potash had flown into Edison's face, nearly blinding him, the newspapers reported that "in order that none of his twenty working hours a day should be wasted," he sat down, as he bathed his eyes, and talked over business matters with William H. Meadowcroft, his "right-hand man." If Edison's assistants did not share this spirit, they at least pretended to. One man in particular, reminisced an ex-employee, "made up for work" every morning "by skillfully spreading a lot of grime upon his manly countenance." Another of the old timers once poked his finger under Edison's nose while he was dozing at his desk and wailed, "Look at this son of a bitch. He tells the world he never sleeps, but he is fast asleep like this pretty near all the time. He just don't believe in nobody else sleeping!" Actually, the Edisonian myth of little sleep became more inaccurate with each passing year.

The second major theme of the birthday interviews was Edison's youthfulness. "Edison, 67, feels like a boy," proclaimed one headline. As he grew older, and the image of youth became more difficult to substantiate, one finds pathetic attempts at proof: "Edison Swings Leg Over Chair 4 Feet High on 76th Birthday." The article went on to attribute to him "the agility of a high school boy." A great many analysts of American character have commented on our tendency to idealize youth. A partial explanation may lie in David Riesman's contention that the internalization of respected parental values, which occurred in the inner-directed, production-oriented society of the nineteenth century, is

replaced by the authority of the peer group in an other-directed consumer society.[2] Moreover, in a technological society where accelerating
flux and constant conceptual reorganization are the rules, the flexibility
of youth is a decided advantage.[3] A hero of technological change, then,
cannot afford the stigma of ossified ideas associated with an infirm
body. A less theoretical explanation, however, is that the values of a
large percentage of Americans—including those of Edison himself—were
still rooted in a nineteenth-century, inner-directed, growth-oriented society in which youth was equated with productiveness. The fact that
both youth and work were the dominant themes in the birthday interviews was not coincidental. Edison's own motive in swinging his leg over
the chair was to avoid the stigma of unproductiveness which the inner-
directed attached to age. In the end, it is only the tradition-directed society which truly reveres age.

The most important aspect of the birthday interviews, however, involved Edison's dogmatic statements of opinion. As pope of the religion
of technological progress, Edison might be expected to make predictions
about the material future. But these quickly became science fiction-like
in scope, and before long Edison was speaking *ex cathedra* on medicine,
politics, music, morality, and finally religion itself. The topics covered
on Edison's seventy-fourth birthday (1921), for example, included not
only the usual technological subjects such as synthetic milk and trolley
cars but sales tax, foreign alliances, disarmament, prohibition, bolshe-
vism, reparations, the possibility of war, and the need to "rearrange and
put on a business basis the stupid and bureaucratic form of government
at Washington." Unemployment, he said, "is largely nonexistent—as it is
merely a psychological state of mind." "The world is progressing and is
moving along faster than ever," he added. Asked about the alleged let-
down in morals, he replied (under the heading: "Bares Moral Views")
that "if people would occupy themselves with other things there would
be no cause to run toward immorality." On his seventy-sixth birthday
(1923), after commenting on the future of the helicopter, he moved right
on to oppose the Ku Klux Klan, newspaper bias, and politicians. "College men," he said, "don't know what's going on." He supported the
British debt-refunding scheme, the French occupation of the Ruhr, and
the American girl, who was "fine—none better." In May of that same
year a newly-formed little magazine called *Time* dubbed Edison—with

the facetiousness that became famous—"the accepted mentor of current civilization." After attending the interview on Edison's seventy-ninth birthday (1926), one reporter was fascinated by the fact that "there never was a moment's hesitation in expressing his opinion, no matter how controversial the subject." The eightieth birthday, in 1927, was covered extensively by *The Literary Digest.* The article describes an army of cameramen shouting orders at Ford and Edison amid the din of clicking shutters and Edison "throwing off answers like the Delphic oracle on a holiday" to questions which were now submitted in writing because of his increasing deafness.

Some of the questions demonstrate the degree to which the birthday interviews had evolved since the turn of the century, when the purpose had been to obtain Edison's expert opinion on some current technological topic. Within a few years, miscellaneous subjects were being brought in briefly and peripherally at the close, until finally, in the late 1920s, questions on every conceivable topic were scribbled upon scraps of paper and submitted as though to some oracular computer: "What do you think of Russia?" "Do you think democracy works?" "How can you stop crime?" "Do you think men will go through the industrial age to a higher civilization, the age of art?" (Edison's written answers, in fact, did tend to be computerlike: "Machine age will not interfere with the productions of art.") "Do you think we are near to solving the mystery and meaning of life?" ("No; it will require centuries before we ever have data enough to make a reasonable guess.") And finally and inevitably: "What is good?"

Although the birthday interview was unique in assuming the form of a national ritual, the same increasing tendency to express opinion on an ever-widening range of topics was characteristic of Edison's interviews in general during the same period. On Edison's part, this development reflected a relaxation in his strenuous work schedule. In 1907, it will be remembered, Ford's Model N interrupted the battery campaign, the business depression hit even the phonograph industry, and Edison announced his "retirement." In 1908 Edison's treasurer shot himself, the poured cement house failed to win acceptance, and Edison underwent the second critical operation on his ear. Four months after the surgery, the no-nonsense *New York Times* printed, for the first time in its pages, an interview centering around a topic on which Edison was not an alleged technical expert. (Such interviews appeared earlier in other papers, but since the *Times* was almost always the last to respond to such sensationalism, it is all the more significant that its first human-interest interview did not appear until 1908. The *Times* did not partici-pate in the birthday interviews until even later.) With the man rapidly falling away from the myth, Edison's subject was predictably "Four Hours Sleep Enough for Anyone." Even the interviews which suppos-edly related to Edison's field of expertise began to resemble science fiction more than fact. The first of these to be found in the *Times*, "The Future's Possibilities Outlined by Edison," also appeared in 1908. (The shift from technological to human interest in the *Times*'s treatment of Edison during the late 1900s is immediately evident from table 2 in the appendix.) Less than two years later came the interview on the immor-tality of the soul.

ONLY ONE MAN GOT ME RIGHT

The religious topic did not die in 1911. After everyone had had their say, the issue lay dormant until 1920. In October of that year, an inter-view suddenly appeared in *American Magazine* entitled "Edison Working on How to Communicate with the Next World." He explained that he was hard at work on "an apparatus" through which any intelligence surviving death might communicate with the living. Although many in-terpreted this as a confession of belief in the immortal soul, Edison had a very detailed and, so he thought, materialistic hypothesis in mind. The theory, as it was developed in succeeding articles, amounted to this: There is no such thing as an individual; "intelligence" is ultimately seated in billions of infinitesimal "life units," or entities (his friend Ford called them "the enities"), which pass from the body at death and even-tually enter other bodies. The entities are molecular phenomena, located throughout the body, and controlled by "master entities" in the brain. Believing that they operate in squads, or "swarms," Edison speculated that "memory swarms" may persist as particles of personality after death; this led him to construct his electrical "apparatus." Ever-practical Edison even did an "experiment" to demonstrate the entities at work: he burned the skin off of his thumb and observed that they caused the exact same thumbprint to grow back. As to their origin, Edison scooped the Von Daniken school by half a century in supposing that the entities originally came from outer space.

It was the thumbprint which had given Edison the idea; and in this sense it was not as ridiculous as it might seem. The "entity" he was actually groping for was the chomosome, or, more basically, the double helix (DNA); but this concept had to await the use of the electron microscope in 1950. At the other extreme, Edison was really only substituting another term for "soul"; instead of passing the buck to "infinity," he passed it to "infinitesimal" (and to outer space, for that matter). But even with these qualifications one is still amazed at the degree to which the American public took the whole episode seriously. "The confidence in you throughout the world is great," wrote one interviewer, "people everywhere are anxiously awaiting word from you." "Ten million men and women," he added, "who have lost dear ones in the war are hungering for word or knowledge as to the existence of life after the life we know." "Edison 'Spirit Finder' Seeks Great Secret," announced one banner line. "Do You Know the 'Little Peoples'?" asked the title of another article. The widespread acceptance of the idea that an "electrical apparatus" might serve such a purpose demonstrates the degree to which the public put its faith in science, technology, and in Edison himself. In *Scientific American* we find the familiar "beaker" type of photograph—Edison pouring the contents of a flask into a beaker—with the caption, "Thomas A. Edison—the world's foremost inventor—who is now at work on an apparatus designed to place psychical research on a scientific basis."

Edison's own thoughts and motives on the whole matter seemed somewhat confused. His "apparatus" never materialized. When asked how the machine worked he replied "What difference does that make? There are half a dozen ways of making a machine or of approaching the problem." A friend finally quoted Edison as saying that B. C. Forbes, the interviewer to whom he first gave the "spirit finder" story, came to see him "on one of the coldest days in the year. His nose was blue and his teeth were chattering. I really had nothing to tell him, but I hated to disappoint him, so I thought up this story about communicating with spirits, but it was all a joke." Continually accused of believing in spirits, Edison finally said "Everybody seems to have misunderstood me, and so far as I know only one man got me right. He was an American rancher down in Mexico."

In 1923 Edison began using the word "soul" for his "entities," which of course resulted in many headlines such as, "Edison Bares Belief in Soul After Death." The first such instance seems to have been at Harding's funeral. (Edison had an affection for Harding; "Harding is alright," he said, "any man who chews tobacco is alright.") Meanwhile, the "Supreme Intelligence" had become the "Supreme Being," and editorials declared that many would be reassured by such a declaration of faith "from a man who has stood so long and conspicuously before them as a symbol of scientific knowledge. Multitudes of persons unconsciously assign authority to what Edison says." Throughout the twenties Edison increasingly used the rhetoric of Christianity in conjunction with a materialistic ideology; consequently, his words became all things to all men, as exemplified in 1926 when Edward Marshall again interviewed him on the subject of immortality. On the basis of a number of vague statements in which Edison never really committed himself, the editors of *Forum,* who printed the interview, commented on the "great advance that has taken place in his opinions." Yet when he was questioned on his eightieth birthday (1927) as to whether his view regarding immortality had really changed, he answered,

No, it has not changed; the reading of the interview [Marshall's] was misconstrued; I propose that, to get some reasonable data, every known fact in favor of immortality should be put in one column and every fact against immortality should be put in an opposite column. Then in time we might find in summing up that there were 56 per cent in favor and 44 per cent against. This would give a hope; as it is now we have no data.

The reaction to this—the old Tom that everyone knew—was almost as great as it had been in 1910. The issue was declared to be science versus religion. Edison, "the representative of cold reason," was contrasted to Lincoln, who was "religious to the core." But, again, the critics were predictably the representatives of reactionary and fundamentalist-oriented groups. A year later, when asked to comment on the report that 11,344 churches in the United States had gained no converts in the last year, Edison replied, "People are drifting away from superstition and bunk; increase in scientific knowledge is responsible."

Perhaps Edison was torn between his own convictions and the desire to measure up to the public image; this may especially have been true in 1923, shortly after his "intelligence questionnaire" had become the target of even greater criticism than his religious views. On the other hand, there may never have been any compromise at all; it may have been entirely the work of reporters and journalists. By the late twenties, at any rate, the compromise seems to have vanished. In the end, it did not matter a great deal. When permitted, the public will assign to the culture hero whatever views it deems most fitting. The convenient ambiguity of his "Supreme Intelligence" and his "entities" probably added large numbers of the comforted to those who already worshiped him for his agnosticism. The motives of the man himself were probably known only to him and the rancher in Mexico.

Edison's last words, as he sat gazing out a window, were purported to be, "It is very beautiful over there." In his semiconscious state his meaning was most likely the simplest. Yet America injected that phrase with the utmost spiritual meaning. The best culture hero is always a dead one. A few weeks later, Henry Ford—who was to Edison what Boswell was to Dr. Johnson—proclaimed to the world: "The greatest thing that has occurred in the last fifty years is Mr. Edison's conclusion that there is a future life for all of us."

LOSING TRACK OF TIME

Whether Edison ever had a theology, he remained a Calvinist in spirit throughout his life. There was a hard streak of Protestant asceticism in Edison's character which led him to declare that a soft bed "spoils a man," that "we should not be guilty of enjoying our meals," and that "Prohibition is eternally correct." "Everyone knows what we do with our pleasures," he said, "we indulge them too much." "I have always lived abstemiously. It is a religion with me." Ironically, the nature of Edison's inventions won him such titles as "the world's new Purveyor of Pleasure." Also amusing is the comment, coming from the living symbol of the machine age, that society seeks too many things "for the stimulation of the nerves."

The biographies asserted that "idleness has no charms for him," that he "indulged in no recreation or amusements except parcheesi," and that he cares "nothing for the pleasures of the flesh, nor for gold, nor fame." "If I were to hazard a guess as to what young people should do to avoid temptation," Edison said, "it would be to get a job and work at it so hard that temptation would not exist for them." President Wilson, as was his wont, summed up the meaning of Edison's labor in the spirit of the old Protestant morality: "His success has been paid for."

A related theme grew out of Edison's belief that "clock watchers never succeed, you can't keep one eye on the clock and the other on your work." This theme received particular emphasis in the youth-oriented literature on Edison in the 1920s—a self-indulgent decade which seems to have compensated by electing Calvin Coolidge and preaching Puritan virtues in the world of business. The anti-clock-watching motif became a cliche: "I'd put it this way," said a large corporation executive in 1924, explaining the promotion of a company officer, "Albert Salt was the best office boy we ever had, the best clerk we ever had, the best salesman we ever had, the best purchasing agent we ever had, and he never knew when the whistle blew." [4] It is in the 1920s that we are frequently told that few of the clocks in Edison's laboratory run, and that those that do have no hands. A father once begged Edison "to say something to the boy which he could remember as having been the most valuable piece of advice given to him in his life." "My boy," Edison said, "never watch the clock."

Edison's aversion to clocks would have been ironic had it not been his way of affirming the degree to which both he and his culture were obsessed with time. Mumford's suggestion that the mechanical clock, invented in a thirteenth-century monastery, was the mainspring of the machine age, and Franklin's admonition that "time is money" remind us of the degree to which measured linear time has shaped the mythology of our culture. Great weight was given to the notion that "never a moment has been lost in Mr. Edison's life," and that his deafness meant that he did not have to "listen to much nonsense which would keep him from his work and waste his valuable time." Edison himself feared that too much leisure "would have a bad effect, particularly on the young" and that the four hour day would turn us into a nation of "loafers."

Another aspect of the older Protestant morality occasionally attached to the Edison image was the sanctity of hearth and home. As one might expect, the theme is difficult to find outside of the juvenile literature.

The fact that it exists at all can be traced to a man named Northrop, who published an article entitled "The Unknown Edison" in *Success* magazine in 1902. The article, which constantly substitutes "husband" and "father" for Edison's name, explains that home life "has become necessary to his work," and that "a new and more potent power than ever before controlled him has gained its mastery over him. This is the power of love." On the basis of this article, F. A. Jones's widely distributed 1907 biography emphasized an ideal family life. In the same year, a large photograph of Edison and his family appeared in the *New York Times* with the caption: "It is in the bosom of his family that Mr. Edison forgets the incessant inventive planning of the day." In 1911, Meadowcroft's prototypical biography for boys also stressed a "happy and perfect domestic life." A year later, another book for juveniles described Edison "romping with his children, whom he loves dearly," and enjoying the company of his wife, "a true helpmate." Thereafter, except for an occasional comment, the theme remains in the juvenile literature. Two books in particular take the idea to unlikely extremes, one (North, 1958) apparently drawing a number of its images from the other (Garbedian, 1947). Edison is depicted liking "above all else" listening to his wife play Beethoven on the piano in the drawing room. Under his wife's "diplomatic maneuvering" he "became more polished," smoked less, and learned to like Dickens and Scott. He never left his house without kissing his wife; and she "returned his love in full measure. She brushed his clothes for him" and "gently scolded him when his tie was not straight." For Edison, we are told, "happiness meant a loving family, an understanding wife, hard work, music, and a chance to putter around his garden." The juvenile literature, in fact, is rife with the everyday imagery of middle-class life; Mrs. Edison and her daughter, for example, "left their hotel, arm in arm, for a shopping spree." In truth, Edison disliked babies, ignored his own children, spent almost all of his days and nights at the laboratory, often failing to return for meals, forgetting social engagements, wedding anniversaries, and even Christmas. In public, many noticed that he seemed to regard his wife as a stranger. The articles stressing his home life, however, tended to juxtapose Prometheus to the Earth Mother, suggesting that she catered to his every whim while he, in turn, became a little boy in her presence.

The real embodiment of the trappings of middle-class culture and domesticity was Mrs. Edison herself, whose father, the cofounder of Chautauqua, was the author of books on self-help, and whose mother was a temperance crusader. Edison was not the only American cultural symbol under his wife's guardianship. She also served, for example, as Chaplain General of the Daughters of the American Revolution. As chairman of the beautification committee of West Orange she declared that "if civic beautification programs were carried far enough, people would live naturally good lives and the Eighteenth Amendment would not be necessary." In 1912 she announced that "continual entertainment will undermine the nation" and that women's suffrage and girls living in flats would destroy the home. In 1915 she stopped Sunday amusements in West Orange in order that people might "hark back to the example" of their forefathers and "cultivate the home idea." But perhaps her finest hour was a radio speech she made in 1930 calling women back to the home. "America is essentially a nation of homes," she said. "The woman who doesn't want to make a home is undermining the nation." Attempting to depict homemaking as a big business demanding diversified abilities, she compared cooking, for example, to chemistry. The irony of it all is that in her concern for the decline of cultural consensus, Mrs. Edison mistook symptoms for causes. In the search for the latter, her husband's laboratory might have been a good starting point; for here was a source not only of much of the uprooting force of the electrical age but also of her own domestic despair, probably the real motivation for her jeremiads.

Mina Edison's reaction to social change reflected the pessimistic, retrogressive side of middle-class reform in the early twentieth century, while her husband's pronouncements exemplified the more optimistic, forward-looking aspects of what was in fact a general search for order. Yet Edison himself also embodied both sides of the Progressive paradox. Seen together, the various ideas which he expounded place him clearly within the pale of American Progressivism, not only in his politics (he was a Bull Mooser in 1912) but in his faith in democracy, his concern for morality and social justice, his exuberant belief in progress, his quest for efficiency, and his urban middle-class outlook. Like Teddy Roosevelt, whom he once named as the greatest man in the modern world, he was the embodiment of middle America. His own values, like those attached to his image, were largely those of the nineteenth-century cultural consensus. As America moved into the postwar period, in fact, the Edison image and Progressivism fell into many of the same contradictions.

WHAT *IS* A CHINESE WINDLASS?

Edison shared with the Prohibitionists, Fundamentalists, Ku Kluxers, and others in the Progressive backwash the frustrating sense of being passed up by the flow of history; thus his views tended ever more to the extreme and encountered increasing ridicule in the press. He was an abstemious dry, a mythologizer of the farmer (who was "still the bulwark of the nation"), a Puritan moralist, a male chauvinist, and an ethnic bigot.

The six most publicized interview topics arising during the last two decades of Edison's life were sleep, immortality of the soul, the intelligence questionnaire, the tour of Europe, diet, and currency. In line with Protestant moderation, Edison maintained that Americans ate too much and that his own diet was scientifically sound (though he died largely because there was little left of his stomach). The currency topic arose in 1921 when Henry Ford proposed financing Muscle Shoals with an issue of paper money. Edison backed him up, apparently completely misunderstanding the purpose of gold, which he declared was "a relic of Julius Caesar." Interest, he said, "is an invention of Satan," and "paper money is the money of civilized people. . . . Humanity and soil—they are the only real basis of money." He proposed issuing currency on the basis of warehouse receipts for farm products. The controversy became heated and filled the papers throughout the first half of 1922. Edison finally declared that "it would be hopeless to get anybody to understand it." One wonders what became of the rancher in Mexico.

Other biases were less innocent: If women had "more imagination, more courage," and were "better able to figure and to calculate," he said, they would simplify their housework with electrical appliances. "It is very difficult to make women believe anything that is so. Women as a class are inclined to be obstinate. They do not seem to want to get out of the beaten paths." His racism was often linked to his hatred of cigarette smoking, which, he once explained, had made the Turks "a race of weak, vicious degenerates." Mexicans also smoked too much; "that is why Mexicans as a race are not clear-headed." Commending President Wilson for his intervention south of the border, he observed that "there will always be trouble and dissension among the Mexicans, for that is their nature." In 1921, of course, he was "absolutely opposed to letting . . . [the Japanese] come over here." As early as 1914 a *Times* editorial took Edison to task for calling the European war a "conflict of races." When he goes out of his field, the editor commented, "he not infrequently reveals the consoling fact that wisdom will not die with him."

Yet Edison's dogmatisms lay in the very areas where the nation itself was engaged in a struggle with modernity. The psychic polarity of the era brought not only Babbitt and bathtub gin, Fitzgerald and Mencken, Freud and the Model T but also isolationism, immigration restriction, Warren Harding, William S. Hart, the Scopes monkey trial, and the Anti-Saloon League. The great culture heroes of the time were those, like Ford, Edison, and Lindbergh, who embodied both past and future, change and continuity, self and society, machine and garden. Thus, when Edison violated one pole of this continuum, he enhanced the opposite side in direct proportion.

In spite of editorial headlines like "His Certainties Far Too Numerous" and regardless of the decision of some journalists in the twenties to go ahead and print the "ain'ts" and the bad grammar, Edison was still referred to in 1927 as "the chief prodder of the American mind." (The "ain'ts" were used primarily to quote Edison's criticism of the press.) When Edison said what the public wanted to hear, he was an American symbol; when he said the opposite, he was the individualistic old man who had given birth to the symbol in his productive years. But the myth now had a glistening immortality of its own. The finger smudges of the mere man could never destroy it; ultimately, they only expanded general awareness of the symbol itself. Perfection has never been demanded of the culture hero. Washington was not disqualified from the American pantheon for his aloofness, nor Franklin for his promiscuity, nor Jefferson for his intellectualism, not to mention the highly specialized appeal of lesser heroes.

The most notorious incident in which the vernacular Edison violated the intellectual Edison involved what came to be known as the "Edison Questionnaire." In 1921, he devised a factual quiz, which he submitted to applicants for positions in his laboratories and factories. Typical questions were: "Where is Kenosha?" "Who was Francis Marion?" "What city in the United States leads in making laundry machines?" "What is copra?" "Where do we get peanuts from?" "What are leucocytes?" "Where is Magdalena Bay?" "Who wrote 'Home, Sweet Home'?" "What are menhaden?" "How far is it from New York to Buffalo?" "What is grape nuts [the Postum's cereal] made of?" "How many square feet in an acre?" and "What is a Chinese windlass?" After only some thirty of several hundred applicants managed to pass the test, Edison commented: "Men who have gone through college I find to be amazingly ignorant. They don't seem to know anything." Edison could put his foot in his mouth on matters of the spirit and come out untarnished because that was not the area of American life symbolically entrusted to him. But on matters of the intellect he might have been more circumspect. When the national symbol of genius declares American higher education to be worthless, a confrontation is inevitable. "Can't Mr. Edison understand," said a *Times* editorial,

that the young graduate whose mind is dwelling on . . . free verse doesn't care to know the ingredients of felt hats or automobile tires? Has it ever been brought to his attention that not a few college men who would be entirely willing to be inscribed temporarily upon his payroll nevertheless look upon his shops, his factories, his materials, his processes, as the mere dross and slag of life, not to be compared with the lofty things to which they aspire? . . . He may enjoy a brief triumph with his catch questions, but he cannot grade the human soul. Mr. Edison should cultivate a little humility.

Other editorials saw in the incident an indication that, out of his domain, "a really notable man can give a startlingly lifelike imitation of mediocrity and unenlightenment," and "a touching faith in higher education and a profound misunderstanding of its aims are often displayed by men who have succeeded without college training. If ever their preconceived notions as to the all-embracing nature of a four-year course of study are shattered, they condemn colleges in general for not being on the job." Yet, in all, the restraint of the critics was significant, a typical comment being that "he himself is so exceptional as to have little understanding of ordinary men."

Nor, of course, was all comment adverse; in fact, the written responses of newspaper readers were about half and half. "Are we Americans losing intelligence?" began one long syndicated interview. "This amazing interview with that greatest of all living Americans, Thomas A. Edison, makes this seem a possibility." * Edison explained to the interviewer that he considered memory vitally important; without facts, one had no food for imagination. Other supporters pointed out that a majority of the questions were of a type which an engineer should be able to answer, and "the man whose being has a thousand antennae bringing him news of the world about him" is just the sort needed as foreman or shop manager.

Edison had always believed not only that the colleges should teach "somep'n useful" but that "if a boy has ambition, he don't need to go to college." "I wouldn't give a penny for the ordinary college graduate," he said, "except those from the institutes of technology. They aren't filled up with Latin, Philosophy and the rest of that ninny stuff." Now he added that the atrophy of the power to observe was the fault of an educational system which was "turning out men who not merely have failed to learn, but have been robbed of the capacity to learn." Although the curriculum of the day was open to much criticism, his claim that the absence of middle-range scores on his quiz had proven his point is doubtful if one assumes the universality of a bell-curve; if anything, it proved the inadequacy of the test. By another measure, however, the quiz was not as impossible as many suggested. The well-informed person of the 1980s would probably have scored around seventy percent; Edison counted a high score at about twenty-five percent.

To the delight of humorists in the press, Edison came out with a second questionnaire in 1922, aimed at a higher caliber applicant such as might serve as a personal assistant. The aspirant was asked if he was "hardboiled," how a particular poker hand should be played, and was confronted with situational dilemmas such as: "You are a salesman making every effort to get an order from a big manufacturer who is married to an unusually jealous wife. One evening you see this prospective customer dining in a restaurant with a chorus girl. What would you do?" Edison not only initiated the pilot model for the research laborato-

* The author was Edward Marshall, veteran of Edison interviews concerning the European tour, the soul, mechanical utopias, and other timely topics. Marshall, with seven periodical articles, and Allan Benson, with eleven, easily head the list of by-line journalists who cashed in on Edison.

ries of modern corporations but also invented the prototype of the "personality test" later used to people those organizations.

By 1929 his search had qualitatively narrowed to the ultimate degree: he now devised a test to locate among the youth of the entire country the one boy who would become his "successor." The public, by this time, seems to have made its peace with Edison on the subject of education, just as it had on the matter of theology. Most writers took the idea of a successor with extreme seriousness, even reverence. "Never in all history has there been such a winnowing of material by a man who sought a disciple," said the *Boston Globe.* "The educational systems of forty-eight states and the District of Columbia have cooperated to find the right youth." *The Commonweal* described the search in imagery suggesting a "Great Conqueror" seeking a successor to a throne of empire. The search culminated on the rolling lawn of Edison's estate where Wilbur B. Huston, an unathletic-looking boy in heavy spectacles, was proclaimed the official "brightest boy in the United States" and handed the Edison scholarship. Whatever his credentials, Huston was bright enough to reply to a question like "What do you consider four of the most important qualifications necessary to success in any pursuit?" with the solidly Edisonian: "Ambition, the will to work, education, and stamina." (If "education" had not originally been Edisonian, it probably was now, along with the "entities.") And like a McGuffey student proudly reciting, "Try, Try Again," Huston replied to another question that if he had failed at an experiment ten times, he would "try again. If then I got no results I would try again with varying procedure." Talk of a successor faded and the high school test for the Edison scholarship became an annual occurrence. The whole episode, in fact, would itself have provided a choice quiz item, had Edison lived to design a test for our own time. Tucked away amid the long columns of numbered examples exposed by the newspapers might be: "147. Whatever became of Wilbur B. Huston?"

Although the biographies barely touch on Edison's venture into intelligence-testing, it was one of the half-dozen most publicized aspects of his life. As an editorial writer in the *Times* perceived, thousands now knew Edison as a self-made authority on education "who could not tell for the life of them what he has invented." Humorists cashed in on the incident, and college presidents answered Edison in commencement speeches. The Book of Knowledge Company devoted a full-page advertising to the point that an owner of their product would have breezed through the test; and Postum Cereal gave similar space to an expression of gratification that Edison considered the ingredients of grape nuts of vital import. The whole issue served to keep Edison in the limelight to a degree that might not otherwise have been possible.

But most important, the fifty percent or more who supported Edison were affirming some fundamental American themes: the efficacy of self-education, practicality, "horse sense," utility, the superiority of doers over thinkers, the concrete over the abstract, and factual data over theory. In a real sense, the publication of the tests was the flinging down of the gauntlet by the great mass of anti-intellectual Americans; and to their minds the challenge was successful. For wasn't the average collegiate score only 28 to 35 percent for women and men, respectively, while grammar-school-educated newspaper readers were reporting scores of 75 and 80 percent? An irony was noted by the *New York Telegram* in one of the few negative comments of 1929. Observing the almost pathological role of science in the situational questions,* the *Telegram* suggested that although Edison was "much too practical and insufficiently imaginative to be a scientist," he "would trade it all for the status of scientist. The bulbs and the phonographs and all the rest he would throw into the discard if only he could have been an Einstein." I believe that there was a degree of truth in this, dating as far back as Edison's failure to comprehend Newton's *Principia* as a boy. Best of all, perhaps, is the postscript: Einstein himself had visited America in 1921 and—for the same reasons one would see the Statue of Liberty or the Grand Canyon—had taken the Edison test. Tucked away in the *Times* was an item reporting his abysmal failure.

ONLY TEN PERCENT OUT

The theme of practicality in American culture was also an obsession of that other genius of electricity, Benjamin Franklin, who wrote in his "Project of arriving at moral Perfection": "Avoid trifling Conversation.

* For example: If you had only food and water enough for three in the desert, whom would you choose from the following: an aged "brilliant scientist," two

. . . Let each Part of your Business have its Time. . . . Lose no Time.
Be always employ'd in something useful. Cut off all unnecessary
Actions. . . . Avoid Extremes." [5] The emphasis on utility—especially on
action over reflection and applied over theoretical knowledge—is one of
the most commonly noted American traits.[6] Explicit not only in the
questionnaire controversy but throughout the Edison material is the
praise of the doer over the dreamer, the pragmatist over the philosopher. Just as pragmatism, the philosophical apologetics for applied science, is a uniquely American doctrine, the reverence for practicality and
know-how echoes the emphasis on means over ends in an atomistically
individualized culture where identity is sought through confrontation.
The theme also has an obvious historical relevance to Puritan proscrip-
tions against idleness and to a rapidly industrializing, open society, rich
in resources but poor in labor.

It is within the moral overtones of the Protestant Ethic, in fact, that
biographers interpreted the intense practical activity associated with
Edison's boyhood. "He was not a youth who had time for idle day-
dreaming," one writer explained, "he had his own way to make in the
world. His mind was not full of soft, fuzzy, vain hopes of tomorrow, but
of hard, clear-cut, practical ideas that would work today." Self-reliance
was the key concept. "It was not unusual for a boy of twelve to strike
out on his own in the fifties," said the same author, for "at this period,
as in pioneer days, life was more work and worry than play"; "boys
early learned to work hard, to do for themselves, to strike shrewd bar-
gains." Practicality, then, was an inseparable part of American individualism, and the tinkering, empirical, vernacular character of Edison
became the ideal vehicle for such a theme.

One of the more homely aspects of Edison as the embodiment of
American practicality is that of the Yankee tinkerer, a figure envisioned
by the average American as a rough-hewn, sinewy New Englander with
a strong resemblance to Uncle Sam himself. In appearance, Ford fit this
image better than Edison. But the description of Edison working all
night and eating his breakfast "from a bench littered with parts of ma-

---

guides, one young and one old, the scientist's wife, "interested mainly in society
matters," her little son, the girl you are engaged to marry, your best friend,
yourself, or "a young man of your own age, who has shown great promise in the
field of science?"

chines," the observation that "fine clothes" were wasted on him because "he prefers to hang over a machine" until "his hands are covered with oil, grease and grime," and his own boast that all the machines he had ever worked on "would cover about twenty-five acres," recalls the vision of the barnyard tinkerer, whose common sense know-how is that of the rugged, self-sufficient pioneer. "A bold spirit," another biographer said of Edison, "unlearned but infinitely audacious, sticking a capable finger into many puzzling pies." A journalist reporting the fiftieth anniversary of the light observed that "of all the types of great mental men, the prophet, the artist, the statesman, the warrior, it is he, the lonely, the eccentric Yankee genius of contrivances and devices who is most intelligible to our minds and most heating to our emotions." Reminiscing on his improvement of the telephone, it was Edison, as always, who communicated the image most directly: "I went to work and monkeyed around, and finally struck the notion of the carbon button."

"He worked all day and all night tinkering with cogwheels and bits of copperwire," lampooned Dos Passos; "whenever he thought of a device he tried it out. He made things work . . . whenever he got a hunch he tried it out." If anything, the satire understated a trait not only associated with Edison's boyhood but often treated as the key to his inventive success. Edison even denied certain Newtonian axioms that he could not test; and once, when he read that a small vial of phosphoric anhydride was enough to suffocate the entire population of Paris, he "took just a little sniff" and went into a blood-spitting convulsion. "The book was right that time," he concluded.

"The way to find out how to do a thing is to try everything you can think of," Edison once said. My suggestion that this method was sealed into his being by the incandescent success is supported by an incident in which a lab assistant, being lectured by Edison on the limitations of theoretical scientists, was asked to guess what material had made the first promising filament. "Limburger cheese!" exclaimed Edison. "Now, can you show me a book of theoretical chemistry that explains why Limburger cheese must be good for the incandescent lamp?" From his travesty of the empirical method came his famous quip: "Genius is one percent inspiration and ninety-nine percent perspiration." As one writer put it: "You, perhaps, have a ten percent greater brain equipment than I, but if I work twelve hours a day and you work only eight, Edison would prefer me to you." The assumption, which was perfectly suited to Edison's method, was that the quantity rather than the quality of the work was most important, the latter automatically following the former.

At the core of Edison's anti-intellectualism seems to have been a hyperactivity which, as we have seen, dates from early childhood. He was indeed a man of action; asked how he made his calculations, he answered: "I don't know exactly; but I can't do them on paper. I have to be moving around." "One thing Edison would not tolerate among his employees was a dreamer," explained one biographer to her young readers. "Dreams are impractical things, and seldom the output of a man who hustles." "Edison never wastes any energy on mere idle curiosity," said another, and "is almost a Gradgrind in squelching any tendency on the part of his experimenters to 'wonder.' " His contempt for the old German professor studying the fuzz on the bee became a favorite quotation. In another anecdote, the inventor of a "sunshine lamp" brought the apparatus to Edison, explaining that he wanted a practical inventor to examine it and not "an expert with a lot of degrees who has never invented a carpet tack."

Edison's hatred of academic abstractions, especially on the part of those he referred to as "*the*-o-retical" scientists, was a subject of praise long before the questionnaire controversy. "Edison is never hindered by theory," American boys were told. "Where others brought forth only ideas, he created actualities." When Edison said that "the value of an idea lies in the using of it," he was not suggesting the philosophical subtleties of pragmatism; rather, as his official biographers said in 1910: "trusting nothing to theory, he acquires absolute knowledge."

Mathematics (in which Edison freely admitted he was "the zero") is the subject of many anti-intellectual anecdotes, such as the one involving the mathematician who produced a solution to a particular problem after four hours of calculating. "I worked only half an hour," said Edison, "and was only ten percent out, which was right enough for my purposes." The favorite anecdote, however, concerns the physicist whom Edison asked to determine the volume of an oddly shaped container. When the solution was brought to him after long hours of measurement, Edison simply checked it by filling the container with water and pouring it into a standard beaker. The lesson which those who cite the story overlook, of course, is not so much Edison's common sense as the value of the theoretical work which went into making the standard beaker. Yet the beaker *was* available to the physicist in question, so perhaps Edison made his point. If not, he would make it another way: "I can always hire mathematicians, but they can't hire me." "No man of a mathematical habit of mind ever invented anything that amounted to much. He hasn't the imagination to do it. He sticks too close to the rules." (Yet he feared that his mathematically trained son, Theodore, "may go flying into the clouds with that fellow Einstein.")*

After one of his men had been trying for months to develop a certain type of wax for phonograph disks, Edison told him that negative results were just what he wanted. "I can never find the thing that does work best until I know everything that *don't* do it," he said. Finally the man declared that he had tried every reasonable thing he could think of without result. "Thank God you can't think up any more reasonable things," Edison retorted, "so you'll have to begin thinking up *un*reasonable things to try, and now you'll hit the solution in no time."

Edison's disdain for the academic scientist, whom he once defined as "a man who would boil his watch while holding on to an egg," was solidly American. Josiah Willard Gibbs, perhaps the greatest of American scientists, was celebrated in Europe while living an obscure life at Yale in his own country. Edison, on the other hand, was called "our country's greatest contribution to the world list of scientific men." "What the country needs now," he said, "is the practical skilled engineer who is capable of doing everything. In three or four centuries when the country is settled and commercialism is diminished, there will be time for the literary men."

The fact that Edison's anti-intellectualism extended to the arts served only to reinforce the practical, democratic, self-educated, vernacular image. His tastes were simple and sentimental. He never went to the theater, was artistically apathetic, and his favorite literary works were *Evangeline* and *Les Misérables*. Shakespeare, he said, had great ideas and would have been "a wonderful inventor, if he had trained his mind to

* If Edison was fortunate in not being a learned man, he could be even more thankful that he was not a poet: a discussion question in a juvenile textbook read: " 'Oft on the dappled turf at ease/ I sit and play with similes/ Loose types of things through all degrees.' Study the above lines. Are the minds of the poet and the inventor alike?"

Camping near Hagerstown, Maryland, 1921, with Henry Ford to his left and President Warren Harding and Harvey Firestone to his right. Firestone Tire and Rubber Co.

On a camping trip in West Virginia, 1918. Left to right: Thomas Edison, Harvey Firestone, Jr., John Burroughs, Henry Ford, Harvey Firestone. Seated is R. J. H. deLoach. Firestone Tire and Rubber Co.

Edison reenacts the making of his incandescent lamp on the second floor
of the reconstructed Menlo Park laboratory at Greenfield, Michigan, on the
fiftieth anniversary of the invention,
October 21, 1929. Ford and Francis
Jehl (a Menlo Park coworker) look on.
Edison National Historic Site.

it." In his leisure moments he read detective stories or the *Police Gazette* and occasionally went to a movie to see Tom Mix, William S. Hart, or Mary Pickford. He believed that paintings depended for their value entirely upon scarcity and conspicuous consumption and would have been pleased at the verdict of a well-known historian of the motion picture that he had "the right to smile at the labors of Leonardo, Rubens, Hals, Rembrandt, Goya, and all those," for he was "their successor—the picture maker to a new and faster age." Edison, in fact, refused to have his portrait painted in 1926 because it would be made without aid of mechanism and therefore could not be "really very good." "Everything in this world should be done by machinery and measurements," he told the painter. The incident was reported in the newspaper under the caption, "Edison Wants His Portrait Made Only With Machinery." His request was granted that same year, though not quite in the way Edison had imagined, when the dust jacket of a new Edison biography featured the painting showing Edison's profile made up entirely of mechanical and electrical parts (p. 1).

Readers were told that Edison had "a deep and genuine sensibility" for the beauty of the natural world "when he has time for it," that he "never troubled himself with philosophy or metaphysics," that he had "a haunting feeling for things," which, rather than people, were the "source of most inspiration," and that he believed all knowledge to be "but a classification of experiences and facts." One of his men referred to his mind as a "mental junkyard." From that junkyard came both the phonograph and the first words spoken into it: "Mary had a little lamb."

INHERITING THE EARTH

"Do you want to know my definition of a successful invention?" Edison once asked. "It is something that is so practical that a Polish Jew will buy it." "I measure everything I do by the silver dollar," he told his secretary, "if it don't come up to that standard then I know it's no good." *
The statement has sometimes been misinterpreted; he was referring to

* The anecdote concerning Edison's first invention—a vote recorder which was rejected by Congress as politically impractical—is almost always coupled with

public demand rather than personal profit. The nation he typified apparently used the same yardstick; for Congress, in 1923, put the "Value of Edison's Genius" at fifteen billion dollars.

Edison's insistence on utility as a criteria for invention became the root of a new aspect in his image which appeared in the years after World War I: the idea of service to the nation and to mankind. His contributions to progress, comfort, and convenience had always been noted; but in the new consumer society of the 1920s, "Service," in the Rotarian sense, acquired an abstract value of its own. A strong part of his service image derived from the publicity given to his alleged egalitarian concern for the common man.

"The poor man with a family," said Edison, "is the man who has my sympathy, and is the man for whom I am working." "Let the poor take heart," wrote Allan Benson, for not only did Edison predict that machinery would take over all their heavy work, but the workingman could purchase Edison's new poured-cement house at extremely low cost. The kinetophone (sound movies) was another of Edison's inventions widely publicized as "a genuine contribution to the advance of democracy." It would now be "possible for the poorest families in Squeedunk to see the same operas and plays that are produced in New York City." In general, Edison was depicted as "the creator of inventions to help the greatest number at the lowest cost." One biographer observed that "the tinkerer ability of the American people" was "slowly but surely turning the world from an Aristocracy into a Democracy"; and Henry Steele Commager saw Edison as "democracy's own inventor, concerned always with things the plain people of the country could use."

In spite of the abundance in the Edison material of such phrases as "democratic simplicity," "most democratic of men," "the great Democrat of Science," and "plain, simple, hard-working, unpretentious American," Edison had an intense fear of being set apart from the plain people. He frequently brushed off questions about his medals with the comment that he had a "couple of quarts" of them up at the house.

Edison's statement that he learned then and there never again to invent anything for which there was no practical demand. This anecdote (with the lesson attached) was the twelfth most frequent to appear out of a total of 74 anecdotes counted relating to Edison's boyhood, youth, and early manhood.

"Knows Nothing About His Medals," reads an 1898 caption in the *Ladies' Home Journal*. Favorite stories tell of him leaving a medal on a ferryboat or throwing them "into a pile of odds and ends that he labeled as his 'useless junk.'" In its most popular form this theme was an expression of belief in the American Adam—in the moral superiority of equalitarian, American democracy itself. The most frequent image, with regard to medals and honors, depicted Edison in his shirt sleeves or stripped to the waist, covered with grime, grease, and sweat, hurrying irritably out to the waiting room to quickly receive a medal from a foreign dignitary who had traveled all the way across the Atlantic to present it. Edison would then stuff it into his pocket and return immediately to his work. He "often begrudges the time he is impressed into wasting in receiving visits from foreign potentates and other celebrities," wrote B. C. Forbes. "He is of the common people and his heart is with the common people." In one instance a Frenchman is depicted with an accent and a "swelling bosom." In all such cases it is implied or stated that the dignitary prizes his medal more than he does Edison. One representative is pictured in a comic strip frame gazing with intense pride not at Edison but at the medal he has just placed in his outstretched hand. At other times the image of Edison as the American Adam is more subtly implied, as, for example, when his wife interrupts his fervent reading with the announcement: "The Prince is here. You will have to get up."

The theme was used extensively in connection with Edison's two tours of Europe, in 1889 and 1911. The most popular anecdote to emerge from his visit to the Paris Exposition in 1889 concerned the presentation of the decoration of the Legion of Honor. Not only did Edison refuse to let the commander pin the sash on him, but he turned the badge under his lapel for fear that he might encounter fellow Americans on the streets of Paris who would "think he was showing off." Many of the honors bestowed on Edison, explains one biographer, "he could not accept because they carried honorary titles unacceptable in American democracy." Yet if he was "embarrassed by the attentions showered upon him" in Europe and by his lionization in the House of Commons, the shouts of "Edison! Edison! Edison!" along the route of the 1916 Preparedness Parade in New York "went straight to his heart. The sincere applause of the multitude, of the rank and file of his own people, was more gratifying to Edison than all the diplomas and parchments and medals in the world."

It was a common observation that Edison "is only one of the workers" who "punches time cards like any employee." "He didn't stand around giving orders," one author tells her juvenile readers, "but worked in the trenches with his men in all the dirt and hurly burly of traffic." It is in the youth-oriented literature, in fact, that the idea of Edison working along with the men is most heavily stressed. His "laboratories were all industrial democracies—republics in themselves," and he was "their democratic 'boss.'" His familiarity with the men and their devotion to him are constantly stressed, especially, of course, in reference to the Menlo Park years.

Repeatedly, readers are told that "a truck driver or a deck hand finds Edison one of their class" and that Edison "is brother to the man in the street." "The best cooking in the country," said Edison, bolstering the image, "is in the West—not in the great hotels, but in the homes of farmers and wage-workers." And reporters relished such an incident as that of the auto mechanic who was reluctant to shake hands, showing Edison that they were covered with grease and grime: " 'What of that,' said Mr. Edison, and he held out his own toil-worn hand palm up. Then they shook hands." Edison is described as "a millionaire who takes a milk train at two o'clock in the morning in order to gain time in going from one of his workshops to another" or who enters a movie hall, "paying his nickel at the door like all the common folks." The question arises as to what a millionaire is supposed to do. Such observations, of course, tell us more about the writers' own snobbery than about Edison.

Perhaps the desire to appear as an "honest and unassuming," "simple, democratic old man" was understandable in one who had remarked that America was an "unorganized mob" and who, in spite of his democratic pose and simple tastes, was a confirmed autocrat. Those close to him knew his raging tantrums and his moody moments when he would march through the laboratory firing men right and left (the old timers knew when to hide). Once, during the ore-milling project, Edison's workers attempted a strike; every last one of them was fired immediately. And then there was the matter of the huge, gabled, Victorian mansion called "Glenmont." An occasional author will suggest that Edison bought it "for his wife's sake" or that it "contained no garish suggestion of wealth." In the end it was not the taint of snobbery that he feared, it was more his thoroughly American desire to avoid self-boundaries and limits. A title, or any hierarchical social rank, no matter how exalted, ultimately suggests finiteness; it provides a handle by which one may be grasped and held to some fixed epitaph. (And it is doubly confining if the status is granted by a European; for one who bestows an honor subtly implies that he lives at some higher jurisdictional level which delimits the honored.)

Once again, then, the American is the archetypal modern man; for above all others he has taken the Copernican revolution to heart. On the surface of that event was a false humility: Man is torn from the center of the universe, allowing Newton to make a monotonous watchwork of his world; he is cast adrift in a vast and indifferent cosmos, much like the individualized American in the New World wilderness. Social and intellectual uprooting, it is argued, has cut man down to size, stripped him of inflated illusions; he has become practical, democratic, American.

But look again. The real implication of the Copernican revolution, as with the American Adam, is that the man who is able to conceive himself in this new existential relationship is *greater* than the cosmos because he is no longer bound by it; he has ceased to be that fixed point at its center or within the Great Chain of Being. He escapes that rigid definition on which the weight of all time, space, and tradition imploded. In short, the post-Copernican, the egalitarian democrat, the self-made-man-to-be, is the equal of God (or perhaps greater, since God cannot feign humility). The unbounded American individualist, soaring like the lone eagle high above all communal consensuses, retains both power and innocence.

SWAPPING YARNS

After the First World War, however, when Americans were temporarily disillusioned with power, the visions of innocence became more overt. It was during the 1920s, especially, that the practical, democratic, "human" Edison began to obscure the Promethean intellectual. As the nation returned to "normalcy," in fact, Edison literally returned to nature.

Edison's camping trips into the Alleghenies with Ford, Firestone, and the naturalist John Burroughs, which began in 1916, became an annual affair with ever-increasing publicity. The trips were apparently Edison's idea; the publicity, not surprisingly, was Ford's. "No one, to tell the absolute truth, wanted to go very much except Mr. Edison," said Burroughs. "He liked roughing it. . . . There can be no doubt about his love for the open air and for wild nature." "John Burroughs and 'Tom' Edison," reported the *San Francisco Chronicle* in 1916, "were sitting together like two happy school boys before a roaring wood fire in front of their tent, discussing the nature of primitive man." Burroughs, however, died in 1921, and the image of the camping trips took on the color of Ford's personality, adding to the general ballyhoo of postwar America. The entourage included limousines, maids, an army of cameramen, and trucks following behind with large placards reading: "Buy Firestone Tires." A mob met them at every village. It was a characteristically American "return to nature": Firestone doubted if they had "ever passed an abandoned mill without Mr. Edison and Mr. Ford getting out to measure the force of the stream, inspect the old wheel, and talk about ways and means of putting the waste power to work."

President Harding's nostalgic return to "normalcy" and Edison's return to nature converged on July 24, 1921, when urban Americans, who now composed more than fifty percent of the population, picked up their morning papers and inhaled their coffee over the headline: "Harding in Camp with Noted Party; Chops Fire Wood." And if Harding could chop wood in the Lincolnesque manner of his midwestern forebears, Coolidge could fetch the "old oaken bucket" from his grandmother's attic in Vermont and present it to Ford against the rural backdrop. "Back of the Coolidge Barn," said the headline; "President, Ford, Edison, and Firestone Swap Yarns as 'Just Folks.' " The papers went on to report that "all leaned back against the woodshed of the old Coolidge home and talked of as many things as the walrus and the carpenter." It was

an exhibition of democracy in which the American people take most delight. Here were four men starting life as poor boys who became known in every corner of the world solely by the development of their own personalities in useful service. Incidentally, three of them became rich and one, at least, very rich. But they are all known not for their riches but for useful work accomplished. None of them is the scion of a great family already well advertised. . . . They are just folks like the rest of us. There are few countries—possibly none except ours—where four such men could meet and chat on a stoney farm which was the ancestral home of one of them.

One of the most publicized camping photographs, showing Edison asleep under a tree, was accompanied by captions to the effect that the pose was a rare one. Actually, as one would expect of a man after age sixty-five, the ratio of sleep to work constantly increased. In spite of Edison's assertion that "there is really no reason why men should go to bed at all" and "sleep is an absurdity, a bad habit," it was observed as early as 1890 that "all night labor is somewhat exceptional with him of late." In 1919, interviewer Isaac Marcosson, arriving at the Edison laboratories in the middle of the work day, encountered the well-worn sign: "Silence. Mr. Edison is asleep." By 1927, if he did not sleep more than eight hours a night he would doze in his chair the next day.

As for work, he seems to have literally "tinkered" in the twenties. Asked by his birthday interviewers in 1923 what he was especially working on, he replied: "Don't ask me. As I get less able to work I take more on." On the following birthday he waved off the question, saying that he had been working on "many things" but that none of them had "come to a head." Three years later the Prince of Sweden inquired what he was engaged in at the present time; "Oh, a great quantity of things," said Edison, and changed the subject. By 1927 his faltering was unmistakable. Uncharacteristically, he sometimes flatly stated that he could not answer some of the usual sorts of questions. The image, it seemed, was beginning to overwhelm the man.

As always, however, Al Edison could not diminish Thomas A. In 1929 a number of writers insisted that he was working sixteen to eighteen hours a day. As late as 1930, *Times* readers were told that he worked fourteen hours a day. This is not to imply that Edison was ever idle. In 1926, for example, he was personally involved, to some degree, in the development of the long-playing record; and in 1928 he stepped up his determination to win one last campaign: the search for a new source of rubber which would provide the United States with an independent supply. The public aspects of this campaign demonstrate the degree to which the Menlo Park years continued to provide the archetypes for the Edison image. In the past, whenever a major problem had arisen Edison had usually reverted to that legendary imagery. In 1912, for example, he had threatened to reinstate his "insomnia squads" in his attempt to perfect a disk phonograph record which would compete with those already existing. Similarly, in 1927, he said he would see the rubber experiments through "if I have to work twenty-four hours a day." All the familiar phrases which grew out of the search for the lamp filament recurred: "To date," said the old inventor, "I have examined fifteen thousand plants, trees, and shrubs growing within the United States to discover their possibilities as rubber producers." And probably he had. Finally, of course, the "emissaries" again went out to various parts of the world to hunt down rubber "facts and specimens." Numerous writers assured America that Edison was working "day and night" on the rubber problem. It is probable, of course, that Edison saw his own situation very clearly. Asked what he would request from Aladdin's genie had he the chance, he said "my health." And after replying that he had not had time to study a certain issue, "he smiled a little. 'Too busy studying rubber,' he chuckled. 'Day and night.' "

YOU CAN'T GO HOME AGAIN

Edison's best friend, Henry Ford, shared with him an aversion to abstractions. Apparently Ford felt that the reliving of the Menlo Park days by Edison and the public should not be confined to vague moments of reverie; it required a tangible, nuts-and-bolts form. Therefore Ford wrote a check and instructed that every remaining scrap of the Menlo Park laboratory, along with the red New Jersey clay on which it had rested, be transported to Dearborn, Michigan, and set alongside a replica of the Sally Jordan boardinghouse where Edison and his men had lived. A short distance from this new Menlo Park was the actual Smith's Creek station where the young editor-chemist had been ejected from the flaming baggage car by the irate conductor. Even the train, the baggage car, and the laboratory and press inside were reproduced down to the most trivial detail. Nor did Ford stop there. Ironically, this man who was himself one of the towering symbols of the machine age, whose flivvers had done so much to destroy the very small-town cohesion he idealized, attempted to reconstruct early America itself. He called it Greenfield Village, purchasing and bringing to it such things as a courthouse where Lincoln had practiced law, a typical log cabin, a typical general store, Burbank's office from Santa Rosa, California, Poe's cottage from Fordham, New York, Patrick Henry's house from Redhill, Virginia, and numerous other authentically furnished and equipped early American structures. Inside the little red schoolhouse where Ford himself was educated was a desk with "H.F." carved in it, and on top of which lay autographed copies of McGuffey's readers. But his prize acquisitions were the Edison buildings. The purpose of the whole project, in fact, was the celebration of the fiftieth anniversary of the invention of the incandescent lamp, to be held on October 21, 1929, and during which Edison was to reenact his success in the reconstructed laboratory.

Ford felt it would be fitting if the final banquet and ceremonies were held in the building in which the Declaration of Independence had been signed; in Philadelphia, however, his agent learned that Independence Hall was not for sale. "Then build me a perfect replica of Independence Hall that will last three times as long as the original," was Ford's reaction. "Build the foundation three times as deep and three times as wide as the one in Philadelphia. That'll show 'em!"

In its pastoral setting, Ford's project for glorifying American invention (which included a huge museum adjacent to the village, containing a visual history of American technology) was one of the purest examples of the attempt to root the machine in the garden. The very name Ford chose, Greenfield Village, functioned as the sort of tag-label which editorial cartoonists use to clarify their caricatures. Here, it said, is the innocent garden of America's childhood, that simple, rural past where relationships were personal, affairs were arranged informally, and cultural values were still intact. Here is that sunny, pre-industrial time when one could remain whole and unique and yet find identity within a larger communal harmony. Most of Ford's props, in fact, were selected not from the Menlo Park years but from the antebellum era of Edison's birth, when the nation's promise seemed infinite, when its boundaries were still undetermined, and mature limits were far off in the next century. With its clean, orderly, unworn structures and its static landscape, the village had the aura of a cemetery—that deathless perfection found only in death itself. Greenfield was the Disneyland of its day, an American Mecca, a cultural transubstantiation. The irony of such attempts to strip away our technological spacesuits and recontact the archetypes in nostalgic settings is that Greenfield, with its freshly painted, oversized Independence Hall, and Disneyland, with its purposely undersized Main Street, fake waterfalls, and mechanical Lincoln, simply raise the artificiality by one more power.

On October 21, 1929, Ford's Fantasyland was an animated *Who's Who*. At the T-shaped dinner table in Independence Hall would sit those whom the newspapers called "the four hundred of the world." Edison himself was met by Ford, President Hoover, and other dignitaries at Dearborn. With reporters and cameramen the party boarded the replica of the Grand Trunk Train on which Edison had been a newsboy and candy vendor. Inside, every minute detail was authentic. Edison picked up the basket of fruit, taffy, and Oh Boy Gum and started down the aisle crying "candy, bananas, apples!" "I'll take a peach!" cried the President, standing up and producing a quarter.

Rolling through a gray mist, ever farther from the main line of the Michigan Central, the wood-burner carried these three symbols of self-made America: Edison, Ford, and Hoover. Within eight days, the economy which they had created would collapse—due largely, in fact, to saturation with automobiles and the pyramiding of power-company ownership. Meanwhile the president of the United States traveled across country to buy a peach from an ex-newsboy. It was as though the chief had come to the medicine man's hut, with the volcanoes smoking in the distance, and together they performed a private ritual of reassurance in the last moments of their world.*

* Yet there is irony in the ridicule no less than in the ritual. To observe that Ford denied the ambiguities and tensions of real history, just as he reduced Al Edison's being to the single act of lighting a bulb, and then to complain that it all represents a fragmented, two-dimensional consumer culture, is to be guilty of the same naiveté of which we accuse Ford. Academia itself seems to grow ever more two-dimensional in this respect—its orthodoxy, in a sentence: "Marx was right; the emperor has no clothes on." The popular jeremiads about the technological society, mass culture, bureaucratic alienation, ad infinitum (a la Theodore Roszak, Charles Reich, Philip Slater, George Leonard, et al.), pursue an Edenic myth which denies a paradoxical and contrapuntal reality. This is not to say that such countercultural diatribes are not solid and fascinating half-truths; it is only to say that if the Edenic myth will not support Ford, neither will it support his critics.

As the entourage disembarked at Smith's Creek station, horse-drawn hacks and high-wheeled bicycles moved about. Crowds cheered them through the rain to the ramshackle wooden building where the real ritual was to take place. Edison was feeling the strain of the day, for he had just gotten over a bout with pneumonia. An old elm stump sat near the structure where it had always been. Edison looked at it and then peered at the ground. "Why Henry's even brought the damn dirt!" he exclaimed. They let him enter first, and then stepped inside, remaining by the door while the stooped old man inspected the room for himself. Every detail was perfect; even Edison's favorite old mortar had been unearthed and cemented back together. A few noticed the old man's lips tremble slightly as he sat down on the wooden chair and folded his arms. "For five, perhaps ten, minutes," wrote a witness, "the scene was unmarred by a word or a gesture, except that now and then Edison looked around him and his eyes dimmed." Perhaps he was recalling the joy of intense activity as others might reflect on enthusiasms shared with childhood companions: Kruesi's disbelief at hearing words from the rotating cylinder he had been told to make, Batchelor's loyalty, cigars and jokes at the late night suppers, Boehm on the zither, the steaming kettle of food from the Woodward farmhouse. Or perhaps he was thinking that just as this was not really Menlo Park, he was not really the Wizard; and all the emissaries, fifteen thousand substances, fantastic endurance, and midnight triumphs of the staunch little band of comrades were fittingly represented by this old mausoleum among the high-wheeled bicycles, log cabins, and other relics. Suddenly he cleared his throat and the spell was broken.

Shortly thereafter, Edison, aided by one of the two surviving assistants from 1879, recreated the first lamp while the event was described over 144 affiliates of the National Broadcasting Company, the greatest radio hookup which had been attempted to date; even Admiral Byrd listened in Antarctica. In their homes, people were listening by candlelight as Edison turned up the replica of the old carbon filament lamp with President Hoover looking on and the announcer proclaimed: "And Edison said: *'Let there be light!'* " At that moment, lights were turned on all over the nation, special lamps in the great cities suddenly blazed up, and the bells pealed atop Independence Hall. With Edison's feat as a pretext, the nation reenacted not so much the invention of the light as the epic of American progress itself. It was a ritual which set the machine in the garden, change within permanence, power within innocence.

As the President preceded him into the banquet hall, Edison sat down on a sofa just outside the door and wept with fatigue. "I won't go in," he said to his wife. Some warm milk was brought and the old man was helped into the hall. He sat grimly through the interminable tributes, too deaf to hear any of them. "Mr. Edison, by his own genius and effort rose from modest beginnings to membership among the leaders of men," said Hoover. "His life gives renewed confidence that our institutions hold open the door of opportunity to all those who would enter." Edison arose, read a short speech written by his son, Charles, and then turned white and slumped into his seat. When he recovered he must have known, if he had not known before, that the Wizard of Menlo Park was no longer in need of Al Edison. "I am tired of glory," the old man said, "I want to get back to work."

6

THE LAST GREAT HAYSEED:
THE POSTHUMOUS IMAGE

Edison, circa 1896. Edison National
Historic Site.

Exactly two years after his collapse at the Jubilee, on the fifty-second anniversary of the incandescent lamp, Thomas A. Edison was buried at sunset beneath a large oak on a hill overlooking his laboratory and factories. As the small funeral party drifted away in the dusk—most of them survivors of the age of steam and gaslight—the cool glitter of the electrical age crept over the valley below.

REPRISE: THE AMERICAN EPIC

Almost to the year, his life had spanned that explosion of human energy which transformed America between the 1840s and the 1920s. In his first memory he had seen wagons set out for California during the gold fever of '49; and in his last months he saw the nation sink ever more deeply into depression. Biographers placed his boyhood in the pre-industrial innocence of Tom Sawyer's Jacksonian America; his drifting adolescence paralleled civil war, Reconstruction, and the birth of a national economy; and the productivity of his early manhood was indispensable to the urban-industrial transformation. It is understandable that twentieth-century America, imbued with a sense of narrowing options, has looked nostalgically to Edison as the embodiment of a Golden Age of youth, hope, and vitality.

Even his boyhood represented the nascent American epic far more than it suggested the simple pastoral milieu of Huck Finn or Tom Sawyer. Set on the Grand Trunk Railroad, the origin of Edison's own electrical epic resembled less the idyll of Huck's raft journey and more the sudden intrusion of a locomotive upon Hawthorne's "Sleepy Hollow":

But, hark! there is the whistle of the locomotive—the long shriek, harsh above all other harshness, for the space of a mile cannot mollify it into harmony. It tells a story of busy men, citizens, from the hot street, who have come to spend a day in a country village, men of business; in short of all unquietness; and no wonder that it gives such a startling shriek, since it brings the noisy world into the midst of our slumbrous peace.[1]

Yet the aura of innocence surrounding the legendary "hustle" of Edison's boyhood suggested that the intrusion of the machine upon the garden had occurred in a fresh dawn under a morning star—that it was the immaculate conception of the American colossus itself.

In the final analysis it was not technological achievement which placed Edison alongside of Washington and Lincoln. For as twentieth-century America became ever more centralized and interdependent, the Promethean drive which had produced the abstract, impersonal society began to seem less appealing than Edison's raw, unbounded individualism. Yet if he became less the promise of utopia and more the surviving symbol of Paradise lost, it was not the loss of the pastoral itself that was mourned. For individuality was swallowed by "Sleepy Hollow" no less than by the technological society. Rather, Edison survived as a memento from that moment of equilibrium in the historical cycle—characteristic of "golden ages"—when forces cancel and the culture is drawn in all directions. In such transitional times, the cultural mainstream becomes a confusion of eddies and whirlpools in which most people drift erratically and some drown, but many discover unprecedented individual freedom. The resulting explosion of creativity and the fragmentation and decay of the Old Order are experienced as one phenomenon, scattering the seeds of new consensuses. Compared to Periclean Athens or Renaissance Italy, of course, the transformation experienced by nineteenth-century America was less fundamental, proceeding as it did within the larger consensus of rational liberalism. Yet there is more than naiveté in the comparison of Greek sculpture, Renaissance painting, and American invention; for the burst of technological creativity had effects greater than those of all previous upheavals put together.

All of this is simply another perspective on the paradoxical function of all culture heroes and the fact that Edison balanced the machine and the garden, power and innocence, isolation and communion. The shifting emphases within the mythology, from Promethean wizard and erudite scientist to the kindly, venerable, and democratic benefactor and finally to the tinkering, vernacular, unreconstructed individualist, was accelerated, as we have seen, after the turn of the century. By the 1920s Edison had become an incongruous blend of the Promethean and the profane, a kind of grandfatherly, senatorial Santa Claus, who, along with his friend Ford, had delivered the modern miracles while America slept—all the trappings of the Jazz Age suddenly discovered by awakened American youth: automobiles, records, telephones, city lights, and silent movies.

During the years immediately surrounding Edison's death, a century of unparalleled expansion seemed to reach its limits and collapse. The

sense of encroaching boundaries, dating perhaps from the symbolic closing of the frontier in 1890, seemed inherent in the very process of mod-
ernization itself. In a larger context, as Walter Webb has argued, the
thirties marked the inevitable end of the four-hundred-year boom in
Western civilization. But from the perspective of a few Depression-
bound Americans, Edison represented the foolish innocence of a late-
maturing society. To them it seemed that he had stolen the fire but escaped the fate, leaving Everyman himself fastened to the rock with the
vulture feeding on his liver. The criticisms of Edison which arose in the
thirties completed the humanization process begun decades earlier. It
was less the negative comment and more the evolution of the twentieth
century itself, however, which eventually caused the image to lose much
of its Olympian aura.

In its place, on one hand, was a nostalgic and reactionary vision of
Edison as the unrestricted individualist of an earlier and better time. On
the other hand, a new view of Edison had begun to emerge in the twenties, though it would not become dominant for almost a half-century.
This was the affirmative and energetic human being which the 1970s
would see as the antithesis to passivity, defeat, and stagnation. We shall
return to this perspective in conclusion; for the moment, we may note
that the idea of "service to mankind," which began to develop in the
Edison image during World War I, was a nascent aspect of this new
dimension.

HUMANIZING THE HUMANITARIAN

It had required the combined assaults of Bright's disease, uremic poison-
ing, diabetes, and a gastric ulcer to bring Edison down, a fact which the
obituaries were quick to relate to his indefatigable industry and perseverance. It was the theme of "service to mankind," however, which
dominated the eulogies.

The reification of "Service," independent of any particular effect such
as comfort or convenience, did not really appear in the image until after
1915. Isolating all of the statements which attribute to Edison's work
some general quality or overall effect upon the world, one finds a significant shift during the post-World War I period. First, the number of
such statements for the years 1915 to 1928 is three times that for the

decades prior to 1915, while the difference in total amounts of material for the two periods is significantly less than three times. Second, while statements in the earlier period stress comfort, convenience, commercial utility, material progress, and national wealth and power (in that order), and although such words as "gift," "giving," "help," "benefit," "contribution," and "mechanical servants" are occasionally encountered, the generalized notion of "service to mankind" and "world benefactor" appears only after 1915, accounting for twenty-three percent of the statements in the period 1915–1928. The only theme ahead of service in this period was progress (predominantly, but no longer strictly, material); those following were: (3) comfort, convenience, and the lightening of labor; (4) increased happiness in general; (5) inspiration to others; (6) national wealth and power; (7) employment; and (8) amusement.*

In 1929 an entire issue of the *National Electric Light Association Bulletin,* devoted to Edison in honor of the Jubilee, was dominated by the idea of service. "Service to humanity," wrote Walter Chrysler, "is the ideal of our modern civilization, and . . . Thomas Alva Edison perfectly personifies the ideal." "His unselfish and untiring efforts to serve mankind," said Ford, "make him today the greatest of all living Americans."

Although the sensational publicity given Edison's work during the First World War, along with the fact that the mass of Americans did not experience electric power in the home until after that time, helps account for the sudden occurrence of the service theme after 1915, its appearance was actually part of the larger cultural transformation.[2] Within the idea of service, as in so many things, Edison's image bridged an older and a newer concept. A fundamental axiom of the nineteenth century held that material progress was prerequisite to moral progress

* The statement count for the categories, from (1) to (8), is as follows: 59, 40, 22, 17, 14, 12, 7, 5. The arbitrariness and overlap of the divisions is obvious, as is the fact that almost any effect of positive value could be included under "service"; the point is only that the latter had become a distinct theme in itself by the 1920s. The shift is reinforced by the words and phrases used in place of Edison's name. Prior to 1915, not one' of them indicates even indirectly the idea of service. In the period 1915–1928, the words "benefactor" and "servant" represent eight percent of the noun substitutes; between 1929 and 1932 the same two, along with "citizen" and "friend" (of mankind), constitute 23 percent.

and human happiness. Thus the ideal of service came to mean the provision of material necessities and conveniences at ever-lower costs; the two symbolic figures in this effort were the manufacturers and technological innovators. Poverty, rather than any limits inherent in man or society, was seen as the source of all evil. "As wealth has accumulated and things have cheapened," said Charles Perkins, president of the Chicago, Burlington, & Quincy Railroad in 1888, "men have improved . . . in their habits of thought, their sympathy for others, their ideas of justice as well as of mercy. . . . Material progress must come first and . . . upon it is founded all other progress." [3]

The concept of service which emerged in this century differed significantly from that of the nineteenth. By the 1920s, when the shift in orientation from production to consumption—from manufacturing to marketing—was complete, the small-business proprietor on the local level and the top managerial executive on the national level had largely replaced the great manufacturers and inventors as the self-proclaimed symbols of service. The word "service" itself had been used infrequently by the late nineteenth-century titans. In the twentieth century, however, it became so standard as to require a capital "S" for easier handling. Rotary International, founded in Chicago in 1905, built its philosophy around such phrases as "He Profits Most Who Serves Best" and "Service Above Self." As the twentieth century moved toward the "post-industrial society," those engaged in actual services would ultimately outnumber those employed in all areas of production. In an ever more interdependent social organism, success depended less on Edisonian industriousness and perseverance and more on other-directed perception and the ability to project a sincere and self-sacrificing image.

Thus the older and newer heroes of service correspond roughly to the builders and the maintainers, the producers and the managers. Both fit the monomythic pattern in that builders extended the area of freedom in a future-oriented society, while the maintainers hold ground against encroaching limits in a present-oriented society—like Coolidge and Edison, they become surrogate parents who persevere while we play.

This perspective had much to do with the fact that the "humanized" Edison of the twenties still retained an Olympian quality. Such portraits as the Shinn photograph or the Silvette painting (p. 129) made him look like a humanitarian United States senator, provoking descriptions of a venerable and wise old man—"the Nestor of American invention"—and a lover of animals and children. The momentum of this image sometimes led to exaggerated assertions that he "was never angry in his life" or that his protective feelings toward baby mice caused lengthy work stoppages in the laboratory. Most pathetic, perhaps, was one writer's attempt to depict "the human Edison," as he titled his piece, by presenting a series of five incidents, each of which climaxed with Edison crying like a baby; the article, which is saturated with adjectives, concludes with the alliterated statement that he left the "sad, sobbing old man traduced by the tyranny of tears."

In spite of the fact that Edison himself, as later writers would note, "did not try to imitate the imaginary figure of a cultured, dignified and benevolent gentleman, created by the media," the image was perpetuated in the twenties under the assumption that such figures symbolize empathy with the common man. A strong part of Edison's service image, in fact, was the publicity given to his alleged equalitarian concern for the plain people. (I found no statement of the democratic-egalitarian theme prior to 1909.) Yet Edison himself "never spoke of 'service to humanity' or his 'mission in life,' " said a former assistant; "commercial demand was his measure of need." He "did not care for money but neither did he care for service that much," added another; he was "a compulsive achiever" who craved fame and prestige. Back in Menlo Park, during the struggle to perfect the light, Edison once told a reporter: "I don't care so much for fortune, as I do for getting ahead of the other fellows."

Ignoring such realities, a number of writers in the 1930s attacked the image of the venerable, benevolent democrat as though it were the man himself. In spite of the numerous articles stressing how little money he made from his inventions relative to the potential involved, and regardless of the frequent claim that his happiness was "not bound up in the making of money," John Dos Passos complained that Edison, like America, had "cashed in gigantically on the machine." He went on to contrast the hunchbacked Steinmetz as the real democrat. The directors of General Electric, with whom he classed Edison,

know in a vague sort of way that they want to make money and to make good; most of them want to play the game according to the rules of their time and not to be a worse son-of-a-bitch than the next man, but the problem of readjustment of human values necessary to fit their world is the last thing they think about. I suppose they would say it was none of their business.

That is why the little crumpled figure of Steinmetz stands out with such extraordinary dignity against this background of practical organizers, rule-of-thumb inventors, patent-office quibblers. Steinmetz felt every moment what his work meant in the terms of the ordinary human being. . . . The officials of G.E. had the attitude of Edison, who when he was asked whether he'd ever studied mathematics, said 'No . . . I can hire a mathematician any time, but the mathematicians can't hire me.' G.E. hired its mathematician, and it was a funny, rare little animal and had to be allowed to range a good deal to be kept happy and contented.

Finally, he wore out and died. If he'd been living, he'd probably have been at Dearborn with his toy thunderstorm, grinning in the limelight with the rest of the grand old men.

But the principal difference, said Dos Passos, was that "Steinmetz was not of the temperament to cash in on anything."

This type of criticism cropped up occasionally in the European press but was not penned by Americans until after the stock market crash in October 1929; even then it was a rare occurrence. *The Christian Century,* commenting that "progress has nothing to do with more human relationships," observed that Ford might have applied the costs of "Light's Golden Jubilee" to aiding the American poor or at least to the thirty thousand employees he dismissed several weeks before the celebration. But it was a German, in 1931, who wrote that Edison "was always convinced that his labors met an urgent human need, but never wondered why. He was one of the most unseeing benefactors of mankind. With religious enthusiasm Edison won humanity to his mechanical music, his lighting effects, and his Portland cement, and now he rises out of the chaos of American Puritanism like an old Indian totem post on the plains of Oklahoma." Such critics tend to commit an error which is the inverse of that made by the writers who were enthralled by Edison paying his nickel at the door "like all the rest"; the question, that is, still remains as to what Edison was supposed to do. One wonders how a man who spends a lifetime in the courts simply trying to prove that his inventions are his own is going to exercise much control over their consequences. Once again, those who argue from an idealism which denies

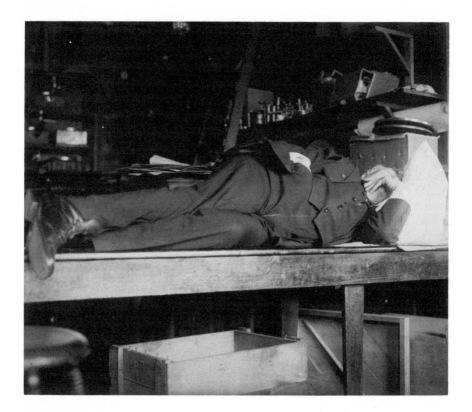

Asleep in the lab, 1911. Edison usually used a book for a pillow. Edison National Historic Site.

Edison and Mina in the West Orange chemistry laboratory, 1906. Edison National Historic Site.

the real tensions of man and history seem to confuse the functions of poetry and politics.

The irony of the stilted stereotypes and shallow criticisms is that, in the end, Edison really *was* at one with the common man. "The birthday interviews, the questionnaires, the annual trips to Florida," said Mary Nerney, who had also been an Edison employee, "all contributed to a stereotyped impression, as did the hackneyed anecdotes, the 'authorized' biographies." They "blurred the rough outlines of his individualism." They made him "a conventional figure, exemplary but dull, the victim of the publicity of flat minds. A great name, a bust in time for the Hall of Fame, but not Edison." The Edison she had in mind was "above everything . . . human, delightfully, charmingly, naively and utterly human." This was the Edison whom Shaw Desmond depicted as an innocent child throughout a series of articles in 1922 and who was called "the best beloved man in America" at the presentation of the Congressional Medal in 1928. It was the same figure whom Spencer Tracy portrayed in the MGM film *Edison the Man* (1940) and who, according to the *New York Times* obituary, was loved for his "fine simplicities and boyishness" and his "warm human presence."

The "human" Edison, first glimpsed in the success theme, took more direct form in the human interest interviews after the turn of the century and finally dominated the image in the 1920s. The human dimension remained incomplete, however, until after his death. The later descriptions of Edison's raw individualism were based almost entirely on an article written for *Harper's Monthly* in 1932 by Martin A. Rosanoff, one of Edison's former assistants. The article, which radically altered the image of Edison for subsequent writers, offers a large number of new anecdotes, the most popular of which occurred during Rosanoff's first day on the job in 1903:

I approached him in a humble spirit: "Mr. Edison, please tell me what laboratory rules you want me to observe." And right then and there I got my first surprise. He spat in the middle of the floor and yelled out, "Hell! there *ain't* no rules around here! We are tryin' to accomplish somep'n!"

Rosanoff describes Edison's high-pitched voice and reproduces his dialect, which included "git," "jist," "turribly," "Eyetalian," "*p*iano," and the constant use of "don't" for "doesn't," "doos" for "does" and "aint no" for "aren't any." Edison constantly spat on the floor in disgust; and when Mrs. Edison reproached him, politely offering to provide a spittoon, he declined, saying that "the floor itself was the surest spittoon because you never missed it." Most of Rosanoff's conversational excerpts bring home Edison's anti-intellectualism and his utter lack of taste in art, music, or literature. But even before Rosanoff wrote, John Chamberlain observed that there was "little beyond the uncanny persistence and imaginative fertility of the man to talk about—no great human conflicts to enhance with selective art."

If anything, this new posthumous dimension in the democratic aspect of the image is more suited to the American idealization of the common man than was the patriarchal humanitarian depicted in the popular press prior to Edison's death. Like Lincoln, who also spoke the frontier dialect, Edison was not merely sympathetic or empathetic to the vernacular Yankee idealized in American tradition, he *was* that figure, writ large through heroic achievement. Rosanoff, of course, only provided the proof for what the public had sensed all along. An occasional writer would candidly state the theme:

He was . . . a neighbor to us all . . . esteemed for his homely virtues as well as admired for his genius. The great American family felt that he was one of them and not remote and above them, and they turned to him in his latter days for counsel in homely things. . . . [His] heroism is something we can understand as we cannot the processes of intellect which produced the high discoveries of pure science or the master works of the arts. We feel closer to Edison than to Einstein.

Thus, when a twenty-five-foot statue of the inventor was to be placed at the base of a twenty-story building, no one questioned that the pose would be "natural" rather than formal. "Here, said the American millions was no cold-blooded scientist, a product of books and the laboratory, learned, inhuman, and detached," wrote one biographer. "Here with his wide-set, kindly eyes, his broad forehead, his generous mouth, was one of themselves, who found mathematics as baffling as they did."

HOW THRILLED HE WOULD BE

As Edison's methods were eclipsed by organized industrial research, conducted by men with professional scientific and technical education, the practical, anti-intellectual image itself gradually drew less praise and more criticism.* In 1927, the inventor Nikola Tesla commented that he was "a sorry witness" to Edison's procedure, "knowing that just a little theory and calculation would have saved him ninety per cent of the labor." "The men who counted in our national development during the last half century," added Dos Passos in 1929, "carried practicality to a point verging on lunacy." Not only were journalists becoming suspicious of Edison's practicality, but, as Rosanoff illustrated, the average twentieth-century youth experienced a profound disillusionment upon meeting Edison, finding "an awfully commonplace sort of man, who could not pass a college entrance examination in math" and who knew less organic chemistry than a college junior.

Some types of criticism, such as that which attacked Edison as a business baron who posed as champion of the common man, did not survive the 1930s; his ignorance of theory, however, was the subject of negative comment well into the post-World War II period. In 1947, on the centenary of Edison's birth, an historian of invention concluded that the advances of science had been "too much for the empirical inventor, too much for the man who could patiently perform ten thousand experiments without ever hitting an invention as big as synthetic rubber or radar." (In addition to a rubber substitute, Edison had sought a device to guide planes in low visibility.) One of the strongest qualifications of the Edison image in a 1964 *Look* magazine series on the men who "made our world" concerned his disinterest in anything that was not useful. "The career of Thomas Edison," observed historian Morrell Heald in the same year, "illustrates the rapidity with which specialization overtook one of this country's legendary scientist-inventors."

In the total image, however, we shall find that skepticism concerning his anti-intellectualism was more than balanced by the degree to which it enhanced his unreconstructed individualism. Edison's attitude was a normal aspect of the nineteenth-century dispute between scientists and

* The figures for "practical" comprise one of the better sets in table 4 (see appendix). The sharp rise early in the century, followed by a slight subsidence and a noticeable decline in the 1960s, corroborates the general impression gained from a chronological reading of the material. The count for "practical" with regard to the inventions themselves (includes "useful," "utility," "commercial," etc.) showed the same tendency, but the differences were not significant.

inventors—a mutual contempt resolved by the contemporary public in favor of the tinkering inventor. This bias was still evident during World War I when Edison's appointment to the Naval Board was viewed by the press as assurance that the best brains would now be available for the application of science to naval problems. Actually, the one scientist on the Board was put there only because Edison had suggested to the President that "we might have one mathematical fellow in case we have to calculate something out." "As late as 1917," writes James Conant, "it was primarily the inventor, not the scientist, who was looked to by the general public as being the prime mover of technology." [4]

During the interwar period, however, the electrical, chemical, and pharmaceutical industries led the way in bringing science into industry. The great research laboratories of General Electric, Bell Telephone, and DuPont are examples. It is ironic that the inventors, who made possible the increased productive capacity and the means of transportation and communication necessary to national markets, would in turn see their kind swallowed into the impersonal obscurity of the "research team" by the very organizations for which they had paved the way. Edison himself established a model for this nonrecognition, building his own team of assistants and sometimes taking credit for their work in much the same way that corporate organizations now reap the publicity for technological achievement. The difference, in Edison's own case, was best phrased in his answer to a visitor's question about the organization and methods of the laboratory: "Organization! Hell! I'm the organization!"

But Edison's most recent biographer, Robert Conot, suggests that Edison lacked the capacity for supervising; he himself always had to be a part of what was going on.

Although his ideas and plans were often boundless, he worked best in intimate surroundings, where a few steps could take him from Batchelor experimenting with the telephone to Upton wrestling with the incandescent light.

What he could not understand, he was not interested in. Despite the camaraderie of the laboratory and the pleasure he obtained from nocturnal socializing, his deafness acted like an auditory veil—his intake of knowledge was overwhelmingly visual. He had difficulty participating in lengthy conversations or absorbing involved explanations.

Essentially, his was a lonely striving, within a social setting. It was alien to his nature to consider that success might depend on the strength and capabilities of his retainers. He was uneasy with men who were too independent, or whose knowledge challenged his. He was indifferent and even antagonistic toward men who wanted to pursue their own ideas under his aegis. He preferred men of limited talent . . . who he knew were dependent on him.

Consequently, men of real talent, men like Nikola Tesla, Frank Sprague, Edward Acheson, and Samuel Mott, stayed at Menlo Park only a short time and then moved on. The problem was compounded at the West Orange laboratory where Edison

assigned projects to people, and tried to make the rounds of the experimental rooms like a hospital physician. But often he became interested in what was happening in one room, and spent the whole week there. Since he disliked employing people with intelligence and initiative to pursue experiments independently, he left men in other rooms, who were deprived of his direction, floundering about.

He continued to measure employees more by their salaries than by their output. He dismissed chemists, but hired hordes of boys with little education on the premise that it was cheaper to train his own workers. . . .

More and more it would become evident that only in those projects in which Edison himself was personally involved was reasonable progress made. Almost never were more than two major projects sustainable simultaneously. Edison's view of the laboratory as a creative cornucopia was impracticable.

These realities qualify to some degree the common observation that Edison invented the modern research laboratory.

By World War II, scientists as scientists were being called upon by the government. The term "scientist" is used here to represent both of the trained communities referred to by Edwin Layton (see p. 34). It was during the Second World War, in fact, that the most conspicuous contradiction of Layton's model occurred. The man in the street now came to see "that the scientist is today taking the place of the inventor; that the 'long-haired' professors who were elaborating highly abstruse mathematical theories had been able to play an important part in the extraordinary development of the atomic bomb." [5]

The impact of the atomic age as such on the Edison image has probably been fourfold. First, the nuclear revolution, being potentially

Last picture taken of Edison, emerging
from his doctor's office in July 1931.
Edison National Historic Site.

Edison writing in one of his 2,500
notebooks, November 5, 1928. Edison
National Historic Site.

comparable to that of steam and electricity, recharged the aura of magic surrounding science and technology. The layman began to realize that the scientist was playing the same role in other fields that he had in the military; medicine was the prime example. Second, the technological race associated with the Cold War, particularly after the launching of Sputnik I in 1957, stimulated a greater emphasis on careers in science. Not only was attention to science increased in elementary and secondary schools, but television programs such as "Mr. Wizard" and "Science in Action" became extremely popular in the 1950s.[6] In this context Edison remained the symbol of "the miracle of America's productive capacity" —the technological superiority which had won the war, and which made "the genius-hungry Russians fret with envy." "Throughout the world the race of science is on, and the pace is fast," said the president of NBC during a tribute to Edison in 1948. "A nation that is slow to meet this challenge imperils its security." Inevitably, the eighth Polaris atomic submarine, launched in 1961, was christened *Thomas A. Edison.*

Equally predictable was the fact that Edison was credited with anticipating the atomic bomb. Former Postmaster General James Farley, among others, quoted Edison's statement that "there will one day spring from the brain of science a machine of force so fearful in its potentialities, so absolutely terrifying, that even man, the fighter, who will dare torture and death in order to inflict torture and death, will be appalled and so will abandon war forever." There was also a pathetic attempt, after the ceremonial opening of Edison's old roll-top desk during the birthday centenary in 1947, to grant Edison a specific knowledge of atomic energy. A glass container labeled "uranium nitrate" had been discovered in the desk among a large number of other bottles and the newspapers asked: "Had Edison, too, speculated on its fearful possibilities? Were they a secret he wished to suppress?" The idea was, of course, absurd, given Edison's total ignorance of atomic theory.

This incongruity raises the third point concerning Edison's image in the new age of theoretical physics: the radical decline of his relevance.*

---

* Words and phrases denoting "scientist" that were used in place of Edison's name rose from 3.1 percent of those found in the period 1876–1889 to 4.4 percent for 1890–1899 and then declined (except for a brief recovery in the Jubilee and obituary years, 1929–1932) to 2.4 percent for 1900–1928, 1.9 percent for 1933–1949, 1.6 percent in the 1950s, and .9 percent in the 1960s.

The fact that Edison remained the American symbol of science while interest in the subject increased and the realities of the man himself became ever more anachronistic resulted in the paradox of most culture
heroes in this century: appreciation without interest. Thus, in 1957,
Edison's birthday was permanently changed to "National Science Youth
Day." Referred to as "a nationwide effort by industry, government and
education to interest young people in science," the stated purpose was
"to focus national attention on the critical shortage of scientists and
engineers"—always in the context of the Cold War. On Science Youth
Day in 1962, for example, the president of the Detroit Edison Company,
after noting the need for technical training, called attention to the rapid
growth of electric power in the Soviet Union during the previous year.
In the 1930s and 1940s, February 11th, Edison's birthday, had been observed, either nationally or in various states (especially New York), as
"Thomas A. Edison Day." Like George Washington, however, Edison
came to exemplify not so much what people were interested in as what
they believed others (especially youth) *should* be interested in. Even the
centenary of his birth took on this character; newspapers reported that
students in schools throughout the country would "study sets of posters
telling in pictures of the life and achievements of the inventor." And in
1952 the so-called 'nationwide observances" in connection with Edison's
birthday took place in industries which had their beginnings in Edison's
work and in service clubs, schools, churches, and the Boy Scouts—groups,
in other words, with an interest in the nostalgic, almost liturgical, pres-
ervation of tradition for its own sake. Stores did not close, nor were
there spontaneous celebrations; it was a back page item.

At Greenfield Village in 1969, on the ninetieth anniversary of the
light bulb, a reenactment of the reenactment of the invention took
place. This time, however, the event was attended not by the president,
the cabinet, major industrialists, and the "500 of the world," but by
busloads of "high school science students and their instructors." Attention to Edison, in other words, had degenerated to the formality of a
field trip.

As early as 1933, in fact, the meeting of the Edison Pioneers, which
had long been a gala, prestigious, widely attended affair, seemed a sad
remnant, preoccupied with Edison's recent death. "Not many young
people attended," noted a reporter. In 1949, on the seventieth anniver-

sary of the bulb, when the Pioneers visited the General Electric laboratories at Schenectady, they "removed their hats, almost unconsciously, as they gazed at the betatron." "On their way back to the train," concluded the brief item, "they asked one another what atomic energy would mean and how quickly changes would come. Nobody had any answers and the incandescent bulb seemed very far away." "Having other marvels of our own day to wonder at," wrote a *Times* editor the day before, "we have long since ceased to consider the electric light bulb a miracle." In 1956, for the first time, the *Times* report of the meeting of the Edison Pioneers did not mention Edison's name except in the title of the group. The article was concerned entirely with a speech by the president of General Dynamics urging atomic aid in foreign policy. Edison was becoming increasingly irrelevant. His picture had disappeared from the light bulb jacket, the label on the phonograph record, and seemed to be fading in the American mind as well.

Yet to become dated is not always to lose relevance and respect. It is possible that the change in attitudes was as much toward science itself as toward Edison. While he had been associated with a millennial view of science, the new aura of scientific magic after Hiroshima may have seemed more black than white. A 1959 public opinion survey about science and scientists indicated at least a more overt ambivalence. The great majority of Americans (92 percent), the study found, believed that science was "making our lives healthier, easier, and more comfortable" and (87 percent) that it was "the main reason for our rapid progress." Medicine received the greatest praise, followed by contributions to human welfare and the military role of science. A large minority (47 percent), however, also felt that science "makes our way of life change too fast" and (40 percent) that the growth of science meant "that a few people could control our lives" (this group had increased by 25 percent over pre-Sputnik responses). A smaller group (25 percent) felt that science destroyed morals. Most of the developments in atomic science were viewed as an area of threat, and "most of the new advances in space were seen much more in the area of an international race with Russia and the total context of the 'cold war,' than as advances in science per se." In sum, the study found "respect and appreciation, but little real curiosity and interest, and . . . a certain amount of distrust and apprehension." [7]

This ambivalence is the fourth and most significant condition affecting the Edison symbol in the postwar era. "For good or ill, others have let loose the Atomic Age from Pandora's box of uranium," said the *New York Times* in 1947. "Since Edison's death, science . . . has hurled us, willing or not, into the blind future of a darker world than that in which he lived." At a meeting of the Pioneers on the centenary of his birth—in spite of Mrs. Edison's opening assurances as to "how thrilled he would be if he were here with us today"—the president of Rutgers University, whose speech followed hers, declared that if Edison were alive "he would look with eyes not free from anxiety upon the contemporary scene. He would look out over the international scene in a world shrunk to a hazelnut by the magic of modern science and witness the incredible farce of great nations splitting hairs in the face of potential extinction." "There was a day when the laboratory was not necessarily considered as the birthplace of death-dealing weapons," wrote the editor of the *Los Angeles Times* that same day, "it was the era of Thomas A. Edison." Even Edison's son, former secretary of the navy and governor of New Jersey, Charles Edison, urged an "effort to curb science's power" and avoid catastrophe. By the 1970s, concern for the environment had joined Cold War anxieties as a counterforce to faith in technology. After a blackout of midtown Manhattan in 1971, Charles F. Luce, chairman of the Consolidated Edison Company of New York, told the public that he could not promise that it would not happen again. "Mr. Luce, who used to agree with Mr. Edison and urged increased use of electricity, now does not," said the *Times*.

During the first half of the twentieth century, although there were few abstract, philosophical attacks on either Edison or the technological society, some negative reaction was inevitable, given the style of Edison's pronouncements. His response in 1927, for example, to complaints about automobiles speeding up the world was that "it serves to stir up our sluggish brain cells." Thus one commentator observed that "sometimes it appears that they [Edison and other inventors] have done little except enable us to run around a little more rapidly in our squirrel cage of civilization." In Eugene O'Neill's little-known play, *Dynamo* (1929), the hero worships the dynamo as a religious idol, "a great, dark mother"; inventors, however, are not implicated.

Even during the depression one must look to Europeans for negative comment of any weight. Dos Passos's "Electrical Wizard" (1930) is the one strong American exception, but a German essay, written the following year and borrowing much of his phrasing, carried the point much further. Speaking from a Marxist point of view, the authors began by criticizing Edison's "brightest boy" scholarship competition and concluded with an attack on the entire American economic philosophy and its idealization of Edison. "Do you want to end in an out-and-out organized ant-existence?" they ask, "subjugated to technique? Shall the imperative be: Machine (profit—for whom?) or Man?" At the end of the "era of expansion," they suggest, it is only the fascist state in which "one needs the most 'useful' men."

More subtle is a Czech play entitled *The Wizard of Menlo* (1934), which contrasts the spirit of Menlo Park with that of the 1930s. In the 1870s Edison's assistants optimistically discuss "the beginning of a new world" in which "everything's being improved." "Are men being improved too?" asks a character called Black. "Yes," answers another.

Life is being improved. We are improving it with our machines. But what we've done so far is nothing to what's going to be done. The machines will get better and better. Life will get easier and easier. Men will get happier and happier. Just think what will happen when machines do away with all hard work. . . . Men will simply bask in prosperity. . . . Can you imagine what life will be like in the year nineteen thirty-four? ["Yes, I can," answers Black.] By that time the world will be a magic garden, an enchanted castle of wonders. Everything'll work by itself, just by pressing a button.

At the end, the scene shifts to the last years of Edison's life. The angry unemployed are heard demonstrating in the streets; a former silent film star bursts in and declares she is going to commit suicide because Edison's talking pictures have put her out of work. Edison himself begins to have misgivings: "I made the machines. . . . Now the machines are beginning to get into people's way. The pace is too rapid. . . . I made their success too easy for them. That's why their success is so unstable. . . . [He laments the weapons race.] I saved people the trouble of thinking. . . . They don't think at all. . . . And I went on inventing just the same." An actor enters wearing the mask of Lenin; removing the mask, he turns out to be Black, unchanged from Menlo Park. Black then recites a poetic speech beginning: "Edison, I am you. I am within you. I am the depths of your soul." He is Prometheus, Socrates, Lucifer, Einstein; he is the individualized, identity-through-conflict side of man. The deaf Edison nods cheerfully, comments on the need for rubber, and turns up Beethoven's Ninth Symphony; police and demonstrators are heard outside.

Kurt Vonnegut, who became a favorite of dissenting youth in the late 1960s, wrote a story for *Collier's* in 1953 entitled "Tom Edison's Shaggy Dog." Written in the first person, it describes an encounter on a park bench with a retired Rotary type called Harold K. Bullard. Bullard is "darn sore" at all the "youngsters these days" who are "mooning around about no frontiers any more. There never have been so many frontiers as there are today. You know what Horace Greeley would say today? . . . 'Go plastic, young man!' That's what Greeley'd say." The narrator then describes how he pulled Bullard's leg with a tale about Sparky, a fictitious dog belonging to Edison. Thinking that "maybe intelligence was just a certain kind of electricity," Edison hooked up an "intelligence analyzer" to the dog. If it worked, said Edison, the next generation would "grow up in the glorious new era when people will be as easily graded as oranges" (the sources, of course, were the questionnaire and Edison's comments on the mechanical nature of the brain). But the dog, after frantic efforts to avoid the test, was revealed to be vastly superior to man—even to Edison himself—in intelligence. This made Edison mad. "Pretty soft, isn't it, Sparky?" he said. "Let somebody else worry about getting food, building shelters and keeping warm, while you sleep in front of a fire or go chasing after the girls or raise hell with the boys. No mortgages, no politics, no war, no work, no worry." Sparky, who pleaded with Edison to keep quiet about the matter, suggested the correct filament material for the lamp. Later, he was torn to bits by a pack of dogs.

Harold K. Bullard, of course, represented the type of right-wing reactionary with whom unqualified praise of most themes in the Edison image had become identified by mid-century. Most of the writing on Edison in the forties and fifties was defensive in tone, reasserting an "American Way" which was believed to be under the attack of powerful groups. Jeremiads lamented the demise of the rugged individual and mourned the loss of opportunity, mobility, initiative, competitive enterprise, and other aspects of late nineteenth-century success mythology.

The nostalgic emphasis on individual freedom over collective organization, in fact, is the last of roughly four phases in the evolution of the success theme within the Edison symbol.

STICKING LIKE HELL

In the first phase, the older Protestant tradition and the idea of competitive mobility dominated explanations for Edison's success until the early years of the twentieth century. One of the better examples of the older emphasis was the 1907 biography by F. A. Jones, translated into several languages, which concluded that "every growing youth who desires to gain a name and fortune by the cultivation of his brains," though "he may not be an Edison," can be assured that "perseverance will carry him a long way on the road to success" and "that it is hard work that tells and that virtue will eventually land one on the topmost rung of Fortune's ladder." Of the older success virtues, hard work is overwhelmingly the most frequently cited. If one breaks the category down into "perseverance," "industry," and "energy," the emphasis shifts over time from the first to the last of these three (see appendix, table 1); there is a gradual and uneven movement, in other words, from morally active to morally passive judgments about Edison's work capacity. Perseverance and industry assume moral choice, while "energy," "activity," "endurance," "capacity for work," and the other terms making up the "energy" subcategory imply biological or predetermined traits. In the juvenile literature, however, the emphasis has remained on industry over energy.[8]

The juvenile literature focused especially on the mobility aspect as an inspiring example for American youth. Sometimes the lesson was implied in the title itself: *Thomas A. Edison: An Inspiring Story for Boys; Edison: Inspiration to Youth; Lives of Poor Boys Who Became Famous; Winning Their Way: Boys Who Learned Self-Help; Biographical Sagas of Will Power;* and *Children of Necessity* are examples. The theme remained strong in all of the Edison literature during the first part of the century. Discussing his "twenty-one world-movers," among whom was Edison, Andrew Carnegie said in 1911: "I want to tell the young men of America that not one of these men who moved the world was rich when he started out on his career. Every one of them began as manual laborers. Every one of them had to earn his own bread . . . and I am proud to think that Thomas Alva Edison was a messenger boy along with me." By a resolution of May 21, 1928, Edison was awarded the Congressional Medal of Honor, and over the radio President Coolidge proclaimed that "although Edison belongs to the world, the United States takes great pride in the thought that his rise from humble beginnings and his unceasing struggle to overcome the obstacles on the road to success well illustrate the spirit of our country." Some of the most dramatic statements appeared in the obituaries: "The world was illuminated from a loop of cotton thread by a former news butcher and telegraph operator whose entire formal education consisted of three months in a Port Huron, Michigan, public school!" said the *St. Louis Post.* And of course any aspects of the success myth in the backgrounds of those competing for the Edison scholarships in 1929 and 1930 were well publicized.

While the older emphases persisted, a second phase in the evolution of the success theme in relation to Edison arose, as we have noted, around the turn of the century, stressing "mind-power," positive thinking, self-confidence, and optimism. Paralleling the economy, writing in this vein peaked in the twenties and resurged again in the fifties.* One of the older themes stressed in this phase was perseverance. "*I* never quit until I git what I'm after," Edison told Rosanoff. "That's the only difference between me, that's supposed to be lucky, and the fellows that think they are unlucky. Then again a lot of people think that I have done things because of some 'genius' that I've got. That too is not true. Any other bright-minded fellow can accomplish just as much if he will stick like hell. . . ." Repeatedly, biographers tell us that the secret of Edison's success might well be "Persistency, more persistency, still more persistency," and "the great lesson which we want to learn from his life is that industry and perseverance are always rewarded." Edison came naturally to David Riesman's mind when he was describing the inner-directed man's freedom to fail in the eyes of others without feeling inadequate: "Like Edison he will try and try again, sustained by his internal judgment of his worth."

* The figures for "optimism and confidence" in table 4 (see appendix) reflect this category. Note the proportional increase of examples in the juvenile literature, following, perhaps, the increasing tendency to view the child as being less a small adult than a potential one, requiring confidence and encouragement.

The ability to forget failures and dismiss the past is a trait natural to the linear, future-oriented liberal tradition which Edison embodied. In 1911, his secretary, Meadowcroft, reported a comment which became one of the all-time favorite Edison quotations: "Spilled milk doesn't interest me. I've spilled lots of it, and, while I have always felt it for a few days, it is quickly forgotten, and I turn again to the future." The ore-milling failure, the ejection of the fifteen-year-old Edison from the burning baggage car by the conductor, and the burning of his laboratory in 1914 are the incidents most frequently cited to demonstrate Edison's professed philosophy of looking "on the bright side of everything." He is "never discouraged," "never worried"; his "gaze is always upward and forward"; he "has always held fast to the belief that 'tomorrow is a new day.' " There was "no such word as 'fail' in his dictionary." "Failure in one direction only stimulated him to more strenuous efforts in another." And he "just keeps on smiling." As he stood watching his West Orange laboratory burn to the ground, he made a statement which was quoted in perhaps ninety percent of the country's newspapers: "I am sixty-seven years old but I am none too old to take a fresh start tomorrow morning. Nobody is ever too old to take a fresh start." "Here is the living incarnation of American spirit and courage," said *American Magazine.* "Not a thought of the past! Not a regret. . . . Was there ever anything finer, more magnificently and truly American than this?" The American quality, added the *San Francisco Chronicle,* lay in the fact that it was "a cheerful rather than a grim determination."

Pollyanna-like at its extremes, American optimism has been rooted in the sense of boundless potential that has characterized the national experience. The buoyant optimism that Edison represented—the denial of limits which we equated with American innocence—has energized the whole thematic spectrum of the national mythology. A mid-century writer who turned his discussion of Edison into a sermon on optimism and confidence illustrates some of the relationships:

Don't permit discouragement to cling to you like a wet garment, dampening your hope and the spirit of progress which is an inherent attribute of every man. If you permit despairing thoughts and debasing fancies to gather like hawks in the fields of your mind, they are likely to prey upon your dreams and desires until all of your energy has been consumed and you flap, loose and slack like a drooping sail [the evil of the fixed and

static]. Stiffen up. . . . Actual utter defeat is found only in the admit-
tance of it. Be stubborn! . . . Rise! Smile! . . . It is your duty, both as
an individual and as a citizen of this great independent Republic to
keep your own life brilliantly shining throughout every moment God allows you the privilege of living here. Regardless of how dictators may
attempt to destroy it, it is only through *private enterprise,* the enterprise of
each individual, that the human family may progress upward on the
thermometer of eternal time. . . . Determine to stand in the sunshine
of progress each day. . . . The best way to reach God . . . is not in the
clammy stagnation of idleness and surrender. . . . So, up! . . . There
is plenty of room at the top of life for good men, for strong men. . . .
Up from the dust alone you must rise . . . from *your own efforts.*

A list of those who have written similarly on Edison—Albert Shaw, edi-
tor of the *Review of Reviews,* B. C. Forbes, Elbert Hubbard, the *Reader's
Digest*—would read like a history of the mind-power theme itself. Even
Norman Vincent Peale wrote a sermon entitled "God's Man, Edison,"
which was distributed to 400 councils of the Federal Council of
Churches of Christ in America.

During the 1930s, a third phase of the success theme in the Edison
image involved the same qualitative increase in negative comment that
we noted in relation to other themes. Along with faith in material
progress, the closely related image of the American businessman suffered
during the depression. Although the standard biographies and many
journalists admitted that "in business he is a babe in the woods," there
were still a great many attempts during the 1920s to present Edison
as a shrewd businessman and a "great captain of industry." In 1933,
however, it was observed that Edison was "at one with the exploitive
capitalist," that he "believed implicitly in the dogma of supply and demand," and that he was completely "immersed in the business view-
point." All this was related to his "general social blindness." The *Nation*
depicted Edison entering heaven amid "the din of riveters and the hiss
of welding machines that surged out through the heavenly gates"; "ban-
ners swung high above the streets of gold," bearing the inscription:
"Forward, Heaven. Business Is Good. Keep It Good." The "Celestial
Rotary Chorus" greeted him with the song that George M. Cohan had
written for the Jubilee ("He's a grand old Wiz," etc.). It was to Edison's
credit that he expressed some misgivings. The gatekeeper thereupon ex-

plained that heaven was perfect—for children; but it was difficult to get into hell; it was "very exclusive. For adults only, you know."

After World War II the image of Edison as businessman again emerged in a positive light. It was said that "he never stopped crediting the American system of business life as an essential factor in what he was able to do for all mankind." And "he himself always pointed out that it was the *cooperation, vitality* and *risk-taking willingness of American business enterprise* that sustained him on the job." As recently as 1971 a writer in *Nation's Business* presented Edison as "a remarkable business-man" who "developed techniques in market analysis, promotion and sales research that are still in use." In the same issue, Edison placed third in a poll of readers to determine the "ten greatest men of Ameri-can business."

Although Edison as a businessman per se was never one of the major themes (see "business acumen" in the appendix, table 4), businessmen comprised an increasingly larger proportion of those who cited Edison as the embodiment of the ideal American traits.* Since World War II, in fact, what constitutes the fourth phase of the success theme in the Edison image has been perpetuated almost entirely by an ultraconserva-tive business faction and its political representatives. (In the 1920s, by contrast, journalists were the dominant spokesmen.) This fact returns us to an earlier observation: By mid-century Edison had become the hero of right-wing reaction, the essence of which amounted to a championing of the unreconstructed individual against what was viewed as an en-croaching, conspiratorial collective.

THE AMERICAN WAY

During the past century, social interdependence has loomed ever larger, limiting the individual in much the same way that the adult world closes in on the adolescent. The desperate denial of such limits—whether by those insulated in innocence or isolated in power—has become the socioeconomic fundamentalism of post-New Deal America. Yet even in

* Note that table 5 in the appendix, which categorizes all statements made about the value of Edison's inventions and ranks them by period, shows that "increased national wealth and investment" ranks progressively higher through-out the twentieth century, placing first in the 1960s.

the 1920s, as we have seen, Edison's own nineteenth-century individualism often seemed closer to the Red Scare, the Scopes Trial, or the Klan rallies than to the cosmopolitan society to which he was ironically prerequisite. He and his associates were often no less reactionary in their own time than his later admirers were in theirs. In 1929, for example, the three Americans whose images best embodied the paradoxical tension between individualism and the machine—Edison, Lindbergh, and Ford—were involved in the judging of the Edison scholarship examinations. Although the top scores were close, one boy had placed five percent ahead of all the rest. In answer to one question, however—"Is the relationship of capital and labor reasonably fair?"—he had expressed mildly the opinion that a different distribution of wealth was inevitable in time; the signs pointed that way. Lindbergh, who had contributed nothing throughout the entire session, was suddenly aroused:

"Read that again," said Lindbergh, leaning forward over the table so as not to miss a word. The Committee exchanged glances as the answer was read and re-read. . . .
"I don't like that boy's answer," he announced; "I don't like it at all. I believe in evolution, not in revolution." . . . Discussion started again. The Colonel talked more than he had talked all day. Some of those who had been friendly to the candidate under dispute began to show signs of wavering; he might be right after all; they must be careful. Did they not represent the foundation of the social order?

The "lone eagle" gave the scholarship to the runner-up.

In his 1938 memoirs, Edison's secretary, A. O. Tate, attacked the New Deal as a threat to "individual initiative." "The power of government," he said, "must be acquired by subtraction from its original source, the individual. To the same degree that government is strengthened by these accretions, individuals are weakened. The process is like a subtle degenerate disease." In the years which followed, the anecdotes of Edisonian individualism gained the status of scriptural readings in the crusade against government paternalism. In 1947 the Virginia Electrical Power Company ran an ad which called attention to the fact, in reference to the invention of the light, that *government didn't do the job. Individuals did.* "No human being ever learned to walk by being carried," said a Pennsylvania Chief Justice in 1950, and "at no time in his life did Thomas A. Edison attempt to snuggle in the arms of paternalistic government." "No American in those days," he went on, "dreamed that the day would come when the government would subsidize scarcity, foster indolence, discourage industry, and promote general disaster instead of general welfare."

Production, of course, was one of the sacred functions of the machine. Edison's belief in "efficiency"—in the idea that "every effort should be made to speed work up," that "the future of the race depends on quantity production," and that "talk of overproduction is a bugaboo"—was frequently cited by postwar spokesmen who accused their contemporaries of "dodging work" and irresponsibly "restricting production and output." Edison's "life's work and accomplishments challenge us to more intelligent efforts, to greater production, . . . to the end that we may make more things cheaper, sell more things faster, create more and more jobs."

In 1946, in a book entitled *Endless Horizons,* Vannevar Bush based an argument against the continuance of wartime social controls on the idea that the kind of opportunity which allowed men like Edison to grow was characteristic of the United States but not of totalitarian states. The anticommunist theme recurs a number of times in the postwar Edison material. "Edison's message for our time" was that we must not "lose our sense of the uniqueness of man's genius, of the supreme value of the individual. In this lies our best safeguard against the deadly regimentation of Communism." "In Edison's day," said one writer, "Communism was no bigger than a man's hand." "There were no class distinctions then, but men passed from class to class—becoming richer or poorer as their talents and abilities merited. American society had not yet become stratified through the working of pseudo-liberalism. And there was no mass, organized movement trying to pit workers against managers and seeking to set up artificial standards by means of which 'common men' could be separated from 'capitalists.' "

Nostalgia of this type was also common. Some of those writing on Edison during the depression praised "the old-time spirit of initiative and self-help that made the typical American so versatile and independent." Greenfield Village, it was said, kept alive "the spirit of the village days of America when great men were born." In the last sentence of his 1938 memoirs, A. O. Tate spoke of "that historic era when, under the inspiration of Individual Initiative and Self-reliance, the foundations of

America's great modern Industrial Empire were laid by its courageous Pioneers." But in 1938 that era did not seem quite so distant nor its passing quite so final. "Contemporary philosophers," said Tate, "are straining their intellects to the bursting point in an effort to identify the values which we have lost. They seem to think that something happened in the period following the Great War. They are mistaken. Nothing escaped. We have lost nothing." After the Second World War, however, few denied the loss. The task, said the president of the Southern California Edison Company in 1947, was to "dedicate ourselves anew to the revival of the ideals and moral atmosphere, the freedom and opportunity, which existed in the America which he [Edison] knew, and but for which it is doubtful that his genius could have flowered." It was fitting that in 1951, on the sixtieth anniversary of the invention of the motion picture camera, the person chosen to announce that "Edison's life work stands as a symbol of the spirit of our nation" was none other than Mary Pickford, the silent-film sweetheart of a more innocent time.

The longing for the frontier individualism of a freer and simpler time, which dominated postwar references to Edison, went hand-in-hand with the popularity of the TV western in the fifties. It also suggested comparisons of Edison to Lincoln, who had become the American archetype of self-reliant success, surpassing even Franklin. Edison was often called "the greatest American since Abraham Lincoln." (Other comparisons, in order of frequency, were made to Franklin, Napoleon, and Columbus.) "Lincoln and Edison," said a radio spokesman for the National Association of Manufacturers in 1949, "hurtled every handicap, alone, unaided." "In these days of universal fear of government control of the individual," Lincoln and Edison "stand as peaks of human liberty." Like Lincoln, "Thomas A. Edison also walked alone. . . . No government subsidized him, no bureau or commission directed him. No RFC made loans to him. He passed no civil service examinations, nor did he ask the consent of any Presidential commission to pursue his experiments. Thomas Edison was a free man. Untutored, unschooled, the master of his personality. . . ." There had been many earlier comparisons of Edison and Lincoln, emphasizing the unpolished originality, the frontier manner, and the love of a good story. One passage summed them up: "He was as shrewd and sensible as Lincoln, as unassuming, as keen a judge of men, and as fond of funny stories." But by far the largest per-

centage of the comparisons fall into the period after World War II and
emphasize self-reliant triumph. The Lincoln parallel brought together
the vernacular, midwestern characteristics that had become prominent
in the image since Edison's death—traits enumerated like rosary beads in
the shadow of communal interdependence.

"I believe that if Lincoln or Edison were here," said George Maxey,
the Pennsylvania chief justice, "they would tell us to dynamically de-
fend the American way of life." One of the primary differences between
the right-wing reaction of the twenties and that of the fifties is that the
latter was far more explicit in grouping its concerns under a reified
"Americanism." On the centenary of Edison's birth, the chairman of the
Commonwealth Edison Company said that "Edison is a prime example
of what a man may accomplish under the American way of life. . . .
His was a country which rewards [sic] initiative and enterprise." Governor Dwight Green of Illinois added that "Edison was historic proof of
opportunity open to all America. Edison lived the American way." During the centennial, Pacific Gas and Electric bought space in the *Wall
Street Journal* and, in a long ode to American opportunity, declared that
" 'made in U.S.A.' labels [Edison] the man as well as his hundreds of inventive marvels." The countless examples declaring that "competitive
enterprise has made America the great nation we are today" and that it
"is inseparable from our American way of life" suggest Will Herberg's
observation that in pluralistic America the religion of the average citizen had ceased to be Catholicism, Protestantism, or Judaism and had
become simply "Americanism." [9] The same might be applied to socioeconomic values in general, for one's final commitment must be made
within the broadest symbolic context available. It is difficult to consider
as an absolute that which is merely one alternative within a more en-
compassing collective experience.

The individual's conflicting roles and identities in an impersonal yet
interdependent society are of course the very condition which has
brought the reactionary obsession with individual autonomy. Edison
"looked on people as individuals and not as numbers in a file case," said
a writer in 1947. And the developer of the radio tube, Lee De Forest, lamented that "the lone inventor will never again have Edison's opportunity for a life work in exploring unknown fields alone. . . . All the seas
are charted; all continents, nay islands, are discovered and surveyed.

There are no more frontiers for lone La Salles and Coronados. Instead armies of scientists flail the garnered wheat together. This spells wealth for humanity; but never again will solitary names blaze singly in a star- less sky." Jonathan Hughes was no less nostalgic when he called Edison "the last great hayseed."

7

REPRISE: THE IMPOSSIBLE
DREAM

On a photograph that survived the
laboratory fire of 1914, Edison wrote
"Never Touched Me!" Edison National Historic Site.

Like Edison himself, the term "hayseed" combines otherwise irreconcilable polar images. The two forms of nostalgia associated with Edison, the pastoral landscape and the unreconstructed individual, have been the antitheses, respectively, to two sets of cultural conditions, corresponding roughly to the paleotechnic and neotechnic eras. But the older form of nostalgia, the pastoral vision of a pre-industrial America, prominent in the success mythology and in the Tom Sawyer aspect of Edison's boyhood, has not disappeared from the image. Nor have the more literal attempts to reconcile the machine with the garden been confined to the hustling boy aboard his train, puffing across fields of fresh-cut hay. In the 1880s, for example, the Edison works at Schenectady—the result of Edison's intention to make the rural setting "more beautiful" by "dotting" it with factories—were described as "lifting themselves boldly up from the level meadows of the Mohawk Valley."

The contrast with the surrounding pastoral scenery does but accentuate all the evidences presented of busy toil. Beyond the factory . . . winds and doubles the placid Mohawk River, hemmed in by green banks and girdled by uprolling mountains well away to the northward. There, in the legendary background, the atmosphere hangs drowsily, as well it might, over the quaint homesteads built by the ancestors and offspring of sundry Rip Van Winkles; but here the air is astir with the sharp outburst of machinery. There, along the circuitous highways, the heavy wagons, with heavier teams, are hauling slowly to market the growth of farm and make of dairy; but here in the forefront, and fixing the eye as insistent energy and bustle always do, especially when on the grand scale, are trains of freight cars alive with men unloading raw material at the factory yard, while others at a half a dozen different points are carrying away the finished product of the works.

One of the stronger expressions of this type of resolution appeared in the 1940 film, *Edison the Man.* As the first successful light continues to burn into the night, Spencer Tracy, as Edison, joins his men around the organ to sing "Sweet Genevieve." The camera pans out the window to the moonlit countryside; and at the window of their nearby cottage, Edison's wife smiles and listens. The song had been a motif in a film on Edison's boyhood, released earlier in the year; it seemed therefore to tie the event to his youth, strengthening the suggestion that technological triumph itself was inseparable from the romantic individualism of an earlier and simpler America. Another example was the farmhouse-

meetinghouse appearance of the Menlo Park laboratory which had enhanced the pastoral setting of Ford's Greenfield Village in 1929. A half-
century later, the reconstructed lab figured prominently in a television
documentary, "Legacy of a Genius," where wistful woodwinds accompanied shots of the quaint exterior set among the trees. The stark, wooden
interior, with its long tables of tubes, jars, and glassware, could almost
be a country kitchen—a frozen moment in the concoction of modern
America. The narrator, Eric Sevareid, followed the scenes with the observation that education "would have spoiled" Edison and Ford, who
enjoyed such simple things as their camping trips into the Adirondacks.

THE NEW PASTORALISM

The second form of nostalgia, a response more to the neotechnic, electronic era than to the paleotechnic age of steam, envisions not the wind-
ing rivers and rolling hills so much as the freedom of the individual to
be as audacious and supremely self-confident as Edison. It is a reaction
less to the physical than to the psychological consequences of technology. It is significant that the pastoral images of the 1880s occurred in relation to Edison's factories rather than to his laboratory or inventions.
The garden, in other words, may have compensated initially and most
directly for the physical sense of Paradise lost which accompanied the
era of grimy sweatshops and chaotic urbanization.

The coming of electricity amid these conditions seemed to promise
the millennium. The conviction arose, after Edison launched the neotechnic century, that the fallen American Adam, having lost the garden
in the age of steam, would now reenter Paradise astride the machine.
The vision still animates at least one hemisphere of the modern mind.
Thus Eric Hoffer—the man admired by Lyndon Johnson as the only intellectual to speak for the silent majority—observed that "it was the machine age that really launched the man-made creation. The machine
was man's way of breathing will and thought into inanimate matter."
But unlike God,

man could not immediately automate his man-made world. He was
not inventive enough. Until yesterday, the machine remained a half-
machine: it lacked the gears and filaments of will and thought, and man
had to use his fellow men as a stopgap for inventiveness. He had to yoke

men, women, and children with iron and steam. . . . Then yesterday, almost unnoticed, the automated machine edged onto the stage. . . . The skirmish with God has now moved all the way back to the gates of Eden. Jehovah and his angels with their flaming swords are holed up in their Eden fortress, and we with our automated machines are hammering at the gates. And right there, in the sight of Jehovah and his angels, we shall declare null and void the ukase that with the sweat of his face man shall eat bread.[1]

Edison stood at the turning point; thus his identity with the American Adam became as necessary within the national mythology as the divinity of Christ within Christianity. (If this has the ring of overstatement, one might recall the instance in the United States Senate on October 21, 1929, when Senator Kean of New Jersey stood up and said: "The light that burst on the civilized world at Menlo Park may be compared with the light that burst from the cradle of the Savior at Bethlehem.") In the national covenant the function of Christ was supplanted by the American experience itself. Because his roots were in the New World Garden, the fallen American Adam was redeemable. As always, he needed only to be industrious, enterprising, and "stick like hell."

The irony is that technology actually *did* recreate the garden, but not quite as envisioned. Paradoxically, while neotechnics expanded the boundaries of the possible beyond previous imagination, the world began to close in on nineteenth-century individuality. The disappearance of the frontier was symbolic, but far more significant was the national organism, and the multitude of urban organisms within it, created by the transportation and communications revolutions. Fragmenting experience and forcing men into tiny specialties of "expertise," the organism became ever more bureaucratized and interdependent, reducing individuals to a childlike dependence on one another and on technology. Though the nineteenth-century world was one of immediate conflicts and limits, there had been an accompanying faith that the quantum effect of everyday triumphs and defeats would lead, with luck, into that promising dawn which seemed to lie on all perimeters—geographic, social, and spiritual. The new social organism, on the other hand, inverted the model: One's world was without immediate limits, but ultimately more finite than medieval cosmology. Enveloping individual autonomy, the technological society, with its gadgets and bureaucratic efficiency, removed everyday obstacles and old-fashioned reality-testing. It tended to encircle and eliminate self-definition-through-conflict in the same way that pastoral harmony is symbolically preserved by hills encircling a valley or lake, or by trees surrounding a meadow. Nurtured by the collective placenta, neotechnic man sprawls before his TV, fantasizing identity-through-conflict in professionalized spectator sports. Seeking out the interstitial sanctuaries between rigid institutions, he sinks into the oblivion of the present instant.

If the nineteenth century was optimistic and future-oriented, the twentieth grew pessimistic, retracting into the "now." The energy of the former might be visualized as a cluster of small arrows, ever running into one another, but from which an explosion of large arrows radiates to infinity; in the contemporary model, on the other hand, the cluster ideally becomes a static dot within a circle (albeit shifting, overlapping circles). The one is Eros, the life principle; the other is Thanatos, the death principle. It was the final irony of the penetration of the locomotive into Sleepy Hollow that, far from destroying the garden, the machine transformed what had been largely fantasy into a Kafkaesque reality.

Or so goes the complaint of many critics of modernity. (A further irony is that some of these critics have offered the circle with the dot as a model for the revitalization of Establishment culture.) We shall return in conclusion to the debate over the validity of such academic jeremiads and the legacy of Edison to that debate. Meanwhile, we may note that writing on Edison in the seventies has stressed his unreconstructed individualism as the antithesis to what might be called the "new pastoralism" of the modern condition.

ANTECHAMBER TO OBLIVION: THE MYTH IN THE SEVENTIES

"Edison Sees This Age Destroying Myths," said a *New York Times* headline in 1927. The "Age of Science," he declared, was responsible for "the passing of the myths of religion and history." It was also responsible, of course, for the passing of his own myth, as flat and two-dimensional as any of those he had disdained. The historical dissection of Edison, which began with Matthew Josephson's biography in 1959 and continued most recently with Robert Conot's more definitive work, has revealed an individuality far greater than the earlier stereotype. A twenty-year, $5 million Edison papers project, started in 1978 under the supervision of Rutgers history professor, Reese Jenkins, promises to uncover the real Edison through an analysis of more than two million documents and artifacts. Meanwhile, books by Conot, Ronald Clark, and others, along with a number of articles on the history of particular inventions, have brought to light an introverted, antisocial egomaniac to whom close personal relationships meant almost nothing, including those within his own family. He was demanding, impatient, tactless, and given to obscene tantrums. He felt awkward with emotion and considered the expression of feeling a weakness; in fact, his inaccurate boasting about little sleep and perfect health was probably a result of misgivings about his manhood due to slow physical development. He was hard-driving, opportunistic, and as ruthless as any robber baron; he befriended those who were useful to him and discarded those who were not. And if he is not demystified by the probability that he stole from Joseph Swan the idea of using carbon in the filament, we also learn that a Frenchman named Cros was ahead of Edison in conceiving on paper the whole principle of the phonograph. Yet as the warts multiply and the complex contradictions within the man continue to surface, the image seems to regain some of its lost appeal.

The waning appeal owed something not only to shifting values and the simple passage of time* but also to the fact that so much of the Edison image, as we have seen, consisted of little more than a series of loosely-joined, often apocryphal anecdotes—a collage of American themes packaged in a black Prince Albert coat, winged collar, and bow tie. Much of the blame for this shallow and inaccurate stereotype lay with a man named George Bliss, who put together a romanticized account from thirdhand material, reading it before the Chicago Electrical

* Although a radical drop in press coverage is to be expected after the death of a celebrity, newspapers and periodicals being oriented primarily toward current events, I believe that if Edison had died at the turn of the century the decline in coverage might have been much more gradual. Edison in a sense outlived his image, serving first as an idol of production and later as an idol of consumption. As with most examples of the latter, the image declined suddenly once the man died and ceased to generate publicity. His recent resurgence, on the other hand, is as an idol of the spirit of production.

Society in 1878. In spite of the fact that those who knew Edison criticized Bliss for his gross distortions, a publisher named J. B. McClure expanded Bliss's article into a book which became source material for almost all subsequent biographical pieces on Edison. Equal responsibility, however, goes to the two-volume "authorized" biography by Dyer and Martin (actually written almost entirely by Edison's secretary, William H. Meadowcroft) which became the definitive work in 1910 in spite of the fact that it suffered from the same kind of distortions and superficiality as the McClure book. Finding their manuscript insufferably dry, the authors had gotten Edison to relate a whole new batch of anecdotes to liven up the story. Some of them had a basis in fact; others, for all purposes, did not. But even those that were true had the effect of again providing a model from which succeeding authors, for lack of talent or incentive, would fear to deviate. The saturation of the book with anecdotes, the explaining away of Edison's failures, and the devotion of only a few sentences to his family are all interrelated conditions: Refusing to accept any failure as final, and viewing the expression of personal feelings as a sign of weakness, he developed the habit of spewing out anecdotes as carelessly as he spit tobacco. They functioned, in other words, like a smoke screen. To the distortions of the McClure and Meadowcroft books one must add not only Edison's own self-advertising but the reminiscences of his former acquaintances and associates (even Rosanoff) who sought to glorify themselves by exaggerating their intimacy with him. As a result, with dozens of books devoted to him by mid-century, Edison still remained an unreal caricature.

In spite of growing academic interest and increased historical dissection, the stereotype and the rituals remain alive, if not completely well. Edison's birthday, celebrated as Science and Engineering Youth Day and as National Inventor's Day, has been used in attempts to encourage careers in science and technology. Most birthday-related activities have taken place at Edison locales—the ten-day Pageant of Light at Fort Myers, Florida, for example, a combination Mardi Gras, sports festival, and fair. The pageant initiated an annual Thomas Edison Great American Award in 1975, conferred for achievement in a field that began with an Edison invention. Echoing the deliberations of Edison, Ford, and Lindbergh over the Edison Scholarship of a half-century before is the fact that the recipient must also "demonstrate high standards of Americanism and moral character." At Menlo Park, where the 131-foot Edison Tower with its 13-foot bulb has stood since 1937, a mobile display of Edisonia arrived annually from the Edison National Historic Site at West Orange—until 1974. In that year the National Park Service canceled the trip "because of the gasoline shortage." Symbolically, the energy crisis had also darkened the bulb on the tower. A year later the Menlo Park Fire Department made its annual visit to the tower to celebrate in the rain. Edison had not received sufficient recognition for his accomplishments, said one member. "That's why we came out here in this bad weather. The man should have a day set aside for him throughout the country, yet we're the only ones who celebrate."

By the 1970s, moreover, much of the exploitation of the Edison myth by less sophisticated spokesmen for the far right seems to have faded away, as had many of the spokesmen themselves. It is primarily among the very young, in fact, that the traditional Edison stereotype survives, although qualifications noting his lack of interest in a personal God, his children, or the feelings of others have become more frequent. Especially since World War II, the ratio of juvenile to adult Edison literature has steadily increased, and the average age level of readers has dropped. The stereotype, in other words, has followed other ossifying values into the elementary school libraries—for culture heroes, the antechamber to oblivion.

Even the centennials of sound and light seemed to be of little interest, per se, to the average American. Articles in 1977 emphasize how Edison "stumbled on his phonograph" while "fiddling in his wood-shack laboratory," and longer items discuss the fact that Cros had anticipated it. In 1979 the *Chicago Tribune* noted that "the centennial of the invention of the incandescent lamp is here without much fanfare. Older people may remember when homes were poorly lit with kerosene and gas lamps; the younger generation takes good lighting for granted." Another article, headed "He Gets Yawns in Milan, Ohio," noted that Edison's birthplace was not bothering to celebrate the centennial. Art Buchwald's syndicated column made a joke of it all, describing a man who, having invented an electric bill, couldn't think of anything to charge people for; he went to "a crazy friend in Menlo Park" and asked him to invent something for the purpose. So ignorant of their topic were some writers and editors that in one case they had Edison living in Menlo

Park, California, in 1887, and in another the man in a headlining photo captioned with Edison's name was actually Heinrich Hertz.

Although the birthday outpourings had become a trickle, and the phonograph centennial had produced little outside of another commemorative stamp,* the Centennial of Light at least evidenced greater efforts. Articles, films, skits, and children's records—including a recorded musical called "The Electric Sunshine Man"—all retained the anecdotal caricature relatively intact. Various power companies capitalized on the occasion, buying ads and offering radio and television commercials "to raise public perception about the value of electricity" and "to rekindle interest and enthusiasm for invention and private enterprise." General Electric hired an actor named Pat Hingle to play Edison in a series of commercials and in a forty-five-minute film. The film, *Thomas Edison: Reflections of a Genius,* might have credited Bliss as technical advisor. Other than mentioning one or two of Edison's mistakes, it presented the anecdotal image unaltered, including the three months of schooling, reading the whole Detroit Library, and the $40,000 surprise. The rounded, grandfatherly Hingle, who might have emerged more believably from an Irish pub than from a laboratory, is closer to Spencer Tracy's Edison than to the man himself.

Most of the centennial publicity and activity during the year-long celebration was instigated by industry—primarily through the International Committee for the Centennial of Light (international because only twenty on its twenty-two-member board were American), made up of industrial leaders, mostly from power companies. The committee directed and coordinated centennial activities under the sponsorship of the Thomas Alva Edison Foundation, a nonprofit organization supported almost entirely by contributions from industry. The foundation had been established in 1946 for the purpose of stimulating youth toward careers in science and technology. This objective became the goal of the committee, its emphasis centering on what the foundation president, James Cook, called the "innovation recession." Appearing around the country for talk shows and newspaper interviews, Cook pointed to the falling patent totals and lagging productivity of the 1970s and to the

* There were two previous stamps, one in 1929, on the fiftieth anniversary of the light, and one in 1947, on the centenary of Edison's birth.

consequent need for new Edisons. The committee issued a bulletin
called the *Edison Centennial News,* the obsessive theme of which was the
decline of American technological superiority. "Edison exemplified the
spirit of American ingenuity" and "the inventive zeal which has made
our country great," said Secretary of Commerce Juanita Kreps. "This
used to be the country of Bell and Edison, of the safety pin and the
atom bomb, of interchangeable parts and built-in obsolescence," lamented the *Washington Post.* "Without our leadership in Yankee know-
how, what are we?"

A pamphlet put out by the committee, *The Search for Tomorrow's Edisons,* explained that the decline of American technology was the result of
industrial cutbacks, government overregulation, a bias against long-
range research as opposed to cheaper investments with quick returns,
and a tendency to fault science and technology for social and environmental ills. The results were inflation, unemployment, and a negative
balance of payments. The same points were stressed in speeches distributed by the committee for use in conjunction with centennial occasions.
"I'm not trying to present Edison to you as a selfless humanitarian," ran
the text of one. "In inventing the light bulb, he wasn't laboring with
some spiritual notion of rolling back the darkness. Simply put, Edison
was competing against the gas utilities." There was "investment money
behind him" and "a chance at a profit." But "more important than
these tangible factors was the spirit of his times. There was a national
belief in growth. People were just as concerned with the future as they
were with the present."

A number of writers suggested that it would have been impossible
for Edison to succeed in today's culture. "His chemically polluted,
explosion-wracked, ill-ventilated laboratories alone would have occupied
all the time of the Environmental Protection Agency and the Occupa-
tional Safety and Health Administration. He would be accused today of
manipulating stock, forming illegal trusts, lying on the witness stand, ex-
ploiting child and immigrant labor, and stealing the ideas of others—all
with some justification." Such phenomena as X-rays—even electricity
itself—would have been considered too dangerous for development. One
of the speeches distributed by the committee attacks the "blind, know-
nothing attitude taken by the anti-technologists" in opposing nuclear
power. Less controversially, *Time* observed that "the once rambunctious

American spirit of innovation and adventurousness is today being paralyzed by the desire to build a risk-free society." And if a passive,
present-bound culture sees no imperative to achieve, neither is it concerned with individual failure. Observing that theorists are "swift to
blame 'society,' poverty or some environmental element when a youngster fails to achieve," the *Cincinnati Enquirer* suggested that "such
theorists would have had an excuse" for the poor and uneducated Edison "if he'd turned out differently."

The "theorists," on the other hand, felt that a thin veneer of miscon-
ceived relevance in centennial rhetoric could not conceal the old right-
wing reaction. Technology, it seemed to them, was not only creating
more problems than it solved but was now solving only those of its own
making. The irony of Edison's statement in 1929 that "today's youngsters are beginning to doubt the myths," and that their "unrest" was
justified by the fact that it produced change rather than "stagnation," is
that the youth who emerged in the 1960s doubted the Edison myth
above all others and saw stagnation as the panacea for all social problems. The cultural illness, they perceived, had grown out of the very fact
of demythologization, which had stripped away all contexts of meaning.
Means had become ends in themselves; the instrumental had replaced
the institutional; and the driving "hustle" of Faustian man resembled
that of the frantic ant whose nest has been destroyed by some microcos-
mic cataclysm.

From this perspective Edison ceased to function even as a negative
symbol; he was simply irrelevant. "The younger generation has presumed to despise genius and heroes and finds Edison quaint," observes
Thomas Hughes. So ambivalent has our view of technology become that
a reviewer of Ronald Clark's 1977 biography could suggest that "Edison
appealed less to needs than to refinements in taste: the desire for clean,
odourless light, or a childish enthusiasm to record scenes and voices," a
comment not so much inaccurate as unphilosophic. (Where do "needs"
begin historically and where do they end psychologically?) During the
Centennial of Light, a columnist for the *Christian Science Monitor* observed
that "as we try to dim the lights—turn on less current, and still less—we
must feel two ways about Edison and the other Promethean geniuses
who played with fire and produced our Big Blaze."

There was something obsessed about the great men of the 19th century. They never doubted. They never hesitated. They never stopped.
. . . What would Edison be today? A nuclear physicist, pushing for
more "nuke" plants? A genetic engineer, chafing at public apprehension
about his experiments?

It would be hard to imagine the drive, the thrust of Edison being converted into, say, conservation. Could his lips ever be taught to pro-
nounce, "Small is beautiful"? He belonged to the last generation of
frontiersmen—the breed who opened up, enlarged, and pushed beyond
(and then beyond), in perfect innocence.

Evaluations of Edison have tended to follow the general polarization
of cultural values. Thus, while technology itself has become overtly suspect, an increased proportion of the attempts to preserve Edison's Olympian aura have also moved to a larger, if less philosophic universe of
discourse. Some of the comments are reminiscent of the observation
made by Treasury Secretary Mellon during the presentation of the Congressional Medal in 1928: Edison, he said, had dominated the electrical
industry so completely that some people believed that electricity itself
was merely another one of Edison's inventions. The same perspective
produced a "poem" on the centenary of his birth which proclaimed:

You will find Edison every day, everywhere—
You turn a switch and he lights your room. . . .
He brings you your radio programs.
He is back of your phonograph.
He is there in every moving picture theater.
He is in your typewriter—the waxed paper for your sandwiches
—the gummed tape that seals your packages.
Every minute of your day, he is with you: making your world
more convenient and more interesting.
YES. HE IS JUST ABOUT EVERYWHERE.

One feels that all the "he's" should have been capitalized. The most recent variation on this motif is the ongoing attempt to maintain Edison
as sole creator of all modernity by linking him in some way, however
obscure or contrived, to each new technological breakthrough. Thus he
is seen as the father of infrared astronomy, "systems" thinking, and the
entire computer industry. The whole attempt may be similar to issuing
a posthumous award to a primordial member of the human species in

recognition of his having peopled the planet with some four billion descendants.

WE'LL GET IT YET: THE MAN IN THE EIGHTIES

While it becomes academic to debate the degree of Edison's responsibility for each new field, there is a less tangible sense in which he directly pervades the present. Eric Hoffer's observation that faith in material progress remained seriously qualified until the neotechnic age suggests that Edison, who launched that age, was perhaps more responsible than any other person for a fundamental change in the world view of the average man. With the new kind of leverage over the environment suggested by the light, the telephone, the phonograph, and the motion picture, the passive resignation which had prevailed throughout man's history began to give way more rapidly than ever to the idea that all things could be changed and controlled. "Thirty years ago when I was a schoolboy," wrote Walter Lippman shortly after Edison's death,

the ancient conservatism of man was still the normal inheritance of every child. We began to have electric lights, and telephones, and to see horseless carriages, but our attitude was a mixture of wonder, fear, and doubt. Perhaps these things would work. Perhaps they would not explode. Perhaps it would be amusing to play with them. Today every schoolboy not only takes all the existing inventions as much for granted as we took horses and dogs for granted, but, also, he is entirely convinced that all other desirable things can and will be invented. . . . No other person played so great a part as Edison in this change in human expectation.

Edison "became the supreme propagandist of science," he added, "and his name the great symbol of an almost blind faith in its possibilities."

Edison's expansive optimism, especially in the context of his raw individuality, remains strong in the image long after other aspects have been interred in musty library basements. Edison believed almost literally that nothing was impossible. His visions always outran his resources. Characteristically, through the winter of 1881–1882, when the city would permit work in the streets only in the late night and wee morning hours, Edison crawled among freezing ditches, ate in all-night dives, and napped on piles of pipe, promising to light all of New York within two and a half years, while struggling simply to light one square mile. Failures for Edison were the fault of extraneous aberrations; total disasters were temporary setbacks. So supreme was his self-confidence that all his talk of persistence, perspiration, and sticking like hell amounted, in fact, to his honest estimate of all that was required to realize any vision that struck him. A point reiterated by biographers from Josephson to Conot is that Edison could not have invented something like the light bulb if he had had the education and sophistication to know that he was attempting the allegedly impossible. Even Rosanoff concluded that it would have been wrong to "tame the eagle." "Had the Wright Brothers been schooled," he said, "they would have known too much to undertake so mad a thing as flying in the sky."

Conot relates one incident in particular which sums up this whole aspect of Edison's personality. Obsessed with the idea of using platinum as a filament substance, he had dispatched prospectors and mailed thousands of inquiries all over the world in search of the rare metal, but without much success. Then, one summer dawn, after an all-night session of telephone experiments broke up at 5:00 A.M., the last man, Frank McLaughlin, tried to leave but "was intercepted at the door by Edison, who had picked up an old milk pan and a spade with a curled edge."

"Come, Mac, let's go out prospecting," Edison said and led the way through the damp grass to the abandoned copper mine a mile away. Handing McLaughlin the shovel, he had him fill the pan with dirt, then waded into the brook and shook the pan so vigorously spray flew in all directions. He peered intently at the pan. Nothing was on the bottom. "Dig away, Mac! We'll get it yet! We'll get it yet!" he urged on his companion. At last, after two hours, he detected a thin residue of black sand on the pan's bottom. "We've got it now!" he murmured joyfully. Gingerly he carried it to Dr. Alfred Haid, the chemist at the lab, and anxiously awaited the result of the assay.

"As fine a specimen of Jersey mud as I have ever seen," Haid reported.

But once again Rosanoff had the anecdote which topped them all: Under Edison's merciless pressure, a big Swede named Roos had been working day and night on a problem for months without results. After awhile he too deemed it prudent to begrime himself every morning till he looked like a locomotive fireman—a part that accorded poorly with his sauvity of manner and the cultured quality of his Swedish voice. Roos dodged the Old Man whenever he could. One day, incautiously, he stepped into my room, and there, talking to me, was Edison. It was too late to back out. The Old Man had caught sight of him and called out, "Come 'ere, Roos, tell me how you are getting along." Roos improvised an expression of intense joy and shouted back, "I've got it, Mr. Edison, I've got it at last! I yoost need another day or two to straighten out some small details. . . ." [Edison assumed] an expression of triumph. "Didn't I tell you right along," he said shrilly, "that you'd git it? I've been telling you *all* the time that all you got to do is stick to it and work like hell, and you'd get it in the end. *Sure* you can have another day or two. . . ." [Roos retreated and Rosanoff congratulated Edison.] The Old Man looked at me as if doubting his ears. "Did *you* believe what he said?"—I opened my eyes wide and stammered, "Why, of course, Mr. Edison; why, what do you mean?"—The Old Man explained cheerfully, "He hasn't got a damn thing. But that's the way to talk!"

It seems likely that Edison's willingness to charge into obstacles which others considered insurmountable went deeper than a simple lack or dislike of theoretical training. Abstraction was not a part of his mental organization. His understanding was extremely visual and concrete; thus, his affinity for "testing out" principles directly—through tangible objects. Lacking the linear, abstract thought necessary to conceptualize a complex problem from beginning to end, he relied on hunches, flashes of associational insight, and tireless trial and error. In neurobiological terms, he resided more in the right hemisphere of the brain than in the left; that is, his consciousness was more gestalt than analytical, more appositional than propositional, more visiospatial than verbal—suggesting that his deafness may have had much to do with his development in this direction.[2] Thus in harping on sleepless perseverance he may have been compensating for his inability to organize his thoughts easily into linear abstractions. Heroic quantities of effort would overcome deficiencies in the quality of method.

The tendency toward the visiospatial, associational, and intuitive is also in line with Edison's habit of thinking in terms of systems: not solitary projects, but an "invention factory"; not a light bulb, but a commercial lighting system; and perhaps most importantly, not a single track of endeavor but a free-associational, let-things-lead-where-they-will approach to inventing. The significance of the last is not just that he worked on many inventions at once but that common principles, such as transferring electrical impulses to treated paper, and common forms, such as the cylinder, ran through many of his activities simultaneously. The possibilities for making associations and for maximizing the potentials of these inchoate forms and principles was thus kept at a high level. Only this type of mind was likely to produce the "electromotograph"—a device in search of a purpose. Unlike most inventions, the electromotograph was not the realization of a linear project toward some preconceived end. Rather, it was the tangible expression (which Edison always sought) for some of the forms and principles which were running through his tinkering. The final result: the serendipitous appearance of the phonograph.

Psychological principles, of course, "explain away" nothing. Edison remains a "poet of matter," regardless of which brain hemisphere is responsible, for the same reason that he qualifies as a "great man" in spite of Swan, Cros, Sprague, Dickson, Armat, and all the others who were shouldering him at the patent office. In the end the language of history consists of the heroes, icons, and images by which the group perceives its existential crossroads—its moments of collective significance.

In the century since Edison's achievements, new crossroads have shifted the emphasis within his image. As we have seen, the erudite intellectual became the humanitarian democrat, the Promethean scientist became the practical individualist, and the prophet of progress emerged as an antidote to its consequences. The cultural shift, to which I have referred in various contexts throughout the book, is ultimately paradoxical. A final clarification of this point should bring together some of the perspectives.

The nineteenth-century reality was one of isolated, essentially autonomous individuals in an open society who were free to expand their limits through confrontation with hostile surroundings. The chronic condition was therefore the exercise of power. The same was true of the industrializing society as a collective whole. The nineteenth-century *vision*, however, looked beyond the immediately hostile to a benevolent universe which rewarded the winners. It was viewed finally as a world without limits, where conflict was no more than the "hustling" which led to inevitable triumph. The present might have been alien and masculine, but the larger transcendent future was benign and feminine. It was a vision of power within a greater context of innocence—of the machine in the garden.

The twentieth-century reality has been one of specialized, highly interdependent individuals enveloped in a technological shell much as the astronaut is sustained by his spacesuit. As dependent on technology and expertise as the fetus is on the maternal organism, the twentieth-century man is thus liberated to a large degree from the necessity for conflict and confrontation. The chronic condition is therefore one of innocence— the new pastoralism. The twentieth-century *vision*, however, has tended to mistake this freedom from conflict for individual autonomy. The nurturing organism is taken for granted while one screams out like an infant at any perception of limits. Thus the instant present has been increasingly viewed as benign and communal, while the larger context of the collective organism itself is seen as hostile and impersonal. It is a vision of innocence within the context of power—of a garden within the machine.

The paradoxes are obvious. In the previous century the reality was the price of the vision; in our time the vision is the price of the reality. Bridging these two conditions, the Edison symbol has shared the same reversal of polarity. Once the embodiment of the promise of technology itself, Edison became more and more the antithesis of its gloomier social implications. It is interesting to note that adjectives of size in descriptions of the laboratory show an average ratio of eight to one in favor of bigness through 1914 (the same ratio applied to the Menlo Park years), while the period from 1929 to 1932, which included the celebration at the laboratory restored by Ford, shows a ratio of two to one in favor of smallness. In 1879 a spacious cave was required for a wizard; in 1929 a quaint little shack was more suited to the precursors of progress and the beginnings of success.

As America moved toward the post-industrial society, then, many began to see that Edison's relevance for the present lay more in what he was than in what he did. In 1931 the *Boston Evening Transcript* admitted that Edison could not be classed with Washington or Lincoln because "on the spiritual side" his "contribution to the country's history is not so great." Two decades later, a similar statement was less insistent: He "may not have enlarged man's spiritual stature," but he made the world more comfortable and more colorful. It began to appear that Edison's own colorfulness had some relation to his relevance. Thus his tobacco-chewing became a favorite prop of reminiscences, such as the report in 1977 that "pianist Ernest Stevens remembered being splattered with the inventor's expectorated tobacco juice as they rode together in cars during the 1920s, but he spoke warmly of his first introduction to Edison." A 1972 play depicting Edison's life took the irresistible title of "The Wizard Who Spat on the Floor."

Accompanying the fascination with Edison's individuality has been a growing perception that it was inseparable from his buoyant, expansive optimism. "His philosophy of life," his son Charles had said, "was the philosophy of dawn, of a new day and of the future." "Grit," common sense, hard work, optimism, and faith were Edison's cures for the 1921 depression; and in 1930 he simply denied that there was a depression—it was all due to "a psychological fear." "I have seen many depressions in business," he said in his last speech. "Always America has come out stronger and more prosperous. Be as brave as your fathers before you! Have faith! Go forward!" The passage is by far the most widely quoted in ceremonial speeches celebrating Edison since his death.

HE KEPT THE SHOP

The passage, however, has an Independence Day ring reminiscent of striped sport coats, barbershop quartets, and watermelon-eating contests. Coming through the pages of history into the late twentieth century, it tends to get lodged with elevator music and catfood commercials. The spirit of the man has long since evaporated from the platitudes. But at a time when so many are abandoning any search for meaning in the collective and are withdrawing as so many atoms into narcissistic fantasy worlds, the incredibly energetic and affirmative figure of "the Old Man" himself looms out of the past—the incarnation of not just an era but of whatever root meaning the American collective may still retain.

The significant increase in the quantity of writing on Edison in the last decade was less a product of the centennial than of the perception which lay beneath the practical theme of that event. The fact that the nineteenth-century vision, however illusory, was prerequisite to building the reality is one of the ironies of the polarity. If there is an American spirit, as I suggested earlier, it has been forged by the immigrant experience, westward movement, urban migration—quests after the impossible dream by people with the courage, hope, and self-confidence to risk change. The nineteenth-century belief that one can break away, that one *can* escape history, is the lifeblood of any collective; for it sustains those who must do the busy work of civilization. Such a faith is necessary to preserve the employee virtues of the Alger hero and the tool-making talents of an otherwise impractical, symbol-making species.

America's demythologization and growing sense of limits have gone hand-in-hand with an increasing polarization in the value structure. The traditional nineteenth-century American mythology clings to the *reactionary* pole, where many experience a feeling of closing limitations—similar to the child's entry into adulthood—in a world which is increasingly impersonal, hyperrational, fragmented, and complex. The resulting sense of impotence generates Disney-like, nostalgic, Edenic fantasies and visions of superheroes. Lodged at this extreme, the Edison myth becomes ever more irrelevant, its real message being that you can't go home again. At the opposite, *radical* pole, however, technological and economic insulation has enabled increasing numbers in the middle- and upper-middle classes to deny the reality of limitation—to retreat to the autocentric world of the child, emphasizing "being" over "doing," immediate over future gratification, inner over outer space, Dionysian over Apollonian.

For the impotent, then, Edison becomes a fatherlike superhero of technological omnipotence; here the myth outweighs the man. For the seemingly omnipotent, on the other hand, he symbolizes the reality of limits, of mortality, of the need to achieve self-definition through conflict; there the man is more than the myth.

As the American Prometheus, Edison was the prophet of the liberal, secularized Protestant gospel of progress with its linear assumption of man's limitless perfectibility. But as "the Old Man"—an indomitable eccentric in pursuit of excellence, dreaming the impossible dream, sticking like hell, tending the machines—he is actually a more transcendent figure. He is the archetypal modern individual, an existential hero choosing the task of Sisyphus over the loss of identity which accompanies flight from conflict. He chooses, in essence, a faith—a faith that the rock placed on the hilltop belongs there and will remain there. Yet it has always been man's ultimate, if unconscious, perception that the rock must roll down and the struggle must be eternally renewed—that the reality of the individual is lesser and linear, while that of the collective is greater and cyclic. It is this root duality which all myths must finally resolve.

In the end, Edison's own myth was unworthy of the man. In the final analysis, heroes exist only in the legends from which they arise. Real life is made up of flesh and blood creatures who are event*ful* rather than event-making. The true heroes, then, are those with a hair more kindness, a mite more hope. They are those whose myopic enthusiasms and pedestrian virtues nurture the world. Like Edison, they work while we sleep. They keep the shop.

BOOKS

The sample of books, pamphlets, and biographical book chapters was gathered from the *Cumulative Book Index,* the *Biography Index,* the *Essay and General Literature Index,* the *Children's Catalog,* the *Junior High School Library Catalog,* the *Standard Catalog for High School Libraries,* the Stanford, University of California, and Library of Congress card catalogs, and from citations and bibliographies. In addition, short excerpts containing value judgments on Edison and his inventions were found through citations, a combing of indexes in all available and relevant American history books, and a search through the obsolete history and science textbooks in the juvenile collections held by the Cubberly Education Library at Stanford University. Other items were added from obvious sources such as encyclopedias, biographical dictionaries, and historical guides. The resulting sample contained 464 items, of which 127 were books and pamphlets devoted to Edison in their entirety. Despite the suggestion by such otherwise responsible writers as Matthew Josephson (*Edison,* p. ix) that "hundreds of books" have been written about Edison, there appear to have been no more than 89 American titles to date and far fewer foreign titles. Approximately 95 percent of the English-language sample was procured for this study, including 62 books, 21 pamphlets, and 326 more chapters and excerpts.

PERIODICALS

All items on Edison listed in the *Reader's Guide to Periodical Literature* since it began publication in 1890 were procured for study. For the period prior to 1890, *Poole's Index to Periodical Literature* is of some value but is very incomplete. Consequently, the fourteen highest circulating, relevant, and available periodicals for the years 1875 to 1890 were thoroughly searched. Some were searched from 1870, and some did not begin publication until later in the period. The search covered the following: *Atlantic* (1875–1890); *Chataquan* (1884–1890); *Harper's Monthly* (1870–1890); *Harper's Weekly* (1870–1890); *Independent* (1875–1890); *Lippincott's* (1879–1890); *North American Review* (1875–1890); *Overland* (1883–1890); *Popular Science Monthly* (1875–1890); *Public Opinion* (1886–1890); *Saint Nicholas* (1875–1900); *Scribner's Magazine* (1887–1890); *Scribner's Monthly* (1870–1890; became *Century* after 1881); *Youth's Companion* (1886–1887). *Collier's* and *Frank Leslie's Weekly* were not available. Citations encountered for *Scientific American* were so numerous that no search was made. Other items were located through citations and special limited searches; for example, *Time* magazine was searched for the years 1923–1935, since it was not indexed in the *Reader's Guide* until the latter year. The final periodical sample, 1870 to 1979, included 936 items (not counting the book reviews).

NEWSPAPERS

The *New York Times* was the only newspaper used for the entire period under study. It was indexed for all the years except 1906–1912, which were searched. For purposes of comparison, Hearst's *New York Evening Journal,* a more sensational paper than the *Times,* was searched for 1915, an active year for Edison. The New York papers carried more items on Edison largely because of their proximity. The *San Francisco Chronicle* was searched for the years 1902 to 1931, and the *London Times Index* provided material for comparison with the American sample. The complete American newspaper holdings of the Stanford Library were searched for their coverage of five special events: the successful test of the carbon filament lamp; the fiftieth anniversary celebration of that event; Edison's death; the centenary of his birth; and the centennial of the light. A scattering of other newspaper items found in citations was also included in the study. The final newspaper sample contained 3,218 items. A list of those located through searches rather than in indexes is included in the bibliography of the original dissertation (Stanford University, 1973).

NOTES ON GRAPH AND TABLES

The line representing press items on Edison in graph 1 was pushed dispro-

portionately upward by three events, two of which fall within one of the three-year averages: the fiftieth anniversary of the light in 1929; Edison's death in 1931; and the centenary of his birth in 1947. It is interesting to note that if a line had been plotted to show coverage by the *London Times,* its trend would have been the inverse of the American press. Almost all of the Edison coverage in the *London Times* occurs from 1878 to 1880, as a result of the invention of the electric light, and from 1888 to 1891, when Edison's representative in London was demonstrating the improved phonograph. The *Times* touched lightly on Edison's other important inventions, but between 1912 and his death in 1931—the peak years of his popularity in America—not a single item on Edison is indexed for the *London Times.* If the *London Times* were plotted on graph 1 it would more closely follow the line representing patents granted to Edison; the *New York Times,* on the other hand, is closer to the line portraying the total patents issued on inventions in the United States. During the first period of *London Times* coverage, 1878 to 1880, the British paper actually gave Edison twenty-six percent more space than the *New York Times.* In the second period, 1881 to 1891, the American paper exceeds the British by forty-five percent only because of the coverage in 1889. Thereafter, British attention becomes negligible, while that of the American press seems to increase almost in proportion to the decline in Edison's inventive activity. The British responded to Edison as an inventor; Americans responded to him as a culture hero.

The final column in table 2 expresses the number of items dealing strictly with Edison's inventions as a percentage of the total Edison items in the *New York Times*. The figures should be qualified by the fact that the "invention" interviews after 1908 deal more often with prophecy than with Edison's own inventions; likewise, after 1908 the figures in the first column often represent reminiscences about older inventions rather than discussions of current ones. In 1909, for example, we find that three of the five *Times* items on inventions are historical, while the one interview concerns "Edison's Picture of the Future of the Aeroplane." In the "human interest" column, three of the items in 1904 and three in 1906 reported incidents involving Edison's wayward son; six of the items in 1908 related to Edison's illness. These qualifications further support the contention that the pivotal point in the shift from "Great Inventor" to "Great American" was closer to 1911.

A content analysis of our entire sample for traits of character attributable to Edison's first sixteen years, stated as adjectives or nouns (see table 3), reveals that the rural, Protestant tradition accounts for about eight percent of all traits. But in general it was found that such an analysis actually distorts the impression received by the reader. For example, the analysis places intellectual precocity and curiosity at the top of the list, above the success virtues; yet this does not accurately reflect the subjective impact of the material, the reason being that curiosity is more naturally stated as an adjective or noun, while the success virtues are not. "Curious" would be counted, while "the boy was not afraid of hard work," or the moral of an entire anecdote, would not. For this reason, the anecdotal analysis is more reliable. Other than curiosity (the synonyms for which totaled approximately 146) and general terms such as "genius" or "bright" (67), the subcategories under "Intellectual Precocity" in descending order of frequency were: creative and imaginative (34), quick to grasp (33), good memory (29), keenness (17), shrewdness and cleverness (17), ingenious (15), concentration (8), and far-sighted (3). Although "ingenious" is redundant here, the word was sufficiently common to warrant its own category. The subcategories not specified in the table under "Success Virtues" were individualism (11), self-confidence and self-assurance (9), aggressiveness (10), ambition (11), business acumen (9), honesty and integrity (7), and thrift and self-discipline (4). These results might be compared with an additional analysis: Isolating all of the statements in the boyhood material which communicate some aspect of the success mythology, we find roughly the following categories in descending order of frequency (the groups of three figures in parentheses refer to the count for adult, youth, and juvenile items, respectively): humble beginnings (28, 4, 2); hard work (14, 8, 10); self-education (24, 5, 0); business acumen (13, 9, 1); ambition, motivation, effort, diligence (12, 4, 5); initiative,

enterprise, "hustle" (7, 8, 3); self-
reliance (12, 5, 1); the older Protestant
virtues of the McGuffey tradition (for
example, thrift, perseverance, punctuality, honesty—but omitting industriousness and diligence, covered
above) (7, 8, 3); self-made, rising by
his own efforts (13, 3, 1); moneymak-
ing (13, 1, 3); "hustle" in the sense of
industry and energy (8, 3, 2); shrewdness, shiftiness (always in relation to
business) (7, 5, 1); self-confidence (including the ability to convince others
of his worth) (6, 5, 0); perceiving the
importance of time (2, 3, 4); and alert
to opportunity (6, 3, 0). These were
followed by nineteen additional
categories.

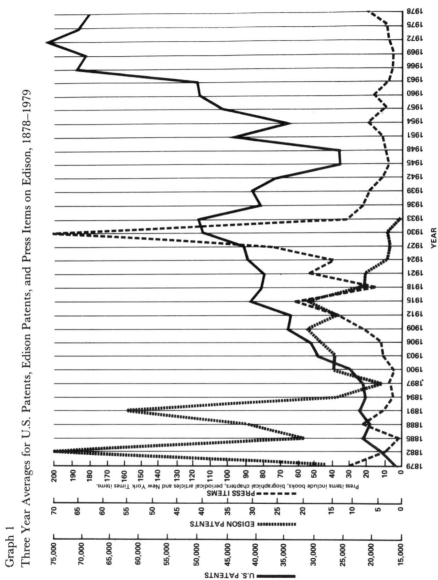

Graph 1
Three Year Averages for U.S. Patents, Edison Patents, and Press Items on Edison, 1878–1979

Table 1
Distribution of Accounts of Edison's Boyhood in Selected Categories by Decade

	Books			Biographical Chapters			Periodicals	NY Times	Total
	A	Y	J	A	Y	J			
1872–1881	1	0	0	2	0	0	4	1	8
1882–1891	1	0	0	1	0	0	4	0	6
1892–1901	1	0	0	2	1	1	7	2	14
1902–1911	2	1	0	2	3	1	3	0	12
1912–1921	3	1	0	4	4	1	13	4	30
1922–1931	4	4	0	4	7	2	21	18	60
1932–1941	5	1	1	4	5	1	8	10	35
1942–1951	2	2	1	8	2	5	27	11	58
1952–1961	1	4	1	5	7	14	20	4	56
1962–1971	6	2	5	6	6	3	4	0	32
Total	26	15	8	38	35	28	111	50	311

Key: A, Y, and J signify adult, youth, and juvenile categories, respectively.
Note: It should be noted that another three dozen or more items which were unprocurable are not listed here. The years 1972–1979 have so far produced seven books, two chapters, five periodical articles, and eight *New York Times* items touching on Edison's boyhood.

Table 2

Distribution of Subject Matter on Edison in the *New York Times*, 1878 to 1928

	A	The Business of Invention		B	The Man		
Year	Inventions	Business and Legal	Interviews	Human Interest	Interviews	Awards and Honors	A as %
1878	5	—	—	1	—	—	83
1879	9	1	—	—	—	—	100
1880	3	—	—	—	—	—	100
1881	1	1	—	—	—	—	100
1882	1	1	—	—	—	—	100
1883	—*	1	—	—	—	—	100
1884	—	1	—	—	—	—	100
1885	—	—	—	—	—	—	—
1886	—	1	—	1	—	—	50
1887	2	—	—	—	—	—	100
1888	4	—	—	—	—	—	100
1889	4	5	2	6	—	1	61
1890	1	2	1	2	—	—	67
1891	6	3	—	—	—	—	100
1892	1	1	—	2	—	1	40
1893	—	—	—	—	—	—	—
1894	—	—	—	2	—	—	0
1895	—	—	—	—	—	—	—
1896	12	—	—	1	—	—	92
1897	2	—	—	—	—	—	100
1898	—	—	—	1	—	—	0
1899	—	1	—	—	—	—	100
1900	—	—	—	1	—	—	0
1901	2	—	1	5	—	—	38
1902	2	1	—	—	—	—	100
1903	3	2	—	3	—	—	63
1904	—	—	—	4	—	—	0
1905	1	—	—	4	—	—	20
1906	1	—	1	8	—	—	20
1907	1	1	—	8	—	—	20
1908	—	1	1	13	1	—	13
1909	5	2	1	5	—	3	50
1910	9	1	—	7	1	1	53

Table 2 (continued)

| Year | A The Business of Invention | | | B The Man | | | |
	Inventions	Business and Legal	Interviews	Human Interest	Interviews	Awards and Honors	A as %
1911	6	1	—	12	4	4	26
1912	5	4	1	6	2	1	53
1913	5	1	1	14	1	1	30
1914	3	3	—	26	5	1	16
1915	22**	1	1	15	6	8	45
1916	9	2	1	18	3	4	32
1917	7	—	—	6	—	2	47
1918	—	—	—	11	—	3	0
1919	—	—	1	8	—	2	9
1920	1	—	—	10	—	2	8
1921	3	1	4	40***	—	—	17
1922	5	—	2	37	—	3	15
1923	1	1	6	27	3	5	19
1924	—	—	3	11	4	2	15
1925	1	—	2	15	1	6	12
1926	1	2	—	30	6	6	7
1927	17	—	—	37	4	1	29
1928	8	—	—	36	6	18	12

* Dashes signify zeros.
** Many of the "invention" items in 1915–1917 are articles on Edison's work with antisubmarine devices and on his role as chairman of the Naval Consulting Board.
*** 1921 and 1922 include many items on Edison's controversial employment quiz.

Table 3
Character Traits Attributed to Edison's First Sixteen Years

Trait groups	1878–1914				1915–1932				1933–1949				1950–1959				1960–1971				Total
	A	J	T	%	A	J	T	%	A	J	T	%	A	J	T	%	A	J	T	%	
Intellectual precocity	75	19	94	26	56	34	90	25	38	36	74	21	16	37	53	15	12	34	46	13	357
Curiosity	23	9	32	22	17	11	28	19	28	16	44	30	5	11	16	11	4	22	26	18	146
Success virtues	22	14	36	29	15	11	26	21	16	15	31	25	5	5	10	8	11	11	22	18	125
Industriousness	5	4	9	31	5	3	8	28	1	4	5	17	2	0	2	7	3	2	5	17	29
Perseverance	5	2	7	33	0	1	1	5	3	3	6	29	1	0	1	5	2	4	6	29	21
Initiative and enterprise	5	0	5	36	3	0	3	21	3	1	4	29	0	1	1	7	1	0	1	7	14
Optimism and enthusiasm	4	1	5	22	2	1	3	13	3	6	9	39	0	5	5	22	1	0	1	4	23
Energy	17	5	22	30	7	4	11	15	13	8	21	29	8	5	13	18	3	3	6	8	73
Practicality	8	1	9	50	1	1	2	11	4	0	4	22	0	1	1	6	0	2	2	11	18
Friendliness and humanity	20	8	28	42	5	11	16	24	4	5	9	14	0	6	6	9	0	7	7	11	66
Withdrawn	13	0	13	33	4	4	8	21	3	2	5	13	2	1	3	8	10	0	10	26	39
Peculiar	2	0	2	17	4	0	4	33	0	0	0	–	2	1	3	25	0	3	3	25	12
Total traits listed	161	48	209		94	66	160		81	72	153		33	61	94		37	60	97		713
Total traits found	176	51	227	29	102	76	178	23	99	76	175	22	35	67	102	13	39	64	103	13	785
Total items in sample (books, articles, etc.)	39	9	48	14	80	18	98	28	75	18	93	27	35	22	57	16	28	22	50	15	346

Key: A = adult literature. J = youth and juvenile literature combined. T = total. % = percent of total in last column.
Note: The high count for "precocity" (usually meaning "horse sense") contradicts the reader's overall subjective impression. Since only nouns and adjectives were counted, many traits which were more easily expressed via phrases or anecdotes score deceptively low. The reader's general impression is that the "success virtues" should top the list.

Table 4
Noun and Adjective Character Traits Attributed to Edison by Period Expressed as a Percentage of the Total Trait Count for Each Period

Traits	1870–1889 A	1870–1889 J	1890–1899 A	1890–1899 J	1900–1914 A	1900–1914 J	1915–1928 A	1915–1928 J	1929–1932 A	1929–1932 J	1933–1949 A	1933–1949 J	1950–1959 A	1950–1959 J	1960–1971 A	1960–1971 J
Intellectual	33.	0	34.8	47.8	33.	27.8	35.6	27.3	38.2	27.2	38.	32.7	41.5	29.3	29.6	29.
Genius	9.7	0	19.4	34.8	13.	25.	16.6	8.8	19.9	12.8	16.7	10.5	12.7	10.9	10.7	9.
Imaginative	15.9	0	5.9	8.7	12.6	0	7.9	8.8	11.6	5.6	13.4	13.5	18.7	4.6	12.2	10.3
Analytical	4.8	0	3.8	4.3	4.4	0	5.	3.5	2.8	5.6	4.1	4.7	5.	8.6	4.6	5.2
Versatile, skill	1.	0	2.	0	1.4	2.8	2.9	3.1	.9	.8	.4	1.8	2.7	.6	1.1	1.9
Open-minded	0	0	.3	0	.1	0	.3	0	.2	.8	.4	0	−.3	0	−1.3	0
Curious	1.	0	2.3	0	1.4	0	1.5	2.2	2.2	1.6	2.4	1.8	1.7	4.	.8	1.9
Concentration	.3	0	1.3	0	.2	0	1.3	.9	.6	0	.7	.6	1.	.6	.2	.6
Human	15.9	0	15.9	26.1	10.2	52.8	11.2	11.	12.6	14.4	10.5	15.8	9.7	14.4	5.4	10.9
Kind, warm	7.3	0	6.4	13.	4.6	16.7	4.8	4.8	7.4	8.8	6.	9.4	6.4	5.2	3.4	5.2
Good-natured	1.7	0	2.	8.7	2.3	2.8	2.3	2.6	1.9	1.6	1.4	3.5	.3	4.6	−.8	0
Sense of humor	2.1	0	5.9	4.3	1.6	0	1.6	1.3	1.1	3.2	2.	1.8	1.3	2.3	2.7	3.9
Encourages others	0	0	0	0	.2	5.6	.2	.4	.2	0	.1	0	.3	0	0	.6
Misc. human	4.8	0	1.5	0	1.5	0	2.2	1.8	1.8	.8	.9	1.2	1.3	2.3	0	1.3
Work	11.4	0	8.7	4.3	10.7	30.6	12.9	17.2	12.5	12.8	10.5	15.2	10.4	14.9	14.1	12.9
Industrious	5.9	0	4.6	4.3	5.3	25.	8.3	10.1	6.2	4.8	4.9	9.4	5.4	12.1	6.3	9.
Energy	5.5	0	4.1	0	5.4	5.6	4.7	7.	6.3	8.	5.6	5.8	5.	2.9	7.8	3.9
Perseverance	9.7	0	5.1	0	4.4	5.6	4.2	9.3	4.5	4.	4.1	2.3	4.	5.7	2.3	4.5
Motivation, interest	4.5	0	6.9	0	6.6	2.8	5.	5.3	6.5	4.	2.5	5.8	3.7	3.4	4.4	3.9
Optimism, confidence	4.2	0	2.3	0	6.1	2.8	5.8	7.5	3.7	6.4	3.3	6.4	2.3	10.3	3.3	5.2
Democratic	6.9	0	5.6	39.1	5.6	0	2.9	6.2	4.3	8.8	3.	9.4	4.3	5.2	1.7	7.1

Practical	1.4	0	1.5	0	4.4	0	5.4	2.6	3.9	3.2	4.2	2.9	4.7	2.9	2.7	5.8
Individualistic	1.	0	1.	4.3	1.4	0	.4	.9	.8	1.6	1.3	1.8	1.	1.1	1.3	1.9
Nonconforming	2.8	0	1.	0	.9	0	.7	.9	.6	1.6	.6	0	.3	.6	0	1.9
Patient	2.8	0	3.8	0	3.5	8.3	2.8	5.3	2.4	3.2	3.2	4.1	2.3	5.2	1.7	2.6
Painstaking	2.1	0	.8	0	2.1	2.8	1.8	3.9	.7	1.6	1.2	2.9	.3	1.7	.6	1.3
Moralistic	1.4	0	1.5	0	2.	0	2.9	.9	3.9	7.2	1.7	1.2	1.7	1.1	1.5	1.9
Moderation	.3	0	1.	0	.5	0	.3	0	.3	0	.1	0	0	0	0	0
Aggressive, bold	1.	0	1.8	0	1.6	0	2.6	1.3	2.4	12.	1.9	.6	1.3	3.4	1.1	1.3
Quiet	.3	0	0	0	.9	0	.6	1.3	-.1	0	.9	2.3	0	.6	-.1	0
Courteous	.7	0	.8	0	.8	0	.6	.9	.3	0	.1	0	0	0	.2	0
Business acumen	.3	0	.3	0	.4	0	.3	.4	-.04	.8	.3	.6	0	0	1.1	-1.9
Misc. success virtues	0	0	.8	0	1.	0	.3	.7	.7	.8	.8	1.2	.3	1.1	1.3	1.3
Misc. Protestant ethic	0	0	0	0	.1	0	.1	0	.04	.8	.5	1.2	.3	0	.2	0
Youthful	0	0	0	0	0	0	0	.4	0	.8	0	0	1.3	1.1	.6	0
Immature	0	0	0	0	0	0	0	0	0	0	0	0	.3	0	.2	0
Total traits	289	0	391	23	1,170	36	1,039	227	2,164	125	1,383	171	299	174	523	155

Key: A and J designate adult and juvenile literature, respectively.

Note: The figure 9.7 for "genius" in the first column, for example, indicates that 9.7% of the total number of traits counted in the adult literature for the period 1870–1889 suggested the idea of genius in connection with Edison. The word "genius" itself accounted for only 7.6% of the traits in the adult literature of the period; the category includes many other words such as "keen" and "intelligent" when used in a positive context. Where two traits have meanings in common, the more narrowly defined trait will not have been included in counting the broader one; thus, words which suggest imagination (creativity) or analytical-mindedness are not included in the "genius" category. This method accounts for the low scores in the "success virtues" and "Protestant ethic" categories. The figures for "intellectual," "human," and "work" represent totals for the traits indented below them. The percentages are derived from net totals; that is, negative traits were subtracted from their positive opposites (e.g. "ignorant" from "informed"); this explains the negative percentages. The tabulation involved some intentional double-counting—between the "optimism, confidence," and "good-natured" categories, for example. The percentages, therefore, will not total 100. Figures for the middle periods are the most reliable due to the larger amount of material. The figure of 39.1% in the J column of the 1890–1899 period for the "democratic" category for example, is not as significant as it might seem.

Table 5
Most Commonly Cited Effects of Edison's Inventions

	1870–1889	1890–1899	1900–1914	1915–1928	1929–1932	1933–1949	1950–1959	1960–1971
Comfort, leisure	7	6	6	1	1	2	1	5
Save expense	2	1	1	2	4	5	4	4
Increase national wealth and investment	4	7	3	3	2	1	2	1
Negative effects	1	3	4	7	7	7	5	2
Create employment	5	4	2	8	6	3	3	3
Improve safety	8	2	7	5	3	6	7	6
Save time	6	5	8	4	8	4	6	7
Benefit to future generations	3	8	5	6	5	8	8	8

Key: Figures indicate rank within each period, the highest being 1.

1

INTRODUCTION

1. Matthew Josephson gives the anecdote in one of its many forms in *Edison: A Biography* (New York: McGraw-Hill, 1959), p. 462. Hereafter, references for citations from the Edison literature may be found in the special note section which follows this one.

2. This is the thesis of John Ward's "The Meaning of Lindbergh's Flight," *American Quarterly* X (Spring 1958), pp. 3–16.

3. A more detailed analysis of a large number of opinion samples, along with attempts to measure popularity through the frequency of Edison items in periodicals, children's literature, etc., may be found in my doctoral dissertation, *A Better Mousetrap: Thomas A. Edison as an American Culture Hero* (Stanford University, 1973).

4. Again, a lengthy quantitative analysis of the treatment of Edison in the American press (and, by comparison, the *London Times*) may be found, along with graphs and tables, in the original dissertation. Also included is a newspaper bibliography on Edison.

5. One of the first to develop this idea was Leo Lowenthal in "Biographies in Popular Magazines" in *Radio Research: 1942–1943*, edited by Paul F. Lazars-

feld and Frank Stanton (New York: Duell, Sloan and Pearce, 1944).

6. Editor Beach relates the entire incident in George S. Bryan, *Edison: The Man and His Work* (Garden City, NY: Doubleday, 1926), pp. 86–87.

2

THE WIZARD OF MENLO PARK

1. Lewis Mumford, *Technics and Civilization* (New York: Harcourt, Brace and World, 1934), chapters iv and v. In that the dynamo is dependent on the internal combustion engine, it is not technologically parallel to the steam engine; but symbolically, each converted energy from more primitive to more efficient forms characteristic of the age.

2. Omitted from the analysis were words such as "wonderful," "astounding," "remarkable," and "magnificent," which describe only the reaction of the beholder and nothing specific about the invention; words in the category of "practical," "useful," and "commercial," which were grouped separately; objective description (size, quantity, etc.); adjectives of size were also counted separately. "Beautiful" placed second only because it was constantly applied to the red glow of the lamp. As one might expect, there was also a disproportionate percentage of negative adjectives

in the period 1870–1889. During the years 1890–1914, adjectives of bigness are in a slight majority only because a few articles dealing with the ore-milling project are saturated with them. It is significant that the years 1915–1971 again show a ratio of 3.4 to 1 in favor of smallness.

3. Nathaniel Hawthorne, *Selected Tales and Sketches* (New York: Holt, Rinehart and Winston, 1964), pp. 301–02, 305, 314. "Ethan Brand" was written in 1850.

4. On the mediating function of the symbol, see Claude Levi-Strauss, "The Structural Study of Myth" in Thomas A. Sebeok, ed., *Myth: A Symposium* (Bloomington, IN: Indiana University Press, 1965), pp. 81–106. Many paired terms have been suggested which appear to reflect the same universal dichotomy. Some of the more interesting models may be found in David Bakan, *The Duality of Human Existence: Isolation and Communion in Western Man* (Boston: Beacon Press, 1966); David Gutmann, "Female Ego Styles and Generational Conflict" in Judith M. Bardwick et al., eds., *Feminine Personality and Conflict* (Belmont, CA: Wadsworth Publishing Co., 1970), pp. 77–96; and Leo Marx, *The Machine in the Garden: Technology and the Pastoral Ideal in America* (New York: Oxford University Press, 1967). The Jungian dimension may be found in Erich Neumann, *The Origins and History of Consciousness* (Princeton, NJ: Princeton University Press, 1970); and Edward F. Edinger, *Ego and Archetype: Individuation and the Religious Function of the Psyche* (Baltimore, MD: Penguin Books, 1973). Another perspective de-

rives from the recent discovery of man's split-brain functions; see, for example, Joseph E. Bogen, "The Other Side of the Brain: An Appositional Mind," in Robert E. Ornstein, ed., *The Nature of Human Consciousness: A Book of Readings* (San Francisco: W. H. Freeman and Co., 1973), pp. 101–125; and Ornstein's *The Psychology of Consciousness* (San Francisco: W. H. Freeman and Co., 1972), chapter iii. A fascinating historical matrix is offered by William Irwin Thompson in *At the Edge of History: Speculations on the Transformation of Culture* (New York: Harper and Row, 1971), chapter iv.

5. Edwin Layton, "Mirror-Image Twins: The Communities of Science and Technology in 19th-Century America," *Technology and Culture* XII (Oct. 1971), pp. 562–580. Layton's thesis, which is concerned with "communities," does not conflict with the idea that science and technology, in their broadest senses, converged in the neotechnic age.

3

INNOCENCE AND POWER:
THE MYTHOLOGY OF EDISON'S
YOUTH

1. Marx, *The Machine in the Garden*. The other titles suggested in note 4 of chapter 2 are again relevant.

2. On the success mythology, see Richard Weiss, *The American Myth of Success: From Horatio Alger to Norman Vincent Peale* (New York: Basic Books, 1969); John B. Cawelti, *Apostles of the Self-Made Man: Changing Concepts of Suc-*

cess in America (Chicago: University of Chicago Press, 1965); Irvin G. Wyllie, The Self-Made Man in America: The Myth of Rags to Riches (New York: The Free Press, 1966); and Richard M. Huber, The American Idea of Success (New York: McGraw-Hill, 1971).

3. An additional 17 percent of the 245-term sample refer to the young "scientist," "experimenter," etc.; another 10 percent explicitly depict action; and most of the remainder imply an early-developed mental aptitude. "The boy" and equivalents such as "lad" were omitted from the count when unqualified by an adjective. A commonly recurring phrase is "editor, manager, compositor, printer and publisher," referring to his Weekly Herald. Used as a subjective complement rather than as a name-substitute, the phrase is one of many which recur as a result of the fact that certain works were widely copied in subsequent Edison material. A few of the more important ones are "A Night With Edison," Scribner's Monthly XVII (Nov. 1878), pp. 88–99; J. B. McClure, Edison and His Inventions (Chicago: Rhoades and McClure, 1879); W. K. L. and Antonia Dickson, The Life and Inventions of Thomas Alva Edison (New York: Crowell, 1892); Frank Lewis Dyer, T. Commerford Martin, and William H. Meadowcroft, Edison: His Life and Inventions, 2 vols. (New York: Harper and Brothers, 1910); and for juvenile literature, William H. Meadowcroft, The Boys' Life of Edison (New York: Harper and Brothers, 1911).

4. Frederick Jackson Turner, The Frontier in American History (New York:

Holt, Rinehart and Winston, 1962), pp. 4, 37.

5. Huber, The American Idea of Success, p. 80.

6. See Roy P. Basler, The Lincoln Legend: A Study in Changing Conceptions (New York: Octagon Books, 1969), pp. 108–109.

7. See Erich Neumann, The Great Mother: An Analysis of the Archetype, 2nd ed. (Princeton, NJ: Princeton University Press, 1972) for an exhaustive elaboration on the archetype.

8. "Drift" is more neutral, though it can connote a transcendent and teleological course of events. The most objective phrases simply state that Edison "worked for a number of railway companies" or "changed jobs many times"; significantly, however, such examples are found disproportionately in the British items and in the books for small children. Words suggesting a quest are generally not stressed in the youth and juvenile literature, with the exception of "wander," the use of which probably reflects only their dependency on the standard biographies (plagiarism, in fact, is more frequent in the juvenile material). Sometimes Edison's drifting will be dismissed in the children's accounts as "traveling" or a desire "to see other parts of the United States." In part this is because the topic hardly reinforces the Protestant virtues; but it also allows that children are unlikely to grasp parallels to the night-journey of the soul.

9. The monomythic hero cycle in classical mythology is treated exhaustively in Joseph Campbell's Hero With a

Thousand Faces (Cleveland and New York: The World Publishing Co., 1956).

10. John Dos Passos, "The Electrical Wizard," from *U.S.A.: The 42nd Parallel* (New York: Random House, 1937), pp. 297–301.

11. David McClelland, *The Achieving Society* (Princeton, NJ: Van Nostrand, 1961), pp. 302–331. On the trickster, see Joseph L. Henderson, "Ancient Myths and Modern Man," in Carl G. Jung, ed., *Man and His Symbols* (New York: Dell Publishing Co., 1968), pp. 103–104; and Orrin E. Klapp, "The Clever Hero," *Journal of American Folklore* LXVII (Jan.–Mar. 1954), pp. 21–34.

4

PROGRESS TOWARD THE ULTIMATE: EDISON AND THE AMERICAN MONOMYTH

1. Marx, *The Machine in the Garden,* pp. 207–208.

2. Charles L. Sanford, *The Quest for Paradise: Europe and the American Moral Imagination* (Urbana, IL: University of Illinois Press, 1961), chapters i–v. The case for the "four-hundred-year boom" is argued by Walter Prescott Webb in *The Great Frontier* (Austin, TX: University of Texas Press, 1952).

3. Examples of the monomyth may be found in Robert Jewett and John Shelton Lawrence, *The American Monomyth* (Garden City, NY: Doubleday, 1977).

4. Marx, *The Machine in the Garden,* pp. 191, 197–198.

5. Hendrik M. Ruitenbeek makes this distinction between medieval and modern history in *The Individual and the Crowd: A Study of Identity in America* (New York: Mentor, 1964), chapter ii. See also Bakan, *The Duality of Human Existence,* chapters ii, iii; and Anton C. Zijderveld, *The Abstract Society: A Cultural Analysis of Our Time* (Garden City, NY: Doubleday, 1971).

6. Rush Welter, "The Idea of Progress in America: An Essay in Ideas and Method," *Journal of the History of Ideas* XVI (June 1955), p. 404.

7. Mumford, *Technics and Civilization,* chapters iv, v.

8. Marx, *The Machine,* p. 220. See, for example, David W. Noble, *The Paradox of Progressive Thought* (Minneapolis: University of Minnesota Press, 1958); John W. Ward, "The Meaning of Lindbergh's Flight," and *Andrew Jackson: Symbol for an Age* (New York: Oxford University Press, 1955); and Marvin Meyers, *The Jacksonian Persuasion: Politics and Belief,* 2nd ed. (Stanford: Stanford University Press, 1960).

9. On the Edenic myth in America, in addition to works by Sanford, Marx, and others previously cited, see Frederic I. Carpenter, " 'The American Myth': Paradise (To Be) Regained," *PMLA* LXXIV (Dec. 1959), pp. 599–606; David Noble, *Historians Against History: The Frontier Thesis and the National Covenant in American Historical Writing Since 1830* (Minneapolis: University of Minnesota Press, 1965), and *The Eternal Adam and the New World Garden: The Central Myth in the American Novel Since 1830* (New York: George Braziller, 1968); R. W. B. Lewis, *The*

American Adam: Innocence, Tragedy and Tradition in the Nineteenth Century (Chicago: University of Chicago Press, 1955); Henry Nash Smith, *Virgin Land: The American West as Symbol and Myth* (Cambridge, MA: Vintage Books, 1950); Paul Shepard, *Man in the Landscape: A Historic View of the Esthetics of Nature* (New York: Alfred A. Knopf, 1967); and Arthur A. Ekirch, Jr., *Man and Nature in America* (New York: Columbia University Press, 1963).

10. On the idea of America's mission, see Ernest Lee Tuveson, *Redeemer Nation: The Idea of America's Millennial Role* (Chicago: University of Chicago Press, 1968); Russel B. Nye, "The American Sense of Mission," in *This Almost Chosen People: Essays in the History of American Ideas* (East Lansing, MI: Michigan State University Press, 1966), pp. 164–207; and Edward McNall Burns, *The American Idea of Mission: Concepts of National Purpose and Destiny* (New Brunswick, NJ: Rutgers University Press, 1957). Also relevant, but confined to the nineteenth century, is Frederick Merk, *Manifest Destiny and Mission in American History: A Reinterpretation* (New York: Vintage Books, 1963).

11. Henry Steele Commager, *The American Mind: An Interpretation of American Thought and Character Since the 1880's* (New Haven, CT: Yale University Press, 1959), pp. 166–167. Winthrop Hudson, *The Great Tradition of the American Churches* (New York: Harper and Row, 1963), pp. 201–202; see also chapter viii, and his *American Protestantism* (Chicago: University of Chicago Press, 1961), chapter iii. Also in-

formative are Stow Persons, "Religion and Modernity, 1865–1914," in James W. Smith and A. Leland Jamison, eds., *The Shaping of American Religion* (Princeton, NJ: Princeton University Press, 1961), pp. 369–401; Arthur M. Schlesinger, "A Critical Period in American Religion, 1875–1900," *Proceedings of the Massachusetts Historical Society* LXIV (June 1932), pp. 523–547; and James Bryce, *The American Commonwealth*, 2nd ed., rev., 2 vols. (New York: The Macmillan Co., 1910), vol. II, pp. 782–785.

12. Quotations are from Herbert Schneider, *Religion in 20th Century America*, rev. ed. (New York: Atheneum, 1964), pp. 123, 126.

5

LOOKING BACKWARD:
FROM GREAT INVENTOR TO
GREAT AMERICAN

1. See Charles E. Skinner, "Lighting the World's Exposition," *Western Pennsylvania Historical Magazine* XVII (1934), pp. 13–22. John Cawelti offers an interesting thesis on the cultural implications of the exposition in "America on Display: The World's Fairs of 1876, 1893, 1933," in F. C. Jaher, ed., *The Age of Industrialism in America: Essays in Social Structure and Cultural Values* (New York: The Free Press, 1968), pp. 317–363.

2. David Riesman, Nathan Glazer, and Reuel Denney, *The Lonely Crowd: A Study of the Changing American Character*, rev. ed. (Garden City, NY: Doubleday, 1956), chapters ii–iv.

3. In *American Civilization in the First Machine Age, 1890–1940* (New York: Harper and Row, 1972), Gilman Ostrander argues that the shift of American society from patriarchy to "filiarchy" became overt in the 1920s.

4. The Albert Salt incident is from John M. Blum, "Exegesis of the Gospel of Work, Success and Satisfaction in Recent American Culture," in Clarence Morriss, ed., *Trends in Modern American Society* (Philadelphia: University of Pennsylvania Press, 1962), p. 22.

5. Leonard W. Labaree et al., eds., *The Autobiography of Benjamin Franklin* (New Haven, CT: Yale University Press, 1964), pp. 149–150.

6. Lee Coleman, examining "a large number of books" on American character in an attempt to determine what traits were most frequently alleged, found that of 57 common traits, "practicality" was among eleven which were mentioned for all four of the periods into which he divided American history ("What is American? A Study of Alleged American Traits," *Social Forces* XIX (May, 1941), pp. 492–499). Tocqueville himself observed that the "Americans are more addicted to practical than to theoretical science," that "in no country in the civilized world is less attention paid to philosophy than in the United States," and that "Practical experience" is "more serviceable to the Americans than book-learning" (*Democracy in America*, 2 vols. [New York: Vintage Books, 1945], vol. I, p. 326, vol. II, p. 42). "Self-examination," Frederick Jackson Turner suggested

"is not characteristic of the historic American. He has been an opportunist rather than a dealer in general ideas. Destiny set him in a current which bore him swiftly along through such a wealth of opportunity that reflection and well-considered planning seemed wasted time. He knew not where he was going, but he was on his way, cheerful, optimistic, busy and buoyant" (*The Frontier in American History*, p. 290). More recently, Daniel Boorstin has reconstructed American history around the boast that American experience has eliminated the European babel of metaphysics and ideology (see especially *The Genius of American Politics* [Chicago: University of Chicago Press, 1953]; and *The Americans: The Colonial Experience* [New York: Vintage Books, 1958]).

6

THE LAST GREAT HAYSEED:
THE POSTHUMOUS IMAGE

1. Marx, *The Machine in the Garden*, p. 13 (quoting Hawthorne's notebooks).

2. The fact that Edison's appointment as chairman of the Naval Consulting Board was motivated by the symbolic impact it would have on the public is corroborated by Josephus Daniels, *The Wilson Era: Years of Peace—1910–1917* (Chapel Hill, NC: University of North Carolina Press, 1946), pp. 490–491; and Theodore A. Thelander, "Josephus Daniels and the Publicity Campaign for Naval and Industrial Preparedness Before World War I," *North Carolina Historical Review* XLIII (1966), pp. 316–320. Daniels thought

that public interest would win Congressional support.

3. Perkins is quoted in Edward C. Kirkland, *Industry Comes of Age: Business, Labor and Public Policy, 1860–1897* (Chicago: Quandrangle, 1967), p. 407.

4. James B. Conant, *Modern Science and Modern Man* (New York: Doubleday, 1953), pp. 18–20.

5. Conant, *Modern Science and Modern Man,* p. 44. The observation is a common one.

6. On the encouragement of science in the schools and the related national concerns, see U.S., Department of Health, Education and Welfare, Office of Education, *Mathematics and Science Education in U.S. Public Schools* (Washington, DC: U.S. Government Printing Office, 1958); *Offerings and Enrollments in Science and Mathematics in Public High Schools* (Washington, DC: U.S. Government Printing Office, 1957); *Digest of Educational Statistics* (Washington, DC: U.S. Government Printing Office, 1964–1966, 1969–1972); and U.S., Federal Security Agency, Office of Education, *The Teaching of Science in Public High Schools* (Washington, DC: U.S. Government Printing Office, 1950). Science enrollment increased significantly relative to total enrollment, 1948–1965 (*Digest,* 1963, p. 16; 1965, p. 27; 1968, p. 34), as compared to almost no increase, 1890–1947 (*The Teaching,* p. 6).

7. Stephen B. Withey, "Public Opinion about Science and Scientists," *Public Opinion Quarterly* XXIII (Fall 1959), pp. 382–388. The study also noted another survey in which 40 percent of the 240 managing editors questioned

reported that their coverage of science news had doubled since Sputnik; another 40 percent reported a 50 percent increase (p. 384). Also, the Withey study revealed that only 12 percent blamed the bad effects of science on scientists themselves; instead, "vague but sinister, powerful, and selfish groups with special interests" were mentioned (p. 387).

8. In the material written for very young children, in fact, hard work and perseverance dominate almost entirely. See, for example, Sue Guthridge, *Tom Edison: Boy Inventor* (Indianapolis: Bobbs-Merrill, 1959 [1947]); Ruth Cromer Weir, *Thomas Alva Edison: Inventor* (New York: Abingdon-Cokesbury, 1953); Mervyn D. Kaufman, *Thomas Alva Edison: Miracle Maker* (New York: Garrard, 1968 [1962]); Charles and Martha Shapp, *Let's Find Out About Thomas Alva Edison* (New York: F. Watts, 1966), p. 46; Patricia Miles Martin, *Thomas Alva Edison* (New York: Putnam, 1971), p. 53; Hattie E. Macomber, *Stories of Great Inventors* (Boston: Educational, 1897), p. 167; Vanza Devereaux, *America's Own Story* (San Francisco: Wagner, Harr, 1954), p. 327; and Raymond F. Yates, *The Young Inventor's Guide* (New York: Harper, 1959). "Work! Work! Work! Think! Think! Think! . . . That was all there was to Thomas Edison's success," said Yates (p. 51).

9. Will Herberg, *Protestant, Catholic, Jew: An Essay in American Religious Sociology,* rev. ed. (New York: Doubleday, 1960). At the center of the creed of "Americanism," he observed, is a faith in faith itself. Eisenhower provided an

example when he said "Our government makes no sense unless it is
founded in a deeply felt religious
faith—*and I don't care what it is*" (pp.
84, 265).

7

REPRISE: THE IMPOSSIBLE DREAM

1. Eric Hoffer, *The Temper of Our Time*
(New York: Harper and Row, 1967),
pp. 34–37.

2. On the split brain see Robert E.
Ornstein, *The Psychology of Consciousness,*
pp. 49–73; Michael S. Gazzaniga,
"The Split Brain in Man," *Scientific
American* CCXVII (Aug. 1967), pp.
24–29; Joseph E. Bogen, "The Other
Side of the Brain: An Appositional
Mind," *Bulletin of the Los Angeles Neuro-
logical Societies* XXXIV (July 1969),
pp. 135–162; Arthur Deikman, "Bi-
modal Consciousness," *Archives of General Psychiatry* XXV (Dec. 1971), 481–
489; and Dorothy Lee, "Codifications
of Reality: Lineal and Nonlineal,"
Psychosomatic Medicine XII (1950), pp.
89–97.

Line numbers refer to the line in which the last word of a quotation or reference appears in the text.

2
THE WIZARD OF MENLO PARK

INTRODUCTORY SECTION
Page 19, line 4:
"An Afternoon with Edison," New York *Daily Graphic,* Apr. 2, 1878. This was apparently the first use of the term "wizard" by the press in connection with Edison.

THE NEOTECHNIC REVOLUTION
Page 23, footnote:
See, for example, *United States Daily,* Oct. 21, 1929, p. 14.

WHILE THE WORLD SLEPT
Page 24, line 1:
"Edison and His Inventions. I.," *Scribner's Monthly,* XVIII (June 1879), 297.

Page 24, line 14:
New York Herald, December 29, 1879, p. 2.

Page 25, line 8:
"Edison in His Workshop," *Harper's Weekly* XXIII (Aug. 2, 1879), 607.

Page 25, line 12:
W. H. Bishop, "A Night with Edison," *Scribner's Magazine* XVII (Aug. 1878), 33.

Page 25, line 12 (alchemy):
See, for example, the *Stockton Daily Independent,* Dec. 23, 1879, p. 2; and the

New York Herald, Dec. 22, 1879, p. 3 [headline].

Page 25, lines 13 and 14:
Examples may be found in the *New York Times,* Oct. 21, 1906, pt. 3, p. 3 [headline]; Sept. 17, 1905, pt. 3, p. 2 [headline]; Jan. 2, 1906, pt. 3, p. 1; *San Francisco Morning Call,* Jan. 3, 1879, p. 3; Frane Bangs Wilkie, *The Great Inventions: Their History from the Earliest Period to the Present* (Philadelphia, 1883), p. 520; and Elbridge Streeter Brooks, *Historic Americans: Sketches of the Lives and Character of Certain Famous Americans Held Most in Reverence by Boys and Girls of America for Whom Their Stories Are Told* (New York, 1940), p. 461.

Page 25, lines 15–18:
Examples are found in the *New York Times,* May 17, 1907, p. 7; William Inglis, "Edison and the New Education," *Harper's Weekly* LV (Nov. 4, 1911), 8; and other citations for this paragraph.

Page 25, line 20 (necromancy):
New York Herald, Dec. 22, 1879, p. 3.

Page 25, line 20 (conjurer):
New Orleans Daily Picayune, Dec. 28, 1879, p. 4.

Page 25, line 20 (caldron):
Horace Townsend, "Edison: His Work and His Workshop," *The Cosmopolitan* VI (Apr. 1889), 605.

Page 25, line 26:
Charles D. Lanier, "Two Giants of the Electric Age: 1. Thomas A. Edison,

Greatest of Inventors," *Review of Reviews* VIII (July 1893), 49.

Page 25, line 28:
Brooks, *Historic Americans,* p. 451.

Page 25, line 29:
New York Times, Jan. 2, 1906, pt. 3, p. 1.

Page 25, line 37:
"Edison and His Inventions," p. 298.

Page 26, line 6:
W. K. L. Dickson and Antonia Dickson, *The Life and Inventions of Thomas Alva Edison* (New York, 1892), p. 105.

Page 26, line 16:
Public Opinion II (Mar. 19, 1887), 504.

Page 26, line 21:
"What's in a Name?" *The Catholic World* LI (Sept. 1890), 803–812.

Page 26, line 24:
New York Times, Oct. 23, 1892, p. 17.

THE PROFESSOR

Page 33, line 11:
"An Electric Railroad," *Harper's Weekly* XXVI (July 15, 1882), 433.

Page 34, line 7:
San Francisco Chronicle, Oct. 23, 1915, p. 7.

Page 35, line 4:
Scientific American Supplement III (Dec. 1878), 11.

Page 35, line 14:
Francis Jehl, *Menlo Park Reminiscences,* 3 vols. (Dearborn, MI, 1937), vol. III, p. 862.

Page 35, line 18:
Harold J. Laski, *The American Democracy: A Commentary and an Interpretation* (New York, 1948), p. 657.

Page 35, line 22:
San Francisco Chronicle, Nov. 17, 1929, rotogravure section, pt. 2, p. 4.

Page 35, line 24:
John E. Rankin, "Thomas Alva Edison," *Vital Speeches of the Day* VI (Apr. 1, 1940), 378.

Page 36, line 3:
San Francisco Chronicle, Dec. 24, 1914, magazine section, p. 7.

Page 36, line 29:
New York Times, May 15, 1910, magazine section, p. 1.

Page 37, line 1:
Frances M. Perry, *Four American Inventors* (New York, 1901), p. 248.

THE BEST YEARS

Page 37, line 26:
"Edison, Thomas Alva," *Annual Cyclopaedia of the Year 1878* XVIII (New York, 1885).

Page 38, line 9:
Nerney, *Thomas A. Edison,* p. 64.

Page 38, line 17:
Henry Ford and Samuel Crowther, *My Friend Edison* (London, 1930), p. 83.

Page 38, lines 25 and 29:
Robert Conot, *A Streak of Luck* (New York, 1979), pp. 184–185.

Page 38, line 30:
Dickson and Dickson, *The Life,* p. 100.

Page 38, line 31:
Frank Lewis Dyer, T. Commerford Martin, and William H. Meadowcroft, *Edison: His Life and Inventions,* 2 vols. (New York, 1910), vol. I, p. 269.

Page 38, line 32:
George S. Bryan, *Edison: The Man and*

His Work (Garden City, NY, 1926), p. 73.

Page 39, lines 25 and 28:
Dickson and Dickson, *The Life,* pp. 100–101.

Page 39, line 35:
Matthew Josephson, *Edison: A Biography* (New York, 1959), pp. 166–167.

Page 40, line 8:
Conot, *A Streak of Luck,* pp. 164–165.

IMAGE TROUBLE

Page 41, line 9:
Stephen Fiske, *Off-Hand Portraits of Prominent New Yorkers* (New York, 1884), pp. 108, 113.

Page 41, line 30:
New York Herald, Dec. 21, 1879, pp. 5–6, 8.

Page 41, line 35:
New York Herald, Dec. 22, 1879, p. 3.

Page 42, line 2:
Boston Daily Advertiser, Dec. 26, 1879, p. 4.

Page 42, line 9:
Washington Post, Dec. 24, 1879, p. 2.

Page 42, line 35:
New York Sun, May 2, 1889, quoted in Dyer and Martin, *Edison,* vol. I, p. 305.

Page 42, line 37:
Scientific American C (Feb. 27, 1909), 171.

Page 43, line 12:
Josephson, *Edison,* p. 236.

Page 43, lines 21, 22, and 26:
"How Publicity Paid Edison," *Literary Digest* LVIII (July 6, 1918), 34.

Page 43, line 27:
T. C. Martin, *Edison at Seventy-Three* (New York, 1920), p. 9.

Page 43, line 32:
New York Times, Dec. 12, 1914, p. 14.

Page 44, line 2:
Josephson, *Edison,* p. 324n.

Page 44, line 12:
New Orleans Daily Picayune, Jan. 7, 1880, p. 2.

Page 44, line 15:
Quoted in "Edison's Light," *Engineering News* VII (Dec. 25, 1880), 443.

THE GREENING OF A WIZARD

Page 46, line 5:
Conot, *A Streak of Luck,* p. 109.

Page 46, line 22:
Hattie E. Macomber, "A Great Inventor," in *Stories of Great Inventors,* Young America Series (Boston, 1897).

3

INNOCENCE AND POWER: THE
MYTHOLOGY OF EDISON'S
YOUTH

INTRODUCTORY SECTION

Page 49, line 3:
Josephson, *Edison,* p. 28.

EVERYTHING COMES TO HIM WHO HUSTLES.

Page 53, line 12:
Esse V. Hathaway, "Thomas A. Edison," in *Partners in Progress* (Freeport, NY, 1935), pp. 207–209.

Page 54, line 3:
Dagobert D. Runes, ed., *The Diary and Sundry Observations of Thomas Alva Edison* (New York, 1948), p. 45.

Page 54, line 6:
"The Anecdotal Side of Edison," *Ladies' Home Journal* XV (Apr. 1898), 7.

Page 54, line 8:
Sue Guthridge, *Tom Edison: Boy Inventor* (Indianapolis, 1959), p. 136.

Page 54, line 20:
Elbridge Streeter Brooks et al., *Great Americans Every Young American Should Know* (n.p., 1910), p. 204.

Page 55, line 15:
Perry, *Four American Inventors*, p. 209.

Page 55, line 18:
Frederick Houk Law, *Modern Great Americans* (New York, 1926), p. 93.

Page 55, line 22:
Ruth Cromer Weir, *Thomas Alva Edison: Inventor* (New York, 1953), p. 38.

Page 55, line 28:
Francis Trevelyan Miller, *Thomas A. Edison: An Inspiring Story for Boys* (Philadelphia, 1940), p. 42.

Page 55, line 37:
Martin, *Edison at Seventy-Three*, p. 5.

Page 56, line 2:
William Adams Simonds, *A Boy With Edison* (Garden City, NY, 1931), p. 70.

Page 56, line 19:
Frederick Houk Law, *Great Lives: Life Stories of Great Men and Women* (New York, 1952), p. 24.

Page 56, line 20:
Miller, *Thomas A. Edison*, p. 58.

Page 56, line 22:
Inez N. McFee, *The Story of Thomas A. Edison* (New York, 1922), p. 15.

Page 56, line 29:
Weir, *Thomas Alva Edison*, p. 28.

Page 56, line 37:
W. E. Wise, *Thomas Alva Edison: The Youth and His Times* (New York, 1933), p. 54.

Page 57, line 1:
Sterling North, *Young Thomas Edison* (Boston, 1958), p. 30.

Page 57, line 3:
Arena XXXIX (June 1908), 70.

Page 57, line 4:
Perry, *Four American Inventors*, p. 219.

OUT OF A BAGGAGE CAR

Page 57, line 25:
James J. Reynolds and Mary A. Horn, *Short Stories of Famous Men* (New York, 1926), p. 207.

Page 57, line 31:
U.S. President (Hoover), *Address of President Hoover in Connection with the Celebration of the 50th Anniversary of Mr. Thomas A. Edison's Invention of the Incandescent Electric Lamp*, at Dearborn, Michigan, October 21, 1929 (Washington, DC, 1929), p. 4.

Page 58, line 22:
James D. Reid, *The Telegraph in America: Its Founders, Promoters, and Noted Men* (New York, 1879), p. 637.

Page 58, lines 22–24:
George C. Hahn, "Thomas A. Edison Commemorative Stamp," *The American Philatelist* LXIII (Aug. 1950), 858.

Page 58, line 27:
H. Addington Bruce, "Great American Inventors," *The Mentor* I (Sept. 1, 1913), 11.

Page 58, line 34:
Waldemar Kaempffert, "Scientist-Magician Who Reshaped a World," *The New York Times Magazine,* Feb. 9, 1947, p. 12.

Page 59, line 4:
New York Times, February 11, 1947, p. 26.

Page 59, line 9:
M. A. Rosanoff, "Edison in His Laboratory," *Harper's Monthly* CLXV (Sept. 1932), p. 409.

Page 59, line 10:
Independent CXVIII (Feb. 9, 1927), 219.

Page 59, line 12:
Lida Rose McCabe, "The Boyhood of Edison," *St. Nicholas,* XX (Aug. 1893), 762.

Page 59, line 14:
" 'Light's Golden Jubilee' Commemorates Edison's Invention of the Incandescent Lamp," *Railway Signaling* XXII (Nov. 1929), 404.

Page 59, line 19:
William Fleming French, "How They Got Their Education," *Illustrated World* XXVIII (Sept. 1922), 29–32.

Page 59, line 32:
Lanier, *Two Giants,* p. 43.

Page 60, line 2:
Charles O. Rice, "Mr. Edison and Science," *Commonweal* XV (Nov. 4, 1931), p. 5.

Page 60, line 6:
Gamaliel Bradford, *The Quick and the Dead* (Boston, 1929), p. 96.

Page 60, line 14:
George W. Maxey, "Thomas A. Edison, Individualist," *Vital Speeches* XVI (March 15, 1950), 332.

TATTERED TOM THE MICHIGAN TRAIN BOY, OR, THE IMPOSSIBLE DREAM

Page 63, line 26:
J. Walker McSpadden, *How They Blazed the Way: Men Who Have Advanced Civilization* (New York, 1939), p. 213.

Page 63, line 34:
Simonds, *Edison,* p. 44.

Page 63, line 36:
Francis Rolt-Wheeler, *Thomas Alva Edison* (New York, 1929), p. 24.

Page 64, line 9:
Enid LaMonte Meadowcroft, *The Story of Thomas Alva Edison* (New York, 1952), p. 48.

Page 64, line 12:
Brooks, *Great Americans,* p. 207.

Page 64, lines 13 and 14:
McFee, *The Story,* p. 16.

Page 64, line 15:
Enid Meadowcroft, *The Story,* p. 51.

Page 64, line 21:
Weir, *Thomas Alva Edison,* p. 70.

Page 64, line 23:
Miller, *Thomas A. Edison,* p. 64.

Page 64, line 34:
The Dial XVIV (Mar. 1, 1908), 126.

Page 65, line 7:
Irving Bacheller, "Making Friends With Luck," *American Magazine* CVII (Jan. 1929), 31.

Page 65, line 13:
A. H. Z. Carr, "Tuning in on Luck," *Coronet* XXXIV (May 1953), 162.

Page 65, line 32:
Mary R. Parkman, *Conquests of Invention* (New York, 1921), p. 163; the quote appears frequently elsewhere.

Page 65, line 34:
George Allison Phelps, *Holidays and Philosophical Biographies* (Los Angeles, 1951), pp. 57–65.

Page 66, line 1:
Amy Cruse, *Boys and Girls Who Became Famous* (New York, 1929), pp. 170–171.

Page 66, line 3:
Maurice Schofield, "The Centenary of Thomas Edison," *Contemporary Review* CLXXI (Feb. 1947), 116.

Page 66, line 4:
Miller, *Thomas A. Edison*, p. 89.

Page 66, line 14:
Mary Childs Nerney, *Thomas A. Edison: A Modern Olympian* (New York, 1934), p. 35.

Page 66, lines 16 and 18:
Rolt-Wheeler, *Thomas Alva Edison*, pp. 45–46.

Page 66, line 25:
J. B. McClure, ed., *Edison and His Inventions Including the Many Incidents, Anecdotes, and Interesting Particulars Connected With the Life of the Great Inventor* (Chicago, 1879), p. 33.

THE ADVENTURES OF TOM EDISON

Page 68, line 15:
Bryan, *Edison*, p. 6.

Page 69, line 11:
Nerney, *Thomas A. Edison*, p. 40.

Page 69, line 13:
McCabe, "The Boyhood of Edison," p. 761.

Page 69, line 14:
Townsend, "Edison: His Work and His Workshop," p. 598.

Page 69, line 27:
Dixon Wecter, *The Hero in America* (Ann Arbor, MI, 1963), p. 417.

Page 69, line 34:
H. Gordon Garbedian, *Thomas Alva Edison: Builder of Civilization* (New York, 1947), pp. 1–2.

Page 69, line 37:
E. Meadowcroft, *The Story*, p. 104.

Page 70, line 2:
Macomber, *Stories of Great Inventors*, p. 149.

Page 70, line 3:
Guthridge, *Tom Edison*, p. 69.

Page 70, line 5:
Law, *Modern Great Americans*, pp. 94–95.

Page 70, line 6:
Wise, *Thomas Alva Edison*, pp. 31–32, 48, 69–70; G. Glenwood Clark, *Thomas Alva Edison* (New York, 1950), p. 34.

Page 70, line 14:
New York Times, Aug. 25, 1929, p. 10.

Page 70, line 20:
Wise, *Thomas Alva Edison*, pp. 101–102.

Page 70, lines 29–32:
See E. Meadowcroft, *The Story*, pp. 3–5; Nerney, *Thomas A. Edison*, p. 31; Caroline Farrand Ballentine, "The True Story of Edison's Childhood and Boyhood," *Michigan History Magazine* IV (Jan. 1920), 168–192; Wise, *Thomas Alva Edison*, p. 25; and Miller, *Thomas A. Edison*, pp. 47, 52–53.

Page 71, line 5:
Francis Arthur Jones, *Thomas Alva Edison: Sixty Years of an Inventor's Life* (New York, 1907), p. 7.

Page 71, line 18:
"Col. Lindbergh Holding Heart of

Young U.S.," *San Francisco Chronicle,*
Dec. 31, 1929, p. 7.

Page 71, line 24:
Mabel Bartlett and Sophia Baker,
*Mothers—Makers of Men: Biographical
Sketches of Mothers of Famous Men,* 2nd
ed. rev. (New York, 1952).

Page 71, line 27:
E. Meadowcroft, *The Story,* p. 34.

EDISON'S NIGHT-JOURNEY

Page 76, lines 28–35; page 77, line 1:
Wise, *Thomas Alva Edison,* pp. 27, 28,
21; Simonds, *Edison,* p. 37.

Page 77, line 5:
Miller, *Thomas A. Edison,* pp. 24–25.

Page 77, lines 31 and 36:
Wise, *Thomas Alva Edison,* p. 173.

Page 78, line 2:
Miller, *Thomas A. Edison,* p. 107.

Page 78, line 25:
Roger Burlingame, "Before and After
Edison," in *Inventors Behind the Inventors*
(New York, 1947), p. 179.

Page 78, line 27:
John Hubert Greusel, *Thomas Alva Edi-
son: The Man, His Work and His Mind*
(Los Angeles, 1913), p. 34.

Page 79, line 2:
Dyer, Martin, and Meadowcroft, *Edison,* vol. I, p. 56.

Page 79, line 22:
Greusel, *Thomas A. Edison,* p. 34.

Page 80, line 4:
Dickson and Dickson, *The Life,* p. 30.

Page 80, line 8:
Luther Stieringer, *Catalogue of the Exhibit of Edison's Inventions at the Minneapolis Industrial Exposition, Minneapolis,*

*Minnesota, 1890, Together With a General
Description of His Work* (New York,
1890), pp. 65–66.

Page 80, lines 10 and 11:
Roselyn Hiebert and Ray Eldon
Hiebert, *Thomas Edison: American Inven-
tor* (New York, 1969), p. 49.

Page 81, line 10:
Miller, *Thomas A. Edison,* pp. 124–125.

Page 81, line 13:
Hiebert and Hiebert, *Thomas Edison,*
p. 60.

Page 84, line 1:
Rolt-Wheeler, *Thomas Alva Edison,* p.
72.

Page 84, line 3:
See Dickson and Dickson, *The Life,* pp.
57–61.

THE POWERFUL INNOCENT

Page 84, line 28:
Dickson and Dickson, *The Life,* p. 30.

Page 84, line 31:
See, for example, Charles Shapp and
Martha Shapp, *Let's Find Out About
Thomas Alva Edison* (New York, 1966),
p. 41, where he still looks twelve years
old in 1869.

4

PROGRESS TOWARD THE
ULTIMATE: EDISON AND THE
AMERICAN MONOMYTH

SEVERAL THOUSAND THINGS
THAT WON'T WORK

Page 90, line 32:
Harold C. Passer, *The Electrical Manu-*

facturers, 1875–1900 (Cambridge, MA, 1953), p. 174.

Page 91, line 25:
Josephson, *Edison*, p. 390.

Page 92, lines 7 and 14:
Alfred O. Tate, *Edison's Open Door: The Life Story of Thomas A. Edison, A Great Individualist* (New York, 1938), pp. 278–279.

Page 93, line 3:
Theodore Waters, "Edison's Revolution in Iron Mining," *McClure's Magazine* V (Nov. 1897), 82–83.

Page 93, lines 35–37; page 98, lines 1–3:
Waters, "Edison's Revolution in Iron Mining," pp. 85–86.

Page 98, line 18:
Dyer, Martin, and Meadowcroft, *Edison*, vol. II, pp. 504–505.

Page 98, line 23:
See Gordon Hendricks, *The Edison Motion Picture Myth* (Berkeley, 1961). In the same manner, Edison's claims with regard to electric traction have been disputed (see Harriet Chapman Jones Sprague, *Frank J. Sprague and the Edison Myth* [New York, 1947]).

Page 99, line 23:
Francis R. Upton, "Edison's Electric Light," *Scribner's Monthly* XIX (Feb. 1880), 535.

Page 99, line 26:
Dyer, Martin, and Meadowcroft, *Edison*, vol. II, 554.

Page 99, line 30:
George Parsons Lathrop, "Talks with Edison," *Harper's Magazine* LXXX (Feb. 1890), 434.

Page 99, line 34:
Dyer, Martin, and Meadowcroft, *Edison*, vol. II, 616.

Page 100, line 4:
Josephson, *Edison*, p. 418.

Page 100, lines 12 and 13:
New York Times, May 19, 1907, p. 6, and section 5, p. 7.

Page 100, line 26:
New York Times, Oct. 5, 1904, p. 1.

Page 100, line 33:
Conot, *A Streak of Luck*, p. 373.

DISINTEGRATORS AND DOOMSDAY MACHINES

Page 101, line 34:
Garrett P. Serviss, *Edison's Conquest of Mars* (Los Angeles, 1947), p. 6. The serial was reissued in book form.

Page 103, line 1:
New York Times, July 19, 1892, p. 1.

Page 103, line 10:
Quoted in Jones, *Thomas Alva Edison,* pp. 196–198.

Page 103, line 16:
New York Times, Apr. 16, 1917, p. 4.

Page 103, line 17:
New York Times, May 25, 1917, p. 3.

Page 103, line 22:
Edward Marshall, "What is Expected of Naval Board," *New York Times Magazine,* Aug. 8, 1915, pp. 14–15.

Page 103, line 23:
New York Times, Mar. 11, 1917, p. 3.

Page 103, line 26:
New York Times, Aug. 21, 1917, p. 2.

Page 103, line 29:
New York Times, Oct. 24, 1915, section 4, p. 1.

Page 103, line 33:
San Francisco Chronicle, Jan. 13, 1918, p. 10.

Page 103, line 35:
San Francisco Chronicle, Mar. 14, 1918, p. 11.

Page 104, lines 2 and 3:
"How Edison Won the War," *Literary Digest* LXVII (Oct. 23, 1920), 26.

Page 104, line 5:
C. H. Claudy, "The Romance of Invention—XX.," *Scientific American,* CXXIV (Mar. 19, 1921), 238.

Page 104, line 7:
New York Times, Jan. 22, 1920, p. 21.

Page 104, lines 11 and 12:
San Francisco Chronicle, Feb. 17, 1923, p. 5. See also Lloyd N. Scott, *Naval Consulting Board of the United States* (Washington, DC, 1920), pp. 160–192.

Page 104, line 15:
San Francisco Chronicle, Aug. 20, 1922, p. 2E.

". . . JUST ABOUT THE PER-FECT GUY, DISREGARDING SEX FOR A SECOND"

Page 108, line 14:
Greusel, *Thomas A. Edison,* p. 11.

Page 108, line 24:
New York Times, Oct. 11, 1908, section 5, p. 6.

Page 108, line 26:
New York Times, Oct. 11, 1914, section 4, p. 1.

Page 108, line 27:
"Mr. Edison's Reminiscences of the First Central Station," *Electrical Review* XXXVIII (Jan. 12, 1901), 63.

Page 108, line 34:
George Iles, "Some Great American Scientists: VI. Thomas Alva Edison," *Chautauquan* IL (Feb. 1908), 396. For a good example of Benson's writing, see "Thomas A. Edison, Benefactor of Humanity," *Munsey's Magazine* XLII (Dec. 1909), 419–425.

Page 109, line 1:
New York Times, Oct. 23, 1892, p. 17.

Page 109, line 4:
Townsend, "Edison: His Work and His Work-shop," p. 605.

Page 109, line 6:
Allan Benson, "Mr. Edison Says Electricity and Machinery Can Make Household Drudgery a Thing of the Past," *The Delineator* LXXVII (Jan. 1911), p. 7.

Page 109, line 7:
San Francisco Chronicle, Sept. 14, 1926, p. 5.

Page 109, line 11:
Edward Marshall, "Machine-Made Freedom, An Authorized Interview with Thomas A. Edison," *The Forum* XXVI (Oct. 1926), 495.

Page 109, line 14:
Samuel Crowther, "T.A.E.—A Great National Asset," *Saturday Evening Post* CCI (Jan. 5, 1929), 7.

Page 109, line 15:
Archibald Henderson, *Contemporary Immortals* (Freeport, NY, 1930), p. 59. Reprinted in 1968. See also Thomas A. Edison, "Inventions of the Future," *Independent* LXVIII (Jan. 6, 1910), 15–18.

Page 109, line 19:
New York Edison Co., *Thirty Years of New York, 1882–1912; Being a History of*

Electrical Development in Manhattan and the Bronx (New York, 1913), p. 19.

Page 109, footnote:
New York Times, May 19, 1907, magazine section, pt. 5, p. 7.

Page 109, line 22:
New York Times, May 19, 1907, pt. 5, p. 7.

Page 109, line 22:
Greusel, *Thomas A. Edison,* p. 10.

Page 109, lines 23–25:
"A Day with Edison at Schenectady," *Supplement to the Electrical World* XII (Aug. 25, 1888), 2.

Page 111, line 15:
Greusel, *Thomas A. Edison,* p. 81.

Page 111, line 18:
New York Times, June 11, 1878, p. 5.

Page 111, line 21:
"Edison in War Time," *American Magazine* LXXVIII (Nov. 1914), 35.

Page 111, line 23:
New Orleans Daily Picayune, Dec. 28, 1879, p. 4.

Page 111, lines 24–25, 29:
"Edison in War Time," p. 35.

Page 111, line 34:
San Francisco Chronicle, July 6, 1919, magazine section, p. 4.

Page 111, line 35:
E. J. Edwards, "The Edge of the Future: Unsolved Problems That Edison is Studying," *McClure's* I (June 1893), 37–39.

Page 111, line 36:
Greusel, *Thomas A. Edison,* p. 62. See also pp. 55–58.

Page 111, line 37; page 112, line 1:
Waters, "Edison's Revolution in Iron Mining," pp. 76, 80, 82, 93.

Page 112, line 2:
"A Night with Edison," *Scribner's Monthly* XVII (Nov. 1878), p. 97. See also Charles Barnard, "Thomas Alva Edison," *The Chautauquan* XVIII (Mar. 1894), 680.

Page 112, line 3:
Dickson and Dickson, *The Life,* p. 111.

Page 112, line 4:
"A Night with Edison," p. 88.

RICE, RICE, RICE, RICE FOREVER

Page 113, line 5:
Charles W. Price, "Thomas Alva Edison," *The Cosmopolitan* XXXIII (May 1902), 37.

Page 113, lines 17 and 18:
Allan Benson, "Edison Says Germany Excels Us," *The World Today* XXI (Nov. 1911), 1358.

Page 113, line 19:
New York Times, Oct. 22, 1911, section 5, p. 10.

Page 113, line 20:
Benson, "Edison Says Germany Excels Us," p. 1358.

Page 113, line 22:
"Thomas A. Edison," *Review of Reviews* VIII (July 1893), 68.

Page 113, line 28:
Benson, "Edison Says Germany Excels Us," p. 1359.

Page 113, line 34:
New York Times, May 15, 1910, magazine section, p. 1.

Page 114, line 10:
Greusel, *Thomas A. Edison,* pp. 56–57, 82, 88–89.

Page 114, line 12:
Ben B. Lindsey, "Mr. Edison and My Little Friend Tony," *Survey* XXX (Sept. 6, 1913), 695.

Page 114, line 14:
New York Times, Jan. 3, 1912, p. 6.

Page 114, line 17:
Allan Benson, "Edison's Dream of the New Music," *Cosmopolitan* LIV (May 1913), 798.

Page 114, line 25:
Bridget Paolucci, "Edison as Record Producer," *High Fidelity* XXVII (Jan. 1977), p. 85.

Page 114, line 26:
New York Times, Dec. 6, 1911, p. 7. The headline read: "Edison Bars Poets from List of Great."

Page 114, line 34:
New York Times, Oct. 2, 1910, magazine section, p. 1.

Page 114, line 35:
Allan Benson, "Edison Tells How to Cook," *Good Housekeeping* LVI (Mar. 1913), p. 401.

Page 114, line 36:
New York Times, Dec. 6, 1911, p. 7.

Page 115, line 6:
New York Herald, Dec. 29, 1879, p. 2.

Page 115, line 12:
Lathrop, "Talks with Edison," pp. 425–426.

Page 115, line 33:
New York Times, Jan. 3, 1912, p. 6.

Page 116, line 5:
Edward Marshall, "Thomas A. Edison on Immortality," *Columbian Magazine* III (January 1911), 612.

Page 116, lines 21–28:
Sarah Bernhardt, *Memories of My Life; Being My Personal, Professional, and Social Recollections as Woman and Artist* (New York, 1968), pp. 395–396. First ed., 1908.

Page 116, line 36:
Townsend, "Edison: His Work and His Work-shop," p. 606.

Page 117, line 16:
Tate, *Edison's Open Door,* p. 140.

TECHNOLOGY AND THE NATIONAL COVENANT

Page 119, lines 2–6:
New York Times, Oct. 8, 1911, section 2, p. 5.

Page 119, line 7:
New York Times, Oct. 22, 1911, section 5, p. 10.

Page 119, line 11:
New York Times, Oct. 29, 1911, section 5, p. 4.

Page 119, line 11:
Benson, "Edison Says Germany Excels Us," p. 1356.

Page 119, lines 12–14:
New York Times, Oct. 22, 1911, section 5, p. 10.

Page 119, line 17:
New York Times, Oct. 29, 1911, section 5, p. 4.

Page 119, line 22:
New York Times, Oct. 26, 1911, p. 10.

Page 119, line 33:
Washington Post, Oct. 22, 1929, p. 6.

Page 120, line 5:
Samuel S. Ullman, *Plays of America's Achievements* (New York, 1940), p. 151.

Page 120, line 13:
Henry W. Ruoff, *Leaders of Men*
(Springfield, MA, 1902), p. 612.

Page 120, line 18:
Rolt-Wheeler, *Thomas Alva Edison*, p. 3.

Page 120, line 19:
New York Times, Feb. 8, 1953, p. 71.

Page 120, line 25:
David Sarnoff, "A Way to Do It Better," in George E. Probst, ed., *The Indispensable Man* (New York, 1962), p. 27.

Page 120, lines 31–32:
George Lawrence Scherger, "Thomas A. Edison," in Mary Griffin Webb and Edna Lenore Webb, eds., *Famous Living Americans* (Greencastle, IN, 1915), p. 163.

Page 120, line 34:
Benson, "Thomas A. Edison, Benfactor of Humanity," p. 419.

Page 120, line 34:
Boston Evening Transcript, Oct. 19, 1931, p. 14.

Page 121, line 1:
Jennie D. Haines, "The Wonderful Century," *St. Nicholas* XXVIII (Feb. 1901), 338.

Page 121, line 3:
Benson, "Edison Says Germany Excels Us," pp. 1356–1357.

Page 121, line 6:
San Francisco Chronicle, Feb. 20, 1916, magazine section, p. 2.

Page 121, line 10:
Marshall, "Machine-Made Freedom," pp. 493–494.

Page 121, line 13:
Herbert Casson, quoted in Alan Sullivan, "Pioneers of Invention," *Collier's* LVI (Nov. 27, 1915), 38–39.

Page 121, line 15:
Henry F. Unger, "Edison—Most Useful American," *Public Utilities Fortnightly* LI (June 4, 1953), 777.

Page 121, line 18:
Thomas Alva Edison, "Thomas A. Edison: Philosopher," *The Golden Book Magazine* XIII (Apr. 1931), 79.

Page 121, line 27:
Ruoff, *Leaders of Men*, p. 624.

Page 121, line 30:
Maxey, "Thomas A. Edison, Individualist," p. 331.

Page 122, line 4:
"Edison in War Time, " p. 36.

Page 122, line 7:
New York Times, May 22, 1915, p. 16.

Page 122, lines 9–11:
New York Times, July 15, 1917, p. 6.

AN EDISONIAN BULL

Page 123, line 4:
New York Times, Oct. 2, 1910, magazine section, p. 1.

Page 123, line 13:
New York Times, Oct. 9, 1910, magazine section, p. 6.

Page 123, line 19:
New York Times, Oct. 17, 1910, p. 7.

Page 123, line 22:
New York Times, Nov. 13, 1910, magazine section, p. 1.

Page 123, line 25:
Marshall, "Thomas A. Edison on Immortality," pp. 603–612.

Page 123, line 28:
New York Times, Dec. 1, 1910, p. 1.

Page 123, line 32:
Marshall, "Thomas A. Edison on Immortality," p. 606.

Page 123, lines 30 and 35:
New York Times, Oct. 2, 1910, magazine section, pp. 1, 15.

Page 124, line 6:
New York Times, Feb. 19, 1911, section 3, p. 9.

Page 125, line 32:
Rufus R. Wilson, "Edison on Inventions: A Remarkable Interview with the Great Inventor," *Monthly Illustrator* XI (Nov. 1895), 344.

Page 125, lines 36 and 37; page 126, line 2:
Marshall, "Thomas A. Edison on Immortality," pp. 605–609.

Page 126, line 8:
Marshall, "Thomas A. Edison on Immortality," p. 605.

Page 126, line 15:
San Francisco Chronicle, Aug. 13, 1922, p. 2E.

Page 126, line 27:
Lathrop, "Talks with Edison," p. 435.

Page 126, line 32:
Wilson, "Edison on Inventions," p. 344.

Page 127, line 31:
Shaw Desmond, "Edison's Views Upon Vital Human Problems," *Strand Magazine* LXIV (Aug. 1922), 155.

Page 127, line 35:
New York Times, June 22, 1921, p. 15.

Page 127, line 36:
"High Jinks on Edison's Eightieth Birthday," *The Literary Digest* XCII (Mar. 5, 1927), 34.

Page 128, line 4:
San Francisco Chronicle, Aug. 6, 1922, p. F3.

Page 128, line 12:
New York Times, Jan. 2, 1906, p. 1.

Page 128, line 23:
Rosanoff, "Edison in His Laboratory," p. 409.

5

LOOKING BACKWARD: FROM GREAT INVENTOR TO GREAT AMERICAN

THE MENTOR OF CIVILIZATION

Page 132, line 18:
See the Association of Edison Illuminating Companies, Committee on St. Louis Exposition, *"Edisonia": A Brief History of the Early Edison Electric Lighting System* (New York, 1904).

Page 132, line 35:
McFee, *The Story of Thomas A. Edison,* p. 165. See also *Scientific American Supplement* LVII (Mar. 5, 1904), 23555–56.

Page 133, line 11:
McFee, *The Story of Thomas A. Edison,* p. 166.

Page 133, line 21:
New York Times, Feb. 12, 1911, p. 5.

Page 133, line 22:
New York Times, Feb. 11, 1913, p. 1.

Page 133, line 23:
New York Times, Feb. 12, 1913, p. 8.

Page 133, line 24:
New York Times, Feb. 12, 1914, p. 1.

Page 133, line 25:
New York Times, Feb. 11, 1920, p. 9.

Page 133, line 25:
New York Times, Feb. 12, 1922, section 2, p. 1.

Page 133, line 26:
New York Times, Feb. 12, 1927, p. 1.

Page 133, line 28:
San Francisco Chronicle, Feb. 18, 1916, p. 5.

Page 133, line 31:
New York Times, Feb. 12, 1926, p. 19.

Page 134, line 1:
New York Edison Co., *Forty Years of Edison Service, 1882–1922* (New York, 1922), p. 32.

Page 134, line 2:
Greusel, *Thomas Alva Edison,* p. 64.

Page 134, line 5:
San Francisco Chronicle, January 31, 1929, sports section, p. 1.

Page 134, line 6:
Chicago Tribune, quoted in National Electric Light Association, "In Memoriam: Thomas Alva Edison, 1847–1931," *National Electric Light Association Bulletin,* Nov. 1931, pp. 3–32. Among other significant comments on work are Barnard, "Thomas Alva Edison," pp. 678, 680; Perry, *Four American Inventors,* p. 295; *New York Times,* Jan. 7, 1906, section 3, p. 1 and May 19, 1907, section 5, p. 7; *San Francisco Chronicle,* Mar. 5, 1922, rotogravure section, p. 6 (photo of Edison punching time-clock on seventy-fifth birthday); and "Another of America's Great Sons," *Industrial Arts and Vocational Education* XXXVI (Feb. 1947), 55.

Page 134, line 9:
Brooks, *Historic Americans,* p. 460.

Page 134, line 14:
New York Times, Aug. 13, 1911, picture section, p. 7.

Page 134, line 18:
New York Times, Aug. 26, 1915, p. 1.

Page 134, lines 21 and 25:
Rosanoff, "Edison in His Laboratory," pp. 404, 408.

Page 134, line 29:
New York Times, Feb. 12, 1914, p. 1.

Page 134, line 33:
New York Times, Feb. 12, 1923, p. 15.

Page 135, line 26:
New York Times, Feb. 10, 1921, p. 13.

Page 135, lines 27 and 28:
New York Times, Feb. 12, 1921, p. 9.

Page 135, line 31:
San Francisco Chronicle, Feb. 12, 1921, p. 3.

Page 135, lines 34 and 36:
San Francisco Chronicle, Feb. 13, 1923, p. 12.

Page 136, line 2:
Time I (May 28, 1923), 19.

Page 136, line 5:
New York Times, Feb. 12, 1926, p. 19.

Page 136, line 9:
"High Jinks on Edison's Eightieth Birthday," pp. 38, 40.

Page 136, lines 18–25:
"High Jinks on Edison's Eightieth Birthday," pp. 38, 40.

Page 137, line 7:
New York Times, May 31, 1908, section 5, p. 1.

Page 137, line 10:
New York Times, Oct. 11, 1908, section 5, p. 6.

ONLY ONE MAN GOT ME RIGHT

Page 137, line 18:
B. C. Forbes, "Edison Working on How to Communicate with the Next World," *American Magazine* XC (Oct. 1920), 10. Details on the hypothesis may also be found in the following: Austin C. Lescarboura, "Edison's Views on Life and Death," *Scientific American* CXXIII (Oct. 30, 1920), 446, 458–460; *New York Times,* Jan. 23, 1921, section 7, pp. 1, 6; *San Francisco Chronicle,* Aug. 27, 1922, p. F5.

Page 138, lines 13–16:
New York Times, Jan. 23, 1921, section 7, p. 1.

Page 138, line 16:
San Francisco Chronicle, Aug. 27, 1922, p. F5.

Page 138, line 17:
Allan Benson, "Do You Know the 'Little Peoples'?" *The Dearborn Independent,* Mar. 21, 1925, p. 2.

Page 138, line 25:
Lescarboura, "Edison's Views on Life and Death," p. 446.

Page 138, line 30:
New York Times, Jan. 23, 1921, section 7, p. 6.

Page 138, line 35:
New York Times, Oct. 15, 1926, p. 11.

Page 139, line 2:
New York Times, Feb. 12, 1922, section 2, p. 2.

Page 139, line 5:
San Francisco Chronicle, Aug. 11, 1923, p. 4. The article which makes it clear that the "soul" meant no more than the "entities" is in the *New York Times,* Oct. 7, 1922, section 4, p. 1.

Page 139, line 7:
Robert K. Murray, *The Harding Era: Warren G. Harding and His Administration* (Minneapolis, 1969), p. 119.

Page 139, line 12:
San Francisco Chronicle, Aug. 13, 1923, p. 18.

Page 139, line 19:
Edward Marshall, "Has Man an Immortal Soul? An Authorized Interview with Thomas A. Edison," *The Forum* LXXVI (Nov. 1926), 640–650, xliii.

Page 139, line 28:
San Francisco Chronicle, Feb. 12, 1927, p. 3.

Page 139, line 31:
San Francisco Chronicle, Feb. 20, 1927, p. 16.

Page 139, line 32:
San Francisco Chronicle, Feb. 14, 1927, p. 22.

Page 139, line 37:
San Francisco Chronicle, Feb. 12, 1928, p. 9.

Page 140, line 21:
Quoted in Nerney, *Thomas A. Edison,* p. 223.

LOSING TRACK OF TIME

Page 140, line 25:
Meadowcroft, *The Boy's Life,* p. 150.

Page 140, line 26:
"Know-Nothing," *Time* XVI (Dec. 22, 1930), 10.

Page 140, line 27:
Benson, "Edison Tells How to Cook," p. 402.

Page 140, line 28:
"Men and Women of the Outdoor

World," *Outing* XLIV (April 1904),
p. 62.

Page 140, line 30:
Dyer, Martin, and Meadowcroft, *Edison*, vol. II, p. 528.

Page 140, line 32:
San Francisco Chronicle, Nov. 29, 1903,
p. 10.

Page 140, line 33:
Price, "Thomas Alva Edison," p. 37.

Page 140, line 34:
B. C. Forbes, *Men Who Are Making America* (New York, 1917), p. 104.

Page 141, line 2:
R. Carville, "Behold the Man," *The Golden Book Magazine* XIII (Apr. 1931),
79.

Page 141, lines 4 and 6:
Forbes, *Men Who Are Making America*,
pp. 95, 103.

Page 141, line 9:
Edmond L. Leipold, *Founders of Fortunes*, 2 vols. (Minneapolis, 1967), vol.
II, p. 16.

Page 141, line 19:
Elbert Hubbard, *Little Journeys to the Homes of the Great* (New York, 1928), p.
335.

Page 141, line 22:
Rolt-Wheeler, *Thomas Alva Edison*, p.
80.

Page 141, line 30:
Mary H. Wade, *Wonder-Workers* (Boston, 1912), p. 116.

Page 141, line 32:
Mathilda Schirmer, *Builders for Progress* (Chicago, 1950), p. 84.

Page 141, line 33:
San Francisco Chronicle, Oct. 18, 1923,
p. 1.

Page 141, line 34:
San Francisco Chronicle, Oct. 19, 1921,
p. 20.

Page 142, line 7:
W. B. Northrop, "The Unknown Edison," *Success* V (Sept. 1902), 497,
517–518.

Page 142, line 8:
Jones, *The Life*, chapter xx.

Page 142, line 11:
New York Times, Aug. 25, 1907, picture section, p. 6.

Page 142, line 13:
Meadowcroft, *The Boys' Life*, p. 237.

Page 142, line 15:
Wade, *Wonder-Workers*, pp. 119–120.

Page 142, lines 19–29:
North, *Young Thomas Edison*, pp. 52–53,
90–91, 117; Garbedian, *Thomas Alva Edison*, pp. 169, 211.

Page 142, line 33:
Conot, *A Streak of Luck*, p. 263.

Page 143, line 9:
New York Times, May 27, 1932, p. 3.

Page 143, line 10:
New York Times, Jan. 7, 1912, section
2, p. 11.

Page 143, line 13:
New York Times, Feb. 28, 1915, section
4, p. 6.

Page 143, line 16:
New York Times, July 8, 1930, p. 1.

Page 143, line 18:
Mrs. Thomas A. Edison, "Home-Making is a Profession," *Pictorial Review* XXXII (Nov. 1930), 2, 90. See also "The Only Person Edison Obeys," *Literary Digest* XLVII (November 15, 1913), 968–969, 976.

WHAT *IS* A CHINESE WINDLASS?

Page 144, line 9:
Thomas H. Uzzell, "The Future of Electricity: An Interview with Thomas A. Edison," *Collier's* LVIII (Dec. 3, 1916), 7.

Page 144, line 15:
On the topic of diet see, for example, Richard Cole Newton, "How Can a Man Keep Well and Grow Old?" *Ladies' Home Journal* XXIX (Feb. 1912), 20.

Page 144, line 20:
New York Times, Dec. 6, 1921, p. 6.

Page 144, lines 20 and 22:
New York Times, July 16, 1922, pp. 1, 2.

Page 144, line 26:
New York Times, July 23, 1922, section 2, p. 4.

Page 144, line 28:
Benson, "Mr. Edison Says," p. 7.

Page 144, line 32:
Edison, "Thomas A. Edison: Philosopher," p. 78.

Page 144, line 34:
San Francisco Chronicle, Nov. 29, 1903, p. 10.

Page 145, line 1:
New York Times, May 11, 1914, p. 20.

Page 145, line 4:
New York Times, Nov. 14, 1913, p. 2.

Page 145, line 5:
New York Times, Feb. 10, 1921, p. 13.

Page 145, lines 7 and 8:
New York Times, Oct. 27, 1914, p. 1. See also Oct. 26, 1914, p. 1.

Page 145, line 20:
New York Times, May 17, 1923, p. 18.

Page 145, line 21:
On the bad grammar see, for example, *New York Times,* Feb. 13, 1923, p. 5.

Page 145, line 22:
New York Times, Feb. 6, 1927, section 4, p. 4.

Page 146, lines 1–7:
New York Times, May 13, 1921, p. 10; May 11, 1921, p. 6.

Page 146, lines 10 and 25:
New York Times, May 8, 1921, section 2, p. 2.

Page 146, line 28:
New York Times, May 11, 1921, p. 16.

Page 146, line 33:
New York Times, May 14, 1921, p. 8.

Page 146, line 35:
W. E. Allen, "Some Points Suggested by the Edison Questionnaire," *School and Society* XIV (Nov. 12, 1921), 433.

Page 147, line 3:
New York Times, May 17, 1921, p. 8.

Page 147, line 8:
New York Times, Aug. 10, 1921, p. 14.

Page 147, lines 11–14:
Archibald Henderson, *Contemporary Immortals* (Freeport, NY, 1930), p. 58; *San Francisco Chronicle,* Feb. 12, 1929, p. 6; *San Francisco Chronicle,* Mar. 13, 1912, p. 1; *New York Times,* Dec. 6, 1911, p. 7; June 14, 1912, p. 1.

Page 147, line 17:
"What Do You Know? The Edison Questionnaire—Its Aim, Its Results, and Its Collateral Significance," *Scientific American* CXXV (Nov. 1921), 16. See also "Mr. Edison's Brain-Meter," *Literary Digest* LXIX (May 28, 1921), 29.

Page 147, line 24:
Ernest Greenwood, "Grading Human Beings: VI. General Information Tests and an Interview with Thomas A. Edison," *Independent* CXV (Dec. 12, 1925), 682.

Page 147, lines 25–33:
On the 1922 questionnaire, see Arthur Dean, "A Point of View: The New Edison Questionnaire," *Industrial Education Magazine* XXIV (Aug. 1922), 37; *New York Times,* June 11, 1922, pp. 1, 2.

Page 148, lines 10, 12, 21, and 25:
"The New Edison's Rocky Road to Success," *Literary Digest* CII (Aug. 24, 1929), 32, 36.

Page 148, line 13:
"Thomas Edison's Successor," *The Commonweal* X (May 15, 1929), 33.

Page 148, line 36:
New York Times, Nov. 22, 1922, p. 20.

Page 149, line 3:
San Francisco Chronicle, May 22, 1921, p. 8F.

Page 149, line 5:
Literary Digest LXXIV (July 1, 1922), 53.

Page 149, line 6:
Among the humorous items was a lengthy pamphlet: E. Judson, *Edison's Phunnygraph, Or, What Happened to One XYZ* (New York, 1921). "XYZ" was Edison's failing grade.

Page 149, footnote:
"Saving the Wanderers in Mr. Edison's Desert," *Literary Digest* CVI (Aug. 23, 1930), 36–37. (Quotes the *New York Telegram.*)

Page 149, line 28:
New York Times, May 18, 1921, p. 12.

ONLY TEN PERCENT OUT

Page 150, lines 20 and 25:
Wise, *Thomas Alva Edison,* pp. 127, 75.

Page 151, line 1:
Lathrop, "Talks with Edison," p. 426.

Page 151, line 3:
Greusel, *Thomas Alva Edison,* p. 10.

Page 151, line 4:
"A Talk with Edison," *Scientific American* LXVI (Apr. 2, 1892), 216.

Page 151, line 8:
Arthur Pound, "Natural-Born Scientists," *The Independent* CXVIII (Feb. 19, 1927), 219.

Page 151, line 12:
"It Could Only Happen Here," *Business Week,* Oct. 26, 1929, p. 29.

Page 151, line 15:
McFee, *The Story,* p. 64.

Page 151, line 19:
John Dos Passos, *U.S.A.: The 42nd Parallel* (New York, 1937), pp. 300–301.

Page 151, line 21:
On his need to "test out" anything and everything see, for example, Parkman, *Conquests of Invention,* p. 179. On Newton see "A Night with Edison," pp. 98–99.

Page 151, lines 24 and 25:
New York Herald, Dec. 31, 1879, p. 3.

Page 151, line 27:
Arthur J. Palmer, *Edison: Inspiration to Youth* (West Orange, NJ, 1928), p. 64.

Page 151, line 33:
Rosanoff, "Edison in His Laboratory," p. 407.

Page 152, line 1:
William Maxwell, "Edison—The 'Original Man from Missouri,' "

American Magazine LXXXV (Feb. 1918), 27.

Page 152, line 8:
Lathrop, "Talks with Edison," p. 434.

Page 152, line 11:
McFee, *The Story*, p. 156.

Page 152, line 13:
W. H. Meadowcroft, "How Edison Would Educate Children," *Leslie's Illustrated Weekly Newspaper*, Sept. 19, 1912, p. 270.

Page 152, line 18:
New York Times, Mar. 14, 1924, p. 8.

Page 152, line 22:
Meadowcroft, *The Boys' Life*, p. 217.

Page 152, line 23:
Forbes, *Men Who Are Making America*, p. 94.

Page 152, line 24:
Hubbard, *Little Journeys*, p. 331.

Page 152, line 26:
Dyer, Martin, and Meadowcroft, *Edison*, vol. II, pp. 619–620.

Page 152, line 32:
Runes, *The Diary*, pp. 45–46.

Page 152, line 36:
On the beaker anecdote see Jones, *Thomas Alva Edison*, pp. 323–324.

Page 153, line 4:
Dyer, Martin, and Meadowcroft, *Edison*, vol. II, p. 26.

Page 153, line 7:
French Strother, "The Modern Profession of Inventing," *World's Work* X (June 1905), 6295.

Page 153, line 8:
New York Times, June 12, 1923, p. 32.

Page 153, line 16:
Rosanoff, "Edison in His Laboratory," p. 408.

Page 153, line 18:
New York Times, Feb. 12, 1952, p. 30.

Page 153, line 22:
Rankin, "Thomas Alva Edison," p. 378.

Page 153, line 26:
Edison, "Thomas A. Edison: Philosopher," p. 78.

Page 153, line 30 (theater):
Paul Kempf, "Thomas A. Edison Sees a Menace for Music in the Radio," *The Musician* XXXII (Jan. 1927), 11.

Page 153, line 31 (*Les Misérables*):
John Burroughs, "Was There Ever Another Vacation Like This?" *System, The Magazine of Business*, XLIX (June 1926), 792.

Page 153, footnote:
Max J. Herzberg and Leon Mones, *Americans in Action* (New York, 1937), p. 183. (The title gives them away.)

Page 157, line 1:
Waldo P. Warren, "Edison on Invention and Inventors," *Century Magazine* LXXXII (July 1911), p. 418.

Page 157, line 1 (detective stories):
James R. Crowell, "What It Means to Be Married to a Genius," *American Magazine* CXI (Feb. 1930), 150.

Page 157, line 3:
New York Times, Feb. 13, 1923, p. 5.

Page 157, line 8:
Terry Ramsaye, *A Million and One Nights: A History of the Motion Picture*, 2 vols. (New York, 1926), vol. I, pp. 51, 63–64.

Page 157, lines 10 and 12:
New York Times, July 4, 1926, section 2, p. 1.

Page 157, line 19:
Bradford, *The Quick and the Dead,* p. 98.

Page 157, line 20:
Rolt-Wheeler, *Thomas A. Edison,* p. 194.

Page 157, line 21:
San Francisco Chronicle, Aug. 6, 1922, p. F3.

Page 157, line 22:
Nerney, *Thomas A. Edison,* p. 243.

Page 157, line 23:
Martin, *Edison At Seventy-Three,* p. 5.

Page 157, line 24:
Rosanoff, "Edison in His Laboratory," p. 411.

INHERITING THE EARTH

Page 157, line 29:
Warren, "Edison on Invention and Inventors," p. 416.

Page 157, line 30:
Tate, *Edison's Open Door,* p. 126.

Page 158, line 3:
New York Times, June 24, 1923, section 8, p. 3.

Page 158, line 13:
George E. Walsh, "With Edison in His Laboratory," *Independent* LXXV (Sept. 4, 1913), 558.

Page 158, line 14:
Benson, "Thomas A. Edison, Benefactor of Humanity," p. 419.

Page 158, lines 19 and 21:
New York Times, Jan. 5, 1913, section 2, p. 16.

Page 158, line 22:
Larston D. Farrar, "The Philosophy of Thomas Edison," *Public Utilities Fortnightly* XXXIX (Feb. 13, 1947), 201.

Page 158, line 24:
Henry Thomas, *The Story of the United States: A Biographical History of America* (New York, 1938), p. 359.

Page 158, line 27:
Henry Steele Commager, "Edison: Typical American," *Scholastic* L (Feb. 10, 1947), 13. See also Isaac F. Marcosson, "The Coming of the Talking Picture," *Munsey's Magazine* XLVIII (Mar. 1913), 958; Forbes, *Men Who Are Making America,* p. 96; *San Francisco Chronicle,* Nov. 13, 1921, p. 10E; and Emil Ludwig, "Edison, the Greatest American of the Century," *American Magazine* CXII (Dec. 1931), 98.

Page 158, line 29:
McFee, *The Story,* p. 113.

Page 158, line 29:
Waldemar Kaempffert, "A Visit to the Home of Thomas A. Edison," *Woman's Home Companion,* XXXI (Feb. 1904), 3.

Page 158, line 30:
Wilson, "Edison on Inventions," p. 344.

Page 158, line 31:
National Electric Light Association, "In Memoriam," p. 31.

Page 158, line 33:
Palmer, *Edison: Inspiration to Youth,* p. 79.

Page 159, line 1:
"The Anecdotal Side of Edison," p. 8.

Page 159, line 3 (ferryboat):
Palmer, *Edison: Inspiration to Youth,* p. 78.

Page 159, line 4:
Henry Thomas, *Thomas Alva Edison* (New York, 1958), p. 83.

Page 159, line 12:
Palmer, *Edison: Inspiration to Youth,* p. 79.

Page 159, lines 13 and 15:
Forbes, *Men Who Are Making America,* p. 96.

Page 159, line 16:
Greusel, *Thomas Alva Edison,* p. 69.

Page 159, line 20:
Palmer, *Edison: Inspiration to Youth,* p. 79.

Page 159, line 23:
New York Times, June 4, 1926, p. 1.

Page 159, line 30:
Brooks, *Historic Americans,* p. 465.

Page 159, line 33:
Dyer, Martin, and Meadowcroft, *Edison,* vol. II, pp. 742–743.

Page 159, line 34:
Harry J. Baker, *Biographical Sagas of Will Power* (New York, 1970), p. 260.

Page 159, line 34 (Commons):
San Francisco Chronicle, Aug. 10, 1911, p. 2.

Page 159, line 35; page 160, line 2:
Forbes, *Men Who Are Making America,* p. 96.

Page 160, line 3:
New York Times, Sept. 17, 1905, section 3, p. 2.

Page 160, line 4:
Thomas A. Edison, "Today and Tomorrow," *Independent* LXXVII (Jan. 5, 1914), 25.

Page 160, line 6:
Grace Humphrey, *Children of Necessity:*

Stories of American Inventions (Indianapolis, 1925), p. 230.

Page 160, line 9:
Miller, *Thomas A. Edison,* p. 264.

Page 160, line 10:
Palmer, *Edison: Inspiration to Youth,* p. 56.

Page 160, line 12:
See, for example, Bradford, *The Quick and the Dead,* p. 106.

Page 160, line 14:
Greusel, *Thomas Alva Edison,* pp. 64–65.

Page 160, line 15:
Pound, "Natural-Born Scientists," p. 219.

Page 160, line 17:
Benson, "Edison Tells How to Cook," p. 402.

Page 160, line 21:
New York Times, Oct. 22, 1916, p. 13.

Page 160, line 23:
Barnard, "Thomas Alva Edison," p. 678.

Page 160, line 24:
New York Times, May 5, 1910, p. 20.

Page 160, line 27:
Scherger, "Thomas A. Edison," p. 173.

Page 160, line 28:
Gamaliel Bradford, "Thomas Alva Edison, Worker," *Nation's Business* XVIII (Sept. 1930), 52.

Page 160, line 29:
Nerney, *Thomas A. Edison,* p. 198.

Page 160, line 37:
Rolt-Wheeler, *Thomas Alva Edison,* pp. 180–181.

Page 161, line 1:
Wade, *Wonder-Workers,* p. 115.

SWAPPING YARNS

Page 162, line 6:
John Burroughs quoted in Harvey S. Firestone and Samuel Crowther, *Men and Rubber: The Story of Business* (Garden City, NY, 1926), pp. 195, 215.

Page 162, line 9:
San Francisco Chronicle, August 30, 1916, p. 20.

Page 162, line 14:
San Francisco Chronicle, July 24, 1921, p. 2. See also Mary B. Mullet, "Four Big Men Become Boys Again," *American Magazine* LXXXVII (Feb. 1919), 39.

Page 162, line 18:
Firestone and Crowther, *Men and Rubber,* p. 226.

Page 162, line 23:
San Francisco Chronicle, July 24, 1921, p. 1.

Page 162, line 28:
San Francisco Chronicle, Aug. 20, 1924, p. 1.

Page 162, line 31:
San Francisco Chronicle, Aug. 21, 1924, p. 22.

Page 163, line 4:
San Francisco Chronicle, Sept. 14, 1924, rotogravure section, p. 3.

Page 163, line 10:
New York Times, Oct. 11, 1914, section 4, p. 1.

Page 163, line 12:
Lathrop, "Talks with Edison," p. 426.

Page 163, line 14:
Isaac F. Marcosson, *Adventures in Interviewing* (New York, 1919), p. 207.

Page 163, line 15:
San Francisco Chronicle, Feb. 12, 1927, p. 6.

Page 163, line 19:
New York Times, Feb. 13, 1923, p. 1.

Page 163, line 21:
New York Times, Feb. 12, 1924, p. 16.

Page 163, line 22:
San Francisco Chronicle, Feb. 12, 1927, p. 6.

Page 163, lines 29 and 30:
See, for example, *N.E.L.A. Bulletin* XVI (Sept. 1929), picture folio; John F. Sinclair, "Some Builders of Prosperity," *Review of Reviews* LXXIX (Jan. 1929), 48; *New York Times,* Mar. 18, 1930, p. 56; June 11, 1930, p. 1.

Page 164, line 5:
New York Times, March 20, 1927, section 9, p. 8.

Page 164, line 9:
Crowther, "T.A.E.—A Great National Asset," p. 129.

Page 164, line 11:
New York Times, Sept. 25, 1927, section 8, p. 4.

Page 164, line 15:
New York Times, Dec. 4, 1929, p. 33.

Page 164, line 17:
New York Times, June 18, 1929, p. 2. It is interesting that Faraday, Edison's boyhood hero, had also sought the chemical formula for rubber.

YOU CAN'T GO HOME AGAIN

Page 164, line 18–page 165, line 12:
Sources for this paragraph are Reynold M. Wik, *Henry Ford and Grass-Roots America* (Ann Arbor, MI, 1972), p. 207; *New York World,* Oct. 22, 1929, p. 2.

Page 165, line 19:
Robert Silverberg, *Light for the World:*

Edison and the Power Industry (Princeton, NJ, 1967), p. 5.

Page 166, line 14 (apples):
New York World, Oct. 22, 1929, section 1, p. 2.

Page 166, line 14 (peach):
New York World, Oct. 22, 1929, section 1, p. 2.

Page 167, lines 1–26:
Sources for this paragraph are *New York World,* Oct. 21, 1929, p. 2; Oct. 22, 1929, p. 2; *New York Times,* Oct. 22, 1929, pp. 1, 2.

Page 167, line 15:
"Edison's Golden Day," *Literary Digest* CIII (Nov. 2, 1929), 10.

Page 168, lines 5 and 11:
New York Times, Oct. 22, 1929, pp. 2, 3; *New York World,* Oct. 22, 1929, p. 1.

Page 168, line 16:
Silverberg, *Light for the World,* p. 8.

6

THE LAST GREAT HAYSEED: THE POSTHUMOUS IMAGE

HUMANIZING THE HUMANITARIAN

Page 174, lines 19 and 20:
N.E.L.A. Bulletin XVI (Sept. 1929), 557, 563.

Page 176, line 1:
Edward Marshall, "Youth of To-day and Tomorrow; An Authorized Interview with Thomas A. Edison," *The Forum* LXXVII (Jan. 1927), 41.

Page 176, line 3:
New York Times, Oct. 18, 1931, p. 2.

Page 176, line 5:
Schirmer, *Builders for Progress,* p. 85.

Page 176, line 10:
John F. O'Hagan, "The Human Edison," *The Commonweal* XIX (Feb. 16, 1934), 437–438.

Page 176, line 13:
J. G. Crowther, *Famous American Men of Science* (Freeport, NY, 1969 [1937]), p. 311.

Page 176, line 20:
Rosanoff, "Edison in His Laboratory," pp. 414–415.

Page 176, line 22:
Jonathan Hughes, *The Vital Few: American Economic Progress and Its Protagonists* (Boston, 1965), p. 165.

Page 176, line 25:
New York Daily Tribune, Sept. 28, 1878, p. 4.

Page 176, line 29:
"A Talk with Edison," p. 216.

Page 176, line 31:
Meadowcroft, *The Boys' Life,* p. 235.

Page 177, line 19:
John Dos Passos, "Edison and Steinmetz: Medicine Men," *The New Republic* LXI (Dec. 18, 1929), 104.

Page 177, line 24:
"A Revealing Episode," *The Christian Century* LXVI (Nov. 6, 1929), 1370.

Page 177, line 33:
Richard Hülsenbeck, "Edison Passes On," *The Living Age* CCCXLI (Dec. 1931), 327.

Page 180, line 13:
Nerney, *Thomas A. Edison,* p. 254; p. 21.

Page 180, line 14:
San Francisco Chronicle, Aug. 6, 1922, p.

F3; Aug. 13, 1922, p. 2E; Aug. 20, 1922, p. 2E.

Page 180, line 15:
New York Times, Oct. 25, 1928, p. 26.

Page 180, line 19:
New York Times, Oct. 18, 1931, p. 3.

Page 181, line 6:
Rosanoff, "Edison in His Laboratory," pp. 403–415.

Page 181, line 9:
John Chamberlain, *New York Times,* Mar. 8, 1931, book review section, p. 5.

Page 181, line 25:
National Electric Light Association, "In Memoriam," pp. 25, 27. (Quotes the *Chicago Tribune.*)

Page 181, line 28:
New York Times, Jan. 23, 1925, p. 1.

Page 181, line 32:
Herman Hagedorn, *Americans, A Book of Lives* (New York, 1946), p. 43.

HOW THRILLED HE WOULD BE

Page 182, lines 3 and 5:
New York Times, Oct. 19, 1931, p. 27.

Page 182, line 7:
Dos Passos, "Edison and Steinmetz," p. 103.

Page 182, line 11:
Rosanoff, "Edison in His Laboratory," p. 411.

Page 182, line 21:
New York Times, Feb. 9, 1947, section 6, p. 45.

Page 182, line 24:
Leo Rosten, "They Made Our World: Edison," *Look* XXVIII (Feb. 25, 1964), 100–102.

Page 182, line 27:
Morrell Heald, "Technology in American Culture," in John A. Hague, ed., *American Character and Culture: Some Twentieth Century Perspectives* (DeLand, FL, 1964), p. 113.

Page 183, line 25:
Simonds, *Edison,* p. 314.

Page 184, lines 7 and 26:
Conot, *A Streak of Luck,* pp. 211–212, 258–259.

Page 187, line 10:
James V. Toner, *The Boston Edison Story, 1886–1951, 65 Years of Service!* (New York, 1951), pp. 8–9.

Page 187, line 12:
Unger, "Edison—Most Useful American," p. 777.

Page 187, line 15:
David Sarnoff, *Edison (1847–1931)* (New York, 1948), p. 16.

Page 187, line 16:
New York Times, June 16, 1961, p. 5.

Page 187, line 23:
New York Times, Feb. 8, 1953, p. 71.

Page 187, line 29:
New York Times, Feb. 10, 1947, p. 28. The *Washington Post* (Feb. 9, 1947, p. 6m) was the most suggestive about the uranium nitrate.

Page 188, line 7:
New York Times, Feb. 12, 1957, p. 14.

Page 188, line 9:
"National Edison Birthday Celebration Planned by Electric Industry," *Edison Electric Institute Bulletin* XXV (Jan. 1957), p. 23.

Page 188, line 12:
Walker L. Cisler, quoted in Probst, ed., *The Indispensable Man,* pp. 93, 95.

Page 188, line 20:
Sacramento Union, Feb. 2, 1947, p. 8.

Page 188, line 21:
"Nation-Wide Observances Honor Anniversary of Thomas Alva Edison's Birth," *Edison Electric Institute Bulletin* XX (Mar. 1952), 70.

Page 188, line 31:
New York Times, Oct. 12, 1969, section 10, p. 21.

Page 188, line 37:
New York Times, Feb. 12, 1933, p. 35.

Page 189, line 6:
New York Times, Oct. 22, 1949, p. 28.

Page 189, line 9:
New York Times, Oct. 21, 1949, p. 24.

Page 189, line 12:
New York Times, Feb. 12, 1956, p. 5.

Page 190, line 6:
New York Times, Feb. 10, 1947, p. 28.

Page 190, lines 8 and 14:
New York Times, Feb. 12, 1947, p. 27.

Page 190, line 17:
Los Angeles Times, Feb. 11, 1947, section 2, p. 4.

Page 190, line 18:
New York Times, July 25, 1949, p. 15.

Page 190, line 25:
New York Times, Feb. 14, 1971, section 4, p. 3.

Page 190, line 31:
New York Times, Nov. 18, 1927, p. 48.

Page 190, line 34:
"Honoring Mr. Edison," *World's Work* LVII (Dec. 1928), p. 122.

Page 191, line 11:
A. Horschitz and Paul Oestreich, *Edison and His Competition: A Critical Study,*

Alice Hohenemser-Salt, trans. (London, 1932), pp. 49, 54.

Page 192, line 5:
Edmond Konrad, *The Wizard of Menlo* (London, 1935), pp. 39–40, 84, 92–96.

Page 192, line 29:
Kurt Vonnegut, Jr., "Tom Edison's Shaggy Dog," *Collier's* CXXXI (Mar. 14, 1953), 46, 48–49.

STICKING LIKE HELL

Page 193, line 13:
Jones, *Thomas Alva Edison,* pp. 346–347.

Page 193, lines 26–29:
Miller, *Thomas A. Edison*; Palmer, *Edison: Inspiration to Youth*; Sarah Knowles Bolton, *Lives of Poor Boys Who Became Famous* (New York, 1962 [1947]); John T. Faris, *Winning Their Way: Boys Who Learned Self-Help* (New York, 1909); Baker, *Biographical Sagas of Will Power*; Humphrey, *Children of Necessity.*

Page 194, line 2:
New York Times, Nov. 26, 1911, p. 1.

Page 194, line 8:
U.S., President, 1923–1928 (Coolidge), *Presentation of a Medal Granted By the Congress of the United States to Thomas A. Edison, Washington, D.C., October 20, 1928* (Washington, 1928), p. 2.

Page 194, line 12:
Quoted in National Electric Light Association, "In Memoriam," p. 25. Passages of this type are numerous; some of the better ones may be found in Kaempffert, "A Visit to the Home of Thomas A. Edison," p. 4; Rolt-Wheeler, *Thomas Alva Edison,* p. 136; McFee, *The Story,* pp. 157, 166, 172;

Scherger, "Thomas A. Edison," p. 163; *Chicago Journal of Commerce and La Salle Street Journal,* Oct. 20, 1931, p. 3; Association of Edison Illuminating Companies, *Edison: Honored Throughout the World* (New York, 1929), p. 43.

Page 194, line 14:
See, for example, the *San Francisco Chronicle,* July 14, 1930, p. 5.

Page 194, line 26:
Rosanoff, "Edison in His Laboratory," p. 406.

Page 194, line 28:
Philip G. Hubert, Jr., *Men of Achievement: Inventors* (New York, 1894), p. 249.

Page 194, line 29:
Brooks, *Historic Americans,* p. 226.

Page 194, line 33:
David Riesman, Nathan Glazer, and Reuel Denney, *The Lonely Crowd: A Study of the Changing American Character* rev. ed. (Garden City, NY, 1953), p. 150.

Page 195, line 6:
Meadowcroft, *The Boys' Life,* p. 236.

Page 195, line 10:
New York Times, Feb. 12, 1924, p. 10.

Page 195, line 11:
"The Anecdotal Side of Edison," p. 7.

Page 195, lines 12 and 13:
Rolt-Wheeler, *Thomas Alva Edison,* pp. 3–4.

Page 195, line 13:
McFee, *The Story,* p. 141.

Page 195, line 14:
Association of Edison Illuminating Companies, "Edisonia," p. 79.

Page 195, lines 15 and 19:
Dyer, Martin, and Meadowcroft, *Edison,* vol. II, p. 566.

Page 195, line 22:
"Edison Under Fire," *American Magazine* LXXIX (Mar. 1915), 11.

Page 195, line 24:
San Francisco Chronicle, Oct. 20, 1915, p. 18.

Page 196, line 12:
Phelps, *Holidays and Philosophical Biographies,* pp. 52–55.

Page 196, line 15:
See Albert Shaw, "Mr. Edison as the Typical American," *Review of Reviews* LXXXIV (Sept. 1931), 17–18; Forbes, *Men Who Are Making America,* pp. 93–95; Hubbard, *Little Journeys,* p. 344; Charles Edison, "My Most Unforgettable Character," *Reader's Digest* LXXIX (Dec. 1961), 172–180.

Page 196, line 24:
New York World Telegram, Aug. 15, 1931, p. 11.

Page 196, line 26:
Henderson, *Contemporary Immortals,* p. 46. See also "Throwing New Light on a Great Inventor," *Current Opinion* LXIX (July 1920), 45–48; and Thomas A. Edison, "How I Would Double the Volume of a Business," *System, the Magazine of Business* XLIV (Sept. 1923), 265–268, 330–332.

Page 196, lines 28–30:
C. Hartley Grattan, "Thomas Alva Edison (1847–1931): An American Symbol," *Scribner's Magazine* XLIV (Sept. 1933), 152.

Page 197, line 2:
James Rorty, "The Inventor Enters

Heaven," *The Nation* CXXX (March 12, 1930), 295–296.

Page 197, lines 6 and 8:
Henry Junior Taylor, "Edison Didn't Succeed Alone," in *An American Speaks His Mind* (Garden City, NY, 1957 [1945]), pp. 118–119.

Page 197, line 11:
Roderic Peters, "Tom Edison's Sales Techniques," *Nation's Business* LIX (Mar. 1971), 52.

Page 197, line 13:
"The 10 Greatest Men of American Business—As You Picked Them," *Nation's Business* LIX (Mar. 1971), 44–50.

THE AMERICAN WAY

Page 198, line 23:
Nerney, *Thomas A. Edison,* pp. 288–289.

Page 198, line 30:
Tate, *Edison's Open Door,* pp. 121, 123.

Page 198, line 35:
Virginia Gazette, Jan. 3, 1947, p. 14.

Page 199, lines 1 and 4:
Maxey, "Thomas A. Edison, Individualist," p. 332.

Page 199, lines 6–8:
Marshall, "Machine-Made Freedom," pp. 493, 495.

Page 199, lines 10–14:
Frank M. Tait, "Thomas A. Edison: Prototype for American Enterprise," *Edison Electric Institute Bulletin* XV (Mar. 1947), p. 86.

Page 199, line 18:
Vannevar Bush, *Endless Horizons* (Washington, DC, 1946), p. 149.

Page 199, line 23:
David Sarnoff, in Probst, ed., *The Indispensable Man,* p. 37.

Page 199, line 30:
Farrar, "The Philosophy of Thomas Edison," p. 202.

Page 199, line 34:
Albert Shaw, "Mr. Edison's Views on Life and Work," *Review of Reviews* LXXXV (Jan. 1932), 31.

Page 199, line 35:
Miller, *Thomas A. Edison,* p. 299.

Page 200, lines 2 and 7:
Tate, *Edison's Open Door,* pp. 312, 288–289.

Page 200, line 12:
Los Angeles Times, Feb. 11, 1947, section 2, p. 2.

Page 200, line 16:
New York Times, Feb. 11, 1951, p. 60.

Page 200, lines 26–33:
George E. Sokolsky, "Lincoln and Edison," *Vital Speeches* XV (Apr. 1, 1949), 377–378.

Page 200, line 35:
For examples of Lincoln comparisons, see, respectively, Greusel, *Thomas Alva Edison,* p. 60; Benson, "Do You Know the 'Little Peoples'?" p. 2; "Naval Consulting Board Personnel," *Engineering Magazine* L (Nov. 1915), 199; and Waters, "Edison's Revolution," p. 83.

Page 200, line 37:
Chase-Shawmut Co., *The Fuse: Its Story from the Sources of Its Invention Through Its Progress to Maturity* (Newburyport, MA, 1943), p. 6.

Page 201, line 8:
Maxey, "Thomas A. Edison, Individualist," p. 334.

Page 201, line 14:
New York Times, Feb. 11, 1947, p. 26.

Page 201, line 16:
Chicago Tribune, Feb. 11, 1947, p. 32.

Page 201, line 20:
Wall Street Journal (West Coast ed.),
Feb. 11, 1947, p. 3.

Page 201, line 22:
Tait, "Thomas A. Edison," pp. 69–70.

Page 201, line 33:
Farrar, "The Philosophy of Thomas
Edison," p. 202.

Page 202, line 4:
New York Times, Nov. 15, 1931, section
9, p. 8.

Page 202, line 5:
Jonathan Hughes, *The Vital Few:
American Economic Progress and its Protag-
onists* (Boston, 1965), p. 150.

7

REPRISE: THE IMPOSSIBLE
DREAM

INTRODUCTORY SECTION

Page 205, line 28:
"A Day with Edison at Schenectady,"
pp. 1–2.

Page 206, line 9:
South Carolina Educational Television, "Legacy of a Genius: The Story
of Thomas Alva Edison," 1979.

THE NEW PASTORALISM

Page 207, line 15:
New York American, Oct. 22, 1929, p. 4.

ANTECHAMBER TO OBLIVION:
THE MYTH IN THE SEVENTIES

Page 208, line 30:
New York Times, Oct. 7, 1927, p. 17.

Page 209, line 17:
See, for example, William J. Broad,
"Rival Centennial Casts New Light
on Edison," *Science* CCIV (Apr. 1979),
32–36.

Page 211, line 1:
Jane M. Hatch, *The American Book of
Days,* 3rd ed. (New York, 1978), p.
164.

Page 211, line 5:
New York Times, Feb. 11, 1974, p. 74.

Page 211, line 11:
New York Times, Feb. 10, 1975, p. 59.

Page 211, lines 16 and 17:
See, for example, Keith Ellis, *Thomas
Edison: Genius of Electricity* (Hove, Sus-
sex, Great Britain, 1974).

Page 211, line 25:
New York Times, Apr. 24, 1977, section
2, p. 27.

Page 211, line 26 (laboratory):
Hans Fantel, "The First 100 Years of
the Phonograph," *Popular Mechanics*
CXLVIII (Aug. 1977), 87.

Page 211, line 26 (Cros):
See Leonard Marcus, "Recordings Be-
fore Edison," *High Fidelity* XXVII
(Jan. 1977), 58–67; and *New York
Times,* Apr. 24, 1977, section 2, p. 31.

Page 211, line 30:
Chicago Tribune, Oct. 22, 1979, section
1, p. 7.

Page 211, line 31:
Sacramento Bee, Oct. 22, 1979, people section, p. A3.

Page 211, line 36:
The Denver Post, Oct. 14, 1979, section B, p. 21.

Page 212, line 1:
Joseph Barbato, "Bringing Edison to Light," *Change* XI (Mar. 1979), 40.

Page 212, line 2:
Fred Shunaman, "Pioneers of Radio," *Radio Electronics* XLIX (Sept. 1978), 46.

Page 212, line 7:
John F. Wilson and Grace Hawthorne, "The Electric Sunshine Man" (Carol Stream, IL, 1978). [LP HR926, Somerset Press]

Page 212, lines 10 and 11:
Edison Centennial News II (Aug. 1979), 7.

Page 212, line 20:
General Electric, *Thomas Edison: Reflections of a Genius,* 1978.

Page 212, line 28:
Thomas Alva Edison Foundation, "Fact Sheet" (printed by the International Committee for the Centennial of Light, Greenwich, CT, 1979).

Page 212, line 32:
Edison Centennial News II (Aug. 1979), 3.

Page 213, line 5:
Edison Centennial News, "Perspectives on Thomas Alva Edison and His Centennial of Light (1879–1979)" (Greenwich, CT, 1979), p. 3.

Page 213, lines 7 and 9:
Washington Post, Nov. 25, 1978.

Page 213, line 16:
International Committee for the Centennial of Light, *The Search for Tomorrow's Edisons* (Greenwich, CT, 1979).

Page 213, line 25:
International Committee for the Centennial of Light, "How We Can Best Honor Edison Today," Sample Speech No. 1 (Greenwich, CT, 1979), pp. 5–7.

Page 213, line 33:
"Thomas Alva Edison: He Lit Up Our Lives," *Business Week* XVII (Apr. 23, 1979), 13.

Page 213, line 36:
International Committee for the Centennial of Light, "Has the Edison Legacy Been Lost in the United States?" Sample Speech No. 2 (Greenwich, CT, 1979), p. 15.

Page 214, line 2:
"The Sad State of Innovation," *Time* CXIV (Oct. 22, 1979), 71.

Page 214, line 8:
Cincinnati Enquirer, Feb. 10, 1979.

Page 214, lines 14 and 15:
Marshall, "Youth of Today and Tomorrow," pp. 41–42, 45.

Page 214, line 26:
Thomas Hughes, "The Man of a Thousand Patents," *New York Times Book Review,* Nov. 13, 1977, p. 4.

Page 214, line 30:
"American Pie," *Economist* CCLXV (Oct. 15, 1977), 132.

Page 215, line 10:
Melvin Maddocks, "Did Edison Invent the 'Off' Switch?" *Christian Science Monitor,* Oct. 22, 1979, p. 22.

Page 215, line 19:
Henderson, *Contemporary Immortals*, p. 65.

Page 215, line 30:
Tait, "Thomas A. Edison: Prototype for American Enterprise," p. 70.

Page 215, lines 35 and 36 (father of . . .):
See, for example, "Science and the Citizen," *Scientific American* CCXXVII (Dec. 1972), 43; "Giants of the Electric Century 1874–1974: Thomas Alva Edison," *Electrical World* CLXXX (July 1, 1973), 29; *The Saturday Evening Post* CCXLVIII (July/Aug. 1976), 49.

WE'LL GET IT YET: THE MAN
IN THE EIGHTIES

Page 216, lines 24 and 26:
Gilbert A. Harrison, ed., *Public Persons* (New York, 1976), p. 111.

Page 217, line 12:
Rosanoff, "Edison in His Laboratory," pp. 409–410.

Page 217, line 33:
Conot, *A Streak of Luck,* p. 145.

Page 218, line 18:
Rosanoff, "Edison in His Laboratory," p. 404.

Page 220, line 36:
Boston Evening Transcript, Oct. 19, 1931, p. 14.

Page 220, line 37:
Louis Untermeyer, *Makers of the Modern World* (New York, 1955), p. 227.

Page 221, line 6:
New York Times, Aug. 13, 1977, p. 47.

Page 221, line 8:
London Times, May 2, 1972, p. 8.

Page 221, line 12 (future):
New York Times, Sept. 5, 1932, p. 13.

Page 221, line 12 (grit):
New York Times, Sept. 29, 1921, p. 1.

Page 221, line 15:
New York Times, July 31, 1930, p. 3.

Page 221, line 18:
San Francisco Chronicle, June 12, 1931, p. 3.

BIBLIOGRAPHY OF EDISON LITERATURE

BOOKS AND PAMPHLETS

Andre, Luc. *Thomas Edison.* Appleton, WI, 1964. [J] *

Association of Edison Illuminating Companies, Committee on St. Louis Exposition. *"Edisonia"; A Brief History of the Early Edison Electric Lighting System.* New York, 1904.

Association of Edison Illuminating Companies. "The Development of the Incandescent Electric Lamp Up to 1879." Unpub. New York: Association of Edison Illuminating Companies, 1929. [Pamphlet]

——— . *Edison: Honored Throughout the World.* New York, 1929. [Pamphlet]

Beasley, Rex. *Edison.* Philadelphia, 1964.

Bellis, Hannah. *Edison and Marconi.* London, 1938. [Y]

A Brief Biography of Thomas Alva Edison. [Pamphlet distributed by the Edison National Historic Site, West Orange, NJ]

Bryan, George S. *Edison: The Man and His Work.* Garden City, NY, 1926.

Campbell, Helen Mary Le Roy. *Story of Edison.* Darien, CT, 1912. [Y]

Clark, G. Glenwood. *Thomas Alva Edison.* New York, 1952. [Y]

Clark, Ronald W. *Edison: The Man Who Made the Future.* New York, 1977.

Compere, Mickie. *The Story of Thomas Alva Edison, Inventor: The Wizard of Menlo Park.* New York, 1964. [J]

Conot, Robert. *A Streak of Luck.* New York, 1979.

Cook, James. *Edison: The Man Who Turned Darkness into Light.* Southfield, MI, 1978. [Pamphlet]

Cooper, Frederic Taber. *Thomas A. Edison.* Great Men Series. New York, 1914.

Cousins, Margaret. *The Story of Thomas Alva Edison.* New York, 1965. [Y]

Davison, George. *Beehives of Invention: Edison and His Laboratories.* Washington, DC, 1977. [Pamphlet]

Denslow, Van Buren, and Parker, P. J. M. *Thomas A. Edison and Samuel F. B. Morse,* n.p.: Cassell, 1887.

Dickson, W. K. L., and Dickson, Antonia. *Edison's Invention of the Kineto-Phonograph.* Los Angeles, 1939. (Orig. pub. in *Century Magazine,* 1894.)

——— . *The Life and Inventions of Thomas Alva Edison.* New York, 1892.

Dyer, Frank Lewis; Martin, Thomas Commerford; and Meadowcroft, William Henry. *Edison: His Life and Inventions.* 2 vols. New York, 1910.

Edgar, C. L. *Edison's Place in the Electrical Industry.* n.p.: Edison Electric Illuminating Company of Boston, 1926. [Pamphlet]

Edison Pioneers. "Addresses Delivered at the Dedication of the Commemorative Tablet Near the Site of the Edison Laboratories and Workshops at Menlo Park, NJ, May 16, 1925." Unpub. (in Library of Congress.) [Pamphlet]

Edison Pioneers. *The Story of Menlo Park.* New York, 1925. [Pamphlet]

Edison, Thomas A. *A Proposed Amendment to the Federal Reserve Banking System: Plan and Notes.* Orange, NJ, [1921?]. [Pamphlet]

——— . *Lighting Country Houses by Electricity.* Orange, NJ, 1911. [Pamphlet]

* Juvenile books are indicated by [J], works for older youths by [Y].

Ellis, Keith. *Thomas Edison: Genius of Electricity.* Hove, Sussex, Great Britain, 1974. [J]

Fritz, Florence. *Bamboo and Sailing Ships: The Story of Thomas A. Edison and Fort Myers, Florida.* Fort Myers, FL, 1949. [Pamphlet]

Frost, Lawrence A. *The Edison Album: A Pictorial Biography of Thomas Alva Edison.* Seattle, 1969.

Garbedian, H. Gordon. *Thomas Alva Edison: Builder of Civilization.* New York, 1947. [Y]

Garbit, Frederick J. *The Phonograph and Its Inventor Thomas Alvah [sic] Edison; Being a Description of the Invention and a Memoir of Its Inventor.* Boston, 1878. [Pamphlet]

Gordon, Sydney. *Thomas Alva Edison, 1847–1931; His Life, Work and Experiments.* Pageant of Scientists Series. n.p.: Blackwell, 1966. [Y]

Graham, Winifred Wise. *Thomas Alva Edison.* New York, 1950. [J]

Greenwood, Ernest. *Edison: The Boy—The Man.* New York, 1929.

Greusel, John Hubert. *Thomas Alva Edison: The Man, His Work and His Mind.* Los Angeles, 1913.

Guthridge, Sue. *Tom Edison: Boy Inventor.* Indianapolis, 1959. (Orig. pub. 1947.) [J]

Hanford, Barbara. *Thomas Edison.* Men of Genius Series. New York, 1964. [J]

Hendricks, Gordon. *Beginning of the Biograph: The Story of the Invention of the Mutoscope and the Biograph and Their Supplying Camera.* New York, 1964.

——— . *The Edison Motion Picture Myth.* Berkeley, 1961.

——— . *The Kinetoscope: America's First Commercially Successful Motion Picture Exhibitor.* New York, 1966.

——— . *Origins of the American Film.* New York, 1972.

Hiebert, Roselyn, and Hiebert, Ray Eldon. *Thomas Edison: American Inventor.* Immortals of Engineering Series. New York, 1969. [Y]

Holland, Maurice. *Edison's Organization Method.* New York, 1933. [Pamphlet]

Horschitz, A., and Oestreich, Paul. *Edison and His Competition: A Critical Study.* Translated by Alice Hohenemser-Salt. London, 1932. (Orig. pub. 1931.)

Hughes, Thomas P. *Thomas Edison: Professional Inventor.* London, 1976. [Pamphlet]

Hutchings, David W. *Edison at Work: The Thomas A. Edison Laboratory at West Orange, New Jersey.* New York, 1969.

International Committee for the Centennial of Light. *The Search for Tomorrow's Edisons.* Greenwich, CT, 1979. [Pamphlet]

Jones, Francis Arthur. *The Life Story of Thomas Alva Edison.* 2nd ed., rev. New York, 1924.

——— . *Thomas Alva Edison: Sixty Years of an Inventor's Life.* New York, 1907.

Josephson, Matthew. *Edison.* New York, 1959.

Judson, E. *Edison's Phunnygraph, or What Happened to One XYZ: A Story.* New York, 1921.

Kaufman, Mervyn D. *Thomas Alva Edison: Miracle Maker.* New York, 1968. (Orig. pub. in Discovery Biography Series, 1962.) [J]

Keim, Albert. *Edison.* Les Grands Hommes Series. Paris, 1913.

Kennelly, Arthur E. *Biographical Memoir of Thomas Alva Edison, 1847–1931.* National Academy of Sciences of the United States of America, Biographical Memoirs Series. Washington, DC, 1932. [Pamphlet]

Kenyon, Edith C. *Thomas Alva Edison: The Telegraph Boy Who Became a Great Inventor.* London, 1895.

Kurland, Gerald. *Thomas Edison: Father of Electricity and Master Inventor of our Modern Age.* Charlotteville, NY, 1972. [Pamphlet]

Literary Digest. Edison's Posers Answered in Various Ways. New York, 1921. [Pamphlet]

Lombard, Rose. *Behind the Biographies; A Personal Study of Thomas Alva Edison.* n.p., 1951.

Lowitz, Sadyebeth, and Lowitz, Anson. *Tom Edison Finds Out.* Rev. ed. Minneapolis, 1967. (Orig. pub. 1940.) [J]

McChesney, L. W. *A Light is Extinguished.* n.p.: by author, 1932. [Pamphlet]

McClure, J. B., ed. *Edison and His Inventions Including the Many Incidents, Anecdotes, and Interesting Particulars Connected With the Life of the Great Inventor.* Chicago, 1879.

McFee, Inez N. *The Story of Thomas A. Edison.* New York, 1922. [Y]

McGuirk, Kathleen L., ed. *The Diary of Thomas A. Edison.* Old Greenwich, CT, 1970.

Marshall, F. J. C. *Thomas Alva Edison 1847–1931.* Makers of History Series. Exeter, England, 1936. [Y]

Martin, Patricia Miles. *Thomas Alva Edison.* New York, 1971. [J]

Martin, Thomas Commerford. *Edison at Seventy-Three.* New York, 1920. [Pamphlet]

Meadowcroft, Enid LaMonte. *The Story of Thomas Alva Edison.* New York, 1952. [Y]

Meadowcroft, William H. *The Boys' Life of Edison.* New York, 1949. (Orig. pub. 1911.) [Y]

——— . *Edison and His Storage Battery.* Orange, NJ, 1928. [Pamphlet]

——— . *Notable Events and Achievements in the Life of Thomas Alva Edison.* New York, 1925. [Pamphlet]

Metro-Goldwyn-Mayer Corporation, Research Department. *Edison the Man.* 2 vols. Los Angeles, 1940. (In the New York Public Library)

Miller, Francis Trevelyan. *Thomas A. Edison: An Inspiring Story for Boys.* Philadelphia, 1940. (Orig. pub. as *Thomas A. Edison, Benefactor of Mankind,* 1931.) [Y]

National Electric Light Association. "In Memoriam: Thomas Alva Edison, 1847–1931." *National Electric Light Association Bulletin,* November, 1931. (pp. 3–32) [Pamphlet]

Nerney, Mary Childs. *Thomas A. Edison: A Modern Olympian.* New York, 1934.

North, Sterling. *Young Thomas Edison.* Boston, 1958. [Y]

Palmer, Arthur J. *Edison: Inspiration to Youth.* West Orange, NJ, 1928. [Y]

Peskind, S[amuel?]. *Thoughts on the Death of Thomas Edison.* n.p.: Meador, 1935.

Presentation of the Congressional Medal for Scientific Achievement to Thomas Alva Edison, October 20, 1928. n.p. (In Library of Congress)

Pringle, Patrick. *The Young Edison.* London, 1963. [Y]

Probst, George E., ed. *The Indispensable Man.* New York, 1962.

Rolt-Wheeler, Francis. *Thomas Alva Edison.* True Stories of Great Americans Series. New York, 1929. (Orig. pub. 1915.) [Y]

Runes, Dagobert D., ed. *The Diary and Sundry Observations of Thomas Alva Edison.* New York, 1948.

Sarnoff, David. *Edison (1847–1931).* New York, 1948. [Pamphlet]

Schultz, Robert F. *Edison Inventions and Related Projects.* Detroit, 1968. [Pamphlet] [Y]

Serviss, Garrett P. *Edison's Conquest of Mars.* Los Angeles, 1947. (Orig. pub. in the *New York Evening Journal,* 1898.)

Shapp, Charles, and Shapp, Martha. *Let's Find Out About Thomas Alva Edison.* New York, 1966. [J]

Shaw, George Bernard. *The Irrational Knot.* New York, 1905.

Silverberg, Robert. *Light for the World: Edison and the Power Industry.* Princeton, NJ, 1967.

Simonds, William Adams. *A Boy With Edison.* Garden City, NY, 1931. [Y]

——— . *Edison: His Life, His Work, His Genius.* Indianapolis, 1934.

Stieringer, Luther. *Catalogue of the Exhibit of Edison's Inventions at the Minneapolis Industrial Exposition, Minneapolis, Minnesota, 1890 To-*

gether With a General Description of His Work. New York, 1890. [Pamphlet]

Stringfellow, George H. Edison's Contributions to Modern Transportation. West Orange, NJ, 1929.

Tate, Alfred O. Edison's Open Door: The Life Story of Thomas A. Edison, A Great Individualist. New York, 1938.

Thomas A. Edison, Inc. A Cubic Foot of Copper. New York, 1937. [Pamphlet]

Thomas, Henry. Thomas Alva Edison. New York, 1958. [Y]

Vanderbilt, Byron M. Thomas Edison, Chemist. Washington, DC, 1971.

Van de Water, Marjorie. Edison Experiments You Can Do. New York, 1960. [Y]

Weir, Ruth Cromer. Thomas Alva Edison: Inventor. Makers of America Series. New York, 1953. [J]

Wise, W. E. Thomas Alva Edison: The Youth and His Times. New York, 1933. [Y]

Wymer, Norman George. Thomas Alva Edison. Lives of Great Men and Women Series. New York, 1957. [J]

Yates, R. F. Edison's Secrets of How to Invent. n.p.: Donley Publishing Co., 193[?]. [Y]

BOOK EXCERPTS: BIOGRAPHICAL

All About the Electric Light. London, [1878?]. (pp. 31–48)

Asimov, Isaac. "Thomas Alva Edison: Bringer of Light." Breakthroughs in Science. Boston, 1959. [Y]

Bachman, Frank P. "Other Famous Inventors of To-Day: Thomas A. Edison." Great Inventors and Their Inventions. New York, 1930. [Y]

Bailey, Carolyn S. Hero Stories. Springfield, MA, 1919. [Y]

Baker, Harry J. Biographical Sagas of Will Power. New York, 1970. (pp. 257–260)

Baldwin, Leland Dewitt. The Stream of American History. New York, 1952. (Vol. II, pp. 157–159)

Bartlett, Mabel, and Baker, Sophia. "Nancy Elliot, Mother of Thomas A. Edison." Mothers—Makers of Men: Biographical Sketches of Mothers of Famous Men. 2nd ed., rev. New York, 1952.

Beard, Charles A., and Bagley, William C. "An American Industrial Romance." A First Book in American History. New York, 1920. [Y]

Bixby, William. "Thomas Edison: Man of Light." Great Experimenters. New York, 1964.

Bjoland, Esther N., ed. "Thomas Alva Edison: Wizard of Electricity." People and Great Deeds. Vol. II of The Child's World. Chicago, 1948. [J]

Bolton, Sarah Knowles. "Thomas Alva Edison." Famous Men of Science. 3rd ed., rev. New York, 1960. [Y]

———. "Thomas Alva Edison." Lives of Poor Boys Who Became Famous. New York, 1962. (Orig. pub. 1947.) [Y]

Bonner, Mary Graham. "Light in Darkness." Wonders of Inventions. New York, 1961. [Y]

Bradford, Gamaliel. "Let There Be Light: Thomas Alva Edison." The Quick and the Dead. Boston, 1929.

Bridges, Thomas Charles. "Electric Light and the Phonograph." The Book of Invention. London, 1925. [Y]

———. "Electric Light and the Phonograph." The Young Folk's Book of Invention. Boston, 1926. [Y]

Brooks, Elbridge Streeter. "The Story of Thomas Alva Edison, of New Jersey: Called 'The Wizard of Menlo Park.' " Historic Americans: Sketches of the Lives and Character of Certain Famous Americans Held Most in Reverence by Boys and Girls of America for Whom Their Stories Are Told. New York, 1940. (Orig. pub. 1899.) [Y]

————, et al. "The Marvelous Genius of Thomas A. Edison, the Greatest Inventor of the World." *Great Americans Every Young American Should Know.* n.p.: W. E. Scull, 1910. [J]

Burlingame, Roger. "Before and After Edison." *Inventors Behind the Inventors.* New York, 1947.

Burnley, James. "Edison–'The Wizard': The Story of America's Greatest Inventor." *Millionaires and Kings of Enterprise: The Marvelous Careers of Some Americans Who by Pluck, Foresight, and Energy Have Made Themselves Masters in the Fields of Industry and Finance.* London, 1901.

Buttre, Lillian C. *The American Portrait Gallery with Biographical Sketches of Presidents, Statesmen, Military and N[aval?] Heroes, Clergymen, Authors, Poets, Etc., Etc.* New York, 1878.

Calhoun, Dorothy D. *When Great Folks Were Little Folks.* New York, 1913. [Y]

Canning, John. "Thomas Alva Edison, 1847–1931." *One Hundred Great Modern Lives: Makers of the World Today from Faraday to Kennedy.* New York, 1965.

Carmer, Carl, ed. "The Great Inventor." *Cavalcade of America: The Deeds and Achievements of the Men and Women Who Made Our Country Great.* New York, 1956. [Y]

Clark, Leonard. "Thomas Alva Edison: American Scientist and Inventor, 1847–1931." *When They Were Children.* New York, 1964. [Y]

Clifford, Harold Burton. "Thomas A. Edison." *American Leaders.* n.p.: American Book Co., 1953. [J]

Cook, Clarence. "Thomas Alva Edison." *Great Men and Famous Women: A Series of Pen and Pencil Sketches of the Lives of More Than Two Hundred of the Most Prominent Personages in History.* Vol. III. New York, 1894.

Cottler, Joseph, and Haym, Jaffe. "Thomas Alva Edison (1847–1931): The Wizard of Menlo Park." *Heroes of Civilization.* Rev. ed. Boston, 1969. (Orig. pub. 1931.) [Y]

Crowther, J. G. "Thomas Alva Edison, 1847–1931." *Famous American Men of Science.* Freeport, NY, 1969. (Orig. pub. 1937.)

————. "Thomas Alva Edison (1847–1931)." *Six Great Inventors.* London, 1954. [Y]

Cruse, Amy. "Thomas Edison: The Boy Who Loved Experiments." *Boys and Girls Who Became Famous.* New York, 1929. [Y]

Curtin, Andrew. "Thomas Edison." *Gallery of Great Americans.* New York, 1955. (p. 27) [J]

Darrow, Floyd L. "Thomas A. Edison." *Masters of Science and Invention.* New York, 1923. [Y]

de Camp, L. Sprague. "Edison and the Electric Light." *The Heroic Age of American Invention.* Garden City, New York, 1961.

Derieux, Mary, ed. "Thomas Alva Edison (1847–1931)." *One Hundred Great Lives: Revealing Biographies of Scientists and Inventors, Leaders and Reformers, Writers and Poets, Artists and Musicians, Discoverers and Explorers, Soldiers and Statesmen, Great Women.* New York, 1944.

Devereaux, Vanza. "The 'Wizard' of America." *America's Own Story.* San Francisco, 1954. [J]

DeWitt, William A. " 'Wizard of Menlo Park': Thomas Alva Edison." *Illustrated Minute Biographies: One Hundred and Fifty Fascinating Life-Stories of Famous People from the Dawn of Civilization to the Present Day Dramatized With Portraits and Scenes from Their Lives.* New York, 1949. [1955 rev. ed. listed Y.]

Dolin, Arnold. "Thomas Alva Edison (1847–1931): Wizard of Electricity." *World Famous Great Men of Science.* New York, 1960. [Y]

Dunlap, Orrin Elmer. "Thomas Alva Edison: America's Greatest Inventor." *Radio's One Hundred Men of Science.* New York, 1944.

Eberle, Irmengarde. "Thomas Alva Edison: The Man Who Made Electricity Useful to

Mankind." *Famous Inventors for Young People.* New York, 1966. (Orig. pub. 1941.) [Y]

Eby, Lois. *Marked For Adventure.* New York, 1960. (pp. 113–114) [Y]

"Edison in His Workshop." *Popular Culture and Industrialism, 1865–1890.* Edited by Henry Nash Smith. Garden City, NY, 1967.

Edison Institute. *Greenfield Village Guide Book.* Dearborn, MI, 1948. (pp. 18–27)

Editors of News Front Year. "Let There Be Light: Edison's Incandescent Lamp Lit Up World." *The Fifty Great Pioneers of American Industry.* Maplewood, NJ, 1964.

Eibling, Harold H.; Gilmartin, John G.; and Skehan, Anna M. "Thomas A. Edison: Electrical Wizard." *Great Names in Our Country's Story.* River Forest, IL, 1959. [J]

Evans, Idrisyn Oliver. "Many Inventions: Thomas Alva Edison (1847–1931)." *Inventors of the World.* London, 1962. [Y]

Evett, Robert. "Thomas Alva Edison." *Those Inventive Americans.* National Geographic Society, Special Publications Division. Washington, DC, 1971.

Fanning, Leonard M. "Thomas A. Edison; 1847–1931; Father of the Electrical Industry." *Fathers of Industries.* Philadelphia, 1962. [Y]

Faris, John T. "Thomas A. Edison, Electrician." *Makers of Our History.* Boston, 1917. [Y]

————. "Thomas Alva Edison." *Winning Their Way: Boys Who Learned Self-Help.* New York, 1909. [Y]

Fiske, Stephen. "Thomas Alva Edison." *Off-Hand Portraits of Prominent New Yorkers.* New York, 1884.

Fitzpatrick, James K. "Thomas Alva Edison: The Wizard of Menlo Park." *Builders of the American Dream.* New Rochelle, NY, 1977.

Foote, Anna Elizabeth, and Skinner, Avery Warner. "Edison and the Electric Light."

Makers and Defenders of America. New York, 1910. [Y]

Forbes, B. C. "Thomas A. Edison." *Men Who Are Making America.* New York, 1917.

Foster, Annie Harvie. *Makers of History.* n.p.: Ryerson Press, 1946. (pp. 62–75)

Fowler, Mary Jane, and Fisher, Margaret. "Thomas A. Edison." *Great Americans.* Grand Rapids, Michigan, 1960. [J]

Gibson, James B. *Great People—Great Americans.* New York, 1959. (pp. 155–174)

Gilmartin, John G., and Skehan, Anna M. "Thomas A. Edison, Electrical Wizard." *Great Names in American History.* New York, 1946. [J]

Glenister, S. H. "Thomas Alva Edison, Electrical Engineer." *Stories of Great Craftsmen.* London, 1939. [Y]

Goebel, Edmund Joseph; Quigley, Thomas J.; and O'Loughlin, John E. "Thomas A. Edison, Electrical Wizard." *Builders of Our Country.* New York, 1951. [J]

Greenwood, Ernest. *Amber to Amperes: The Story of Electricity.* New York, 1931.

Griffith, Ward. "Thomas A. Edison: Miracle Man of Electricity." *Fifty Famous Americans.* Racine, WI, 1946. [J]

Grigson, Geoffrey, and Gibbs-Smith, Charles Harvard, eds. "Technological Wizard: Thomas Alva Edison." *People: A Volume of the Good, Bad, Great & Eccentric Who Illustrate the Admirable Diversity of Man.* 2nd American ed. New York, 1957.

Hagedorn, Hermann. *Americans, A Book of Lives.* New York, 1946. (pp. 43–62)

Haine, Edgar A. "The Great Inventor— Thomas Edison." *Man's Great Achievements.* New York, 1976. [Y]

Harrington, Marshall C. "Thomas Alva Edison." *Vocations and Professions.* Creative Personalities, vol. 1. Edited by Philip Henry Lotz. New York, 1940. [Y]

Harris, Jeremy. "Thomas Alva Edison: The Boy Wizard." *A Cavalcade of Young Ameri-*

cans. Edited by Carl Carmer. New York, 1958. [J]

Hartman, Gertrude. "A New Light for the World." *Machines and the Men Who Made the World of Industry.* New York, 1959. [Y]

Hatch, Jane M. "Thomas Alva Edison's Birthday." *The American Book of Days.* 3rd ed. New York, 1978.

Hathaway, Esse V. "Thomas A. Edison." *Partners in Progress.* Freeport, NY, 1935.

Henderson, Archibald. "Thomas Alva Edison: The Genius of Invention." *Contemporary Immortals.* Freeport, NY, 1930. (Reprinted in 1968.)

Herzberg, Max J., and Mones, Leon. "Thomas A. Edison." *Americans in Action.* New York, 1937. [Y]

Heyn, Ernest V. "Thomas Alva Edison—1,093 Patents!" *Fire of Genius: Inventors of the Past Century.* Garden City, NY, 1976.

Hoff, Carol. "Thomas A. Edison." *They Served America.* Austin, TX, 1966. [J]

Holland, Rupert S. "Edison and the Electric Light." *Historic Inventions.* Philadelphia, 1911. [Y]

Hoover, Eva Hood. "Thomas Alva Edison: The Inventor: 1847–1931." *Sixteen Exceptional Americans.* New York, 1959.

Hubbard, Elbert. "Thomas Edison." *Little Journeys to the Homes of the Great.* New York, 1928.

Hubert, Philip G., Jr. "Thomas A. Edison." *Men of Achievement: Inventors.* New York, 1894.

Hughes, Jonathan. "The Wizard of Menlo Park." *The Vital Few: American Economic Progress and its Protagonists.* Boston, 1965.

Humphrey, Grace. "Why Don't You Know? Thomas Alva Edison: 1847–   ." *Children of Necessity: Stories of American Inventions.* Indianapolis, 1925. [Y]

Hylander, C. J. "Thomas Alva Edison." *American Inventors.* New York, 1936. (Orig. pub. 1934.) [Y]

Larsen [Lehrburger], Egon. "Ninety-Eight Per Cent Perspiration." *The Pegasus Book of Inventors.* London, 1965. [Y]

———. "Thomas Alva Edison, The Man of Practical Genius." *Children's Book of Famous Lives.* Edited by Eric Duthrie. n.p., 1960. [J]

———. "Thomas Alva Edison: The Man with Twenty-Five Hundred Patents." *Men Who Changed the World: Stories of Invention and Discovery.* London, 1952. [Y]

Law, Frederick Houk. "Thomas A. Edison: The Boy Who Found Many Opportunities." *Great Lives: Life Stories of Great Men and Women.* New York, 1952. [J]

———. "Thomas Alva Edison." *Modern Great Americans.* New York, 1926. [Y]

Leipold, L. Edmond. "Thomas A. Edison: He Made a Thousand Things." *Heroes of a Different Kind.* Minneapolis, 1978. [J]

———. "Thomas A. Edison: The World's Most Useful Citizen." *Founders of Fortunes.* Vol. II. Minneapolis, 1967. [Y]

Lewis, I. A. "Thomas Alva Edison: The Wizard." *Our American Inventors.* New York, 1953. [J]

Macomber, Hattie E. "A Great Inventor." *Stories of Great Inventors.* Young America Series. Boston, 1897. [J]

McFee, Inez N. *Stories of American Inventors,* Chapters 7, 8, 10. New York, 1921. [Y]

McSpadden, J. Walker. "The 'Wizard' Who Gave More Light to Men: Thomas Alva Edison (1847–1931)." *How They Blazed the Way: Men Who Have Advanced Civilization.* New York, 1939. [Y]

Manning, Harold G. "Thomas A. Edison—The World's Greatest Inventor." *Inventive America.* Waterbury, CT, 1940. [Y]

Martin, T. Commerford, and Coles, Stephen Leidy, eds. *The Story of Electricity; A Popular and Practical Historical Account of the Establishment and Wonderful Development of the Electrical Industry.* 2 vols. New York, 1919–1922.

Mason, Miriam E., and Cartwright, William H. "Thomas Alva Edison." *Trail Blazers of American History.* New York, 1961. [J]

Matschoss, C. "Thomas Alva Edison, 1847–1931." *Great Engineers.* London, 1939.

Meadowcroft, William H. "Thomas A. Edison, the Inventor." *My Vocation: By Eminent Americans.* Edited by Earl G. Lockhart. New York, 1938.

———. "Thomas Alva Edison: The Traveling Newspaper Office." *Roads to Greatness.* Edited by Louise Galloway. Junior Classics Series. New York, 1962. [Y]

Melbo, Irving R. "Thomas Alva Edison, He Gave the World a New Light." *Our America.* Indianapolis, 1937. [J]

Morello, Theodore, ed. "Thomas Alva Edison." *The Hall of Fame for Great Americans at New York University.* New York, 1967.

Morris, Charles. "Thomas A. Edison, The Wizard of Invention." *Heroes of Progress in America.* Philadelphia, 1906.

Mowry, William A., and Mowry, Arthur May. "Thomas A. Edison, 1847– ." *First Steps in the History of Our Country.* New York, 1900. (Orig. pub. 1898.) [Y]

Murthi, A. N. S. "Thomas Alva Edison." *Names You Should Know.* Ambala, Cantt. [India], 1954. [Y]

Parkman, Mary R. "The Franklin of Our Times: Thomas Alva Edison (1847–)." *Conquests of Invention.* New York, 1921.

Paton, Graham, ed. "The Wizard of Menlo Park: Young Tom Edison Was a Poor Student." *Great Men and Women of Modern Times.* London, 1966. [Y]

Patterson, John C. "Thomas Alva Edison: World's Most Prolific Inventor." *America's Greatest Inventors.* New York, 1943. [Y]

Pereira, Arty. *They Won Fame and Fortune.* New York, 1973. (pp. 52–58) [Y]

Perry, Frances M. *Four American Inventors.* New York, 1901. [Y]

Pim, Paul. "Telling Tommy About Thomas A. Edison: Inventor of the Incandescent Light." *Telling Tommy About Famous Inventors.* New York, 1942. [J]

Poole, Lynn, and Poole, Gray. "Thomas Alva Edison, 1847–1931, American." *Men Who Pioneered Inventions.* New York, 1969. [Y]

Powell, Lucille Rader. *Ten All-American Boys.* New York, 1971. (pp. 18–22) [J]

Pratt, Edwin A. *Successful Lives of Modern Times.* London, 1906. (pp. 92–105)

Pratt, Fletcher. *All About Famous Inventors and Their Inventions.* New York, 1955. (pp. 84–91) [J]

Pringle, Patrick. "A Multiple First." *They Were First.* New York, 1965. [Y]

———. *One Hundred and One Great Lives.* n.p.: Ward, Lock, 1963. [Y]

———. *When They Were Boys.* New York, 1954. (pp. 155–172) [Y]

Radford, Ruby L. "Thomas Alva Edison: America's Greatest Inventor." *Inventors in Industry.* New York, 1969. [J]

Reid, James D. "Three Prominent Inventors." *The Telegraph in America: Its Founders, Promoters, and Noted Men.* New York, 1879.

Reynolds, James J., and Horn, Mary A. "Thomas A. Edison." *Short Stories of Famous Men.* New York, 1926. [J]

Rhodes, James A. "Thomas Alva Edison." *Teenage Hall of Fame.* Indianapolis, 1960. [Y]

Ruoff, Henry W. "Thomas Alva Edison." *Leaders of Men.* Springfield, MA, 1902.

Savage, Robert M. " 'I Tried to Warn You!' " *Scientists and Inventors.* Vol. II of *Childcraft: The How and Why Library.* Chicago, 1968. [J]

Scherger, George Lawrence. "Thomas A. Edison." *Famous Living Americans.* Edited by Mary Griffin Webb and Edna Lenore Webb. Greencastle, IN, 1915.

Schirmer, Mathilda. "Benefactor of Civilization: Thomas Alva Edison." *Builders for Progress.* Chicago, 1950. [J]

Schu, Pierre. "Thomas Alva Edison, 1847–1931." *The World of Great Men: History Told Through the Lives of the Men Who Made It.* North Easton, MA, 1967. [Y]

Sewell, W. Stuart. "Thomas Alva Edison." *Brief Biographies of Famous Men and Women.* New York, 1949.

Shepard, Walter. *Heroes of Science.* New York, 1964. [J]

Simmons, Sanford. "Thomas Edison: The Wonderful Wizard of Electricity." *Great Men of Science.* New York, 1955. [J]

Southworth, Gertrude Van Duyn, and Southworth, John Van Duyn. "Thomas A. Edison." *Heroes of Our America.* Syracuse, NY, 1952. [J]

Steedman, Amy. "Thomas Alva Edison." *When They Were Children: Stories of the Childhood of Famous Men and Women.* New York, 1926. [J]

Strong, Jay. "Thomas Edison: Wizard of Electricity." *Famous Heroes of the Ages.* New York, 1958. [J]

Tappan, Eva March. "Thomas Alva Edison, Inventor, 1847– ." *Heroes of Progress: Stories of Successful Americans.* New York, 1921. [Y]

Tharp, Edgar. "Thomas Alva Edison (1847–1931): Electricity Becomes Man's Servant." *Giants of Invention.* New York, 1963. [Y]

Thomas, Eleanor, and Kelty, Mary Gertrude. *Heroes, Heroines and Holidays.* Boston, 1947. (pp. 115–122) [J]

Thomas, Henry. "Thomas A. Edison, Engineer in God's Workshop." *The Story of the United States: A Biographical History of America.* New York, 1938.

Thomas, Henry, and Thomas, Dana Lee [Schnittkind]. "Thomas Alva Edison (1847–1931)." *Great Americans: Their Inspiring Lives and Achievements.* Garden City, NY, 1948.

——— . "Thomas Alva Edison: 1847–1931." *Life Stories of the Great Inventors.* Garden City, NY, 1948.

——— . "Thomas Alva Edison." *Living Biographies of Famous Americans.* Garden City, NY, 1941. (pp. 203–215)

Untermeyer, Louis. "Thomas Alva Edison." *Makers of the Modern World.* New York, 1955.

Wade, Mary H. "The Magician of Sound." *Wonder-Workers.* Boston, 1912. [J]

Wall, C. B. "Incandescent Genius." *Great Adventures in Science.* Edited by Helen Wright and Samuel B. Rapport. New York, 1956.

Wildman, E. "Thomas Alva Edison: Electrical Wizard and World's Greatest Inventor." *Famous Leaders of Industry: The Life Stories of Boys Who Have Succeeded.* Boston, 1920.

Williams-Ellis, Anabel. "A Great Inventor: Thomas Edison 1847–1931." *They Wanted the Real Answers.* New York, 1958. [J]

Wilson, Mitchell. "The Wizard of Menlo Park." *American Science and Invention: A Pictorial History.* New York, 1954.

BOOK EXCERPTS: GENERAL

A Guide Book for the Edison Institute Museum. Dearborn, MI, 1948.

Aiken, Duncan. *The Turning Stream.* Garden City, NY, 1948. (p. 202)

Alexander, Charles C. *Nationalism in American Thought 1930–1945.* Chicago, 1969. (p. 111)

American Inventors. 2 vols. n.p.: F. A. Owens, [1912?].

Athearn, Robert G., and the editors of American Heritage. *Age of Steel. The American Heritage New Illustrated History of the*

United States, vol. X. New York, 1963. [J]*

Bailey, Thomas A. *The American Pageant.* Rev. ed. New York, 1961. (p. 529)

Baker, Ray Stannard. "The Story of the Phonograph." *The Boy's Book of Inventions.* New York, 1899. [J]

Barwick, E. Buller. "The Phonograph." *Man's Genius: The Story of Famous Inventions and Their Development.* London, 1932.

Beard, Charles A., and Bagley, William C. "Men of Industry: Inventors, Business Men, and Artisans." *The History of the American People.* Rev. ed. New York, 1970. [J]

Beard, G. M. *American Nervousness, Its Causes and Consequences.* New York, 1881. (pp. 96–129)

Berger, Josef, and Berger, Dorothy, eds. *Diary of America.* New York, 1957. (pp. 520–522)

Blow, Michael, and the editors of *American Heritage. Men of Science and Invention.* American Heritage Junior Library Series. New York, 1960. (pp. 87–88, 90–96, 99–101) [J]

Boorstin, Daniel J. *America and the Image of Europe: Reflections on American Thought.* Cleveland, 1960. (p. 131)

Bowen, H. G. *The Edison Effect.* West Orange, NJ, 1950.

Boyd, James P. "Wonders of Electricity." *Triumphs and Wonders of the Nineteenth Century.* Philadelphia, 1899.

Bright, Arthur A., Jr. *The Electric Lamp Industry: Technological Change and Economic Development from 1800 to 1947.* New York, 1949.

Brown, Harriet McCune; Ludlum, Robert P.; and Wilder, Howard B. *This Is America's Story.* Rev. ed. Boston, 1964. (p. 446) [J]

Brown, William R. *Imagemaker: Will Rogers and the American Dream.* Columbia, MO, 1970. (pp. 221–222)

Burlingame, Roger. *Henry Ford: A Great Life in Brief.* New York, 1954. (pp. 181–182)

Burns, Elmer E. *The Story of Great Inventions.* New York, 1910. (pp. 95–96, 121, 147)

Bush, Vannevar. "Our Tradition of Opportunity." *Endless Horizons.* Washington, DC, 1946.

Byrn, Edward W. "The Phonograph." *The Progress of Invention in the Nineteenth Century.* New York, 1970. (Orig. pub. 1900.)

Calder, Ritchie. *The Evolution of the Machine.* New York, 1968. (pp. 11, 72–75, 77–79, 96–97, 147–148)

Caldwell, Otis, and Curtis, Francis. *Everyday Science.* Boston, 1949. (p. 396) [J]

Casner, Mabel B., and Gabriel, Ralph H. *Story of the American Nation.* Sacramento, CA, 1963. (pp. 463–464, 558) [J]

Casson, Herbert N. *The History of the Telephone.* Chicago, 1910. (p. 69)

Chamberlain, John. "The Age of Edison." *The Enterprising Americans: A Business History of the United States.* New York, 1961.

Chandler, Maurice Henry. *Inventions That Made the Modern World.* London, 1966. [J]

Chase-Shawmut Company. *The Fuse: Its Story From the Sources of Its Invention Through Its Progress to Maturity.* Newburyport, MA, 1943.

Chesterton, G. K. "On a Negation." *Generally Speaking: A Book of Essays.* London, 1928.

Coffin, Robert Peter Tristram. "Tom Was Just a Little Boy." (poem). *Primer for America.* n.p., 1943. [J]

Conot, Robert. *American Odyssey.* New York, 1974. (pp. 62–64, 86–88)

Cooke, David Coxe. *Inventions That Made History.* New York, 1968. [J]

Coppersmith, Fred. *Patent Applied For.* London, 1949. (pp. 20, 86)

Curt, Ralph Henry. *The Story of Discovery*

---

* The symbol [J] in this category combines [Y] and [J].

and Invention. New York, 1937. (pp. 352–355)

Daniels, Jonathan. *The End of Innocence.* Philadelphia, 1954. (pp. 175–176, 321)

Darrow, Floyd L. *Thinkers and Doers.* New York, 1925. (pp. 258–263)

———, and Hylander, C. J. *The Boy's Own Book of Great Inventions.* New York, 1941. (pp. 26, 311, 314) [J]

David, Ira C.; Burnett, John; and Gross, E. Wayne. *Science: Experiment and Discovery.* Vol. II. New York, 1954. (p. 33) [J]

Dos Passos, John. "The Electrical Wizard." *U.S.A.* New York, 1937.

———. "The Electrical Wizard." *A Reflective Reader.* Edited by H. James Rockel. New York, 1956.

Dunaway, Philip, and Evans, Mel, eds. " 'I Do Believe I Have a Big Bump for Cookies' —Thomas Alva Edison." *A Treasury of the World's Great Diaries.* Garden City, NY, 1957.

Dyer, Frank L., and Martin, T. C. "Edison's Electric Light Invention." *America: Great Crises in Our History Told by Its Makers.* Edited by the Veterans of Foreign Wars Committee on Americanization. Chicago, 1925.

Ebon, Martin. "Thomas Edison: A Machine to Contact the Dead." *They Knew the Unknown.* New York, 1971.

Edison Institute of Technology; Greenfield, Michigan, the Early American Village; Menlo Park; Industrial Museum. n.p., [?].

Edison Portland Cement Company. *The Romance of Cement.* New York, 1926. (pp. 20–22)

Edison, Thomas A. "Introduction." *The Life and Works of Thomas Paine.* By Thomas Paine. New Rochelle, NY, 1925.

Editors of *American Heritage. The American Heritage Pictorial History of the Presidents of the United States.* Vol. II. New York, 1968. (p. 650)

Editors of *Time. Time Capsule/1923.* New York, 1967. (pp. 195, 197)

Editors of *Time. Time Capsule/1929.* New York, 1967. (pp. 17, 131, 151–152)

Ellis, Edward S. *The People's Standard History of the United States: From the Landing of the Norsemen to the Present Time.* New York, 1895. (p. 1548)

Fahie, J. J. *A History of Wireless Telegraphy.* London, 1901. (pp. 102–111)

Farmer, Robert, et al. "Thomas Alva Edison." *The Last Will and Testament.* New York, 1968.

Fiske, Bradley A. *Invention: The Master Key to Progress.* New York, 1921. (pp. 123, 285, 291–292, 310–312, 328–329, 342)

Foote, Irving P. *The Story of Our Republic.* Yonkers-On-Hudson, NY, 1932. (p. 376) [J]

Ford, Henry, and Crowther, Samuel. *Moving Forward,* Garden City, NY, 1930.

Fraser, Charles G. "The American School of Acoustics," and "The Edison Lamp." *Half Hours with Great Scientists: The Story of Physics.* New York, 1948.

Fraser, Hugh Russell. "Edison." Unpub.

Garraty, John A. *The American Nation: A History of the United States Since 1965.* New York, 1966. (pp. 93–94, 100–101, 160)

Gelatt, Roland. *The Fabulous Phonograph: From Edison to Stereo.* Rev. ed. New York, 1965. (Orig. pub. 1954.)

Gies, Joseph and Frances. *The Ingenious Yankees.* New York, 1976. (pp. 330–341)

Ginger, Ray. *Age of Excess: The United States from 1877 to 1914.* New York, 1965. (p. 312)

Greenleaf, William. "The Emergence of Modern Industry: The Threshold of the Electrical Age." *American Economic Development Since 1860.* New York, 1968.

Halsey, Francis Whiting, ed. "Edison's Electric Light Invention, A Contemporary Account." *Our Own Recent Times, 1877–1911.* Great Epochs in American History, vol. x. New York, 1912.

Hammond, John Winthrop. *Men and Volts: The Story of General Electric.* New York, 1941.

Hatfield, H. Stafford. *The Inventor and His World.* West Drayton, Middlesex, England, 1948. (Orig. pub. 1933.) (pp. 30–37, 60–61)

Heald, Morrell, "Technology in American Culture." *American Character and Culture: Some Twentieth Century Perspectives.* Edited by John A. Hague. DeLand, FL, 1964.

Heath, Monroe. *Great Americans at a Glance.* Menlo Park, CA, 1956.

Hofstadter, Richard. *Anti-Intellectualism in American Life.* New York, 1963. (p. 25)

Holmes, George S. "And Yet Fools Say." *Poems for Modern Youth.* Cambridge, MA, 1938. [J]

Howell, John W., and Schroeder, Henry. *History of the Incandescent Lamp.* Schenectady, 1927.

Hubbard, Elbert. *Elbert Hubbard's Scrapbook.* New York, 1923. (p. 21)

Hurd, Charles, and Hurd, Eleanor. "Thomas A. Edison—' . . . my first mailing phonogram.' " *A Treasury of Great American Letters: Our Country's Life and History in the Letters of Its Men and Women.* New York, 1961.

Iles, George. *Inventors at Work.* New York, 1906. (pp. 310–313, 414–415, 432–433)

Jones, Payson. *A Power History of the Consolidated Edison System, 1878–1900.* New York, 1940.

Josephson, Matthew, ed. "Thomas Alva Edison: On the Industrial Research Laboratory." *An American Primer.* Edited by Daniel J. Boorstin. New York, 1966.

Kaempffert, Waldemar, ed. *A Popular History of American Invention.* 2 vols. New York, 1924.

———. "The Great Dilemma." *The American Story.* Edited by Earl Schenck Miers. Great Neck, NY, 1956.

Keating, Paul W. *Lamps for a Brighter America: A History of the General Electric Lamp Business (1892–1954).* New York, 1954.

Kelly, Fred C. *The Wright Brothers.* New York, 1943. (p. 3)

Kelty, Mary G. *Life in Modern America.* New York, 1943. (Orig. pub. 1941.) (pp. 327–333) [J]

Kerr, J. Ernest. "Thomas A. Edison." *Imprint of the Maritimes: Highlights in the Lives of One Hundred Interesting Americans Whose Roots are in Canada's Atlantic Provinces.* Boston, 1959. (p. 90)

Kingsbury, Edward M. "Prospero is Dead." *The Treasure Chest: An Anthology of Contemplative Prose.* New York, 1946.

Kirkland, Edward C. *Industry Comes of Age: Business, Labor, and Public Policy, 1860–1897.* Chicago, 1967. (Orig. pub. 1961.) (p. 167)

Lansing, Marion F. *Great Moments in Science.* New York, 1926. (pp. 246–249)

Laski, Harold J. *The American Democracy: A Commentary and an Interpretation.* New York, 1948. (pp. 12, 166, 231, 262, 275, 339, 365, 628, 657)

Leithauser, Joachim G. *Inventors' Progress.* Translated by Michael Bullock. Cleveland, 1959. (Orig. pub. 1954.) (pp. 63, 235–237, 260–262)

Lewis, Floyd A. *The Incandescent Light: A Review of Its Invention and Application.* Rev. ed. New York, 1961. (Orig. pub. 1949.)

Lippmann, Walter. "Thomas A. Edison." In Harrison, Gilbert A., ed., *Public Persons.* New York, 1976. (pp. 110–112)

Low, Archibald Montgomery. *Thanks to Inventors.* London, 1954. (p. 91, 157–158)

Lubschez, Ben J. *The Story of the Motion Picture 65 B.C. to 1920 A.D.* New York, 1920. (pp. 37–49)

Lynd, Robert, and Lynd, Helen Merrell. *Middletown in Transition: A Study in Cultural Conflicts.* New York, 1937. (p. 413)

McDonald, Forrest. *Insull.* Chicago, 1962. (pp. 15–51, 63)

MacFarlane, Lloyd [Ira Lee Cochrane]. *The Phonograph Book.* New York, 1917.

Maloney, John A. "The Incandescent Lamp." *Great Inventors and Their Inventions.* Chicago, 1938. [J]

Maule, Harry E. *The Boy's Book of New Inventions.* Garden City, NY, 1912. (p. 290) [J]

May, Henry F. *The End of American Innocence.* Chicago, 1959. (pp. 14–15, 137)

Meadowcroft, William H. "A New Light in the World." *Science in Literature* by Frederick H. Law. New York, 1929. (Excerpt from *Boys' Life of Edison.*) [J]

Meister, Morris. *Magnetism and Electricity.* New York, 1930. (p. 142) [J]

Meyer, Jerome Sydney. *World Book of Great Inventors.* New York, 1950. (pp. 183–184)

Montgomery, Elizabeth Rider. "Talking Tinfoil." *The Story Behind Great Inventions.* New York, 1944. [J]

Mott, Frank Luther. *A History of American Magazines.* 5 vols. Cambridge, MA, 1930–1968. (Vol. III, pp. 118–121)

Mowry, William A., and Mowry, Arthur May. *American Inventions and Inventors.* New York, 1900. (pp. 86–89) [J]

Muldoon, Sylvan Joseph. "Thomas A. Edison Approved Seership." *Psychic Experiences of Famous People.* n.p., Aries Press, 1947.

Murray, Robert K. *The Harding Era: Warren G. Harding and His Administration.* Minneapolis, 1969. (p. 119)

Nevins, Allan, and Hill, Frank Ernest. *Ford: The Times, the Man, the Company.* New York, 1954. (pp. 531–532, 544)

———. *Ford: Expansion and Challenge, 1915–1933.* New York, 1957. (pp. 312, 486)

———. *Ford: Decline and Rebirth, 1933–1962.* New York, 1962. (p. 24)

New York Edison Company [T. Commerford Martin]. *Forty Years of Edison Service, 1882–1922.* New York, 1922.

———. *Thirty Years of New York: 1882–1912; Being a History of Electrical Development in Manhattan and the Bronx.* New York, 1913.

O'Brien, Robert, and Editors of *Time-Life Books. Machines.* New York, 1964. (pp. 126–129) [J]

Oliver, John W. "Thomas A. Edison, 1847–1931." *History of American Technology.* New York, 1956.

Passer, Harold C. *The Electrical Manufacturers, 1875–1900.* Cambridge, MA, 1953.

Phelps, George Allison. "The Luminary of Light." *Holidays and Philosophical Biographies.* Los Angeles, 1951.

Platt, Orville H. "Invention and Advancement." *Popular Culture and Industrialism, 1865–1890.* Edited by Henry Nash Smith. Garden City, NY, 1967.

Pope, Franklin Leonard. *Evolution of the Electric Incandescent Lamp.* Elizabeth, NJ, 1889. (pp. 12–23, 52–54)

Prescott, George B. *The Speaking Telephone, Talking Phonograph and Other Novelties.* New York, 1878. (pp. 300–308)

Ramsaye, Terry. *A Million and One Nights: A History of the Motion Picture.* 2 vols. New York, 1926.

Riesman, David, et al. *The Lonely Crowd: A Study of the Changing American Character.* Garden City, NY, 1956. (Orig. pub. 1950.) (p. 150)

Robbin, Irving. *The How and Why Wonder Book of Basic Inventions.* New York, 1965. [J]

Rogers, Agnes. *From Man to Machine.* Boston, 1941. (pp. 104, 119)

Rolt-Wheeler, Francis. *A Boy With the U.S. Inventors.* Boston, 1929. (p. 327) [J]

Ross, Ishbel, *Grace Coolidge and Her Era: The Story of a President's Wife.* New York, 1962. (p. 132, 203)

Rossman, Joseph. *The Psychology of the Inventor.* Washington, 1931. (pp. 28–31, 48–49, 152–153)

Russell, Francis, and the Editors of *American Heritage. The American Heritage History of the Confident Years.* New York, 1968. (pp. 134–138)

Schlesinger, Arthur Meier. *The Rise of the City, 1878–1898*. New York, 1933. (p. 99)

Schroeder, Henry. *History of the Electric Light*. Smithsonian Miscellaneous Collections, vol. LXXVI, no. 2. Washington, DC, 1923. (pp. 43–46)

Scott, Lloyd N. *Naval Consulting Board of the United States*. Washington, DC, 1920. (pp. 160–192)

Shannon, Fred Albert. *Economic History of the People of the United States*. New York, 1934. (pp. 531, 536, 569–570)

Sharlin, Harold I. "Applications of Electricity." *Technology in Western Civilization*. Edited by Melvin Kranzberg. London, 1967. (Vol. I, pp. 563–578)

————. *The Making of the Electrical Age*. New York, 1963. (pp. 153–155)

Simonds, William Adams. *Henry Ford and Greenfield Village*. New York, 1938. (pp. 98, 135)

Sipley, Louis Walton. *Photography's Great Inventors*. Philadelphia, 1965. (pp. 93–94)

Sparks, Edwin Erle. *National Development*. American Nation Series, vol. XXIII. New York, 1907. (p. 45)

Sprague, Harriet Chapman Jones. *Frank J. Sprague and the Edison Myth*. New York, 1947.

Steinberg, Samuel. *The United States: Story of a Free People*. Boston, 1958. (p. 342) [J]

Steinmetz, Charles P. "Edison: The Genius." *Transactions of the Illuminating Engineering Society*, August 30, 1916. Reprinted in Edison Illuminating Companies, *Edison Honored Throughout the World*, p. 31.

Sward, Keith. *The Legend of Henry Ford*. New York, 1968. (Orig. pub. 1948.) pp. 89, 112, 114)

Talbot, Frederick A. *All About Inventions and Discoveries: The Romance of Modern Scientific and Mechanical Achievements*. New York, 1917. [J]

Taylor, Henry Junior. "Edison Didn't Succeed Alone." *An American Speaks His Mind*. Garden City, NY, 1957. (Orig. pub. 1945.)

Thompson, Holland. *The Age of Invention: A Chronicle of Mechanical Conquest*. Yale Chronicles of America Series, vol. XXXVII. New Haven, CT, 1921. (pp. 205, 212, 215)

Thompson, Robert Luther. *Wiring a Continent: The History of the Telegraph Industry in the United States, 1832–1866*. Princeton, NJ, 1947. (p. 246)

Toner, James V. *The Boston Edison Story, 1886–1951, 65 Years of Service!* New York, 1951. (pp. 8–9)

Venable, John D. *Out of the Shadow*. East Orange, NJ, 1978.

Wallace, Archer. *The Religious Faith of Great Men*. Freeport, NY, 1967. (Orig. pub. 1934.) (pp. 165–167)

Waller, Leslie. *American Inventions*. n.p. [J]

Walsh, Richard J. *The Making of Buffalo Bill: A Study in Heroics*. Indianapolis, 1928. (p. 304)

Wecter, Dixon. "Gods From the Machine: Edison, Ford, Lindbergh." *The Hero in America*. Ann Arbor, MI, 1963. (Orig. pub. 1941.)

Weisberger, Bernard A., and the Editors of *Life*. "The Amazing Men of Many Marvels." *The Age of Steel and Steam*. The Life History of the United States, vol. VII. New York, 1964. [J]

Wik, Reynold M. *Henry Ford and Grass-roots America*. Ann Arbor, MI, 1972. (pp. 113–114, 158, 176, 207–208, 216)

Wilkie, Frane Bangs. "Thomas A. Edison." *The Great Inventions: Their History from the Earliest Period to the Present: Their Influence on Civilization*. Philadelphia, 1883.

Williams, Archibald. *The Romance of Modern Invention*. Philadelphia, 1903. (p. 54)

Woodbury, David O. *A Measure for Greatness: A Short Biography of Edward Weston*. New York, 1949. (pp. 4, 67, 99, 111–112, 126–127, 132, 206)

Yates, Raymond F. "Edison's Methods of Inventing." *The Young Inventors' Guide*. New York, 1959. [J]

REMINISCENCES

Bernays, Edward L. *Biography of An Idea: Memoirs of Public Relations Counsel Edward L. Bernays*. New York, 1965.

Bernhardt, Sarah. *Memories of My Life: Being My Personal, Professional, and Social Recollections as Woman and Artist*. New York, 1968. (Orig. pub. 1908.)

Burroughs, John. "October, 1917: Edison and Ford." *John Burroughs Talks: His Reminiscences and Comments*. New York, 1922.

———. *Our Vacation Days*. Akron, 1926.

Croffut, William A. *An American Procession, 1855–1914: A Personal Chronicle of Famous Men*. Freeport, NY, 1968. (Orig. pub. 1931.)

Daniels, Josephus. *The Wilson Era: Years of Peace—1910–1917*. 2 vols. Chapel Hill, NC, 1946. (Orig. pub. 1944.)

Edison, Charles. "The Electric Thomas Edison." *Great Lives, Great Deeds*. New York, 1964.

Firestone, Harvey S., and Crowther, Samuel. *Men and Rubber: The Story of Business*. Garden City, NY, 1926.

Fleming, Sir Ambrose. *Memories of a Scientific Life*. London, 1934.

Fleming, J. A. *Fifty Years of Electricity: The Memories of an Electrical Engineer*. London, [1921 ?].

Ford, Henry, and Crowther, Samuel. *My Friend Mr. Edison*. London, 1930.

Ford, Henry. *My Life and Work*. Garden City, NY, 1922.

Jehl, Francis. *Menlo Park Reminiscences*. 3 vols. Dearborn, MI, 1937.

Johnson, Robert Underwood. *Remembered Yesterdays*. Boston, 1923.

Marcosson, Isaac F. *Adventures in Interviewing*. New York, 1919.

Marshall, David Trumbull. *Recollections of Edison*. Boston, 1931.

McAdoo, William G. *Crowded Years: Reminiscences of William G. McAdoo*. Boston, 1931.

Phillips, Walter P. "From Franklin to Edison." *Sketches Old and New*. New York, [?].

PERIODICALS

Abrams, Ernest R. "The Inquisitive Thomas Edison." *Public Utilities Fortnightly* XXXIX (January 30, 1947), 135–142.

"Academic Honors for a Wizard." *Outlook* CXIV (Novmeber 1, 1916), 481–482.

Acheson, Edward G. "My Days with Edison." *Scientific American* CIV (February 11, 1911), 142–143.

"Achievements of Thomas A. Edison." *Proceedings of the New Jersey Historical Society* XIV (new series) (July 1929), 331–334.

"The Age of Edison." *Outlook* CXLV (February 23, 1927), 227.

"Adult Illiterates." *Time* II (October 15, 1923), 18.

Alexander, Jack. "Ungovernable Governor." *Saturday Evening Post* CCXV (January 23, 1943), 9–10, 51, 53–54.

Allen, W. E. "Some Points Suggested by the Edison Questionnaire." *School and Society* XIV (November 12, 1921), 433–435.

American Inventor I–XVI (June 1, 1898–December, 1907).

The American Magazine XCIII (February 1922), 46.

"The Anecdotal Side of Edison." *Ladies' Home Journal* XV (April 1898), 7–8.

"Anecdotes of Edison." *Review of Reviews* XVII (April 1898), 458.

"Anniversary of Edison Lighting." *Public Utilities Fortnightly* LXVII (January 19, 1961), 118–119.

Anton, Mark. "To the Memory of Thomas A. Edison." *Edison Electric Institute Bulletin* XXII (June 1954), 183–186.

"Another of America's Great Sons." *Industrial Arts and Vocational Education* XXXVI (February 1947), 55.

Antiques CXVI (September 1979), 546–547.

"Are We in Danger from Materialism?" *Current Literature* XLIX (November 1910), 536–538.

"Are Your Trees Worth Saving?" *Time* (March 12, 1928), 49.

Arnold, Bion J. "The Edison Medal." *Science* XIX (May 27, 1904), 835–836.

Asimov, Isaac. ". . . And There Was Light." *Science Digest* LXXXIV (October 1978), 13–17.

——— . "Edison . . . Bringer of Light." *Senior Scholastic* LXXIV (March 6, 1959), 14–15.

Aunt Fanny. "A Wonderful Candle." *St. Nicholas* VI (March 1879), 309–311.

"Award and Presentation of the Rumford Premium." *Science* III (June 19, 1896), 891–893.

"Awards to American Electricians." *Scientific American,* August 19, 1882. Reprinted in Association of Edison Illuminating Companies, *Edison Honored Throughout the World* (New York, 1929), 12.

B., H., and S., R. "Thomas Edison Talks on Invention in the Life of Today." *Review of Reviews* LXXXIII (September 1931), 38–40.

Bacheller, Irving. "Making Friends with Luck." *American Magazine* CVII (January 1929), 54–57.

——— . "Making Good with Lady Luck." *The Literary Digest* C (February 16, 1929), 54–57.

Baker, Joseph B. "Thomas A. Edison's Latest Invention, A Storage Battery Designed and Constructed from the Automobile User's Point of View." *Scientific American* CIV (January 14, 1911), 27, 30, 45–47.

Baker, Ray Stanndard. "Edison's Latest Marvel: The New Storage Battery." *Windsor Magazine* XVI (November 1902), 603–609.

Ballentine, Caroline Farrand. "The True Story of Edison's Childhood and Boyhood." *Michigan History Magazine* IV (January 1920), 168–192.

Banning, Kendall. "Men and Methods." *System* XXVI (November 1914), 522–524.

Barbato, Joseph. "Bringing Edison to Light." *Change* XI (March 1979), 40–43.

——— . "Robert Conot." *Publisher's Weekly* CCXV (March 19, 1979), 8–9.

Barber, DeWitt D. "The Edison Questionnaire." *Scientific American* CXXIV (May 28, 1921), 429.

Barnard, Charles. "Thomas Alva Edison." *The Chautauquan* XVIII (March 1894), 677–680.

Barney, Mary Wilbur. "Milan's First Century." *The Firelands Pioneer* XX (new series) (December 25, 1918), 2047–2053.

Barrett, William F. "Edison's Telephone." *Nature* XIX (March 20, 1879), 471–472.

——— . "Mr. Edison's Inventions." *The Electrician* II (November 23, 1879), 76–77.

——— . "The Telephone, Its History and Its Recent Improvements: II." *Nature* XIX (November 7, 1878), 12–14.

——— . "The Telephone, Its History and Its Recent Improvements: III." *Nature* XIX (November 21, 1878), 56–59.

Beach, Frederick E. "Thomas Alva Edison (1847–1931)." *American Journal of Science* XXIII (5th series) (January 1932), 94–96.

Beard, George M. "The Nature of the Newly Discovered Force." *Scientific American* XXXIV (January 22, 1876), 57.

——— . "The Newly-Discovered Force." *Archives of Electrology and Neurology* II (1875), 257–282.

Beardsley, Harry M. "Self-Made Genius." *Facts* II (April 1943), 99–107.

Bell, Louis, "The Relation of Electric Inventions to Human Activity." *Engineering Magazine* XXVI (March 1904), 967–978.

Benjamin, Park. "Communication at Sea." *Public Opinion* IV (December 10, 1887), 207.

Benson, Allan L. "Do You Know the 'Little Peoples'?" *The Dearborn Independent,* March 21, 1925, p. 2.

———. "Edison on How to Live Long." *Hearst's Magazine* XXIII (February 1913), 266–269.

———. "Edison Says Germany Excels Us." *The World Today* XXI (November 1911), 1356–1360.

———. "Edison Sees the 200-Year-Old Man." *The Dearborn Independent,* March 14, 1925, p. 2.

———. "Edison Tells How to Cook." *Good Housekeeping* LIV (March 1913), 401–404.

———. "Edison's Dream of New Music." *Cosmopolitan* LIV (May 1913), 797, 800.

———. "Edison's Substitute for Schoolbooks." *The World Today* XXI (March 1912), 1923–1927.

———. "Mr. Edison Says: Electricity and Machinery Can Make Household Drudgery a Thing of the Past." *The Delineator* LXXVII (January 1911), 7, 67.

———. " 'O Sleep! It is a Gentle Thing'." *The Dearborn Independent,* April 11, 1925, p. 2.

———. "Thomas A. Edison, Benefactor of Humanity." *Munsey's Magazine* XLII (December 1909), 419–425.

———. "The Wonderful New World Ahead of Us." *Cosmopolitan* L (February 1911), 294–306.

[Bernays, Edward L.] "Men at the Top: A Bernays'-Eye View." *Fortune* LXXII (October 1965), 138–139.

Better Homes and Gardens XII (March 1934), 42.

Birkinbine, John, and Edison, Thomas Alva. "The Concentration of Iron-ore." *American Institute of Mining Engineers Transactions* XVII (1888), 728–744.

Blackton, J. S. "An Interview with Thomas Alva Edison." *The School Arts Magazine* XXXI (December 1931), 9–12.

Boelio, Robert C. "The Golden Years of Thomas A. Edison." *Antiques Journal* XII (October 1957), 22–26.

Bongartz, R. "Ladies and Gentlemen, It Lights!" *Americana* VII (September 1979), 68–72.

The Bookman XXVII (June 1908), 389.

Boone, Andrew R. "Edison on the Screen: Famous Experiments Recreated in Movie." *Popular Science Monthly* CXXXVII (July 1940), 102–105.

Bowen, Harold G. "Thomas Alva Edison's Early Motion-Picture Experiments." *Journal of the Society of Motion Picture and Television Engineers* LXIV (September 1955), 508–514.

Bowie, Beverley M. "The Past is Present in Greenfield Village." *National Geographic Magazine* CXIV (July 1958), 96–127.

"Boy's Own Hero." *The Publisher's Weekly* CXX (October 24, 1931), 1919.

Brackett, C. F., and Young, C. A. "Notes of Experiments upon Mr. Edison's Dynamometer, Dynamo-Machine and Lamp." *Journal of Science* XIX (June 1880), 475–479.

Bradford, Gamaliel. "Thomas Alva Edison, Worker." *Nation's Business,* XVIII (July, September 1930), 15–17, 49–52, 156–157, 210–214.

Braucher, Howard. "Mrs. Thomas A. Edison." *Recreation* XLI (November 1947), 361.

———. "Thomas A. Edison." *Recreation* XL (March 1947), 625.

"Brightest Boys." *Time* XIV (August 12, 1929), 14, 16, 18.

Broad, William J. "Rival Centennial Casts New Light on Edison." *Science,* CCIV (April, 1979), 32–33, 35–36.

"Bronze Bust of Edison to Appear in NYU's Hall of Fame for Great Americans." *Electrical Engineering* LXXIX (December 1960), 1067–1068.

Brooks, Herbert Baron. "Electrical Indicating Instruments Used in Early Edison Central Stations (1880–88)." *Journal of the Franklin Institute* CCLVI (November 1953), 401–422.

Brown, S. "Electricity as an Executioner." *Scientific American,* XXXIV (February 12, 1876), 100.

Brownell, W. C. "The Paris Exposition: Notes and Impressions." *Scribner's Magazine* VII (January 1890), 18–35.

Bruce, H. Addington. "Great American Inventors: Eli Whitney, 1765–1825; Robert Fulton, 1819–1867; S. F. B. Morse, 1791–1872; Alex. Graham Bell, 1847– ; Thomas Alva Edison, 1847– ." *The Mentor* I (September 1, 1913), 1–11; frontpieces.

Buckingham, Charles L. "The Telegraph of Today." *Scribner's Magazine* VI (July 1889), 3–22.

Bulletin of the Edison Electric Light Company, New York, 1882–1883.

Burritt, Richard C. "Another Edison Makes Some Discoveries." *The New York Times Magazine,* October 12, 1941, pp. 16, 27.

Burroughs, John. "Was There Ever Another Vacation Like This?" *System, The Magazine of Business* XLIX (June 1926), 790–794.

"But the Cupboard Was Pretty Bare." *Business Week* [?] (February 15, 1947), 32.

Byrn, Edward W. "The Progress of Invention During the Past Fifty Years." *Scientific American* LXXV (July 25, 1896), 82–83.

Carr, A. H. Z. "Tuning In On Luck." *Coronet* XXXIV (May 1953), 160–162.

Carroll, T. J. "Mr. Edison and Science." *The Commonweal* XV (November 25, 1931), 105.

The Canadian LXXVIII (November 1932), 11.

Canby, Edward Tatnall. "The Golden Voices of Edison." *Harper* CCXIII (July 1956), 95–96.

"The Carbon Telephone." *Scientific American* XXXIX (June 8, 1878), 353.

Carville, R. "Behold the Man." *The Golden Book Magazine* XIII (April 1931), 78–79.

Cary, R. "Thomas Alva Edison." *Literary Digest* CXI (November 14, 1931), 41.

"Celebration of the Twenty-Fifth Anniversary of the Invention of the Edison Incandescent Lamp." *Scientific American Supplement* LVII (March 5, 1904), 23555–23556.

"The Centennial of Two Great Men: Alexander Graham Bell and Thomas A. Edison." *Educational Screen* XXVI (March 1947), 144–145.

Cessna, Ralph. "Edison Institute: Pageant of Progress." *Christian Science Monitor,* May 10, 1941, pp. 4, 12.

Chamberlain, John. "A History of American Business." *Fortune* LXV (February 1962), 127–130, 132, 136, 138, 143–144.

Channing, William F. "Popular Miscellany: Anticipations Concerning the Phonograph." *The Popular Science Monthly* XII (April 1878), 756–757.

The Chautauquan XLIX (February 1908), 301.

——— LXIV (September 1911), 81.

Churchill, Arthur. "Edison and His Early Work." *Scientific American Supplement* LIX (April 1, 1905), 24451–24452.

Clark, Delbert. "What Makes a Genius?" *Saturday Review* XXXVIII (November 12, 1955), 9–10, 49–52.

Clarke, C. L. "Edison's Electric Railway Economically Considered." *Van Nostrand's Engineering Magazine* XXXIII (1880), 515–517.

Claudy, C. H. "The Romance of

Invention–XX." *Scientific American* CXXIV (March 19, 1921), 230, 238–239.

Coakley, John C. F. "Thomas Edison's 102 Years." *Public Utilities Fortnightly* XLIII (February 3, 1949), 156–159.

"Coffin." *Time* VIII (July 26, 1926), 26.

Colby, F. M. "What Nobody Ought to Know." *Harper's* CXLIII (September 1921), 479–484.

Collier's LXXIV (November 29, 1924), 21.

——— CXXXVI (December 9, 1955), 68.

Collins, F. L. "Mrs. Thomas A. Edison as the Wife of a Genius Has a Full-time Job." *Delineator* CXI (July 1927), 8, 74, 77.

Collins, James H. "My Interview with Edison." *Public Utilities Fortnightly,* LXIV (July 2, 1959), 43–51.

"The Columbia." *The Electrician* V (May 29, 1880), 15.

Coman, Martha, and Weir, Hugh. "Home Can Make or Break You." *Collier's* LXXVI (August 1, 1925), 17.

———. "The Most Difficult Husband in America." *Collier's,* LXXVI (July 18, 1925), 11, 42–43.

"The Coming Vocal Type-writing Machine." *Public Opinion* IV (December 3, 1887), 184.

Commager, Henry Steele. "Edison: Typical American." *Scholastic* L (February 10, 1947), 13.

Compton, Karl T. "Edison's Laboratory in War Time." *Science* LXXV (January 15, 1932), 70–71.

Conant, James B. "The Advancement of Knowledge in the United States in the Nineteenth Century." *Colorado Quarterly* XI (Winter 1963), 229–244.

"The Conferring of the Congressional Medal on Mr. Edison." *School and Society* XXVIII (October 27, 1928), 510–511.

"Conferring of the Congressional Medal on Mr. Edison." *Science* LXVIII (October 26, 1928), 398.

Connery, Thomas B. "Reminiscences of Two Modern Heroes." *The Cosmopolitan* XI (June 1891), 150–151.

Conot, Robert. "Twin of a Feeble Edison 1879 Light Bulb Casts One-candlepower Glow For Centenary." *Smithsonian* X (September 1979), 34–43.

"Conquest of Culture!" *Time* XII (November 19, 1928), 13.

"Contemporary Portraits. New Series.–No. 23. Thomas Alva Edison." *Dublin University Magazine* IV (November 1879), 584–598.

Coolidge, Calvin. "Address of President Coolidge in Honor of Mr. Edison." *Science* LXVIII (October 26, 1928), 389–390.

Cormack, J. D. "Edison." *Good Words* XLII (1901), 157–163.

"The Correct Answer to Mr. Edison's Question: 'What Is Grape-Nuts Made of?' " *Literary Digest* LXXV (July 1, 1922), 53.

"Correspondence: Edison's Electrical Generator." *Scientific American* XLI (November 1, 1879), 476.

Cosmopolitan IL (June 1910), 46.

Cowan, Thomas H. "Mr. Edison Didn't Like It." *American Heritage* VI (August 1955), 82.

Crawford, Remsen. "Patents, Profits, and Pirates." *The Saturday Evening Post* CCIII (September 27, 1930), 3–5, 135, 137–138.

Crosby, Otis A. "Edison Pioneered Audio-Visual Learning." *The Nation's Schools* LXVII (February 1961), 92–96.

Crowell, James R. "What It Means to Be Married to a Genius." *American Magazine* CXI (February 1930), 24–26, 150–153.

Crowther, Samuel. "Educating for Leadership: Henry Ford Explains His New Schools for a Million Children." *Ladies' Home Journal* XLVII (August 1930), 12, 69.

———. "My Vacations with Ford and Edison." *System, The Magazine of Business* XLIX (May 1926), 643–645, 722–725.

——— . "T. A. E.–A Great National Asset." *Saturday Evening Post* CCI (January 5, 1929), 6–7, 124, 126, 129.

——— . "What Vacations Have Taught Me About Business." *System, The Magazine of Business* L (July 1926), 47–49, 106–107.

Current History XXIX (March 1929), 939.

Current Opinion, July, 1930.

Dacy, G. H. "Edison's Rubber." *Scientific American* CXLII (May 1930), 384–385.

Darrell, R. D. "Mr. Edison's Phonograph: A Post-Mortem." *The Sewanee Review* XLI (January–March 1933), 91–103.

"A Day with Edison at Schenectady." *Supplement to the Electrical World* XII (August 25, 1888), 1–12.

Dean, Arthur. "A Point of View." *Industrial Education Magazine* XXIV (August 1922), 37–38.

"Death of a Titan." *Time* XVIII (October 26, 1931), 52.

DeFonvielle, W. "Le Phonographe d'Edisson [sic]." *L'Illustration* LXXI (March 3, 1878), 196.

DeLoach, Robert John Henderson. "In Camp with Four Great Americans." *The Georgia Review* XIII (Spring 1959), 42–51.

Depinet, Ned E. "The Position of the Film Director." *The Rotarian* XLVIII (February, 1936), 42–44.

Desmond, Shaw. "Edison's Views Upon Vital Human Problems." *Strand Magazine* LXIV (August 1922), 155–162.

"Development Days at Menlo Park–1880." *Edison Monthly* XV (June 1923), 118–119.

De Vogue, Eugene-Melchoir. "Electricity at the Paris Exposition." *The Chautauquan* X (November 1889), 193–197.

Dickson, Antonia, and Dickson, W. K. L. "Edison's Invention of the Kineto-phonograph." *Century Magazine* XLVIII (June 1894), 206–214.

"Did Mr. Edison Flunk You? Try This One." *The Independent* CV (June 4, 1921), 603–607.

"The Discovery of Another Form of Electricity." *Scientific American* XXXIII (December 25, 1875), 400–401.

"Distinguished Inventors." *Scientific American* LXXV (July 25, 1896), 84–86.

"Dr. Steinmetz." *Time* II (November 5, 1923), 22.

Dodds, Laurence B., and Crotty, Francis W. "The New Doctrinal Trend." *Journal of the Patent Office Society* XXX (February 1948), 83–120.

Dos Passos, John. "Edison and Steinmetz: Medicine Men." *The New Republic* LXI (December 18, 1929), 103–105.

"Double Deuce." *Time* XVII (January 12, 1931), 34.

Dow, Carl S. "American Engineering: I. Engineers and Engineering." *The Chautauquan* LXIV (September–November 1911), 72–81.

Drake, James. A. "The Parallel Careers of Edison and Bell." *High Fidelity Magazine* XXVII (January 1977), 68–72.

Dunlap, Orrin E., Jr. "Edison Glimpsed at Radio in 1875." *Scientific American* CXXXV (December 1926), 424–425.

Dyer, Frank L., and Martin, T. Commerford. "Edison's Inventions: Their Commercial Value to the World." *Scientific American Supplement* LXVII (April 3, 10, 1909), 210–211, 230–231.

——— . "Impressions of American Inventors. I. Thomas A. Edison." *Scientific American* C (February 27, 1909), 171.

"The Eclipse of the Sun, July 29, 1878." *Scientific American* XXXIX (August 17, 1878), 96.

Edgar, Charles L. "An Appreciation of Mr. Edison Based on Personal Acquaintance." *Science* LXXV (January 15, 1932), 59–65.

"Edison." *The Christian Century* XLVIII (October 28, 1931), 1336–1337.

"Edison." *The Nation* CXXXIII (October 28, 1931), 449–450.

"Edison." *The Telegraphic Journal* IX (November 5, 1881), 440–441.

Edison, Charles. "My Experiences Working for Father." *American Magazine* LXXXVI (August 1918), 33–35, 91.

———. "My Father and Music." *Etude* LXV (February 1947), 64–65, 80, 113.

———. "My Most Unforgettable Character." *Reader's Digest* LXXIX (December 1961), 172–180.

Edison, Mrs. Thomas A. "Home-Making Is a Profession." *Pictorial Review* XXXII (November 1930), 2, 90.

———. "Leisure and Contentment." *Playground* XXIII (January 1930), 607–609.

———. "Recreation and Wholesome Living." *Recreation* XXIX (December 1935), 443, 469–470.

———. "Share Your Christmas." *Parents Magazine* IX (December 1934), 11.

Edison, Thomas Alva. "The Air-Telegraph: System of Telegraphing to Trains and Ships." *North American Review* CXLII (March 1886), 285–291.

———. "The Beginning of the Incandescent Lamp." *Scientific American Supplement* LVII (May 14, 1904), 23711–12.

———. "Beginnings." *The Saturday Evening Post* CCL (July–Aug. 1978), 44–45.

———. "A Better Idea." *The Saturday Evening Post* CCXLVIII (July–Aug. 1976), 49.

———. "The Dangers of Electric Lighting." *North American Review* CXLIX (November 1889), 625–634.

———. "Dangers of Electric Lighting." *Public Opinion* VIII (November 9, 1889), 113–114.

———. "Edison's Impressions of European Industries." *Scientific American* CV (November 18, 1911), 445.

———. "Edison's New Art of Generating Electricity." *Scientific American* LXVIII (February 18, 1893), 99.

———. "How I Would Double the Volume of a Business." *System, The Magazine of Business* XLIV (September 1923), 265–268, 330–332.

———. "How the Movies Got Their Start." *Science Illustrated* III (July 1948), 33–35, 79.

———. "Inventions of the Future." *Independent* LXVIII (January 6, 1910), 15–18.

———. "Letters from Eminent Americans Endorsing 'The Golden Hour'." *Etude* XXXIX (May 1921), 295.

———. "Mr. Edison on the Microphone." *Scientific American* XXXIX (July 13, 1878), 20.

———. "Mr. Edison's New Force." *Scientific American* XXXIV (February 5, 1876), 81.

———. "On a New Method of Working Polarised Relays." *The Telegraphic Journal* II (November 15, 1874), 361.

———. "On the Use of the Tasimeter for Measuring the Heat of the Stars and of the Sun's Corona." *American Journal of Science* CXVII (1879), 52–55.

———. "The Perfected Phonograph." *North American Review,* CXLVI (June 1888), 641–650.

———. "The Perfected Phonograph." *Public Opinion* V (June 9, 1888), 202–203.

———. "The Phonograph and Its Future." *North American Review* CXXVI (May–June 1878), 527–536.

———. "Photographing the Unseen—A Symposium on the Roentgen Rays." *Century Magazine* LII (May 1896), 120–131.

———. "Recollections of My Boyhood." *Continent* XX (May 1891).

———. "The Storage Battery and the Motor Car." *North American Review* CLXXV (July 1902), 1–4.

———. "The Success of the Electric

Light." *North American Review* CXXXI (October 1880), 295–300.

———. "Telephone Relay." *Chemical News* XXXVIII (October 18, 1878), 198.

———. "Telephonic Repeater." *Chemical News* XXXVIII (July 26, 1878), 45.

———. "Thomas A. Edison: Philosopher." *The Golden Book Magazine* XIII (April 1931), 78–79.

———. "Today and Tomorrow." *Independent* LXXVII (January 5, 1914), 24–27.

———, and Porter, Charles T. "Description of the Edison Steam Dynamo." *The Electrician* IX (July 15, 1882), 199–201.

"Edison and His Inventions: I." *Scribner's Monthly* XVIII (June 1879), 297–306.

"Edison and Immortality." *The Nation* CXXXIII (November 18, 1931), 534.

"Edison and the Electric Light." *Nature* XXI (February 12, 1880), 341–342.

"Edison and the Incandescent Lamp." *Cassier's Magazine* XXV (April 1904), 545–549.

"Edison and the Incandescent Lamp." *Science Monthly* LXIX (October 1949), 221.

"Edison and the Investor." *Review of Reviews* LXXX (July 1929), 80, 82.

"Edison and the Mutoscope in Court." *Scientific American* LXXXVI (March 22, 1902), 210.

"Edison and the Unseen Universe." *Scientific American* XXXIX (August 24, 1878), 112.

"Edison as Music Critic." *The Literary Digest* CXI (November 14, 1931), 18.

"The Edison Centennial." *Compressed Air Magazine* LII (February 1947), 39–42.

"The Edison Centennial Celebration 1847–1947." *School Life* XXIX (January 1947), 16–17.

"The Edison Concentrating Works." *The Iron Age* II (October 28, 1897), 1–8.

"Edison: De Rebus Sanitatis." *Time* XVII (January 5, 1931), 30.

"The Edison Electric Lighting Station." *Scientific American* XLVII (August 26, 1882), 127, 130.

"Edison Enters Heaven." *Time* XV (March 17, 1930), 69.

"Edison Flayed." *Time* XI (May 21, 1928), 22.

"The Edison Fluorescent Lamp." *The Electrical Engineer*, XXI (June 3, 1896), 596.

"Edison Giant Roll Patents Sustained." *Scientific American* CV (July 1, 1911), 13.

"Edison Hunting for Rubber in Weeds." *The Literary Digest* XCV (November 26, 1927), 18–19.

"Edisonia." *Time* XIII (February 25, 1929), 54.

"Edison Illuminates Lower Manhattan by Electricity." *Electrical World* CLV (June 5, 1961), 48–49, 89.

"Edison in Hall of Fame." *Science News Letter* LXXIX (June 17, 1961), 372.

"Edison in His Workshop." *Harper's Weekly* XXIII (August 2, 1879), 607.

"Edison in Pictures." *Science Digest* LIV (August 1963), 6–13.

"Edison in War Time." *American Magazine* LXXVIII (November 1914), 35–36.

"Edison Invented These, Too." *Science Illustrated* II (February 1947), 40–43.

"Edison Laboratory National Monument Opened." *Electrical Engineering* LXXVI (July 1957), 651.

"Edison Makes a Dress Suit Comfortable." *McBride's Magazine* XCVII (April 1916), 60.

"The Edison Memorial Tower." *The Scientific Monthly* XLVI (April 1938), 386–389.

"Edison—One of His Co-Workers Supplies an Anecdote." *Scientific American* CVXIII (September 1940), 145.

"Edison Plaque Unveiled at Site of Inventor's First Headquarters in New York City." *Edison Electric Institute Bulletin* XIX (November 1951), 378.

"The Edison Portland Cement Works."
Scientific American Supplement LVII (January 30, February 6, 1904), 23469–70, 23488–90.

"Edison's Camera Eye." *Reader's Digest* XL (March 1942), 77.

"Edison's Defense of His Questionnaire." *The Literary Digest* LXXI (November 26, 1921), 47.

"Edison's Early Inventive Genius." *World's Work* X (July 1905), 6441–6442.

"Edison's Electric Light." *Harper's Weekly* XXIV (January 3, 1880), 6–7.

"Edison's Electrical Generator." *Scientific American* XLI (October 18, 1879), 242.

"Edison's Electro-Chemical Telephone." *Scientific American* XL (April 26, 1879), 260.

"Edison's Electro-Motograph." *Scribner's Monthly* XVIII (May 1879), 154–155.

"Edison's Foresight Put Raw Ideas to Work." *Electrical World* CLV (June 5, 1961), 50.

"Edison's Gift to Humanity." *Literary Digest* LI (October 2, 1915), 707–708.

"Edison's Golden Day." *Literary Digest* CIII (November 2, 1929), 10–11.

"Edison's Greatest Invention Half Century Old." *Popular Mechanics* XLVIII (August 1927), 203–207.

"Edison's Handwriting." *Mentor* XVII (June 1929), 67.

"Edison's Home Becomes Historic Shrine." *Edison Electric Institute Bulletin* XXV (February 1957), 47.

"Edison's Improvement of the Transmission of Power." *Scientific American* LXVIII (May 13, 1893), 296.

"Edison's Inventions." *Nature* XVIII (October 24, 1878), 674–676.

"Edison's Inventions: II." *Scribner's Monthly* XVIII (July 1879), 446–455.

"Edison's Laboratory Tests for Human Nature." *Literary Digest* LVI (March 9, 1918), 52–56.

"Edison's Light." *Engineering News* VII (December 25, 1880), 443.

"Edison's Microtasimeter." *Chemical News* XXXVIII (August 2, 1878), 56–58.

"Edison's Microtasimeter." *Scientific American* XXXVIII (June 22, 1878), 385.

"Edison's Microtasimeter and Carbon Telephone." *Chemical News* XXXVIII (November 15, 1878), 241.

"Edison's Mill for Iron Ore." *Review of Reviews* XVI (November 1897), 603–604.

"Edison's Most Important Discovery." *Harper's Weekly* XLV (December 21, 1901), 1302.

"Edison's New Electrical Railway." *Scientific American* XLII (June 5, 1880), 354.

"Edison's New Method of Telegraphing Without Wires." *Scientific American* LXVI (January 16, 1892), 36.

"Edison's New Steam Dynamo." *Scientific American* XLV (December 10, 1881), 367.

"Edison's Patents Sustained by the United States Circuit of Appeals." *Scientific American* LXVII (October 15, 1892), 245.

"Edison's Phonographic Doll." *Scientific American* LXII (April 26, 1890), 263.

"Edison's Phonomotor." *Scientific American* XXXIX (July 27, 1878), 51.

"Edison's Posers Answered—in Various Ways." *Literary Digest* LXIX (May 28, 1921), 38–44.

"Edison's Prophecy: A Duplex, Sleepless, Dinnerless World." *Literary Digest* IL (November 14, 1914), 966–968.

"Edison's Religion." *Literary Digest* CXI (November 7, 1931), 19–20.

"Edison's Revolutionary Education." *Literary Digest* XLVII (October 4, 1913), 576–577.

"Edison's System of Concrete Houses." *Scientific American* XCVII (November 16, 1907), 356.

"Edison's System of Fast Telegraphy."

Scribner's Monthly XVIII (October 1879), 840-846.

"Edison's Views on Immortality Criticized." *Current Literature* XLIX (December 1910), 644–647.

"Edison's Working Hours." *Literary Digest* CXI (November 28, 1931), 18–19.

"The Edison System of Electric Illumination." *Engineering* XXXIII (March 10, 1882), 226–228.

"Edison the Experimenter." *Science News Letter* LXXI (February 1957), 90–91.

"Edison: The Man Behind the Genius." *Reader's Digest* CIII (July 1973), 160–164.

"Edison to Be Installed in Hall of Fame June 4." *Edison Electric Institute Bulletin* XXIX (May 1961), 134.

"Edison Toy Manufacturing Company." *Scientific American* LXIII (December 6, 1890), 353.

"Edison Under Fire." *American Magazine* LXXIX (March 1915), 11–14.

"Editor's Outlook: Edison's Wonderful Phonograph." *The Chautauquan* IX (October 1888), 53.

"Editor's Scientific Record." *Harper's New Monthly Magazine* LVI (December 1877), 154.

"Editor's Scientific Record." *Harper's New Monthly Magazine* LVII (September 1878), 635.

"Editor's Scientific Record." *Harper's New Monthly Magazine* LVIII (February 1879), 475.

"Editor's Scientific Record." *Harper's New Monthly Magazine* LIV (July 1879), 314.

"Editor's Table: American Contributions to Electrical Science." *The Popular Science Monthly* XII (April 1878), 744–745.

Edwards, E. J. "The Edge of the Future: Unsolved Problems that Edison is Studying." *McClure's* I (June 1893), 37–39.

———. "The Great Promoters." *Munsey's Magazine* XXX (October 1930), 73–81.

Einstein, Albert. "Thomas Alva Edison." *The Outlook and Independent* CLIX (October 28, 1931), 261.

"Electric Exhibition." *Leisure Hour* XXX (1881), 763.

"Electric Illumination." *The Popular Science Monthly* XIV (December 1878), 234–237.

"The Electric Light in Houses." *Harper's Weekly* XXVI (June 24, 1882), 394.

"The Electric Pen." *Engineering* XXII (December 15, 1876), 511.

"An Electric Railroad." *Harper's Weekly* XXVI (July 15, 1882), 433–439.

"Electrical Apparatus Presented by Columbia University to Edisonia." *Science* LXX (December 27, 1929), 628.

"The Electrical Exhibition." *Harper's Weekly* XXVIII (September 13, 1884), 597.

"The Electro-Motograph." *The Telegraphic Journal* II (October 1, 1874), 321–322.

Electron. "Mr. Edison's New Force." *Scientific American* XXXIV (January 29, 1876), 69.

Emery, E. W. "A Plea." *Literary Digest* CXI (November 14, 1931), 41.

"End of the Edison Era." *Literary Digest* CXI (October 31, 1931), 8–10.

Engel, Leonard. "Thomas Edison, American Wizard of the Industrial Age." *Science Digest* XXXIV (October 1953), 84–89.

"The English Press and Mr. Edison." *Bulletin of the Edison Electric Light Company* X (1882), 12.

Erichsen, Hugo. "How the Edison Phonograph Came to Michigan." *Michigan History Magazine* XVI (1932), 59–67.

Espenshade, A. H. "Edison, Benefactor of Mankind." *The Saint Nicholas Magazine* LVI (February 1929), 291–292, 331.

Esteourt, R. "Light," *Time* V (April 6, 1925), 28. [Letter to editor]

"Etheric Force and Weak Electric Sparks." *Scientific American* XXXIV (January 1, 1876), 2.

Etude L (June 1932), 391–392, 452. [Portrait with comment]

"Execution By Electricity." *Public Opinion* VII (July 27, 1889), 336.

"Extremely Bright Boys." *Time* XVI (August 11, 1930), 34.

F., M. "How to Make a Telephone." *St. Nicholas* V (June 1878), 549–551.

"Facts About the Only Recording of Mr. Edison's Voice." *Hobbies* LXXVI (January 1972), 37–38; (February 1972), 37–38.

Fales-Curtis, [?]. " 'Graphing' and 'phoning' a Concert." *Harper's Weekly* XXXIII (February 16, 1889), 127.

"Famous Edison Suit Settled." *The Talking Machine World*, April 15, 1909, p. 49.

"A Famous Vacation." *Life* XXVIII (January 2, 1950), 44–45.

Fantel, Hans. "The First 100 Years of the Phonograph." *Popular Mechanics* CXLVIII (August 1977), 87, 126, 128.

Farrar, Larston D. "The Philosophy of Thomas Edison." *Public Utilities Fortnightly* XXXIX (February 13, 1947), 201–209.

Favia-Artsay, Aida. "Edison Historical Souvenirs." *Hobbies* LXV (July 1960), 32.

"The Fiftieth Anniversary of the Incandescent Light and Mr. Edison." *Science* LXIX (May 10, 1929), 489–490.

"The First Forty Hours." *Scholastic* LXV (October 20, 1954), 12.

"First Practical Stencil Process Invented by Thomas A. Edison." *Speed-o-Print Merchandiser*, June 1944, p. 4.

Fish, Carman. "He Lighted the World's Pathways." *National Safety News* LV (February 1947), 20–21, 81–83.

Fiske, Bradley A. "The Electric Railway." *Popular Science Monthly* XXIV (April 1884), 749–750.

Floyd, Candy. "Birthday of the Lightbulb: An Enlightened Celebration." *History News*, XXXIV (March 1979), 67–69.

Flynn, John T. "Up and Down with Sam Insull." *Collier's* XC (December 3, 1932), 10–11, 32–33.

Forbes, B. C. "Edison Working on How to Communicate with the Next World." *American Magazine* XC (October 1920), 10–11, 82, 85.

————. "Why Do So Many Men Never Amount to Anything?" *American Magazine* XCI (January 1921), 10–11, 85–86, 89.

Forbes, Leslie. "SOS in the Night." *Coronet* XXXII (June 1952), 139.

"Ford and Edison on the Inventions of the Future." *Literary Digest* CIII (December 7, 1929), 28, 30.

Fraser, Hugh Russell. "Edison's 'First 100 Years'." *Pathfinder* LIV (February 12, 1947), 22–29.

Freeman, Effie C. "Mr. Edison's Doll." *Antiques Journal* X (May 1955), 38–39.

French, William Fleming. "How They Got Their Education." *Illustrated World* XXVIII (September 1922), 29–32.

"Gas and the Electric Light." *The Popular Science Monthly* XVI (April 1880), 859.

[Gentry, William D.] "Edison's Accidental Discoveries." *Scientific American* LXIII (October 11, 1890), 225.

Gessner, Robert. "The Moving Image." *American Heritage* XI (April 1960), 30–35, 100–104.

"Giants of the Electric Century, 1874–1974." *Electrical World* CLXXX (July 1, 1973), 29.

Gibbons, Cardinal. [Interview.] *Columbian Magazine, A Treasury of Entertainment and the Latest Useful Information* III (1911).

Giddings, Franklin H. "The Right to Be Ignorant." *The Independent* CV (May 28, 1921), 562–563.

Goebel, H. "The Edison Incandescent Lamp Patent Attacked." *Scientific American* LXVIII (February 11, 1893), 82–83.

"Golden Jubilee." *Time* XIII (May 27, 1929), 44, 46, 48, 50.

"Goldenrod Rubber." *Time* XIV (December 16, 1929), 63.

Gordon, Isobel. "Thomas Alva Edison." *Hobbies* LII (February 1948), 131, 133.

Gorman, Mel. "Charles F. Brush and the First Public Electric Street Lighting System in America." *Ohio Historical Quarterly* LXX (April 1961), 44, 128.

Grattan, C. Hartley, "Thomas Alva Edison (1847–1931): An American Symbol." *Scribner's Magazine* XLIV (September 1933), 151–156, 186–192.

Gray, Andrew, and Gray, Thomas. "The Tasimeter and Magnetization." *Scientific American* XXXIX (September 7, 1878), 143.

"The Great Edison Scare." *The Saturday Review of Politics, Literature, Science, and Art* (London) XLIV (January 10, 1880), 41–43.

"The Great Promoters." *Munsey's Magazine* XXX (October 1903), 78-81.

Greenwood, Ernest, "Grading Human Beings." *The Independent* CXV (December 12, 1925), 681–689.

"Guilty Conscience?" *Time* I (March 17, 1923), 24.

H., P. J. "The New Force." *Scientific American* XXXIV (January 29, 1876), 69.

Hahn, George C. "Thomas A. Edison Commemorative Stamp." *The American Philatelist* LXIII (August 1950), 857–871.

Haines, Jennie Day. "The Wonderful Century." *St. Nicholas* XXVIII (February 1901), 338–339.

"Hall of Fame Welcomes Thomas A. Edison." *Electrical World* CLV (June 5, 1961), cover, 47.

Hammer, Edwin J. "Edison Electric Railways of 1880 and 1882." *Electrical World and Engineer* XXXIII (June 19, 1899), 797–801.

Hammer, W. J. "James U. MacKenzie." *The Electrical Engineer* XIX (1895), 56.

——— . "William Wallace, and His Contributions to the Electrical Industries." *The Electrical Engineer* XV (February 1, 1893), 103–106.

Hammond, John Winthrop. "The Edison Pioneers." *Mentor* XVI (June 1928), 1–13.

——— . "The Historic Pearl Street Generating Station." *General Electric Review* X (October 1932), 499–502.

——— . "An Industry and a City." *New York History* XIII (1932), 236–246.

Hazard, Patrick. "Listenables and Lookables." *Senior Scholastic* LXX (February 8, 1957), 19-T.

Head, Walter D. "Thomas A. Edison, Rotarian." *The Rotarian* LXXVIII (February 1951), 25, 59.

"He Doubled the World's Working Hours." *Time* XIV (September 30, 1929), 63. [Advertisement]

Hendricks, Gordon. "A Collection of Edison Films." *Image* VIII (September 1959), 156–163.

"Henry Ford, Historian; At Ford's Edison Institute." *House and Garden* LXXIX (February 1941), 24–25, 63.

Hidden, W. E. "On Edisonite, a Fourth Form of Titanic Acid." *American Journal of Science* XXXVI (3rd series) (October 1888), 272–274.

"High Jinks on Edison's Eightieth Birthday." *The Literary Digest* XCII (March 5, 1927), 34–40.

"His Diary Reveals an Unsuspected Mr. Edison." *American Heritage* XXII (December 1970), 68–74.

Holland, Walter E. "The Edison Storage Battery. Its Pre-eminent Fitness for Vehicle Service." *Electrical World* LV (April 28, 1910), 1080–1083.

Holmes. G. S. "And Yet Fools Say." *Literary Digest* CXI (November 14, 1931), 41. [poem]

"Honoring Mr. Edison." *World's Work* LVII (December 1928), 121–122.

Hoover, Herbert Clark, "Mr. Hoover's Tribute to Mr. Edison." *Science* LXX (November 1, 1929), 411–413.

————. "The Progress of Science." *The Scientific Monthly* XXIX (December 1929), 566–571.

"An Hour With Edison." *Scientific American* XXXIX (July 13, 1878), 17.

Housley, J. Elmer. "Edison and the AIEE." *Electrical Engineering* LXVI (February 1947), 118.

Houston, E. J., and Thomson, Elihu. "Electrical Phenomena. The Alleged Etheric Force-Test Experiments as to Its Identity with Induced Electricity." *Scientific American Supplement* I (May 20, 1876), 326.

"How Edison 'Won the War'." *The Literary Digest* LXVII (October 23, 1920), 26–27.

"How Edison Worked." *Literary Digest* CXI (November 21, 1931), 17.

"How Publicity Paid Edison." *The Literary Digest* LVIII (July 6, 1918), 34–35.

"How to Find a Genius." *Literary Digest* CI (June 8, 1929), 20–21.

Hubert, Philip G., Jr. "The New Talking-Machines." *Atlantic Monthly* LXIII (February 1889), 256–261.

Hughes, Thomas P. "Harold P. Brown and the Executioner's Current: An Incident in the AC-DC Controversy." *Business History Review* XXXII (Summer 1958), 143–165.

"Hughes' Microphone an Alleged Piracy." *Scientific American* XXXIIX (June 22, 1878), 388.

Hulsenbeck, R. "Edison Passes On." *The Living Age* CCCXLI (December 1931), 327–329.

Huyck, Dorothy Boyle. "Over Hill and Dale with Henry Ford and Famous Friends." *Smithsonian* IX (June 1978), 88–95.

Iles, George. "Some Great American Scientists: VI. Thomas Alva Edison." *Chatauquan* IL (February 1908), 389–396.

"Imaginary Interviews: Thomas A. Edison." *Time* I (May 28, 1923), 22.

"Imaginary Interviews: Thomas A. Edison." *Time* III (February 4, 1924), 22.

"Imaginary Interviews: Thomas Edison." *Time* III (February 25, 1924), 30.

"In Memoriam: Thomas Alva Edison." *Punch* CLXXXI (October 28, 1931), 457.

"In Memory of Mr. Edison." *Recreation* XXV (January 1932), 582.

The Independent XLI (March 28, 1889), 8.

————— LXXXIII (July 26, 1915), cover page.

—— XCVIII (June 21, 1919), 44. [Portrait with comment]

"Industrial Preparedness for Peace—An Interview with Thomas Alva Edison." *Scientific American* CXV (December 2, 1916), 497.

Inglis, William. "Edison and the New Education." *Harper's Weekly* LV (November 4, 1911), 8.

"The Installation of the Edison Light." *The Electrician* ILX (February 11, 1882), 202–203.

International Studio XXXI (June 1907), cxxii–cxxx.

"An Interview with Mr. Edison." *Open Court* XXVIII (June 1914), 380–381.

"In the Driftway" *The Nation* CXXXIII (November 11, 1931), 517–518.

"In the Interpreter's House: A New View of Thomas A. Edison." *American Magazine* LXVII (November 1908), 101–104.

"The Invention of the Incandescent Lamp Awarded to Edison." *Scientific American* LXVII (October 22, 1892), 259.

"Inventions Do Not Come by Chance." *Public Opinion* VII (September 21, 1889), 495–496.

"The Inventor and the World." *The New Republic* LXVIII (November 4, 1931), 312–313.

"Is the Old-Fashioned Home Gone Forever?" *Literary Digest* CVI (April 2, 1930), 18.

"Is There a Dearth of Great Men?" *The Literary Digest* XCIV (August 6, 1927), 12–13.

"It Could Only Happen Here." *The Business Week* [?] (October 26, 1929), 29–30.

Jacks, Maston M. "Edison Started Something." *Popular Mechanics* LXXXVII (February 1947), 153–157.

Jehl, Francis. "Birth of the Bulb." *Boardwalk Illustrated News* [IX?] (June 1929).

——— . "The First Three-wire Central Station." *Edison Monthly,* July 1927, pp. 165–166.

——— . "How Edison Discovered the Three-wire System." *Edison Monthly,* May 1927, pp. 117–118.

Jewett, F. B. "Edison's Contributions to Science and Industry." *Science* LXXV (January 15, 1932), 65–68.

Johnson, Edward H. "Address to Kansas City Electric Light Convention." *The Electrical World* XV (February 22, 1890), 154.

——— . "Letter to the Editor on Phonograph." *Scientific American* XXXVII (November 17, 1877), 304.

Johnston, Alva. "Profiles—the Wizard." *The New Yorker* V (December 28, 1929), 21–24; (January 4, 1930), 24–26; (January 11, 1930), 22–25.

Jones, Ernest. "How to Tell Your Friends from Geniuses." *Saturday Review* XL (August 10, 1957), 9–11, 39–40.

Josephson, Matthew. "Edison: Last Days of the Wizard." *American Heritage* X (October 1959), 32–45.

——— . "Edison's Struggle to Build a Better Battery." *Popular Science* CLXXV (December 1959), 132–135.

——— . "The Invention of the Electric Light." *Scientific American* CCI (November 1959), 98–106, 108, 110, 112, 114.

"A Jubilee to Be Noted." *Industrial Arts and Vocational Education* XLIII (December 1954), 336.

Kaempffert, Waldemar. "The Light of Edison's Lamp." *The Survey* LXIII (October 1, 1929), 12–16, 58–59.

——— . "Scientist-Magician Who Reshaped a World." *The New York Times Magazine,* February 9, 1947, pp. 12–13, 45–47.

——— . "A Visit to the Home of Thomas A. Edison." *Woman's Home Companion* XXXI (February 1904), 3–4.

Kempf, Paul. "Thomas A. Edison Sees A Menace for Music in the Radio." *The Musician* XXXII (January 1927), 11–12.

Kennelly, Arthur E. "The Edison Storage Battery Described." *Electrical Review* XXXVIII (May 25, 1901), 666–669.

——— . "The New Edison Storage Battery." *American Institute of Electrical Engineers* XVIII (May 21, 1901), 219–243.

Kettering, Charles F. "Thomas Alva Edison." *The Scientific Monthly* LXIV (February 1947), 109–116.

"The Kinetograph." *Public Opinion* LX (April 19, 1890), 37.

Kluckhohn, Frank L. "Another Edison Helps Build the Navy." *The New York Times Magazine,* January 14, 1940, pp. 9, 16.

Knight, Edward H. "Review of Recent Inventions." *Harper's Weekly* XIX (April 10, 1875), 298.

"Know-Nothing." *Time* XVI (December 22, 1930), 10.

Kolodin, Irving. "Edison's Baby: From Tinfoil to Tape." *Saturday Review* IV (July 23, 1977), 20–22.

"A Lady on Electric Lights." *Operator,* August 15, 1882. Reprinted in Association of Edison Illuminating Companies, *Edison Honored Throughout the World* (New York: Association of Edison Illuminating Companies, 1929), p. 12.

Lake, E. J. and Vaughn, S. J., eds. "The Edison Questionnaire." *Industrial-Arts Magazine* XI (November 1922), 440.

Lane, Winthrop D. "Edison Vs. Euclid: Has He Invented a Moving Stairway to

Learning; A Symposium." *Survey* **XXX** (September 6, 1913), 681–695.

Langfeldt, Bent. "Edison Og Dally." *Medicinhistorik Arsbok* **XXXIII** (1966), 87–91.

Lanier, Charles D. "Two Giants of the Electric Age: 1. Thomas A. Edison, Greatest of Inventors." *Review of Reviews* **VIII** (July 1893), 40–53.

Larned, E. S. "The Edison Concrete House: Conclusions of Engineers Concerning Practability of the Project. The Purpose of the Inventor." *Scientific American Supplement* **LXV** (April 18, 1908), 249–251.

"The Latest About the Edison Battery." *The Horseless Age* **XI** (April 8, 1903), 442.

Latham, Frank. "Builders of America: Thomas A. Edison (1847–1931), 'The Most Useful American.' " *Scholastic* **XLII** (March 15, 1943), 10.

Lathrop, George Parsons, "Edison's Kinetograph." *Harper's Weekly* **XXXV** (June 13, 1891), 446–447.

———. "Talks with Edison." *Harper's Magazine* **LXXX** (February 1890), 425–435.

"Laureates from Two Centuries." *Fortune* **CXI** (January 1975), 70.

Lawler, Joseph J. "Thomas A. Edison Stamp." *Hobbies* **LII** (March 1947), 110.

"Leading Men in Many Fields Agree That Restful Sleep is of Vital Importance." *Time* **XIV** (November 25, 1929), 36.

Lee, A. "Edison." *Poetry* **XXXIX** (December 1931), 128.

Leidy, Thomas W., and Shenton, Donald R. "Titan in Berks; Edison's Experiments in Iron Concentration." *Historical Review of Berks County* **XXIII** (Fall 1958), 104–110.

Lescarboura, Austin C. "Edison's Views on Life and Death." *Scientific American* **CXXIII** (October 30, 1920), 446, 458–460.

Leslie, Eric. "Inventors of Radio—Thomas A. Edison." *Radio-Electronics* **XXXI** (April 1960), 48–49.

Lewis, Joseph, and O'Hagan, John F.

"Communications: Edison and Religion." *The Commonweal* **XVII** (December 14, 1932), 188–189.

Lieb, John W. "The Work of Thomas Alva Edison in the Field of Illumination with Relation to the Contemporary State of the Art." *General Electrical Review* **XIX** (May 1916), 332–341.

"Life Doesn't Begin at 40." *Time* **LXII** (August 31, 1953), 38.

"Light on Edison." *Newsweek* **XXIX** (February 17, 1947), 27.

"Light's 80th Birthday." *Edison Electric Institute Bulletin* **XXVII** (October 1959), 351–352, 356.

" 'Light's Golden Jubilee' Commemorates Edison's Invention of Incandescent Lamp." *Railway Signaling* **XXII** (November 1929), 403–406.

"The Light That Changed the World." *Scholastic* **LXIX** (December 13, 1956), 12.

"Like to See Edison's Laboratory?" *Popular Science* **CL** (May 1947), 142–143.

The Literary Digest **XCVIII** (August 11, 1928), 9. [Portrait with comment]

"London Electrical Exhibition." *Telegraph & Telephone*, February 15, 1882. Reprinted in Association of Edison Illuminating Companies, *Edison Honored Throughout the World* (New York: Association of Edison Illuminating Companies, 1929), 12.

Long, Robert. "The Life and Labs of Thomas A. Edison." *High Fidelity Magazine* **XXVII** (January 1977), 73–80.

Lucker, Jay E. "Phonograph is Now Perfect: The Edison-Mayer Letters." *Princeton University Library Chronicle* **XXV** (Summer 1964), 220–224.

Ludwig, Emil. "Edison: Studie über Genie und Charakter." *Die Neue Rundschau* **XLIII** (January 1932), 52–69.

———. "Edison, the Greatest Man of the Century." *American Magazine* **CXII** (December 1931), 66–67, 96–97.

Lungren, C. M. "Electric and Gas Illumination." *The Popular Science Monthly* XXI (September 1882), 557–587.

McCabe, Lida Rose. "The Boyhood of Edison." *St. Nicholas* XX (August 1893), 761–766.

McClung, Littell. "What Can Henry Ford Do with Muscle Shoals?" *Illustrated World* XXXVII (April 1922), 184–191, 292.

McClure's Magazine I (July 1893), 124–125.

McCormick, Richard C. "Our Success at Paris in 1878." *North American Review* CXXIX (July 1879), 1–22.

McGinty, Brian. "The Great Invention: Thomas Edison Creates a Light for the World." *American History Illustrated* XIV (August 1979), 34–38.

"McGraw's Book: He Has Written a Piercing Satire, More Brilliant than Mr. Edison's." *Time* I (May 28, 1923), 25.

McGuire, Philip. "Technology and Commerce: The Gas Light Industry's Response to Edison's Electric Bulb." *Potomac Review* VI (1973), 70–75.

McHugh, F. D. "Ford's Friend Edison." *Scientific American* CXLI (November 1929), 377–380.

MacKaye, Percy. "Edison." *The Independent* LXXII (May 10, 1915), 244.

McLaurin, Richard C. "Mr. Edison's Service For Science." *Science* XLI (June 4, 1915), 813–815.

McNicol, Donald. "Thomas A. Edison." *Proceedings of the Institute of Radio Engineers, Inc.* XXXV, no. 2 (February 1947), 106.

Maguire, Franck Z. "The Graphophone." *Harper's Weekly* XXX (July 17, 1886), 458–459.

"Maladie du Siecle." *Time* VIII (July 12, 1926), 16.

Man, Albon. "Communications: 'Edison's Electric Light'—A Reply." *Scribner's Monthly* XIX (March 1880), 795.

"A Man I Admire: Notes on Two Members of Rotary's Board . . . and on Lives That Have Inspired Others." *Rotarian* LXXIII (December 1948), 43.

"Man of Light." *Time* XVIII (October 28, 1929), 15.

"The Man Who Made Jobs for Millions." *Popular Mechanics* LVI (December 1931), 906–908.

Marcosson, Isaac F. "The Coming of the Talking Picture." *Munsey's Magazine* XLVIII (March 1913), 956–960.

Marshall, Edward. "Has Man An Immortal Soul? An Authorized Interview with Thomas A. Edison." *The Forum* LXXVI (November 1926), 640–650, xliii.

———. "If the Answer is Easy It's Wrong." *Collier's* LXXIV (December 6, 1924), 5–6.

———. "Machine-Made Freedom, An Authorized Interview with Thomas A. Edison." *The Forum* LXXVI (October 1926), 492–497.

———. "The Scientific City of the Future, An Authorized Interview with Thomas A. Edison." *The Forum* LXXVI (December 1926), 823–829.

———. "Thomas A. Edison on Immortality." *Columbian Magazine* III (January 1911), 603–612.

———. "The Woman of the Future." *Good Housekeeping* LV (October 1912), 436–444.

———. "Youth of To-day and Tomorrow; An Authorized Interview with Thomas A. Edison." *The Forum* LXXVII (January 1927), 41–53.

Martin, Thomas Commerford. "The Edison of To-day." *Harper's Weekly* XLVII (April 18, 1903), 630.

———. "Edison's Pioneer Electric Railway Work." *Scientific American* CV (November 18, 1911), 451, 465–466.

"Master Inventors Discuss Some Revolutionizing Projects." *Current Opinion* LXXII (January 1922), 120–121.

Maxey, George W. "Thomas A. Edison, Individualist." *Vital Speeches* XVI (March 15, 1950), 330–334.

Maxwell, William. "Edison—the 'Original Man from Missouri.'" *American Magazine* LXXXV (February 1918), 25–27, 80.

May, George S., and Lemmer, Victor F. "Thomas Edison's Experimental Work with Michigan Iron Ore." *Michigan History* LIII (1969), 109–130.

Mayer, Alfred M. "On Edison's Talking-Machine." *The Popular Science Monthly* XII (April 1878), 719–724.

Meadowcroft, W. H. "How Edison Would Educate Children." *Leslie's Illustrated Weekly Newspaper,* September 19, 1912, pp. 270, 280–281.

——— . "The Wizard of Modern Invention: Thomas A. Edison." *Chamber's Journal* LXXXIX (April 1912), 260–264.

"Medals." *Time* III (February 25, 1924), 22, 24.

"Memorial to Thomas Alva Edison." *Science* LXXV (February 26, 1932), 233.

"Men and Women of the Outdoor World." *Outing* XLIV (April 1904), 60–62.

Mendenhall, T. C. "On the Influence of Time on the Change in the Resistance of the Carbon Disc of Edison's Tasimeter." *The Telegraphic Journal and Electrical Review* XI (December 9, 1882), 447–448.

Metz, John J. "An Anomaly." *Industrial Arts and Vocational Education* XXVII (April 1939), 148–149.

Metzler, Paula Wilens. "In Nature's Laboratory." *The Conservationist* XXXII (July–August 1977), 30–33, 47.

"Milan Honors a Native Son." *The Rotarian* LXX (April 1947), 32–33.

Millard, Bailey. "Our Twelve Great Scientists: VI. Thomas Alva Edison." *Technical World* XXII (October 1914), 278–285, 316.

——— . "Pictures that Talk." *Technical World* XIX (March 1913), 16–21.

Miller, Harry F. "I Worked for Thomas Edison." *The Christian Science Monitor,* January 24, 1942, pp. 6, 15.

Millikan, Robert Andrews. "Edison as a Scientist." *Science* LXXV (January 15, 1932), 68–70.

Mills, Joseph B. "History Lives at Greenfield." *The Rotarian* XLIV (May 1934), 27–29, 52.

"The Mind That Carried Music to Millions." *Etude* LXV (February 1947), 63, 80.

"Miscellaneous. Edison's Instrument for Measuring the Heat of Heavenly Bodies—Improvements in the Telephone." *Chemical News* XXXVIII (July 12, 1878), 26.

Mitchell, E. P. "The Edison Battery." *The Horseless Age* XI (April 8, 1903), 458.

"Mitten's Scheme." *Time* VII (October 4, 1926), 13.

"A Momentous Musical Meeting." *Etude* XLI (October 1923), 663–664.

Moore-Smith, Elizabeth. "Precocious." *Time* V (January 5, 1925), 30. [Letter to Editor]

Morris, Paul J. "Making Music More Musical: An Interview with Thomas A. Edison." *The Musician* XXI (May 1916), 263–265.

Morton, Henry. "Electricity in Lighting." *Scribner's Magazine* VI (August 1889), 176–200.

——— . "Notes on Recent Progress in Applied Science." *North American Review* CXXVII (April 1879), 526–536.

——— . "Storing Electricity." *Harper's Monthly Magazine* LXVI (December 1882), 92.

Moses, Otto A. "Edison's Ore Separator: To the Editor of the *Electrician.*" *The Electrician* V (September 18, 1880), 211.

"The Most Useful Americans: A Referendum of *Independent* Readers on the Most Deserving of Their Contemporaries." *Independent* LXXIV (May 1, 1913), 956–963.

"Movies." *Time* I (May 28, 1923), 19.

"The Movies Are Growing Up." *Scholastic* XXXV (October 2, 1939), 25E.

"Mr. Edison and Science." *The Commonweal* XV (November 4, 1931), 5–6.

"Mr. Edison Asks Some More Questions." *Literary Digest* LXXIV (July 1, 1922), 50–53.

"Mr. Edison—Humanity's Friend." *Recreation* XLII (February 1949), 520.

"Mr. Edison on Storage Batteries." *Bulletin* (The Edison Electric Light Company), No. 16 (1883), 275–280.

"Mr. Edison's Brain-Meter." *Literary Digest* LXIX (May 28, 1921), 28–29.

"Mr. Edison's Brick and Concrete." *Literary Digest* L (March 20, 1915), 606–607.

"Mr. Edison's Candid Opinion." *The Electrician* (London) X (March 10, 1883), 396–397.

"Mr. Edison's Electric Discovery." *Scientific American* XXXIV (January 8, 1876), 17.

"Mr. Edison's Forty Years of Litigation." *Literary Digest* XLVII (September 13, 1913), 449–450.

"Mr. Edison's Improved Phonograph." *Public Opinion* IV (October 29, 1887), 63–64.

"Mr. Edison's Pyromagnetic Dynamo." *The Popular Science Monthly* XXXII (November 1887), 138.

"Mr. Edison's Reminiscences of the First Central Station." *Electrical Review* XXXVIII (January 12, 1901), 60–63.

"Mr. Edison's Torpedo Boat." *Public Opinion* IX (July 26, 1890), 369.

"Mr. Thomas A. Edison." *Scientific American* XXXIX (new series) (July 6, 1878), 5.

"Mrs. Edison's Hallowe'en Party." *Woman's Home Companion* XXXI (October 1904), 8.

Mullett, Mary B. "Four Big Men Become Boys Again." *American Magazine* LXXXVII (February 1919), 34–37, 86, 88–92.

"Music and Drama Demonstrations at the Recreation Congress." *Recreation* XXIV (January 1931), 555.

N., H. B. "Burning Light." *Christian Science Monitor Magazine* (October 22, 1949), 12.

"Nation Pays Homage to Edison's Genius on 102nd Anniversary." *Edison Electric Institute Bulletin*, XVII (February 1949), 33–34.

"National Edison Birthday Celebration Planned by Electric Industry." *Edison Electric Institute Bulletin* XXV (January 1957), 23.

N.E.L.A. Bulletin XVI (September 1929), 546–547, 549–563, 567–571, and picture folio.

Nation's Business XXV (May 1937), 85. [Portrait with comment]

"Nation-Wide Observances Honor Anniversary of Thomas Alva Edison's Birth." *Edison Electric Institute Bulletin* XX (March 1952), 70.

"The Naval Advisory Board of Inventions—I: A Brief Biographical Summary of Its Membership." *Scientific American* CXII (October 2, 1915), 301, 312.

"Naval Consulting Board Personnel." *Engineering Magazine* L (November 1915), 199.

Nelson, Henry Loomis. "The Electric Motor Applied to Street Cars." *Harper's Weekly* XXXIII (September 14, 1889), 749–752.

"The 'New Edison's' Rocky Road to Success." *Literary Digest* CII (August 24, 1929), 32, 34, 36.

"A New Invention in Telephones." *Scientific American* XXXVII (July 28, 1877), 56.

"New Light on the Edison Questionnaire." *Review of Reviews* LXIV (December 1921), 659–660.

"The New Phase of Electric Force." *Scientific American* XXXIII (December 25, 1975), 401.

"New Ways of Using Electricity." *Public Opinion* III (May 14, 1887), 112–113.

Newsweek VI (August 31, 1935). [Thomas A. Edison, Jr., obituary]

————— XXX (September 1, 1947), 46.

Newton, Byron R. "Edison Himself Answers a Questionnaire." *Collier's* LXXII (July 14, 1923), 10.

Newton, Richard Cole. "How Can a Man Keep Well and Grow Old?" *Ladies' Home Journal* XXIX (February 1912), 20.

Nichols, Herbert R. "Edison's Heritage." *The Christian Science Monitor,* February 8, 1947, p. 6.

"A Night with Edison." *Scribner's Monthly* XVII (November 1878), 88–89.

Northrop, W. B. "The Unknown Edison." *Success* V (September 1902), 497, 517–518.

Norwig, E. A. "The Patents of Thomas A. Edison." *Journal of the Patent Office Society* XXXVI (March–April 1954), 213–232, 275–296.

"Not Only the Incandescent Lamp." *Electrical World* CXXXII (October 15, 1949), 16–17.

"Notes." *Public Opinion* I (August 7, 1886), 335.

"Notes." *Public Opinion* III (May 21, 1887), 137.

"Notes." *Public Opinion* III (May 28, 1887), 160.

"Notes." *Public Opinion* III (September 3, 1887), 445.

"Notes." *Public Opinion* VI (November 17, 1888), 119.

"Notes." *Public Opinion* VII (October 12, 1889), 14.

"Notes." *Public Opinion* VII (October 17, 1889), 41.

"Notes." *Public Opinion* VIII (February 22, 1890), 474.

"Notes." *Time* V (March 30, 1925), 17.

"Notes and Comment." *The New Yorker* XXII (February 1, 1947), 17–18.

"Notes of Thomas A. Edison." *Science Digest* XXIV (August 1948), 1–5.

Novick, Sheldon. "The Electric Power Industry." *Environment* XVII (November 1975), 7–9, 11–13, 32–34.

O'Hagan, John F. "Edison and Religion." *The Commonweal* XVI (October 26, 1932), 612–614.

—————. "The Human Edison." *The Commonweal* XIX (February 16, 1934), 437–438.

Olken, H. "Invention—A Coming Profession." *Scientific American* CXLVIII (January 1933), 28–30.

"One Dollar." *Time* XI (February 27, 1928), 32.

"100-Year-Old Revolution in Light." *U.S. News* LXXXVII (October 22, 1979), 94.

"One-Hundredth Anniversary." *American City* LXII (February 1947), 5–6.

"One of Mr. Edison's Curious Experiments." *Scientific American* XXXIV (January 15, 1876), 33.

"The Only Person Edison Obeys." *Literary Digest* XLVII (November 15, 1913), 968–969, 976.

Operator, January 15, 1882.

"Our Wizard and His Lamp." *Literary Digest* XCIX (November 24, 1928), 24.

Outlook CXIII (May 31, 1916), 260.

————— CXXXIX (February 25, 1925), 298. [Portrait with comment]

————— CXLIX (August 15, 1928), 609. [Portrait with comment]

Paddock, Paul D. "Edison to Remake First Light." *Popular Mechanics* LI (June 1929), 940–944.

Pan American Magazine XLII (November 1929), 154.

Paolucci, Bridget. "Edison as Record Producer." *High Fidelity Magazine* XXVII (January 1977), 85–89.

Paris, Leonard. "He Heralded a Modern World." *Senior Scholastic* LXII (February 21, 1958), 46.

"Patent for Extracting Rubber From Goldenrod." *Science News Supplement* LXXI (February 21, 1930), xiv.

Pepper, Robert K. "Edison's Life in Florida." *Hobbies* LVI (December 1951), 20–21.

Peters, Roderic. "Tom Edison's Sales Techniques." *Nation's Business* LIX (March 1971), 52–56.

Philips, H. J. "Thomas Alva Edison." *Literary Digest* CXI (November 14, 1931), 41.

Phillips, Walter P. "Edison, Bogardus and Carbolic Acid." *Electrical Review and Western Electrician* LXXV (November 14, 1914), 965–966.

"The Phonograph." *Harper's Weekly* XXII (March 30, 1878), 249–250.

"The Phonograph." *Scientific American* LXXV (July 25, 1896), 65–66.

"The Phonograph." *Scribner's Monthly* XV (April 1878), 899.

"Physical Society, November 9." *Nature* XLX (November 21, 1878), 68.

Pope, Franklin Leonard. "The Electric Motor and Its Applications." *Scribner's Magazine* III (March 1888), 306–321.

Pope, James Chester. "Ten Biggest." *Time* IX (January 3, 1927), 4.

Pope, Ralph W. "The Rise of the Stock Reporting Telegraph." *The Electrical World* XXXIII (March 4, 1899), 268–270.

Popular Mechanics Magazine L (October 1928), 529.

"Popular Miscellany: Edison's Electro-Chemical Telephonic Receiver." *The Popular Science Monthly* XV (October 1879), 854–855.

"Popular Miscellany: Progress of the Electric Light." *The Popular Science Monthly* XVI (February 1880), 570–571.

Potter, Robert D. "Edison's Magnificent Fumble." *Popular Science* CL (February 1947), 130–133.

Preece, William Henry. "Electric Lighting at the Paris Exhibition." *Van Nostrand's Engineering Magazine* XXVI (January 1882), 151–163.

——— . "Electrical Science at the British Association: The Telephone." *The Telegraphic Journal* V (September 1, 1877), 199–200.

——— . "Recent Advances in Electric Lighting." *The Popular Science Monthly* XIX (July 1881), 380.

——— . "Recent Progress in Telephony." *The Telegraphic Journal and Electrical Review* XI (September 2, 1882), 175–177.

"Prescient Edison." *Time* XXX (September 6, 1937), 34–35.

Prescott, George B. "Edison's Telephonic and Acoustic Inventions." *Popular Science Monthly* XIV (December 1878), 129–142.

——— . "Edison's Telephonic Researches." *Scientific American* XXXIX (July 6, 1878), 10–11.

——— . "The Telephone and the Phonograph." *Scribner's Monthly* XV (April 1878), 848–858.

"Presentation of a Congressional Medal to Mr. Edison." *Science* LXVIII (October 12, 1928), 345.

"President Hoover Dedicates Edison Institute." *Ford News* IX (November 1, 1929), 242–245.

Price, Charles W. "Thomas Alva Edison." *The Cosmopolitan* XXXIII (May 1902), 35–37.

"Problems Raised by Edison's Questionnaire." *Current Opinion* LXXI (July 1921), 77–80.

"Prof. Edison's Induction Balance for Telephone Lines." *Scientific American* XL (April 19, 1879), 245.

"Professor Morton on the Electric Light." *Scientific American* XXXIX (November 9, 1878), 288–289.

"Progress of the Telephone." *Scientific American* XL (March 22, 1879), 176.

"The Progress of the World." *Review of Reviews* LXXXI (April 1930), 35–36.

Public Opinion II (March 12, 1887), 479.

——— II (March 19, 1887), 504.

—— II (March 26, 1887), 528.

—— III (April 16, 1887), 16.

—— III (June 4, 1887), 183.

—— III (August 27, 1887), 421–422.

—— VII (April 20, 1889), 34.

—— VIII (October 17, 1889), 40.

Pupin, M. I. "Dr. Pupin on the Edison Fluoroscopes." *The Electrical Engineer* XXI (April 1, 1896), 337.

Putnam's Monthly I (October 1906), 90.

"Quadruplex Telegraphy." *Scientific American* XXXVI (June 16, 1877), 369.

"The Quintessential Innovator." *Time* CXIV (October 22, 1979), 72–73.

Radio Broadcast VI (November 1924), 36. [Portrait with comment]

"Radio V. Phonograph." *Time* VIII (October 4, 1926), 36.

Ramsaye, Terry. "The Industry." *Theatre Arts Monthly* XIII (September 1929), 633, 656–663.

Rankin, John E. "Thomas Alva Edison." *Vital Speeches of the Day* VI (April 1, 1940), 378–379.

Read, Oliver, and Riley, James. "Evolution of the Phonograph." *Radio and Television News* LIV (November 1955), 58–59, 149–153.

"Real Labor." *Time* XVI (December 8, 1930), 44.

"Rebuilding Edison's Great Plant." *Scientific American* CXII (January 9, 1915), 50.

"Rebuilding the Edison Plant." *The Literary Digest* L (May 15, 1915), 1149.

"Recent Improvements in Telephony." *Scribner's Monthly* XVI (August 1878), 600–602.

"Report of the Committee on Edison Fire." *Journal of the American Concrete Institute* III (1915), 585, 674–688.

"Report on the Incandescent Lamps Exhibited at the International Exposition of Electricity." [Paris, 1881] *Van Nostrand's Engineering Magazine* XXVII (July 1882), 372–376.

"A Revealing Episode." *The Christian Century* LXVI (November 6, 1929), 1369–1370.

Review of Reviews XXV (April 1902), 422.

—— LXX (December 1924), 669.

—— LXXV (March 1927), 226. [Portrait with comment]

—— LXXX (August 1929), 67. [Portrait with comment]

—— XCI (June 1935), 31.

Rice, E. W., Jr. "Edison's Greatest Contribution: Birth of the Electric Street-Car." *System, The Magazine of Business* LIV (November 1928), 523–525, 594–600.

Riordan, R. "Recent Advances in Telegraphy." *The Popular Science Monthly* IX (May 1876), 71–79.

Rosanoff, M. A. "Edison in His Laboratory." *Harper's Monthly Magazine* CLXV (September 1932), 402–417.

—— "Edison Vivo." *Revista Bimestre Cubana* XLVI (1940), 57–82.

Ross, Ron. "Edison's Genius Lives On." *Science News Letter* LI (February 8, 1947), 90–91.

Rosten, Leo. "They Made Our World . . . . Edison." *Look* XXVIII (February 25, 1964), 100–102.

"Rubber-Producing Plants." *Science News Supplement* LXIX (March 1, 1929), x, xii.

Ruckle, Marie L., and Hanton, Gladys. "Edison's Two Ways of Gardening." *Better Homes and Gardens* X (February 1932), 26, 58–60.

Sachs, Joseph. "The Evolution of Safe and Accurate Fuse Protective Devices." *American Institute of Electrical Engineers* XVII (March 28, 1900), 131–203.

Sandison, G. H. "The Real Edison." *Columbian Magazine* III (1911).

Saturday Evening Post CCXXVI (October 3, 1953), 17.

—— CCXXVII (May 21, 1955), 17. [Portrait with comment]

Savary, A. W. "Connection of the Family of Edison, the Inventor, with Digby, Nova Scotia." *New England Historical and Genealogical Register* XLVIII (April 1894), 199–200.

"Saving the Wanderers in Mr. Edison's Desert." *Literary Digest* CVI (August 23, 1930), 36–37.

Sawyer, W. E. "The 'Etheric' Force." *Scientific American* XXXIV (January 15, 1876), 36.

—— . "The 'Etheric' Phenomenon." *Scientific American* XXXIV (February 19, 1876), 116.

Schofield, Maurice. "The Centenary of Thomas Edison." *Contemporary Review* CLXXI (February 1947), 115–117.

—— . "Edison—Master Inventor." *Discovery* VIII (February 1947), 59–60.

School Arts LVI (February 1957), 7. [Portrait with comment]

Schonberg, Harold C. "Edison Started the Big Noise a Century Ago." *Smithsonian* IX (May 1978), 111–112, 114, 116, 118–125.

Schwartz, Tony. "Edison's Sound Predictions." *Popular Photography* LIX (July 1966), 34.

"Science and the Citizen." *Scientific American* CCXXVII (December 1972), 43.

Scientific American C (February 27, 1909), 165.

—— CXII (June 5, 1915), 515-516.

—— CXII (June 5, 1915), 536.

"Scientific: Electricity and the Inventors." *Public Opinion* I (April 15, 1886), 4.

Scientific Monthly XV (December 1922), 588.

—— XXV (October 1927), 380.

"Second Brightest Boy." *Time* XIV (September 16, 1929), 59.

"Seeing History Through American Achievements: Incandescent Lamp." *Scholastic* L (February 10, 1947), 36.

"Selection of Able High-School Students by Mr. Edison." *School and Society* XXIX (May 11, 1929), 604.

Sevey, Robert. "Edisoniana." *Time* XI (November 9, 1931), 4.

Sharp, Clayton H. "First Milestone of the Electronic Era: How 'Edison Effect' Was Discovered 60 Years Ago." *Electronic Industries* II (September 1943), 214, 216, 218.

Shaw, Albert. "Mr. Edison, A Typical American." *Review of Reviews* LXXXIV (September 1931), 17–18.

—— . "Mr. Edison's Views of Life and Work." *Review of Reviews* LXXXV (January 1932), 30–31.

—— . "The Progress of the World." *Review of Reviews* LXXXI (April 1930), 30–31.

—— . "The Progress of the World." *Review of Reviews* LXXXIII (February 1931), 29–31.

Shaw, G. M. "Sketch of Thomas Alva Edison." *Popular Science Monthly* XIII (August 1878), 487–491.

Shunaman, Fred. "Pioneers of Radio." *Radio Electronics* XLIX (September 1978), 46, 57.

—— . "A Question of Semantics: Who Did Invent the Radio?" *Popular Electronics* XXXIII (October 1970), 27–30.

"Sidelights on Ford and Edison as Seen by John Burroughs." *Current Opinion* LXXI (December 1921), 742–743.

Sinclair, John F. "Some Builders of Prosperity." *Review of Reviews* LXXIX (January 1929), 46–50.

Sloane, Madeleine Edison. "The Edison Birthplace." *Edison Electric Institute Bulletin* XXII (August 1954), 294.

"Smart Son." *Time* VIII (September 20, 1926), 31.

Smith, Winifred S. "Thomas Alva Edison." *Museum Echoes* XXVIII (December 1955), 91–93.

Snow, R. F. "From Pearl Street to Main

Street." *American Heritage* XXX (October 1979), 76–79.

"Social Equal." *Time* IV (December 29, 1924), 30. [Letter to Editor]

Sokolsky, George E. "Lincoln and Edison." *Vital Speeches* XV (April 1, 1949), 377–378.

"Some New Features of the Edison Test." *Literary Digest* CII (August 31, 1929), 18.

"Special Observances to Mark 'Edison Day' Both Here and Abroad." *Edison Electric Institute Bulletin* XVII (January 1949), 2, 22.

"Speech." *Time* VI (September 28, 1925), 26.

Spehr, Paul C. "Edison Films in the Library of Congress." *Library of Congress Quarterly Journal* XXXII (January 1975), 33–50.

——— . "Motion Pictures." *Quarterly Journal of the Library of Congress* XXIII (1966), 70–74.

Speiden, Norman R. "Thomas A. Edison: Sketch of Activities, 1874–1881." *Science* CV (February 7, 1947), 137–141.

"The Spotlight Shines on Edison: A Review of the Nationwide Observance During the Thomas A. Edison Centennial." *Industrial Marketing* XXXII (May 1947), 36–37, 148–150.

Sprague, Frank J. "The Electric Railway, First Paper: A Resume of the Early Experiments." *The Century Magazine* LXX (July 1905), 434–451.

Stahl, G. Allan. "The Centennial of the Phonograph." *Chemistry* L (December 1977), 10–12.

——— . "Edison's Chase and Discoveries." *SciQuest* LII (October 1979), 6–11.

Stanton, William. "Telegraph Reminiscences." *Operator*, August 15, 1880.

Stearns, Royall R. "Notable Suburbanites and Their Homes." *Suburban Life* V (October 1907), 199–202.

"Stratton and Edison." *Time* I (June 25, 1923), 19.

Strother, French. "The Modern Profession of Inventing." *World's Work* X (June 1905), 6289–6298.

Struther, J. "Thomas Alva Edison." *Literary Digest* CXI (December 12, 1931), 22.

Sullivan, Alan. "Pioneers of Invention." *Collier's* LVI (November 27, 1915), 21–22, 37, 40, 43.

Sunset Magazine LX (January 1928), 14.

Sutton, Horace. "The Wizard of Orange." *Saturday Review* III (May 15, 1976), 53-55.

System XXVII (April 1915), 377.

——— XLVII (June 1925), 730.

——— LI (January 1927), 30.

Tait, Frank M. "Thomas A. Edison: Prototype for American Enterprise." *Edison Electric Institute Bulletin* XV (March 1947), 69–70, 86.

Talbot, Frederick A. *World's Work* [London], October 1911.

"Tales of Edison." *Compressed Air Magazine* LVIII (November 1953), 317.

"A Talk with Edison." *Scientific American* LXVI (April 2, 1892), 216.

Talking Machine World, April 15, 1909, p. 49.

"The Talking Phonograph." *Scientific American* XXXVII (December 22, 1877), 384–385.

[Tattler]. "Edison." *The Nation* CI (October 28, 1915), 517–518.

Taylor, A. Hoyt. "Thomas A. Edison and the Naval Research Laboratory." *Science* CV (February 7, 1947), 148–150.

Taylor, Warren. "The Home and Workshop of Edison." *Munsey's Magazine* VI (November 1891), 185–192.

"The Telegraph." *Scientific American* LXXV (July 25, 1896), 58–59.

"The Telephone." *Scientific American* LXXV (July 25, 1896), 89–91.

"The 10 Greatest Men of American Business—as You Picked Them." *Nation's Business* LIX (March 1971), 44–50.

"Terrifying Invention." *Time* LXXVIII (July 21, 1961), 33–34.

Thelander, Theodore A. "Josephus Daniels and the Publicity Campaign for Naval and Industrial Preparedness Before World War I." *North Carolina Historical Review* XLIII (July 1966), 316–332.

"Thomas A. Edison." *Review of Reviews* VIII (July 1893), 67–68.

"Thomas A. Edison 'A Man of the Half-Century.' " *Edison Electric Institute Bulletin* XVIII (January 1950), 17, 31.

"Thomas A. Edison and the Founding of Science: 1880." *Science* CV (February 7, 1947), 142–148.

"Thomas A. Edison—and What He Has Contributed to Human Progress." *Popular Mechanics* LVI (October 1931), 614–619.

"Thomas A. Edison at Home." *Review of Reviews* XXVI (September 1902), 347–349.

"Thomas A. Edison—A Tribute." *Illuminating Engineering* XLII (February 1947), 141–142.

"Thomas A. Edison Automobiling to the South." *Scientific American* XCIV (June 2, 1906), 460.

"Thomas A. Edison: Creator of an Era." *Electrical World* CXXVII (February 8, 1947), 17–20.

"Thomas A. Edison in Los Angeles." *Journal of Education* LXXXII (November 25, 1915), 523.

"Thomas A. Edison: Inventor." *Electrical Engineering* LXVI (February 1947), 113–117.

"Thomas A. Edison Made First Honorary Member of Academy of Motion Picture Arts and Sciences." *Photo-era* LXIII (December 1929), 337.

"Thomas A. Edison Post Cards." *Hobbies* LXI (February 1957), 117, 121.

"Thomas A. Edison: The Story of a Great American." *American Childhood* XXXII (February 1947), 19–22.

"Thomas Alva Edison." *Popular Science Monthly* CXX (January 1932), 68.

"Thomas Alva Edison." *Science* VI [old series] (August 21, 1885), 145–148.

"Thomas Alva Edison." *Science* LXXIV (October 23, 1931), 404–405.

"Thomas Alva Edison." *Scientific American* LXXXVII (December 27, 1902), 463.

"Thomas Alva Edison." *Scientific American* CXLV (December 1931), 365.

"Thomas Alva Edison." *The Telegraphic Journal* IX (November 5, 1881), 432–433.

"Thomas Alva Edison—American." *Bulletin of the Pan American Union* LXX (February 1936), 153–155.

"Thomas Alva Edison Born 100 Years Ago." *Power Plant Engineering* LI (February 1947), 105–107.

"Thomas Alva Edison (1847–1931)." *Nature* CLIX (February 8, 1947), 191–192.

"The Thomas Alva Edison Foundation." *Science* LXXXI (March 1, 1935), 222–223.

"Thomas Alva Edison, One of the First Radio Experimenters." *Scientific American* CXXXV (December 1926), 405.

"Thomas Alva Edison: Tributes Forming A Memorial Program Given at the New Orleans Meeting of the American Association for the Advancement of Sciences." *Science* LXXV (January 15, 1932), 59–71.

"Thomas Edison Memorial Mural Presented to State by Ohio Electric Companies." *Edison Electric Institute Bulletin* XVIII (June 1950), 186.

"Thomas Edison's Successor." *The Commonweal* X (May 15, 1929), 33–34.

Thompson, Ralph. "Thomas A. Edison: The Man and His Work." *Current History* XXXV (December 1931), 372–376.

Thornburgh, George. "Edison Outdone: Wonderful Effect of Electricity." *Harper's Weekly* XXV (April 16, 1881), 260.

Thorndale, Theresa. "The Birthplace of Edison Dreams of her Fallen Greatness."

The Firelands Pioneer XIII (December 1, 1900), 716–723.

"Throwing a New Light on a Great Inventor." *Current Opinion* LXIX (July 1920), 45–48.

Time VII (February 22, 1926), 19.

———— VIII (October 18, 1926), 30.

———— VIII (November 1, 1926), 32.

———— VIII (November 29, 1926), 31.

———— XI (February 13, 1928), 17.

———— XIII (January 28, 1929), 10.

———— XIII (April 22, 1929), 60.

———— XIII (May 6, 1929), 47.

———— XIV (October 28, 1929), 11.

———— XV (February 17, 1930), 58.

———— XV (March 17, 1930), 16.

———— XV (April 21, 1930), 54.

———— XV (June 23, 1930), 34.

———— XVI (July 21, 1930), 48.

———— XVI (September 15, 1930), 62.

———— XXII (December 1, 1930), 32.

———— XVII (June 1, 1931), 21.

———— XVIII (August 10, 1931), 22.

———— XVIII (November 9, 1931), 38.

———— XXVI (September 2, 1935), 36.

———— XXVIII (November 9, 1936), 14.

———— L (September 1, 1947), 78.

Other items in *Time* for the period searched, varying from a sentence to a paragraph, were: *1925*: 3/16: 31; 4/6: 17; 4/13: 26; 5/4: 30; 6/1: 16; 7/20: 32; 9/14: 8, 26; *1926*: 2/22: 9; 3/15: 26; 4/19: 22; 11/29: 19, 31; *1927*: 1/31: 24; 2/21: 24; 3/7: 4; 7/4: 29; 11/7: 30; 11/21: 23; *1928*: 1/2: 5; 1/16: 25; 1/23: 22; 1/30: 24; 4/14: 40; 6/18: 32; 7/30: 32; 8/6: 28; 9/3: 28; 10/8: 26; 10/29: 7; 11/12: 50; 12/3: 36; *1929*: 1/7: 13; 2/18: 10; 5/13: 55; 8/12: 42; 9/2: 64; 9/23: 11; 10/28: 22; 11/4: 45; *1930*: 2/17: 54; 3/3: 58; 10/6: 54; *1931*: 2/16: 50; 3/23: 32; 5/25: 44; 7/13: 23; 12/21: 8; *1932*: 5/16: 25; 8/29: 9; 9/12: 42; *1933*: 1/23: 15; *1934*: 8/20: 36; *1935*: 7/8: 31; 11/11: 71.

Townsend, Horace. "Edison: His Work and His Work-shop." *The Cosmopolitan* VI (April 1889), 598–607.

"Tribute to Edison." *Outlook* CLIII (October 30, 1929), 337.

"True Genius Never Dies." *Industrial Arts and Vocational Education* XXI (January 1932), 11.

Tuttle, Florence Piper. "A Child's Calendar of Famous Birthdays." *American Childhood* XXXI (February 1946), 10.

————. "Dramatic Incidents in Edison's Early Life." *American Childhood* XXXI (February 1946), 10–11.

"Twelve-Year-Old Edison Rides Rails to Library: Inventor on Track of Early Experiments." *American Libraries* VI (December 1975), 637.

Tyndall, John. "The Electric Light." *The Popular Science Monthly* XIV (March 1879), 567–569.

"Ultimate Musical Choice." *Etude* XLIX (January 1931), 9–10.

Unger, Henry F. "Edison—Most Useful American." *Public Utilities Fortnightly* LI (June 4, 1953), 777–783.

"The Universal Ignoramus." *The Weekly Review* IV (May 21, 1921), 485.

"The University of the State of New York and Mr. Edison." *School and Society* IV (October 28, 1916), 665–666.

"Unsolved Problems that Edison is Studying." *Scientific American* LXIX (July 8, 1893), 25.

"The Unveiling of a Tablet in Honor of Thomas Alva Edison." *Science* LXI (June 5, 1925), 584–585.

Upton, Francis R. "Edison's Electric

Light." *Scribner's Monthly* XIX (February 1880), 531–544.

Uzzell, Thomas H. "The Future of Electricity: An Interview with Thomas A. Edison." *Collier's* LVIII (December 2, 1916), 7–8.

Vander, Weyde P. H. "The Nature of the Phenomena Discovered by Mr. Edison." *Scientific American* XXXIV (February 5, 1876), 89.

Vanderbilt, Byron M. "America's First R&D Center." *Industrial Research,* XVIII (November 15, 1976), 27–31.

———. "Thomas Edison: Pioneer of Applied Chemistry." *Chemistry* XLIII (October 1970), 8–11.

Varney, Walter. "Edison the Sleep Wizard." *Time* XIV (September 30, 1929), 51.

"Voices." *Time* X (August 22, 1927), 20.

Vonnegut, Kurt, Jr. "Tom Edison's Shaggy Dog." *Collier's* CXXXI (March 14, 1953), 46, 48–49.

Wade, Herbert T. "The Transophone and the Telescribe: Two New Inventions of Thomas A. Edison." *Scientific American* CXI (September 12, 1914), 216, 219.

Wall, C. B. "Incandescent Genius." *Reader's Digest* LXIV (April 1954), 145–168.

Walsh, George Ethelbert. "With Edison in His Laboratory." *Independent* LXXV (September 4, 1913), 557–559.

Walsh, Jim. "Favorite Pioneer Recording Artists: An Enchanted Evening at the Thomas A. Edison's Laboratory." *Hobbies* LXXXI (January 1977), 35–36, 126–127; (February 1977), 35–36, 126–127; (March 1977), 35–36, 117, 126–127, 130.

———. "Favorite Pioneer Recording Artists: An Evening in Thomas A. Edison's Laboratory." *Hobbies* LXXX (March 1975), 37–38, 119–120; (April 1975), 35–36; (May 1975), 35–37; (June 1975), 35–37.

———. "Favorite Pioneer Recording Artists: More About the History of the Phono-graph." *Hobbies* LIX (December 1954), 26–27.

———. "Favorite Pioneer Recording Artists: 'Professor Edison' Invents the Phonograph." *Hobbies* LVII (August 1952), 22–25, 27, 35, 37, 55, 61.

———. "Favorite Pioneer Recording Artists: Some Mysterious Edison Diamond Discs." *Hobbies* LXX (August 1965), 34–36.

———. "Favorite Pioneer Recording Artists: Walter Van Brunt (Walter Scanlan) II." *Hobbies* (January 1952), 20–23, 25.

Walsh, W. T. "Can Edison Reconstruct Our National Defenses?" *Illustrated World* XXIV (September 1915), 8–11.

Warner, Robert M. "Miss Newcomb and the Talking Machine." *Ohio Historical Quarterly* LXVII (April 1958), 148–151.

Warren, Arthur. "Edison: Boy Printer and Newspaper Proprietor." *The Inland Printer* CXIX (April 1947).

Warren, Waldo P. "Edison on Invention and Inventors." *Century Magazine* LXXXII (July 1911), 415–419.

Waters, Theodore. "Edison's Revolution in Iron Mining." *McClure's Magazine* (November 1897), 77–89.

Watkins, T. H. "A 200-Foot Tower is Scarcely Adequate." *American West* III (Spring 1966), 20–23.

Weir, Hugh. "The Story of the Motion Picture: Edison, Its Great Inventor, Tells How the Idea Came to Him and How He Worked It Out." *McClure's Magazine* LIV (November 1922), 81–85.

———. "Thomas A. Edison Goes to School." *Collier's* LXXV (January 3, 1925), 14.

———. "What Edison Would Like to Do With the Movies." *Collier's* LXXV (February 21, 1925), 20–21.

"The Werdermann Electric Light." *Popular Science Monthly* XIV (February 1879), 545.

Westinghouse, George. "A Reply to Mr.

Edison." *North American Review* CXLIX (December 1889), 653–664.

———. "Sir Wm. Thomson and Electric Lighting." *North American Review* CL (March 1890), 320–329.

Wetzler, Joseph. "The Electric Railway of Today." *Scribner's Magazine* VII (April 1890), 426, 433.

"What Do You Know? The Edison Questionnaire—Its Aim, Its Results, and Its Collateral Significance." *Scientific American* CXXV (November 1921), 16–17.

"What Edison Learned in Germany." *Literary Digest* XLIV (June 1, 1912), 1156–1157.

"What Edison Said About Music and Radio Five Years Ago." *The Musician* XXXVI (November 1931), 7.

"What Edison Thinks of Gold." *The Mentor* IX (January 1922), 29.

"What Others Think: Side Lights on Edison." *Public Utilities Fortnightly* XXXIX (February 13, 1947), 246–247.

"What's in a Name? An Astonishing and Entertaining Analysis of the Name of the Great Electrician, Thomas Alva Edison." *The Catholic World* LI (September 1890), 803–812.

"What Will Come of the Phonograph?" *Public Opinion* V (July 21, 1888), 337.

Wheeler, Schuyler S. "The Phonograph." *Harper's Weekly* XXXII (June 9, 1888), 415.

"When Edison Was Almost Ready to Give Up and to Go Back to Telegraphing." *Current Opinion* LXII (January 1917), 18.

"When Edison Was Sure." *Literary Digest* XLIV (March 2, 1912), 447–448.

"When Thomas Edison Groped in the Dark." *Time* XIII (April 22, 1929), 48.

"When Zero=Infinity." *Newsweek* LIV (November 2, 1959), 98, 100.

"Where Americana Museum is Being Constructed." *Ford News* IX (June 15, 1929), 135, 137.

White, Frank Marshall. "Edison and the Incandescent Light." *The Outlook* XCIV (February 26, 1910), 487–496.

White, W. C. "Electronics . . . Its Start from the 'Edison Effect' Sixty Years Ago." *General Electric Review* XLVI (October 1943), 537–541.

"Who Is Henry Ford?" *Time* I (May 19, 1923), 19.

"Why Edison Chooses to be Deaf." *The Literary Digest* LXXXVI (August 8, 1925), 38, 40.

Wile, Raymond R. "At the Creation." *American Record Guide* XL (February 1977), 6–10.

———. "Genius to Genius." *American Record Guide* XL (September 1977), 6–8; XLI (December 1977), 10–12.

Wilson, Eleanor Robbins. "A Modern Columbus: A Poem." *Education* XXXVI (November 1915), 156.

Wilson, Rufus R. "Edison on Inventions: A Remarkable Interview with the Great Inventor." *Monthly Illustrator* XI (November 1895), 340–344.

Windesheim, Karl A. "The Evolution of Speech Recording Machines." *Quarterly Journal of Speech* XXIV (1938), 257–265.

"Wizard of Menlo Park." *Time* V (May 25, 1925), 16.

"Wizards of Science Astonish Edison." *Current Opinion* LXXIII (December 1922), 777–778.

Woman's Home Companion XLIII (September 1916), 35.

"A Wonderful Invention—Speech Capable of Indefinite Repetition from Automatic Records." *Scientific American* XXXVII (November 17, 1877), 304.

"Work Begins." *Time* VII (March 15, 1926), 21.

"World Citizen." *Time* XVIII (October 12, 1931), 25.

World's Work XXVII (February 1914), 365.

The World Today XXI (October 1911), 1137.

Wyman, William I. "Age of Production in Invention and Other Fields: Genius of Inventors Culminates Early Life." *Scientific American Supplement* LXXVIII (September 5, 1914), 154–155.

——— . "What Are the Ten Greatest Inventions of Our Time?" *Scientific American* CIX (November 1, 1913), 337–339, 350, 352.

Yorke, Dane. "The Rise and Fall of the Phonograph." *The American Mercury* XXVII (September 1932), 1–12.

Young, Victor. "Edison and Music." *The Etude* L (June 1932), 399, 453.

——— . "Edison's Contribution to Musical Appreciation." *The Etude* LXIII (December 1945), 677, 680.

DOCUMENTS

Illinois Committee on Public Information. "Thomas Alva Edison, America's Best-Known Private Citizen." Chicago, 1930.

U.S. House of Representatives. Committee on Coinage, Weights, and Measures. *Report, Authorizing a Gold Medal in Commemoration of the Achievements of Thomas A. Edison.* Report No. 1131. 70th Congress, 1st Session, April 4, 1928. [To accompany H.J.Res. 243; identical to Senate Report No. 1285]

U.S. Senate. Committee on Banking and Currency. *Report, Authorizing a Gold Medal in Commemoration of the Achievements of Thomas A. Edison.* Report No. 1285. 70th Congress, 1st Session, May 3, 1928. [To accompany H.J.Res. 243; identical to House Report No. 1131.]

U.S. President (Coolidge). *Address of President Coolidge Speaking Over the Radio Especially for an Audience Gathered At West Orange, New Jersey on the Occasion of the Presentation of a Medal Granted By the Congress of the United States to Thomas Alva Edison,* Washington, DC, Saturday, October 20, 1928, 9 o'clock

P.M. Washington, DC: Government Printing Office, 1928.

U.S. President (Hoover). *Address of President Hoover in Connection with the Celebration of the 50th Anniversary of Mr. Thomas A. Edison's Invention of the Incandescent Electric Lamp,* Dearborn, MI, October 21, 1929. Washington, DC, 1929.

U.S. Department of the Interior. National Park Service. "Edison National Historic Site." Washington, DC, 1968.

MANUSCRIPTS

Nye, David. "Edison's Reification at Light's Golden Jubilee." Paper presented at the Edison Symposium, Newark, NJ, October 20, 1979.

Wachhorst, Wyn. "A Better Mousetrap: Thomas A. Edison as an American Culture Hero." Unpublished Ph.D. dissertation, Stanford University, 1973.

PLAYS

Adams, Robert K. *Young Tom Edison.* New York, [?].

Konrád, Edmond. *The Wizard of Menlo.* Trans. from Czech by Paul Selver. London, 1935.

Ullman, Samuel S. "The World is Lighted (Edison and the Incandescent Lamp)." In Ullman, *Plays of America's Achievements.* New York, 1940. (pp. 139–152)

RADIO, TELEVISION, MOTION PICTURES, RECORDS

CBS Television. "Let's Take a Trip." February 10, 1957.

——— . "You Are There: Edison and the Miracle of Light." October 17, 1954.

General Electric Corp. *Thomas Edison:*

Reflections of a Genius. 1978. [Motion picture]

Metro-Goldwyn-Mayer. *Edison the Man.* 1940. [Motion picture]

———. *Young Tom Edison.* 1940. [Motion picture]

"My American Heritage: An exciting cast of characters captures the lives of famous Americans with song, story and sound effects. Thomas Alva Edison 1847–1931/ Inventor." Minneapolis: Pickwick Records, 1978. [SPC–5159]

NBC Radio. "Biography in Sound." February 11, 1957.

National Educational Television. "Edison: The Old Man." 1975.

Screen News Digest. *The Endless Search.* 1978. [Motion picture]

Smithsonian Institution. *Thomas A. Edison and His Amazing Invention Factories.* 1978. [Motion picture]

South Carolina Educational Television. "Legacy of a Genius: The Story of Thomas Alva Edison." 1979.

Wilson, John F., and Hawthorne, Grace. "The Electric Sunshine Man." Carol Stream, IL: Somerset Press, 1978. [LP record HR926]